Fodor's 92
Alaska

Fodor's Travel Publications, Inc.
New York and London

Grateful acknowledgment is made to the following for permission to reprint previously published material:

Farrar, Straus and Giroux, Inc.: Excerpt from COMING INTO THE COUNTRY by John McPhee. Copyright © 1976, 1977 by John McPhee, Reprinted by permission of Farrar, Straus and Giroux, Inc. Random House, Inc.: Excerpt from ALASKA by James A. Michener. Copyright © 1988 by James A. Michener. Reprinted by permission of Random House, Inc.

Fodor's Alaska

Editor: Alison Hoffman
Contributors: Suzanne E. De Galan, Mary Ann Hemphill, Barbara Hodgin, Mike Miller, Stanton Patty, Mary Pritchard, Kent Sturgis, Peggy Wayburn, Howard Weaver
Art Director: Fabrizio La Rocca
Cartographer: David Lindroth
Illustrator: Karl Tanner
Cover Photograph: E. Muench/Photoresearchers

Design: Vignelli Associates

Special Sales

Fodor's Travel Publications are available at special discounts for bulk purchases (100 copies or more) for sales promotions or premiums. Special editions, including personalized covers, excerpts of existing guides, and corporate imprints, can be created in large quantities for special needs. For more information write to Special Marketing, Fodor's Travel Publications, 201 East 50th St., New York, NY 10022, or call 1–800–800–3246. Inquiries from the United Kingdom should be sent to Fodor's Travel Publications, 20 Vauxhall Bridge Rd., London, England SW1V 2SA.

MANUFACTURED IN THE UNITED STATES OF AMERICA
10 9 8 7 6 5 4 3 2 1

Contents

Maps and Plans

Foreword

Bigness and remoteness aren't the only things that set Alaska apart from the "lower 48" states. Alaska can be considered America's last wilderness, with its glimmering glaciers, abundant wilderness, towering mountains, and waterfront communities. This guidebook will help you explore and conquer them all.

Because more than 85% of Alaska's visitors see this wilderness by cruise ship, *Fodor's Alaska* is also a complete guide to cruising to and in Alaska. But other modes of transportation are certainly not ignored. Whether you see Alaska by plane, train, motor vehicle, cruise ship, or even dogsled, this guidebook will help you get the most enjoyment out of your trip.

While every care has been taken to assure the accuracy of the information in this guide, the passage of time will always bring change and, consequently, the publisher cannot accept responsibility for errors that may occur.

All prices and opening times quoted here are based on information supplied to us at press time. Hours and admission fees may change, however, and the prudent traveler will avoid inconvenience by calling ahead.

Fodor's wants to hear about your travel experiences, both pleasant and unpleasant. When a hotel or restaurant fails to live up to its billing, let us know and we will investigate the complaint and revise our entries where the facts warrant it.

Send your letters to the editors of Fodor's Travel Publications, 201 E. 50th Street, New York, NY 10022.

Highlights '92 and Fodor's Choice

Highlights '92

To commemorate the 50th anniversary of the completion of the **Alaska Highway,** every community along the 1,422-mile route will feature festivities, exhibitions, and shows. Additionally, museums throughout the state will highlight the social, political, and economic aspects of the highway's creation.

The event, **Rendezvous '92,** will also sponsor a reunion for those soldiers who worked on the route, as well as exhibit the tanks, airplanes, and trucks that were used to build the road half a century ago. Other celebrations are planned in Alaska as well as on stretches of the highway in Canada through British Columbia, Yukon Territory, and Alberta. Once known as the Alcan, the Alaska Highway was built in just eight months during World War II as a military supply route.

Two new developments are making it easier for visitors to Alaska to take side trips to the Soviet Union in 1992.

In Nome, **Bering Air** now offers tours to the Siberian city of Providenya. A U.S. Customs Service agent was posted in Nome in 1990 so visas can be obtained there, instead of sending to Anchorage. The cost of the tour depends on how many passengers are going.

In Anchorage, Alaska's largest city, **Alaska Airlines** is running an air route between Anchorage and the U.S.S.R. cities of Magadan and Khabarovsk. Five- and six-day packages serve both cities, while an eight-day package to Khabarovsk includes a trip on the Trans-Siberian railway, passing through Irkutsk and Lake Baikal.

Due to popular interest in the area of **Prince William Sound,** some local tour operators now include **Bligh Reef,** the site of the *Exxon Valdez* grounding, in their itineraries. Three years following the devastating oil spill, the sound again has many beautiful bays, glaciers, and wildlife to offer the visitor. Cruise ship passengers who toured the area in 1991 now report seeing little or no evidence of damage in the sound.

The 200-passenger *Ptarmigan* (named after Alaska's state bird) continues to cruise from the west side of Portage Lake to the face of **Portage Glacier,** one of Alaska's top attractions, just some 50 miles from Prince William Sound. **Westours Motorcoaches Inc.** operates the day boat in a 20-year permit from the U.S. Forest Service.

Summertime service on the **Alaska Railroad** between Anchorage and the port of Seward offers riders one of the world's most scenic rail views. Self-propelled rail-diesel cars depart Anchorage in summer daily at 7 AM for the four-hour trip south to Seward. Rails follow the Turnagain Arm, climb into the mountains of the Kenai Peninsula near Harding Icefield, and pass within a mile of Spencer Glacier. The route bores through half a dozen tunnels, skirts several lakes, and makes a spectacular hairpin turn. Cost for the round-trip journey is about $70 per person.

This Alaska Railroad service is in addition to the heavily traveled traditional run between Anchorage and Fairbanks, which stops at Denali National Park, and includes a view of North America's highest peak, 30,320-foot Mt. McKinley. Besides Alaska Railroad's regular service, two major tour operators—Princess Tours and Holland America Line-Westours—hitch their own luxury dome cars to the railroad's train.

X 20,320 X

In other rail travel, the **White Pass & Yukon Route** (WP & YR) in Skagway, Southeast Alaska, keeps chugging along. Dating back to the turn-of-the-century Klondike gold rush, the revived narrow-gauge railroad offers scenic excursions between Skagway and the 2,865-foot summit of the gold trail called White Pass—20 miles each way. The WP & YR has extended the trip 8 miles to Fraser, British Columbia, and has provided connections for motorcoach passengers traveling between Whitehorse, capital of Canada's Yukon Territory, and Skagway. The rail line also offers a rail-motorcar service for hikers crossing the famed Chilkoot Pass, a main route to the Klondike gold fields in 1897-98. Motorcars (small work cars on rails) depart Lake Bennett, British Columbia, for the 41-mile trip to Skagway each morning from mid-June to mid-September.

Alaska's native peoples—Eskimos, Indians, and Aleuts—are now taking charge of tours in their communities. No longer are they content to play the role of "quaint" camera subjects. In Kotzebue, the Eskimo-owned **NANA** (North Alaska Natives Association) Development Corp. features **Tour Arctic,** which conducts all excursions there. In the tiny village of Gambell on remote St. Lawrence Island, about 150 air miles north of Nome, native residents have formed **Alaska Village Tours Inc.** to organize and run cultural tours of their village, which is only 40 miles from the Siberian coast. Also run by the indigenous people of the area are tours of the Pribilof Islands, on St. Paul Island, where you can see hundreds of species of birds, and visit the walrus and seal rookeries.

Fodor's Choice

No two people will agree on what makes a perfect vacation, but it's fun and helpful to know what others think. We hope you'll have a chance to experience some of Fodor's Choices yourself in Alaska. For detailed information about each entry, refer to the appropriate chapters.

Special Moments

The throbbing of an Eskimo drum in Kotzebue

The howl of a train whistle near Skagway

Blazes of purple fireweed near Fairbanks

The roll of a humpback whale in Glacier Bay

The northern lights on a winter night

Russian Orthodox church domes flashing in the sun

Clown-face puffins in the Pribilof Islands

A misty morning in Sitka with bald eagles on high

The scream of a salmon reel near Ketchikan

Helicopter flightseeing over Juneau's glaciers

Moonlight on Mt. McKinley

Evening fish stories on the deck of the Talaview Lodge near Skwentna

Brown bears on the road in McKinley Park

Climbing an unnamed peak in the Brooks Range and standing where no one has stood before

Caribou crossing the Glenn Highway near Lake Louise

Taste Treats

Halibut "beer bits" at Glacier Bay Lodge

Reindeer steak at the Fort Davis Roadhouse in Nome

Shrimp cocktails anywhere in Petersburg or Wrangell

Smoked salmon

Coconut salmon appetizers and Double Musky pie at the Double Musky in Girdwood

Any fish you caught yourself cooked over a cottonwood fire on the riverbank

Any chocolate dessert at A Moveable Feast in Fairbanks

Chinook beer from the microbrewery in Juneau

Cocktails with glacier ice you collected from Portage Lake

Off the Beaten Track

Canoeing on the Yukon River

Riding a dogsled in Nome and cuddling a husky pup

Rafting through an eagle sanctuary near Haines

Salmon fishing in the company of brown bears
in Katmai National Park

Watching Indian totem carvers at Ketchikan

Hiking the route of the gold rush on the Chilkoot Trail
near Skagway

Driving the McCarthy Road and pulling yourself across
the river on a hand cart to the little historic towns
of McCarthy and Kennicott

Setting out across the tundra to any peak in Thompson
Pass north of Valdez

Driving the Denali Highway from Paxson to Cantwell

After Hours

The Red Dog Saloon in Juneau

Hot-air ballooning over Anchorage on a summer night

The Red Onion Saloon in Skagway

Walking up to Flattop Mountain, above Anchorage,
at midnight on the summer solstice (June 21)

Hotels

Glacier Bay Lodge, Glacier Bay National Park
(Expensive)

Westmark Fairbanks *(Expensive)*

Reluctant Fisherman Inn, Cordova *(Moderate)*

Tides Inn, Petersburg *(Moderate)*

Skagway Inn Bed & Breakfast, Skagway *(Moderate)*

Silver Bow Inn, Juneau *(Inexpensive)*

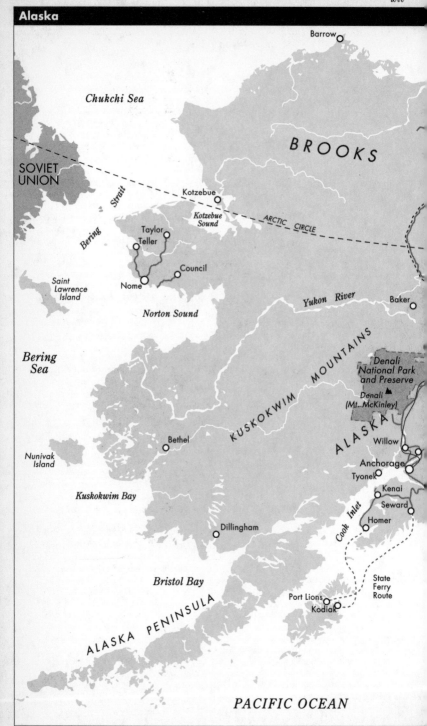

Alaska

Barrow

Chukchi Sea

B R O O K S

SOVIET
UNION

Kotzebue

ARCTIC CIRCLE

*Kotzebue
Sound*

Taylor
Teller
Council
Nome

*Saint
Lawrence
Island*

Norton Sound

Yukon River

Baker

*Bering
Sea*

K U S K O K W I M   MOUNTAINS

Denali
National Park
and Preserve

*Denali
(Mt. McKinley)*

A L A S K A

Willow

*Nunivak
Island*

Bethel

Anchorage
Tyonek

Kenai

Kuskokwim Bay

Seward

Homer

Cook Inlet

Dillingham

Bristol Bay

State
Ferry
Route

Port Lions
Kodiak

A L A S K A   PENINSULA

PACIFIC OCEAN

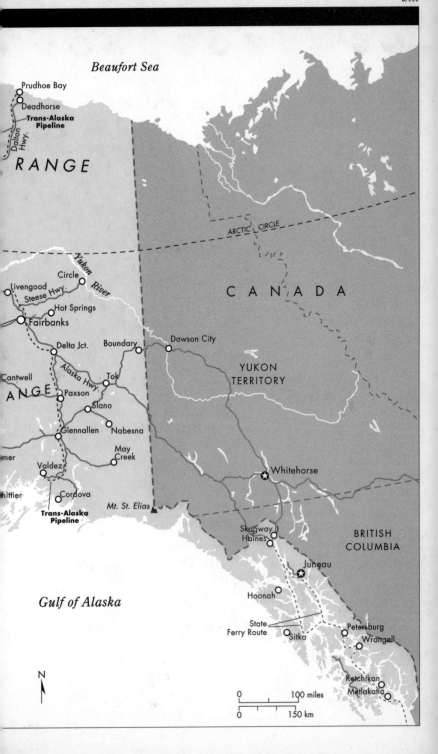

Beaufort Sea

Prudhoe Bay
Deadhorse
Trans-Alaska Pipeline
Dalton Hwy.

RANGE

ARCTIC CIRCLE

Yukon River
Circle
Livengood
Steese Hwy.
Hot Springs
Fairbanks
Delta Jct.
Boundary
Dawson City

CANADA

YUKON TERRITORY

Cantwell
Alaska Hwy.
Tok
Paxson
Slano
ANGE
Glennallen
Nabesna
mer
Valdez
May Creek
hittier
Cordova
Trans-Alaska Pipeline
Mt. St. Elias

Whitehorse

Skagway
Haines

BRITISH COLUMBIA

Juneau

Gulf of Alaska

Hoonah

State Ferry Route
Sitka

Petersburg
Wrangell

N

Ketchikan
Metlakatla

0   100 miles
0   150 km

World Time Zones

Numbers below vertical bands relate each zone to Greenwich Mean Time (0 hrs.).
Local times frequently differ from these general indications,
as indicated by light-face numbers on map.

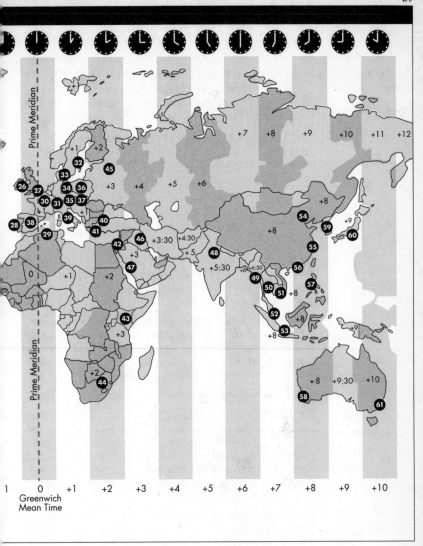

Introduction

By Stanton H. Patty

Born and raised in Alaska, Stanton H. Patty is a retired assistant editor of the Seattle Times *in Seattle, WA.*

Alaska! It is detached, like a severed limb, from the rest of the United States. Its nearest neighbors are Canada and the Soviet Union. Some of its citizens live closer to Japan than to their own state capital, Juneau.

And it is big. A map of Alaska superimposed on one of the continental United States would reach from the Atlantic to the Pacific, and from Canada to Mexico.

Alaskans enjoy telling how they could cut Alaska in half and make Texas the third-largest state. Then they brag about having the highest mountain in North America (Mt. Mc-Kinley) and the nation's biggest oil field (Prudhoe Bay) in the High Arctic.

But it is more than scale and geography—more than a tired list of superlatives—that sets Alaska apart from the rest of the country. For the visitor, Alaska is youth, energy, space, wildness.

A traveler to Alaska senses excitement, a feeling of adventure, the moment he or she steps ashore from a cruise ship in a misty port or arrives by jetliner in a northern city where the architecture is a haphazard blend of back-home modern and frontier shabby.

There is something different about Alaska.

For many visitors, it is almost like a first trip to a foreign land. Yes, the language is the same. There are Big Macs and J.C. Penney stores. Summertime temperatures are comfortable, about the same as in Seattle or Vancouver, B.C., along the coast; even warmer in the interior, where welcome hotel air conditioners hum. Alaska is not the stuff of icy legends in all seasons.

But there is also something almost unsettling about Alaska for the first-time visitor. It seems to be a land of many places, many kinds of experiences—too big to comprehend.

That is the key—the many Alaskas.

A grandmother rides a tourist helicopter to walk on a glacier near Juneau, unaware that a few yards from the safe zone selected by the pilot there are deep crevasses that could gulp a house. "Scary," she says, "but exhilarating."

A young couple straps on backpacks for a hike on a wilderness trail in Chugach State Park. The visitors catch glimpses of mountain sheep and moose just 10 eagle-flight miles from downtown Anchorage, Alaska's largest city.

A youngster pans for gold at a tourist stop in the old goldrush town of Nome. He yells out when he finds a shiny flake among the swirling sands, never dreaming that the pan was "salted" by a kindly miner with a bit of guaranteed gold for his Alaskan souvenir.

Late on a June night in Barrow, at the top of the continent, a vacationing couple watches the midnight sun dip almost to the horizon and then bounce upward again like a fiery ball. They turn and look into the leathery, brown faces of the Arctic's proud people, the Eskimos.*

Rafters on the fabled Yukon River drift with the current, spellbound, watching the high-speed dives of peregrine falcons above rocky cliffs. They camp for the night, swatting mosquitoes, hoping for a breeze to chase away the bugs. The breeze comes, and they unpack a skillet to grill a fresh-caught Arctic grayling.

Near Fairbanks, in Alaska's heartland, other visitors reach out to touch a silvery tube, the trans-Alaska oil pipeline, which transports crude from the Arctic oil field at Prudhoe Bay 800 miles across Alaska to a tidewater tanker terminal in the little town of Valdez. The pipeline, they know from news reports, was the subject of an epic environmental controversy in the 1970s. Here it is, zig-zagging through the wilderness like a giant snake.

Deep in Denali National Park, fickle weather hides the crown of Mount McKinley. There is disappointment aboard the tour bus. But Denali, Alaska's number one visitor attraction, a guide says, is more a wildlife park than a mountain park. On the drive back to the hotel, at the park entrance, the visitors are treated to the sight of grizzly bears bounding across the tundra and moose munching on willows by the road. Disappointment becomes delight.

In Glacier Bay National Park, down in fjord-laced Southeast Alaska, a small cruise ship is anchored for the night right off the face of a booming glacier. There are volleys of sound, like gunshots, then huge slabs of ice from the glacier break away and tumble into the bay, creating waves to rock the vessel with the motion of gentle sea swells. Harbor seals ride the ice rafts like stowaways. Bald eagles ride the air currents above. In the ship's lounge, passengers are cooling their cocktails with slivers of slow-to-melt glacier ice that is millions of years old.

Near the town of Cordova, in South Central Alaska's Prince William Sound, another realm of glaciers, a lone birder on the delta of the Copper River trains binoculars on a trio of trumpeter swans. The swans are like delicate figurines, resting in the quiet waters of a wilderness pond. Nowhere else in the world can a visitor see such a concentration of

---

*Eskimo *is the approved term for Arctic natives of Alaska, according to the Alaska Federation of Natives.* Inuit *is the proper word for Canadian Eskimos.*

trumpeters—as many as 1,000 nest there from late spring into fall.

And out in the Pribilof Islands, dots in the Bering Sea between Alaska and Siberia, where the Aleut people were brought as virtual slaves by Russian fur hunters in the 18th century, the surf crashes on rookeries swarming with northern fur seals. It is breeding time. Jealous bulls guard their harems. Glossy newborn pups are like appealing stuffed toys in a gift shop. Once the seals were hunted almost to extinction for their pelts. Now, thanks to many years of intelligent management by the North Pacific sealing nations (the United States, Canada, the Soviet Union, and Japan), their numbers are swelling. The Aleut natives, slaves no longer, make their livings now mainly from tourism.

This is the real Alaska—many Alaskas—a destination for personal discoveries.

Writers, always seeking convenient categories, like to divide Alaska into six regions. The boundaries are arbitrary, but this is how the regions might be organized:

Southeast Alaska. For most travelers, "Southeast," as Alaskans call the Panhandle in verbal shorthand, is the introduction to Alaska. Glaciers, fjords, vast forests, Indian totems, salmon fleets, cities and towns clinging to shorelines under lofty mountains, mild and often damp weather—these are what define Southeast Alaska. Because there are no highways connecting the communities, the state operates a marine highway, a ferry system for passengers and vehicles. Ports of call include Ketchikan, Juneau, Sitka, Petersburg, Wrangell, Haines, and Skagway.

South Central Alaska. It sweeps from sophisticated Anchorage (pop. 225,000, roughly half of Alaska's total population) down to Prince William Sound and the coast of the Gulf of Alaska, plus the Kenai Peninsula and the Kodiak Island area in the Gulf of Alaska. Major communities, in addition to Anchorage, are Palmer, Wasilla, Whittier, Valdez, Cordova, Yakutat, Seward, Homer, Kenai, Seldovia, and Kodiak. Anchorage's climate is similar to that of Helsinki, Finland, with pleasant summers and chilly winters.

Interior. A region of extremes, with warm summers and frigid winters, this huge piece of Alaska includes the Brooks Range in the north and the Alaska Range in the south, as well as historic waterways such as the Yukon and Tanana rivers. Fairbanks, the hub, was born of an early-day gold rush and still has an edge-of-the-frontier feeling, with old log cabins in the shadows of up-to-date office buildings. The main campus of the University of Alaska is in the Fairbanks area, along with important army and air force bases.

The Arctic. This is the home of the hardy Eskimo people, grouped mostly in villages on the bleak coastlines of the Chukchi and Beaufort seas. The coastal plain—the North Slope in oil-field jargon—has a desertlike environment, with little precipitation and sparse vegetation. Bright wildflowers carpet the tundra during the short summer season. Destinations for visitors include Barrow, Kotzebue, and Nome. (Technically, Nome is just south of the Arctic Circle, but is included on so-called Arctic tours.) The Prudhoe Bay oil field is just to the east of Barrow, America's northernmost community. Tourist motor coaches operate on the all-gravel oil-pipeline construction road, now called the Dalton Highway, between Prudhoe Bay and Fairbanks in the summer season.

Alaska Peninsula–Aleutian Islands. This is a region of steaming volcanoes and fast-changing, often stormy weather. "If you don't like the weather, wait 15 minutes," bush pilots joke. But temperatures are milder than might be expected. There is even a species of orchid in the bleak Aleutians. The region is lightly traveled, and was the scene of Japanese invasions in World War II. The major community is Dutch Harbor/Unalaska. The former is a busy commercial-fishing port. Unalaska is the site of an ancient Aleut community. A travel highlight in this region is Katmai National Park, on the Alaska Peninsula, with its volcanic Valley of Ten Thousand Smokes, trophy fishing for rainbow trout, and an abundant population of brown bears.

Bering Sea Coast. Sometimes called Western Alaska, this region arcs for more than 100,000 square miles from Bristol Bay to the Arctic Circle. It is a watery wilderness that includes the enormous deltas of the Yukon and Kuskokwim rivers and islands (St. Lawrence Island, the Pribilof Islands, Nunivak Island, and others) adrift in the Bering Sea. This region also is a center of the Eskimo people, in communities with such unfamiliar names as Bethel, Dillingham, Naknek, Hooper Bay, St. Michael, Unalakleet, St. Paul, St. George, Gambell, Savoonga, and Mekoryuk. Weather can range from winter harsh to summer mild.

But there is more to Alaska for the traveler than spectacular scenery and wilderness experiences. Returning visitors say Alaska's best asset may be its warm, welcoming hosts—the people.

That is easy to understand when one realizes that Alaska, in many ways, still is a frontier. Communities are widely scattered, linked mostly by airplanes instead of roads. Residents still depend on each other as in pioneer times; hardly a family in village Alaska has not been touched by violent death. There still are gentle places where doors never are locked and car keys are left in ignitions.

There are only about 520,000 Alaskans (just a few more people than in the entire state of Wyoming) spread across 586,400 square miles.

Alaskans socialize with each other in the same way residents of rural America gather for Sunday church services and county fairs. They are on a first-name basis with their politicians—the United States senators are "Ted" (Stevens) and "Frank" (Murkowski) to folks on the streets of the smallest villages. They are not in awe of their leaders; in fact, they hold them as accountable as they would salesmen on expense accounts. Walter J. Hickel, a former governor and President Richard Nixon's first secretary of the interior, will always be "Wally" to families from Ketchikan to Barrow. The late Bill Egan, Alaska's first elected governor after statehood, used to turn down courtesy upgrade invitations from Alaska Airlines to ride first class. Egan always chose to travel in the coach section with economy passengers. "That's where the votes are," he said with a wink.

Because there are so few Alaskans, they band together for common causes—but they also scrap like family.

Anchorage and Fairbanks (the two largest cities) thrive on feuding. Hometowners in Fairbanks think Anchorage is too glitzy for Alaska. They joke that "the real Alaska begins about 10 miles outside of Anchorage." It isn't so, of course. Anchorage is Alaskan in style, with sled-dog races and mountain scenery, but it also has high-rise hotels and posh restaurants for travelers.

Anchorage residents fire back, calling Fairbanks "a hick town, the ice fog capital of the world." That isn't so, either. Fairbanks has a frontier flavor along with its own medley of visitor attractions.

The squabbling is all in fun—most of the time.

In 1982, when forces in the Anchorage area made their most recent try to move the state capital from Juneau, in Southeast Alaska, to Willow, 70 miles or so north of Anchorage, it was a case of Anchorage versus most of the rest of Alaska. That was a serious dispute. Majorities of voters in Fairbanks, Southeast Alaska, and rural Alaska (known in Alaska as the bush) joined to defeat the capital-move measure soundly.

The scars haven't healed yet from that fray. If Alaska in general has a malady, it would be called regionalism.

That's pretty easy to understand, too. Alaska is so big that it has conflicting resource interests. The commercial fishermen of coastal Alaska don't want oil tankers endangering their salmon, halibut, and crab harvests. Business leaders in Anchorage and Fairbanks are unabashed boosters for the petroleum industry that fuels their economies. It doesn't mean much to an Eskimo villager in the Arctic when he hears Southeast Alaska timbermen hundreds of miles away complaining about soft markets for logs in Japan. And it doesn't mean a whole lot to the timbermen when they read about an oil spill in the Arctic. Despite kind words for public consumption, there still is a residual of racism in Alaska. The native peoples—Eskimo, Indian, and Aleut—continue á long struggle to gain equal footing with Caucasian Alaskans. Alaska, in other words, is like many states in one.

Old-timers remember not-so-long-ago signs in shop windows that read: "No dogs or natives allowed." They also remember how native children were punished in U.S. Bureau of Indian Affairs schools for daring to speak their traditional languages.

Those days of overt discrimination are over. Today's brand of racism is far more subtle—the diner in a fancy hotel sniggering about drunken natives wobbling down Fourth Avenue in Anchorage or Second Avenue in Fairbanks. The diner fails to give credit where it's due: Native leaders are in the forefront of campaigns to battle alcoholism. The statewide native newspaper, *Tundra Times*, refuses to accept advertisements for liquor. But city bootleggers continue to sneak booze into concerned native villages that have voted to be "dry."

However, there is one thing that unites the Alaskans—their shared memories of being held back as a territory until statehood in 1959.

Those were the days when Alaskans called themselves "second-class citizens." They couldn't vote for a U.S. president. In territorial times, their governors, ranging from wise to foolish, were appointed by the president without a vote of the people. When prestatehood Alaskans traveled by air between Alaska and Seattle, they were subjected to customs and immigration inspections. From the time the first statehood bill was introduced in Congress, it took Alaskans 40 years to pin a star to the U.S. flag.

The hard feelings from the statehood fight may help explain some of the headlines outsiders read during the oil-pipeline debate. Environmental leaders and outside editorial writers were about as welcome as influenza when they organized a well-orchestrated (but failed) battle against construction of the pipeline. Most Alaskans wanted the line, viewing it as a source of revenue for their money-short state—money for schools and social programs. Angry Alaskans fastened bumper stickers to their cars, reminding environmental worriers that they, too, needed petroleum products for their homes and automobiles. One particularly colorful bumper strip said: "Let the bastards freeze in the dark."

Well, the pipeline was built (completed in 1977), and the Prudhoe Bay oil still flows, supplying America with about one-fourth of its crude. And all but the most reluctant Alaskans will admit that thanks to the pressure from conservationists, the pipeline was "overdesigned" to make it safer for the Alaska they all love.

While the pipeline was being built, environmentalists were winning a bigger battle: getting more of Alaska set aside by the federal government for national parks, wildlife refuges, wild rivers, and other wilderness areas. Today, Alaska's national parklands stretch from the jade fjords of Southeast Alaska to the tundra of the lonely Arctic—50 million acres covering about 13% of the state. Alaska holds 70% of all parklands in the nation and 90% of all wildlife refuges.

That federal action didn't win enthusiastic support from most Alaskans, those who feel that Uncle Sam, now controlling 60 percent of Alaska's land area, still has too much say over the affairs of a sovereign state.

For visitors and the tourist industry, however, those parks, refuges, and wild rivers are treasures. They belong to the nation, not just Alaska.

This is the Alaska you will see today—young, high-spirited, and mostly untrampled.

There was another kind of Alaska back in the mists of time.

First, perhaps 12,000 to 14,000 years ago (scientists still are trying to fix a time), came early man, the forebears of today's native peoples. The first travelers to Alaska trekked across land bridges that long ago disappeared under the choppy waters of the Bering Sea, traveling from Asia to the North American continent. They came in small waves, migrating, following fish and game for food. Some of the nomads continued across the Arctic to Canada and Greenland. Some stayed in what today is Alaska. Others moved on, as far as the American Southwest.

You'll find their traces in Alaska's museums and in the native villages, where traditions such as ivory carving and totem carving still are living art.

In an Arctic community, you can meet Eskimo whaling captains and ceremonial dancers. In Southeast Alaska, you can meet master Tlingit and Haida Indian carvers shaping cedar into dramatic totems and masks. In the Aleutian Islands, stepping stones toward Siberia, you can meet Aleut women who still weave grass baskets so fine and tight they can hold water. In the interior, you can meet Athabascan Indians whose beadwork can turn a pair of moosehide slippers into museum-quality keepsakes.

The peaceful life of the native peoples ended in 1741, when the Russians "discovered" Alaska. (The natives, naturally, say they knew it was there all the time.) Alaska became Russian America for 126 years. The Russians came, spreading out as far as northern California, to gather the furs of sea otters and fur seals. At first the natives fought back—

the Tlingits massacred the residents of Russian outposts at Sitka and Yakutat, even took Russian scalps where the town of Haines is today at the northern end of Alaska's Inside Passage. But it was a losing battle.

Russia sold Alaska to the United States in 1867—for $7.2 million, or about 2¢ an acre. (Ironically, $7.2 million was the value of the first shipment of crude oil moved by tanker after the trans-Alaska pipeline was completed.) Alaska's biggest holiday, Alaska Day, October 18, celebrates the remarkable real estate transaction of 1867.

Alaska's Russian heritage remains a vivid thread in Alaskan life. You can find it in the family names of the native peoples who were crushed by their Russian rulers. Left behind, in addition to mixed-blood offspring, were onion-domed Russian Orthodox churches all across Alaska.

You can see dazzling old icons in St. Michael's Cathedral in Sitka, once the capital of Russian America. You can climb the steps of Castle Hill in Sitka to the spot where the double-eagle czarist flag was lowered for the last time in 1867. You can find prized Russian artifacts in a museum in Kodiak, the Russians' headquarters before Sitka. And out in the Aleutian Chain, on the island of Unalaska, is Alaska's oldest remaining Russian church, the Holy Ascension Russian Orthodox Cathedral, dating back to 1825.

Events moved quickly, almost in a blur, soon after Alaska became American territory: gold stampedes through Alaska to the Klondike in Canada's Yukon Territory, followed by gold rushes down the Yukon River to the beaches of Nome on the Bering Sea and into the hills and valleys around Fairbanks in the heart of Alaska.

During World War II, Japanese planes bombed the U.S. Navy base at Dutch Harbor in the Aleutians in 1942, and a few days later enemy troops occupied the Aleutian islands of Attu and Kiska. A terrible battle was fought at Attu the next year to win back the island. Military records say the percentage of American casualties was second only to the fight for Iwo Jima in the Pacific combat theater.

Some of the GIs stayed in Alaska after the war, rearing families and homesteading. They opened small businesses, put down roots, and joined the pioneers in building a new kind of Alaska. And then came the final momentum that led to statehood in January 1959.

But some folks still aren't convinced that Alaska is in the United States. Not long ago, a Fairbanks man had a letter returned from an aviation school in Miami, where he had applied for entrance. It said: "We are enclosing proper forms for clearance with the American consulate and for obtaining your visa."

And then there was the traveler from California who wrote the Alaska Division of Tourism recently to ask if American currency could be used in Alaska.

Oh, well. You're going to love Alaska, USA.

You have to applaud a place where the first session of the first territorial legislature (in 1913) approved voting rights for women as one of the first orders of business. It would be another seven years before the woman-suffrage amendment was added to the U.S. Constitution.

In this colorful land called Alaska, where it sometimes is difficult to tell tall tales from true stories, that one is on the record.

1 Essential Information

Before You Go

Visitor Information

The **Alaska Division of Tourism** (Box E-701, Juneau 99811, tel. 907/465–2010) publishes an annual Travel Planner, a comprehensive information source for those wishing to vacation in Alaska and Canada's Yukon. The A.D.O.T. also can give you the numbers and addresses of various local tourist centers and chambers of commerce that can assist you if you are planning to visit their specific communities.

For additional information on Canada's Yukon, contact **Tourism Yukon** (Box 2703, Whitehorse, Yukon Territory, Canada Y1A 2C6, tel. 403/993–5575) or the **Tourism Industry Association** (102–302 Steele St., Whitehorse, Yukon Territory, Canada Y1A 2C5, tel. 403/668–3331).

Tour Groups

Tour packages to Alaska have been proliferating in the last few years, and there are many fine ones. Give or take a few adjectives and glowing terms, the brochures put out by the tour operators, cruise ships, and airlines pushing escorted and independent tours paint a reliable picture of Alaska's grand-scale settings. It is wise to compare packages, though; sometimes the lowest price is not the best value, considering what is included and what is extra.

When evaluating a tour, be sure to find out exactly which expenses are included (particularly tips, taxes, side trips, additional meals, and entertainment); ratings of all hotels on the itinerary and the facilities they offer; cancellation policies for you and for the tour operator; and, if you are traveling alone, the cost for a single supplement.

The following is a small sampling of packages from some respected Alaska operators. For additional resources, contact your travel agent or the Alaska Division of Tourism. Most tour operators request that bookings be made through a travel agent—there is no additional charge for doing so.

General-Interest Tours Several major cruise lines are very active in the "cruise/tour" market, packaging a sea passage between Seattle or Vancouver and Alaska, a journey on the state's inland waterways, or both, along with more traditional touring (*see* Cruise Tours in Chapter 3).

Princess Tours (2815 Second Ave., Suite 400, Seattle, WA 98121, tel. 206/728–4202) offers 37 packages combining air, sea, and land travel. The focuses of the tours are well described by their names: "Wilderness Adventure," "Klondike Gold Rush," "Native Cultures," and the like. Princess also serves up a "Midnight Sun Express" luxury train ride from Anchorage to Fairbanks.

Holland America Westours (300 Elliott Ave. W, Seattle, WA 98119, tel. 206/281–0511 or 800/426–0327) cruises the Inside Passage and Glacier Route and offers a choice of 10 escorted cruise itineraries. Most of the tours include first-class rail service between Fairbanks and Anchorage, with an overnight stay and wildlife tour in Denali National Park.

Of course, cruise companies have no monopoly on Alaska packages. **Maupintour** (Box 807, Lawrence, KS 66044, tel. 913/843–1211 or 800/255–4266) offers quality escorted tours touching on most of the best-known sights. Other experienced operators include **Alaska Northwest Travel Service** (130 2nd Ave. S, Edmonds, WA 98020, tel. 206/775–4505) and **Alaska Travel Bureau** (15375 S.E. 30th Pl., Suite 350, Bellevue, WA 98009, tel. 206/644–2526 or 800/426–0082), which can book several different land tours and cruises. **CampAlaska Tours** (Box 872247, Wasilla AK 99687, tel. 907/376–9438) offers 20 itineraries that may include camping, rafting, canoeing, and hiking. Tour size is limited to 12 people. These tours are a good option for people seeking an active, outdoor experience.

Special-Interest Tours
The Division of Tourism's "Alaska Vacation Planner" includes a comprehensive listing of tour operators specializing in outings for travelers wanting to pan for gold, go on photo safaris, run rivers, fish, hunt, go dog-sledding, mountaineering, skiing, and flightseeing.

Adventure **Sobek's International Explorers Society** (Box 1089, Angels Camp, CA 95222, tel. 209/736–4524) is an established international adventure tour operator. Alaska offerings include kayaking, trekking, rafting, climbing, and wildlife viewing tours. **Glacier Bay Sea Kayaks** (Box 26, Gustavus, AK 99826, tel. 907/697–2257) has one-day to two-week treks to destinations such as Glacier Bay and Admiralty Island for novices as well as more experienced adventurers.

Conservation/ Education
Conservation-minded travelers should look into the packages put together by groups like the **American Wilderness Alliance** (7600 E. Arapahoe Rd., Suite 114, Englewood, CO 80112, tel. 800/322–9453 or 303/771–0380), the **National Audubon Society** (950 Third Ave., New York, NY 10022, tel. 212/546–9140), and the **Sierra Club** (730 Polk St., San Francisco, CA 94109, tel. 415/776–2211). You generally have to join these organizations to participate in their special tours, but part of your trip and membership fees will be put to preserving the wild areas you explore.

Fishing **Alaska Sportfishing Packages** (1308 187th Ave. N.E., Bellevue, WA 98008, tel. 206/644–2301 or 800/426–0603) knows where the salmon and other game fish are running, and they will take you there with packages ranging from one to seven nights. **Ketchum Air Service** (Box 190588, Anchorage, AK 99519, tel. 907/243–5525) can equip you and fly you to a number of their remote cabins and camps. **Sportfishing Alaska** (c/o Russ Redick, 1401 Shore Dr., Anchorage, AK 99515, tel. 907/344–8674) can custom-design a fishing trip to match your interest and experience.

Wildlife The **Alaska Wilderness Guides Association** (Box 141061, Anchorage, AK 99514, tel. 907/276–6634) is an association of professional guides that offers guided fishing, photography, and adventure travel throughout the state.

Package Deals for Independent Travelers

Both **Alaska Northwest Travel Service** and **Alaska Travel Bureau** (*see* General-Interest Tours, above) will custom-tailor packages for individuals and small groups. **Alaska Sightseeing Tours** (4th Ave. and Battery Bldg., Suite 700, Seattle, WA 98121, tel.

206/441–8687 or 800/426–7702) offers custom tours matching
varied modes of transportation (such as boat, bus, and jeep) to
your travel budget. **Alaska Airlines** (tel. 800/426–0333) has a
variety of air/hotel packages.

Tips for British Travelers

Visitor Information
Contact the **U.S. Travel and Tourism Administration** (22 Sack-
ville St., London W1X 2EA, tel. 071/439–7433).

Passports and Visas
You will need a valid passport (cost: £15). You do not need a visa
if you are staying for less than 90 days, have a return ticket,
and are flying with a participating airline. There are some exceptions to this visa-waiver rule, so check with your travel
agent or with the U. S. Embassy (Visa and Immigration Dept.,
5 Upper Grosvenor St., London W1A 2JB, tel. 071/499–3443).
No vaccinations are required.

Customs
Visitors 21 or over can take in 200 cigarettes or 50 cigars or two
kilograms of tobacco; one liter of alcohol; and duty-free gifts to
a value of $100. Do not try to take in meat or meat products,
seeds, plants, fruits, etc. Avoid illegal drugs like the plague.

Returning to Britain, you may bring home (1) 200 cigarettes or
100 cigarillos or 50 cigars or 250 grams of tobacco; (2) two liters
of table wine and, in addition, (a) one liter of alcohol over 22%
by volume (most spirits), or (b) two liters of alcohol under 22%
by volume (fortified or sparkling wine) or (c) two more liters of
table wine; (3) 50 grams of perfume and 250 milliliters of toilet
water; and (4) other goods up to a value of £32, but not more
than 50 liters of beer or 25 lighters.

Insurance
We recommend that you insure yourself against health and motoring mishaps. **Europ Assistance** (252 High St., Croydon, Surrey CRO 1NF, tel. 081/680–1234) is a firm that offers this
service. It is also wise to take out insurance to cover loss of luggage (though check that this isn't already covered by any existing home-owner's policies you may have). Trip-cancellation
insurance is another wise buy. **The Association of British Insur-
ers** (Aldermary House, 10-15 Queen St., London EC4N 1TT,
tel. 071/248–4477) will give comprehensive advice on all aspects
of vacation insurance.

Tour Operators
Twickers World (22 Church St., Twickenham TW1 3NW, tel.
081/892–8164) offers the best range of tours to Alaska.

They offer a 16-day "Yukon and Alaska" tour by 15-seater *Explorer* bus that includes historic Dawson City, Fairbanks, and
Denali, Kenai Fjords, and Wrangells-St. Elias National Parks;
an 11-day "All-Alaskan" adventure; a wilderness adventure
tour to follow the caribou migration in the Arctic National
Wildlife Range; and a trip to Glacier Bay and Admiralty Island.
All tours focus on wildlife and bird-watching.

Arctic Experience Ltd (29 Nork Way, Banstead SM7 1PB, tel.
0737/362321) offers an 18-night "Grand Yukon & Alaska Tour"
that follows one of the great overland routes from the Arctic
coast of the Northwest Territories through the Yukon to Alaska and the Pacific, featuring wildlife, historical sites, and all of
Alaska's major national parks.

Kuoni Travel (Kuoni House, Dorking, Surrey RH5 4AZ, tel.
0306/76711) offers a 14-day escorted coach tour of Alaska that
features Fairbanks, the Eskimo village of Barrow, Denali Na-

tional Park, Mt. McKinley, Anchorage, Skagway, Glacier Bay, and Sitka. Also available are tours of the Canadian Rockies followed by a 7-night Alaskan cruise.

Electricity 110 volts. You should take along an adapter, because American razor and hair-dryer sockets require flat, two-prong plugs.

When to Go

Each season in Alaska offers the visitor unique activities and experiences. Most visitors choose summer because of the temperatures and long evenings of midnight sun. From June through August, visitors can expect pleasantly warm, long days—Fairbanks shines under a staggering 22 hours of daylight in late June—and cool, comfortable nights. Alaska's coastal regions, always prone to rain, don't get quite as wet during summer months; the opposite is true of the state's interior. Of course, with the fair weather comes an onslaught of tourists and generally higher prices for rooms, tours, and transportation. Summer, particularly June, also brings on periodic plagues of mosquitoes thanks to "break-up," the time when frozen ground thaws, creating the soggy little bogs these nuisances just love.

Spring and fall offer fewer crowds, fewer mosquitoes, and generally lower prices. Early September brings special fall bonuses: above the brilliant foliage, skies may be unbelievably blue, and the mountains and glaciers are often enhanced by fresh dustings of snow. Daytime temperatures should still be quite pleasant, though evenings get progressively nippier—be prepared with some warmer clothes. Sitka hosts a major fall festival in October, commemorating the day in 1867 that Russia transferred all its holdings in Russian America to the United States. For three days, residents celebrate **Alaska Day** with contests, a parade, a pageant, and a costume ball.

Contrary to popular belief, Alaska does not close down for winter. Yes, it gets cold, and the nights grow long, but Alaskans have come up with some rousing means of taking their minds off the weather. Winter is the season for skiing, sledding, ice skating, ice fishing, and other winter sports. Major events such as the **Iditarod Trail Sled Dog Race,** held in March, help natives and visitors shrug off the cold. The annual **Fur Rendezvous** in Anchorage each February is a raucous, action-packed celebration, highlighted by the traditional Miner's and Trapper's Costume Ball.

Climate Current weather information on more than 750 cities around the world is only a phone call away. Dialing **WeatherTrak** at 900/370–8728 will connect you to a computer with which you can communicate by touch tone—at a cost of 95¢ per minute. The local number plays a taped message that tells you to dial the three-digit access code for the destination you're interested in. The code is either the area code (in the United States) or the first three letters of the foreign city. For a list of all access codes, send a stamped, self-addressed envelope to Cities (9B Terrace Way, Greensboro, NC 27403). For further information, phone 800/247–3282.

What follows are the average daily maximum and minimum temperatures for Alaskan cities.

Anchorage									
	Jan.	22F	− 6C	**May**	55F	13C	**Sept.**	55F	13C
		7	−14		38	3		40	4
	Feb.	25F	4C	**June**	62F	17C	**Oct.**	41F	5C
		9	13		47	8		27	− 3
	Mar.	31F	− 1C	**July**	65F	18C	**Nov.**	27F	− 3C
		14	−10		50	10		14	−10
	Apr.	43F	6C	**Aug.**	63F	17C	**Dec.**	20F	− 7C
		27	− 3		49	9		6	−14

Barrow									
	Jan.	− 9F	−23C	**May**	24F	− 4C	**Sept.**	34F	1C
		−22	−30		13	−11		27	− 3
	Feb.	−12F	−24C	**June**	39F	4C	**Oct.**	22F	− 6C
		−25	−32		29	− 2		12	−11
	Mar.	− 8F	−22C	**July**	46F	8C	**Nov.**	7F	−14C
		−22	−30		33	1		− 5	−21
	Apr.	7F	−14C	**Aug.**	44F	7C	**Dec.**	− 4F	−20C
		− 8	−22		33	1		−17	−27

Fairbanks									
	Jan.	− 2F	−19C	**May**	59F	15C	**Sept.**	54F	12C
		−20	−29		35	2		33	1
	Feb.	11F	−12C	**June**	71F	22C	**Oct.**	35F	2C
		−10	−23		46	8		18	− 8
	Mar.	23F	− 5C	**July**	72F	22C	**Nov.**	12F	−11C
		− 4	−20		48	9		− 5	−21
	Apr.	42F	6C	**Aug.**	66F	19C	**Dec.**	1F	−17C
		17	− 8		44	7		−16	−27

Festivals and Seasonal Events

Top seasonal events include the Anchorage Fur Rendezvous in February, the Iditarod Trail Sled Dog Race in March, Juneau's Alaska Folk Festival in April, Sitka's Alaska Day Celebration in October, and Fairbanks's Oktoberfest in the fall. For exact dates, request a copy of *Alaska Official Vacation Planner* from the Alaska State Division of Tourism (Box E-701, Juneau 99811, tel. 907/465–2010). Additional details are available from local visitors bureaus—the appropriate phone number follows each listing.

Mid-Jan.: Russian New Year and Masquerade Ball celebrates a unique heritage in Kodiak. Tel. 907/486–4782.
Late Jan.: Sled Dog Racing, in Anchorage, gives a good introduction to competitions that are held almost everywhere during the winter months. Tel. 907/276–4118.
Early Feb.: Tent City Winter Festival, in Wrangell, recalls the flavor of Alaska's early days. Tel. 907/874–3770.
Early Feb.: Cordova Ice Worm Festival features a 100-foot ice worm parading through the city streets. Tel. 907/474–2248.
Mid-Feb.: Fur Rendezvous, in Anchorage, includes more than 140 events, from the world's largest outdoor fur auction to the World Championship Sled Dog Races. Tel. 907/276–4118.
Mid-Feb.: Taku Rondy at Eaglecrest, in Juneau, celebrates the history of gold mining. Tel. 907/586–2284.
Mid-Feb.: International Ice Climbing Festival, in Valdez, is not for the faint of heart. Tel. 907/835–2984.
Early Mar.: North Pole Winter Carnival takes place in North Pole, just outside of Fairbanks. Tel. 907/456–5774.

Early to mid-Mar.: Iditarod Trail Sled Dog Race stretches from Anchorage to Nome—1,049 miles. More than 70 dog teams compete. Tel. 907/276–4118.

Mid-Mar.: Bering Sea Ice Classic Golf Tournament is actually held on the pack ice of the Bering Sea near Nome. Tel. 907/443–5535.

Early Apr.: Alyeska Spring Carnival holds court at the Alyeska Resort & Ski Area, 40 miles southeast of Anchorage. Tel. 907/783–2222.

Early Apr.: Alaska Folk Festival, in Juneau, is an unusual mix of music, handmade crafts, and foods. Tel. 907/586–2284.

Early Apr.: Nome to Kotzebue Sled Dog Race. Tel. 907/443–5535.

Mid-May: Little Norway Festival, in picturesque Petersburg, salutes its Scandinavian heritage. Tel. 907/772–3646.

Late May: Kodiak King Crab Festival, on the island of Kodiak, means good food and a cold swimming race, with participants in all-weather survival suits. Tel. 907/486–4782.

Early to late June: Sitka Summer Music Festival. Tel. 907/747–5940.

Mid-June: Basically Bach Festival, in Anchorage. Tel. 907/276–4118.

July 4: Mount Marathon Race in Seward is a rugged climb/foot race up the mountain behind the town. The best vantage is right below the trail starting point.

Mid-July: Valdez Gold Rush Days. Tel. 907/835–2984.

Late–Aug.: Alaska State Fair in Palmer is a traditional state fair with cooking, handicraft, livestock, and brewing competitions. The giant vegetables are the sight to see.

Oct. 13: Alaska Day Celebration brings out the whole town of Sitka to celebrate the day the United States acquired Alaska from Russia. Festival includes a period costume ball and a parade. Tel. 907/747–5940.

Mid-Oct.: Oktoberfest is celebrated in Fairbanks. Tel. 907/456–5774.

Mid-Oct.: Quiana Alaska Native Dance Festival, in Anchorage, provides a taste of Alaska's native culture. Tel. 907/276–4118.

Late Nov.: Great Alaska Shootout takes place at Sullivan Arena, in Anchorage, where some of the best college basketball teams in the country compete. Tel. 907/276–4118.

Late Nov.: Athapaskan Old-Time Fiddling Festival enlivens Fairbanks. Tel. 907/456–5774.

Early Dec.: Bachelor Society Ball, in Talkeetna, is a curious mix of mountain men and city folk. Tel. 907/465–2010.

Late Dec.: Barrow Christmas Games include the world's most northerly golf tournament, dog and mukluk races, Eskimo games, and dancing. Tel. 907/852–5211.

What to Pack

With porters and luggage trolleys seemingly joining the list of endangered species, your best bet is to pack light. Luggage allowances on domestic flights vary slightly from airline to airline. Most allow three checked pieces and two carry-on bags. Check-in luggage cannot weigh more than 70 pounds per piece or be larger than 62 inches (length + width + height). Carry-on luggage cannot be larger than 45 inches (9″ × 14″ × 22″) to fit under the seat, 60 inches (10″ × 14″ × 36″) to fit in the overhead luggage compartment, or 72 inches (4″ × 23″ × 45″) to fit in the storage closet. Items exceeding these dimensions will generally be rejected as carryons, and handled as checked baggage.

Not all sections of Alaska have the fierce winters that are usually associated with the state. The winters in the Southeast and South Central coastal regions are relatively mild—Chicago and Minneapolis tend to experience harsher weather than Anchorage. It's a different story in the interior, where temperatures in the subzero range and biting winds keep most visitors indoors. The best way to keep warm under colder conditions is to wear layers of clothing, starting with thermal underwear and socks. When wearing snow boots, be certain they are not too tight. Restricting your circulation will only make you colder. Bring along a lotion to protect yourself from windburn.

Alaskan summers are mild, though it's a good idea to bring along some rain gear, as sudden storms are common. An extra sweater or jacket for cool evenings will come in handy. And don't forget suntan lotion and plenty of insect repellent.

Sunglasses are a good idea year-round, especially when touring the glaciers. A pair of binoculars will help you track any wildlife you encounter. Pack enough film and personal supplies to see you through your trip, as purchasing these items in Alaska tends to be pricier than in the contiguous United States.

Befitting its frontier image, dress is mostly casual and informal both day and night. Bring along one outfit that is appropriate for "dress up," if you enjoy doing so, though it's not necessary. An extra pair of glasses, contact lenses, or prescription sunglasses is always a good idea. It is important to pack any prescription medicines you use regularly as well as any allergy medication you may need.

Cash Machines

Virtually all U.S. banks belong to a network of ATMs (Automatic Teller Machines), which gobble up bank cards and spit out cash 24 hours a day in cities throughout the country. There are some eight major networks in the United States, the largest of which are **Cirrus,** owned by MasterCard, and **Plus,** affiliated with Visa. Some banks belong to more than one network. These cards are not automatically issued; you have to ask for them. Cards issued by Visa and MasterCard may also be used in the ATMs, but the fees are usually higher than the fees on bank cards, and there is a daily interest charge on the "loan," even if monthly bills are paid on time. Each network has a toll-free number you can call to locate machines in a given city. The Cirrus number is 800/4–CIRRUS; the Plus number is 800/THE–PLUS. Check with your bank for fees and for the amount of cash you can withdraw on any given day.

Traveling with Film

If your camera is new, shoot and develop a few rolls of film before leaving home. Pack some lens tissue and an extra battery for your built-in light meter. Invest about $10 in a skylight filter and screw it onto the front of your lens. It will protect the lens and also reduce haze.

Cold winter weather presents challenges for photographers; Alaska professionals carry their camera gear inside their jackets to keep it working. Lenses also frost up from changes in temperature. Check yours before shooting; let it adjust to the temperature and wipe it clear before you snap the shot.

On a plane trip, never pack unprocessed film in check-in luggage; if your bags get X-rayed, you can say good-bye to your pictures. Always carry undeveloped film with you through security and ask to have it inspected by hand. (It helps to isolate your film in a plastic bag, ready for quick inspection.) Inspectors at American airports are required by law to honor requests for hand inspection; abroad, you'll have to depend on the kindness of strangers.

The old airport scanning machines—still in use in some Third World countries—use heavy doses of radiation that can turn a family portrait into an early morning fog. The newer models—used in all U.S. airports—are safe for anything from five to 500 scans, depending on the speed of your film. The effects are cumulative; you can put the same roll of film through several scans without worry. After five scans, though, you're asking for trouble.

If your film gets fogged and you want an explanation, send it to the National Association of Photographic Manufacturers (550 Mamaroneck Ave., Harrison, NY 10528). They will try to determine what went wrong. The service is free.

Traveling with Children

Publications *Family Travel Times* is an eight- to 12-page newsletter published 10 times a year by **TWYCH** (Travel with Your Children, 80 8th Ave., New York, NY 10011, tel. 212/206–0688). A one-year subscription costs $35 and includes access to back issues. The organization also offers a free phone-in service with advice on specific destinations.

Great Vacations with Your Kids: The Complete Guide to Family Vacations in the U.S., by Dorothy Ann Jordan and Marjorie A. Cohen (E.P. Dutton, 2 Park Ave., New York, NY 10016; $12.95), details everything from city vacations to adventure vacations to child-care resources.

Hotels Alaska's population is young, and families are welcome at most hotels and private lodgings.

Home Exchange Exchanging homes is a surprisingly low-cost way to enjoy a vacation in another part of the country. **Vacation Exchange Club, Inc.** (Box 820, Haleiwa, HI 96712, tel. 800/638–3841) specializes in domestic home exchanges. The club publishes three directories a year and updated, late listings. Membership ($50 per year) includes your listing in one book, a newsletter, and copies of all publications. **Loan-a-Home** (2 Park La., #6E, Mount Vernon, NY 10552, tel. 914/644–7640) is popular with academics and businesspeople. There's no annual membership fee or charge for listing your home, but a directory and supplement cost $35.

Getting There On domestic flights, children under age 2 not occupying a seat travel free. Various discounts apply to children aged 2–12. Regulations about infant travel on airplanes are in the process of changing. Until they do, however, if you want to be sure your infant is secured in his/her own safety seat, you must buy a separate ticket and bring her own infant car seat. (Check with the airline in advance; certain seats aren't allowed. Or write for the booklet "Child/Infant Safety Seats Acceptable for Use in Aircraft," from the Federal Aviation Administration, APA-200, 800 Independence Ave., SW, Washington, DC 20591 tel. 202/267–3479). Some airlines allow babies to travel in their own safety seats at no charge if there's a spare seat on the plane available, otherwise safety seats will be stored and a parent will have to hold the child. If you opt to hold your baby on your lap, do so with the infant outside the seatbelt so he or she won't be crushed in case of sudden stop.

Also inquire about special children's meals or snacks. See the February 1990 and 1992 issues of *Family Travel Times* for "TWYCH's Airline Guide," which contains a rundown of the children's services offered by 46 airlines.

Hints for Disabled Travelers

Challenge Alaska (Box 110065, Anchorage 99511, tel. 907/563–2658) is a nonprofit organization that will answer accessibility questions and provide recreation opportunities for individuals with various disabilities. Write for a free brochure and a quarterly newsletter.

Access Alaska (Suite 900, Anchorage 99517, tel. 907/248–4777) is a statewide information-referral service for accommodations and transportation for the disabled.

The Information Center for Individuals with Disabilities (Fort Point Pl., 1stFloor, 27–43 Wormwood St. Boston, MA 02210, tel. 617/727–5540; TDD 617/727–5236) offers useful problem-solving assistance, including lists of travel agents that specialize in tours for the disabled.

Moss Rehabilitation Hospital Travel Information Service (1200 W. Tabor Rd., Philadelphia, PA 19141, tel. 215/456–9600; TDD 215/456–9602) provides information on tourist sights, transportation, and accommodations in destinations around the world for a small fee.

Mobility International USA (Box 3551, Eugene, OR 97403, tel. 503/343–1284) has information on accommodations, organized study, etc. around the world.

The Society for the Advancement of Travel for the Handicapped (26 Court St., Penthouse Suite, Brooklyn, NY 11242, tel. 718/858–5483) offers access information. Annual membership costs $45, or $25 for senior travelers and students. Send $1 and a stamped, self-addressed envelope.

The Itinerary (Box 2012, Bayonne, NJ 07002, tel. 201/858–3400) is a bimonthly travel magazine for the disabled. Subscriptions cost $10 for 1 year, $20 for 2.

Greyhound (tel. 800/752–4841; TDD 800/345–3109) will carry a disabled person and companion for the price of a single fare.

Amtrak (tel. 800/USA–RAIL) requests 12-hour notice to provide redcap service, special seats, and a 25% discount.

Hints for Older Travelers

The **American Association of Retired Persons** (AARP, 1909 K St. NW, Washington, DC 20049, tel. 202/662–4850) has two programs for independent travelers: (1) the *Purchase Privilege Program,* which offers discounts on hotels, airfare, car rentals, and sightseeing; and (2) the *AARP Motoring Plan,* provided by Amoco, which offers emergency aid and trip-routing information for an annual fee of $33.95 per couple. The AARP also arranges group tours, through **American Express Vacations** (Box 5014, Atlanta, GA 30302, tel. 800/241–1700 or 800/637–6200 in GA). AARP members must be 50 or older. Annual dues are $5 per person or per couple.

When using an AARP or other identification card, ask for a reduced hotel rate at the time you make your reservation, not when you check out. At participating restaurants, show your card to the maître d' before you're seated, because discounts may be limited to certain set menus, days, or hours. When renting a car, be sure to ask about special promotional rates that may offer greater savings than the available discount.

National Council of Senior Citizens (925 15th St. NW, Washington, DC 20005, tel. 202/347–8800) is a nonprofit advocacy group with some 5,000 local clubs across the country. Annual membership is $12 per person or per couple. Members receive a monthly newspaper with travel information and an ID card for reduced-rate hotels and car rentals.

Mature Outlook (6001 N. Clark St., Chicago, IL 60660, tel. 800/336–6330), a subsidiary of Sears Roebuck & Co., is a travel club for people over age 50, with hotel and motel discounts and a bimonthly newsletter. Annual membership is $9.95 per couple. Instant membership is available at participating Holiday Inns.

Golden Age Passport is a free lifetime pass to all parks, monuments, and recreation areas run by the federal government. People 62 and over should pick one up in person at any national park that charges admission. A driver's license or other proof of age is required.

September Days Club is run by the moderately priced Days Inns of America (tel. 800/241–5050). The $12 annual membership fee for individuals or couples over 50 entitles them to reduced car rental rates and reductions of 15%–50% at about 95% of the chain's more than 350 motels.

Greyhound (tel. 800/752–4841) and **Amtrak** (tel. 800/USA–RAIL) offer special fares for senior citizens. Amtrak has a free "Access Guide."

Publications *The Senior Citizen's Guide to Budget Travel in the United States and Canada* is available for $4.95, including postage, from Pilot Books (103 Cooper St., Babylon, NY 11702, tel. 516/422–2225).

The Discount Guide for Travelers over 55, by Caroline and Walter Weintz, lists helpful addresses, package tours, reduced-rate car rentals, etc., in the United States and abroad. If the book is unavailable from your local bookstore, send $7.95 plus $1.50 shipping and handling to NAL/Cash Sales (Bergenfield Order Dept., 120 Woodbine St., Bergenfield, NJ 07621, tel. 800/526–0275).

Further Reading

Alaska has long been a fitting setting for tales of heroic characters, great journeys, and man's epic struggle with nature. Novels richly describing the state and its people include the classic *Call of the Wild* by Jack London; Ivan Doig's *The Sea Runners,* an adventure set in 1853, when Alaska belonged to Russia; *Athabasca,* an Alister MacLean thriller set around the

Alaska pipeline; and *Sitka,* by the popular chronicler of the American frontier, Louis L'Amour.

Coming Into the Country, by John McPhee, describes three different areas of Alaska. *The Wake of the Unseen Object,* by Tom Kizzia, is a sensitive description of little-visited settlements and people in rural Alaska. *I'd Swap My Old Skidoo for You,* by Nan Elliot, tells the stories of interesting and eccentric contemporary Alaskans.

Arriving and Departing

By Plane

Alaska, Continental, Delta, Northwest, and **United** airlines are the major U.S. carriers serving Alaska. Outside of the West Coast, your airline options are not likely to be overwhelming, as the different carriers fly out of different gateway cities. This arrangement reduces the kind of direct competition that ignites fare wars—a situation that is good for the airlines, but not so good for the bargain-hunting vacationer.

The majority of Alaska-bound flights touch down in Anchorage. Nonstop service is also available to Fairbanks, Juneau, and Ketchikan. Southeastern Alaska cities are connected through Seattle, while northern locations are reached through Anchorage or Fairbanks.

Anchorage is also an international air crossroads. **Air France, British Airways, China Airlines, KLM, Korean, Lufthansa, Sabena,** and **SAS** offer stopovers on their way between the United States and the Far East, or over the polar route to Europe.

When booking reservations, keep in mind the distinction between nonstop flights (no stops, no plane changes), direct flights (no plane changes, but one or more stops), and connecting flights (one or more plane changes at one or more stops). Connecting flights are often the least expensive, but they are the most time-consuming and the biggest nuisance.

Smoking   As of early 1990, smoking was banned on all routes within the 48 contiguous states, within the states of Hawaii and Alaska, and on flights of under six hours to and from Hawaii and Alaska. The rule applies to both U.S. and foreign carriers.

On a flight where smoking is permitted, you can request a seat in the nonsmoking section. Department of Transportation regulations require carriers to find seats for all nonsmokers on the day of the flight, provided check-in restrictions are met.

Lost Luggage   Airlines are responsible for lost or damaged property only up to $1,250 per passenger on domestic flights, $9.07 per pound (or $20 per kilo) for checked baggage on international flights, and up to $400 per passenger for unchecked baggage on international flights. If you're carrying valuables, either take them with you on the airplane or purchase additional insurance for lost luggage. Some airlines will issue additional luggage insurance when you check in, but many do not. Insurance for lost, damaged, or stolen luggage is available through travel agents or directly through various insurance companies. Two that issue luggage insurance are **Tele-Trip** (tel. 800/228–9792), a subsidiary of Mutual of Omaha, and **The Travelers Insurance Corporation** (tel. 203/277–0111 or 800/243–3174). Tele-Trip operates sales booths at airports and also issues insurance through travel agents. Tele-Trip will insure checked luggage for up to 180 days; rates vary according to the length of the trip. The Travelers Corporation will insure checked or hand luggage for $500–$2,000 valuation per person, and also for a maximum of 180 days. For more information, write The Travelers Insurance Corporation (Ticket and Travel Dept., 1 Tower Sq., Hartford, CT 06183). Both companies offer the same rates on domestic and international flights. Check the travel pages of your Sunday newspaper for the names of other companies that insure luggage. Before you go, itemize the contents of each bag in case you need to file an insurance claim. Be certain to put your home address on each piece of luggage, including carry-on bags. If your luggage is lost and later recovered, the airline will deliver the luggage to your home free of charge.

By Car

You'll need ample vacation time to motor to Alaska. Though journeying through Canada on the Alaska Highway can be exciting and is viable, the trek from the lower 48 states is a long one. It's a seven-day trip from Seattle to Anchorage or Fairbanks, covering close to 2,500 miles. From Seattle and the Canadian port of Prince Rupert, you can link up with ferry service along the Marine Highway to reach Southeastern Alaska.

If you are planning to drive to Alaska, you should come armed with patience. In the summer, for instance, heavy rains can close the road near the Canadian border for up to a week. While such delays are uncommon, a tight schedule will be more difficult to keep in this huge, wilderness state.

Car Rentals Touring Alaska's vast interior by car is a tempting but frustrating proposition. There are a limited number of highways or, in many places, no roads at all. The Anchorage–Fairbanks corridor, for instance, simply does not connect by road with southeastern cities like Juneau and Ketchikan. However, there is enough to see in this southcentral/interior triangle to warrant having a car. Most southeast communities can be visited on foot or by public transportation. Despite this potential hassle, there are enough worthwhile day trips from most Alaskan cities to make having a car attractive.

Summer rentals should be booked well in advance of your arrival. Most agencies are sold out during tourist season. Expect to pay $40–$50 daily in Anchorage (more in smaller cities) for a subcompact, usually with 100 free miles. Those miles go quickly in much of Alaska, so try to find a weekly unlimited mileage special. Don't worry too much about mileage charges in southeast Alaska–there just isn't much road to drive on, and no two cities connect.

Avis (tel. 800/331–1212), **Budget** (tel. 800/527–0700), **Hertz** (tel. 800/654–3131), and **National** (tel. 800/328–4567) maintain airport and city locations throughout Alaska. Local companies, often a good source for low rates, include **Affordable** (tel. 907/561–1750) and **Practical** (tel. 800/663–6722) in Anchorage; **Artic** (tel. 907/451–0111) and **Rainbow** (tel. 907/457–5900) in Fairbanks; **Ugly Duckling** (tel. 907/586–3825) in Ketchikan; **Kohring's** (tel. 907/376–5784) and **Wasilla** (tel. 907/376–6993) in the Matanuska Valley; **Cheepie** (tel. 907/283–7865) at the Kenai Airport. Budget renter **Rent-A-Dent** (tel. 800/426–5243) serves the major cities, plus Petersburg, Wrangell, Kenai, and Seward.

It's always best to know a few essentials before you arrive at the car-rental counter. Find out what the collision damage waiver (usually an $8 to $12 daily surcharge) covers and whether your corporate or personal insurance already covers damage to a rental car—if so, bring a copy of the benefits section along. More and more companies now also hold renters responsible for theft and vandalism damages if they don't buy the CDW. In response, some credit card and insurance companies are extending their coverage to rental cars. These include **Access American** (tel. 800/851–2800), **Chase Manhattan Bank Visa** (tel. 800/645–7352), and **Dreyfuss Bank Gold and Silver** Master-Cards (tel. 800/847–9700).

When making your reservation, ask about promotional, weekend, and 14-day advance reservation rates; also make sure you get a reservation number. Find out, too, if the rental agency charges you for a full tank of gas whether you use it or not.

By Boat

From the ports of Seattle and Prince Rupert, B.C., you can take a frequent oceangoing passenger and vehicle ferry to reach Alaska. These relatively comfortable vessels connect Bellingham, WA, north of Seattle with principal towns and villages of Southeast Alaska. From Haines or Skagway at the northern end of the ferry route, you can drive on mostly paved highways through British Columbia and the Yukon into the rest of Alaska. *Alaska Marine Hwy., Box R, Juneau 99811, tel. 907/465–3941/42 or 800/642–0066; fax 907/465–2476.*

Another option is the *Queen of the North,* a ferry connecting Port Hardy on Vancouver Island with the Alaska ferries at Prince Rupert, B.C. Sailings are every other day in summer; once a week in winter. *British Columbia Ferries, 1112 Fort St., Victoria, B.C., Canada V8V 4V2; tel. 604/386–3431, or their Seattle office, 206/441–6865.*

By Bus

Island and coastal towns of the southeast Panhandle are not accessible by bus, except for the two ports at the northern end of the Inside Passage, Haines and Skagway. From there, highways connect with overland routes to South Central and interior destinations, and with the Alaska Highway.

Motor coaches, independently or in connection with major tour companies, travel to and throughout Alaska from U.S. and Canadian points. Contact: **Gray Line of Alaska** (300 Elliott Ave. W, Seattle, WA 98119, tel. 800/544–2206) or **Royal Hyway Tours** (2555 76th Ave. SE, Mercer Island, WA 98040, tel. 206/232–1388).

By Train

The only way you can't get to Alaska is via train. Although there are trains *in* Alaska, there are no trains *to* Alaska. The closest train stations for making connections with other means of transportation are in Seattle (tel. 203/464–1930), which is served by **Amtrak;** Vancouver, B.C. (tel. 604/669–3050), served by **Via Rail Canada;** and Prince Rupert, B.C. (tel. 604/627–7304), also served by Via Rail Canada.

Getting Around Alaska

By Plane

Commercial air travel within Alaska is usually by jet or turbo prop. Scheduled air taxi and air charter services provide quick and easy access to smaller towns and remote locales, using propeller-driven "bush aircraft" that land on wheels, on floats, or on skis. Helicopters are increasingly popular for flightseeing and fast transport (*see* the Getting Around sections of each regional chapter for more specific information).

By Train

The state-owned **Alaska Railroad** provides passenger service on the scenic 350-mile route between Fairbanks and Anchorage via Denali National Park and Preserve. The railroad also operates between Anchorage and Whittier, connecting with South Central Alaska ferry liners, and from Anchorage to Seward (three times a week).

The Denali Express has dining, bar, and dome cars for sightseeing (some tour companies operate their own rail cars). Other trains are equipped with vending machine snacks.

Travel aboard the railroad is leisurely (Anchorage to Fairbanks is an all-day trip) so you can enjoy spectacular scenery along the way. And unlike traveling by bus, you can get up and stretch your legs. Some private tour companies that offer a more glitzy trip between Anchorage and Fairbanks hook their luxury rail cars to the train.

Except for the Anchorage–Seward route, the Alaska Railroad operates year-round, but services are reduced from September to May. *Alaska Railroad, Box 1-7500, Anchorage 99510, tel. 907/265–2623 or 800/544–0552.*

By Boat

Ferry liners travel the **Alaska Marine Highway,** providing year-round ferry service for passengers and vehicles in Alaska. Onboard amenities—food service, sightseeing, solariums, and staterooms—keep the ride as pleasant as the passing scenery is. Forest service naturalists ride the larger ferries in summer and provide a running narrative on the sights you see.

The state ferry service covers two separate route networks. On the Southeast Alaska routes, mainline ferries connect Bellingham, WA, and Prince Rupert, B.C., with Ketchikan, Wrangell, Petersburg, Sitka, Juneau, Haines, and Skagway. Smaller vessels serve the smaller towns of Hoonah, Tenakee Springs, Angoon, Pelican, Kake, Hollis, Metlakatla, and Hyder.

Ferries on the South Central route call at Kodiak, Port Lions, Homer, Seldovia, Seward, Valdez, Cordova, and Whittier. In summer, ferries also travel between Kodiak and Dutch Harbor in the Aleutian Islands, stopping at Chignik, Sand Point, King Cove, and Cold Bay. There are no connections between the Southeast and South Central routes.

Schedules and fares vary greatly according to time of year. Reservations are required for summer travel from Seattle or Prince Rupert. In fall, winter, and spring, rates are lower, and senior citizens travel free between Alaska ports (passage only—meals and staterooms are additional). On smaller ferries without staterooms, senior citizens travel free year-round. *For information and reservations: Alaska Marine Hwy., Box R, Juneau 99811, tel. 907/465–3941/42 or 800/642–0066.*

By Car

The **Alaska Highway** begins at Dawson Creek, B.C., and stretches roughly 1,520 miles through Canada's Yukon to Fairbanks. The two-lane highway, Alaska's primary access road, is hard-surfaced for nearly all of its length and is open year-round. You can plan to drive comfortably through stunning wilderness. Highway services are available about every 50 miles (frequently at shorter intervals). *The Alaska Milepost* is a mile-by-mile guide to sights and services along Alaska's highways.

The rest of the state's roads are found almost exclusively in the South Central and Interior regions. They vary from four-lane freeways to nameless two-lane gravel roads and tend to be open and maintained year-round. The **George Parks Highway** connects Anchorage and Fairbanks, passing Denali National Park en route. The **Steese Highway** runs northwest of Fairbanks, to the gold-rush town of Circle. The **Richardson Highway** parallels the Alaska pipeline from Fairbanks south to the port city of Valdez.

Alaska honors valid drivers' licenses from any state or country, and the speed limit on most state highways is 55 mph. Gasoline prices can be higher than in the lower 48 states, especially in smaller towns and remote highway stations.

Hints to Motorists Driving in Alaska is much less rigorous than it used to be, although it still presents some unusual challenges. Alaskan moose, no longer terribly shy of people, often stray inquisitively onto less traveled highways. The best thing to do if you come across one while driving is to stop your car and wait. The moose will usually move on its own.

Flying gravel is a hazard to watch for along the Alaska Highway, especially in summer. Rubber matting can help protect your gas tank. A bug screen will help keep gravel and kamikaze insects off the windshield. Use clear, hard plastic guards to cover your headlights. (These are inexpensive and are available from almost any garage or service station along the access routes to the Alaska and Mackenzie highways.) Don't cover headlights with cardboard or plywood because you'll need your lights often, even in daytime, as dust is thrown up by traffic passing in both directions.

If you get stuck on any kind of road, be careful about pulling off; the shoulder could be soft. In summer it stays light late, and though traffic is also light, one of Alaska's many good samaritans is likely to stop to help and send for aid (which may be many miles away). In winter there are checkpoints for keeping track of motorists, and roads are patrolled. Bringing along some high-energy food (such as nuts or chocolate), flasks of hot beverages, and extra-warm clothing and blankets will help you through the wait for aid, should you need it.

Cars Unless you plan to undertake one of the remote highways (such as the Dempster into Canada's Northwest Territories), you won't need any special equipment. The equipment you do have should be in first-class condition, though, from tires and spare to brakes and engine. Carrying spare fuses, spark plugs, jumper cables, a flashlight with extra batteries, a tool kit, and an extra fan belt is recommended.

RVs The secret to a successful RV trip to Alaska is preparation. Expect to do some driving on gravel and on rougher roads than you are accustomed to. Batten down everything; tighten every nut and bolt in and out of sight, and don't leave anything out to bounce around inside. Travel light and your tires and suspension system will take less of a beating. Protect your headlights and the grill area in front of the radiator. Mike and Marilyn Miller, authors of a helpful motorists' guide titled *Camping Alaska and Canada's Yukon*, recommend that you carry adequate insurance to cover the replacement of your front windshield. "Without a doubt you will pick up at least one chip or crack, if not more. Trying to cover the windshield proves to be more trouble than its worth," they write.

Most of Alaska's roadside campgrounds accommodate trailers, but there are few hookups. Water is available at most stopping points, but it may be limited for trailer use. Think twice before deciding to pull an RV during the spring thaw. Facing the rough, boggy roadbed can be a trial.

Staying in Alaska

Shopping

In many respects, shopping in Alaska is not unlike shopping in the continental United States. Most of the larger cities have department stores and malls with conventional goods, and they accept the same credit cards you use at home. The postal rates for sending gifts home are the same as anywhere else in the country.

The best buys in Alaska are products of native materials made by natives and other artists and craftspeople living in the state. The state has adopted two symbols that guarantee the authenticity of crafts made by Alaskans. A hand symbol indicates the item was made by one of Alaska's native peoples. A dipper-shaped flag symbolizes that the item was made in Alaska by a resident, of materials found in the state. If some items with these tags seem more expensive than you expected, examine them closely and you'll probably find that they are handmade, one-of-a-kind pieces.

Native Crafts Look for carvings out of walrus ivory, soapstone, jade, and wood, and items made of fur. You'll find a wide choice of jewelry, mukluks (seal- or reindeer-skin Eskimo boots), masks, totem poles, paintings, and baskets.

Each of the native cultures is noted for particular skills. Eskimo art, native to the Arctic and Fringes of the state, includes

animal carvings from walrus ivory, baskets made of baleen (a
fibrous material found in the mouths of bowhead whales), and
jewelry made of walrus ivory, jade, baleen, or a combination of
the three.

The Tlingit of Southeast Alaska are known for their totems and
other wood carvings, as well as for baskets and hats woven from
spruce root and cedar bark. Tsimshian Indians also work with
spruce root and cedar bark. Haida Indians, also found mainly in
Southeast Alaska, are noted totem carvers, basket makers,
and slate carvers.

Athabaskans specialize in skin-sewing and beadwork. Grass
basketry, considered among the best in the world, is the principal art of the Aleuts.

Although these native groups are typically concentrated in a
certain region, their wares are sold throughout the state.

Seafood Salmon—smoked, dried, or otherwise—is a true Alaskan
product. Alaskan king crab is a close second. You can have both,
and other seafood items, frozen and shipped from Anchorage,
Fairbanks, and most of the bigger towns in Southeast Alaska.

Furs This is still frontier territory, and hunting is still a way of earn-
ing a living (as well as feeding the family) for some Alaskans.
Look for more fashionable and refined products in the bigger
cities, particularly Anchorage and Fairbanks. In the Fringe areas, you are likely to find more traditional pieces (such as mukluks) and raw pelts.

Participant Sports and Recreation

Boating Rivers, lakes, and saltwater inlets abound for canoeing,
kayaking, and rafting expeditions. Most Alaskan waters require a great deal of experience; having a local guide along is a
good idea. You can find guides, outfitters, and rental agencies
in Parks, Wilderness Areas and Wildlife Refuges/Chapter 4,
and under Guided Tours in each regional section.

Diving Popular along the Southeast and Gulf of Alaska coasts, despite
the fact that divers here must wear no less than quarter-inch
wetsuits. You'll find equipment rental shops in Sitka, Ketchikan, Juneau, Kodiak, and Anchorage.

Dog-sledding Several outfitters take visitors on treks lasting an hour, a day,
or overnight via this most traditional mode of Alaskan transportation. The following are some of the outfitters that can get
you sledbound. **Alaska Mountain Treks** (Box 600-AT, Moose
Pass 99631, tel. 907/288–3610) serves the Denali National Park
and the Kenai Wilderness areas. **Chugach Express Dog Sled
Tours** (Box 261-AT, Girdwood 99587, tel. 907/783–2266) tours
around Anchorage. **Flat Dog Kennels** (Box 1103-AT, Nome
99762, tel. 907/443–2958) mushes through the Seward Peninsula.

Fishing Fishing is one of the major pastimes (and occupations) of Alaskans. It can be pursued at various levels of sophistication and
expense. Deep pools and riffles in the streams along the highway system frequently offer good grayling fishing, and access
is easy. Half-day and day-long charter boat trips are available
in many communities, as are major fly-in expeditions to remote
fishing camps, complete with cabins, boats, and guides.

A nonresident who wants to fish in Alaska will need a license, available from sporting goods stores and many other businesses that serve visitors. A license good for the calendar year costs $36. Short-term licenses are available at $10 for 3 days and $20 for 14 days. Sportfishing licenses are required for salt-water or freshwater fishing. Licenses also are required to take marine shellfish, such as crabs or clams.

You may want to look over a copy of the state's sportfishing regulations, which are updated annually and are available from licensed vendors. To get a copy of the regulations and other information about fishing, write the Alaska Department of Fish and Game (Box 3-2000, Juneau 99802, tel. 907/465–4112). In the Fairbanks area, the agency maintains a where-the-fish-are-biting hot line (tel. 907/452–1525) at all times.

Grayling can be found in most of the clear-water streams of Interior and South Central Alaska. Fishing is likely to be poor in the immediate vicinity of campgrounds, but you might be surprised how prospects improve a bend or two up or down the river. Grayling will take a small floating fly that resembles a mosquito if the water is clear. In murkier water, a small spinner bait should work.

In the Southeast Panhandle, salmon is king—and also red (sockeye), pink (humpback), chum (calico), and silver (coho). The best time of year varies with the species you're angling for. June and July are the best months for hooking the fighting king, the most prized salmon. They average 20 pounds; trophy-size kings weigh in at 45 pounds or more. One of the largest ever caught lies in state at the museum in Petersburg—126.5 pounds.

Most other kinds of salmon are caught during the summer months. Huge Pacific halibut, red snapper, ling cod, and rockfish are caught almost any time of the year.

Some of the best trophy trout fishing awaits in the lakes, streams, and rivers of South Central Alaska, including the Kenai Peninsula. These remote areas are reached mostly by hiking trail or float plane. Fly-in trips for a day or more offer a variety of action-packed angling for Dolly Varden, lake trout, northern pike, Arctic grayling, and rainbow trout. The Kenai River is famous for its huge king salmon. A number of outfitters based around Soldotna and Cooper Landing can guide visitors on shore or in oar-powered drift boats.

Fishermen who have thrown out their lines around the world say that some of the top sportfishing anywhere is in the major rivers and lakes of the Bristol Bay region, less than an hour's flight time southwest of Anchorage. Most of the world's sockeye salmon come out of Bristol Bay waters, and the region is also noted for grayling, Arctic char, Dolly Varden, northern pike, and rainbow trout. Book air travel early for the feverish July season or risk not having any transportation.

Around the northern and western Fringes of Alaska there are some special treats. At some spots, you may be able to fish through the ice for tomcod and tanner crab along with the Eskimos in late spring before the ice pack moves out. Dress for it. If you're with a tour, they'll lend you warm clothing. Otherwise bring your own parka, insulated pants, and boots.

Other sportfish common to the regions include sheefish, a cousin to the salmon and generally found only in larger streams and a favorite among residents who like to fish through the ice; whitefish, usually taken by spearfishing in the fall as they migrate from smaller streams into deep water; and northern pike, a fierce fighting fish that inhabits the larger rivers and lakes.

A successful fishing trip, particularly for salmon, must be well planned. Timing is crucial. Through most of the summer, salmon will be running somewhere in the state, but each particular area is subject to peak runs. Missing that peak by just a few days or in some cases by a few hours may mean an empty creel.

Contacting guides or charter services ahead of time during the off-season can be helpful in planning your trip, and in scheduling the best dates. Once you've arrived in Alaska, check out the local newspapers, particularly late in the week, for information on day-to-day fishing conditions throughout the region.

Alaska Sportfishing Packages is one of the more experienced tour operators specializing in fishing packages. *1308 187th Ave. N.E., Bellevue, WA 98008, tel. 206/644–2301 or 800/426–0603.* (*See* also the tour operators and outfitters listed in Chapter 4, and under Guided Tours in each regional section.)

Hiking Follow the historic trails of gold miners, or cover territory so remote, it may well be that no one has ever walked on the same spot. There are wilderness trails in and around almost every Alaskan city and town (*see* the Exploring sections in each regional chapter) and major trekking can be done in the vast state and national parks (*see* Chapter 4 for a guide to the best hiking).

Hunting Some of the most spectacular trophy hunting is provided in western Alaska, where many of the best-known guides and outfitters accommodate visiting shooters. The most-prized Kodiak, or Alaska brown bear, the largest land carnivore, is taken on Kodiak Island and on the Alaska Peninsula.

Grizzly (brown) bears are often taken in the Interior, where the forest and mountains also provide shelter for black bears, moose, caribou, and Dall sheep. Deer, black and brown bears, moose, and mountain goats are found in Southeast Alaska.

August through November is hunting season for most game. There is also some hunting in the spring. Seasons and bag limits vary considerably between game management units, so it's best to contact local Fish and Game Department offices for details (*see* Chapter 4 for a listing of federal and state agencies). These sources can also give you information on closed areas and restricted species.

Though Alaska's big game take gets most of the attention, it's outnumbered in quantity, if not in bulk, by the small-game harvest. Small-game outings hunt hares and rabbits, beavers, and mink.

Game birds native to the state include three species of ptarmigan and four species of grouse. They're found all over the state. Of the migratory birds, the majority of more than 25 species that nest and are hunted in Alaska are ducks: mallard, pintail, American widgeon, green-winged teal, and shoveler. Canada geese, white-fronted geese, and black brant are the migratory birds most sought.

Your best bet if you are serious about hunting is to sign on with an expert. A list of registered Alaska guides is available from the **Department of Commerce** (Guide Licensing & Control Board, Box D, Juneau 99811). Also write the **Alaska Department of Fish and Game** (Box 3-2000, Juneau 99802) for current regulations. Fish and Game Department offices don't sell licenses; these are issued by designated agents. Write the Licensing Section, Alaska Department of Revenue (1107 W. 8th St., Juneau 99801).

All nonresidents must have a valid license and tags in their possession while taking or attempting to take game. These are considerably more expensive than fishing licenses: $60 for the license, plus $150 to $1,150 for locking tags or "trophy fees."

Skiing Alaska's powder snow offers an exciting challenge for any skier. At Juneau, **Eaglecrest** is across from the city on the slopes of Douglas Island. It has two chair lifts, a platter pull, and a day lodge. There is also skiing on the glaciers of the Juneau Ice Field, reached by helicopter. **Turnagain Pass,** 59 miles from Anchorage on the Seward Highway, is popular with cross-country skiers and snowmobilers. The snowfall here is often greater than 12 feet. **Mt. Alyeska,** south of Anchorage, is a world-class ski resort with hopes of hosting a future Winter Olympics. **Hilltop Ski Area** and **Alpenglow** are small alpine ski areas within 10 miles of downtown Anchorage.

State and National Parks

The Statewide Headquarters Office of **Alaska State Parks** (3601 C St., Suite 1200, Anchorage 99510; mailing address Box 7001) offers an informative folder and map describing Alaska's state park system. The system includes campgrounds, recreation areas, waysides, and historic sites.

For general information on national parks, preserves, and monuments, contact the **National Park Service** (2525 Gambell St., Anchorage 99503) or the **U.S. Forest Service Information Center** (Centennial Hall, 101 Egan Dr., Juneau 99801). For wildlife refuges, contact the **U.S. Fish and Wildlife Service** (1011 E. Tudor St., Anchorage 99503).

For an in-depth review of Alaska's most spectacular state and national parks, plus listings of the state and federal agencies, tour operators, and outfitters that serve them, *see* Chapter 4.

State Parks **Wood-Tikchik State Park,** reached by air from Dillingham, is the largest state park. **Chugach State Park,** the next largest, is easily accessible from Anchorage. Other notable parks include **Chilkat State Park,** south of Haines; **Denali State Park,** about 140 miles north of Anchorage; and **Kachemak Bay State Park** and **Kachemak Wilderness Park** on the Kenai Peninsula.

Plentiful campgrounds throughout the state offer boating, fishing, hunting, hiking, bird watching, and other outdoor activities. The following are some of the best. **Bird Creek,** on Seward Highway 26 miles south of Anchorage, is one of Alaska's most popular recreation areas—noted for its fishing near the road with a view across Turnagain Arm to the small village of Hope and the Chugach Range. **Eklutna Lake** is nestled in an Alpine canyon, 23 miles north of Anchorage on Glenn Highway, eight miles east on a gravel road. There is a popular 13-mile mountain bike and hiking trail around the turquoise lake.

Freshwater glacial streams with waterfalls, spruce and cotton-wood trees, Dall sheep, moose, and bear are all part of the scene. **Chatanika River** is 39 miles north of Fairbanks on the Steese Highway. Located in an area of extensive mining operations, visitors can see where huge gold dredges separated gold from gravel. Even beginners can pan and come up with an occasional nugget.

Stariski is 22 miles north of Homer, at Mile 154 on Sterling Highway. The campground's grassy areas are framed by spruce trees. Bluebells and fireweed bloom in June and July. This campground is crammed with anglers during salmon season. There are excellent views of Mt. Iliamna and other peaks on the Alaska Peninsula across Cook Inlet. **Captain Cook Recreation Area,** 30 miles north of Kenai, offers fishing, boating, and hiking around numerous lakes and stream; it's a quiet alternative on the Kenai Peninsula.

National Parks   Two national forests—the **Chugach** and the **Tongass**—comprise a total of more than 23 million acres, more national forest land than in any other state. **Denali National Park and Preserve** is a remote wilderness in the heart of the state, dominated by Mt. McKinley. **Glacier Bay National Park and Preserve,** 40 miles northwest of Juneau, boasts 16 active glaciers touching tidewater. **Katmai National Park and Preserve** is on the Alaska Peninsula across from Kodiak Island and home to ocean bays, fjords, lagoons, volcanic crater lakes, and glacier-covered peaks.

Klondike Gold Rush National Historical Park commemorates the gold rush, extending all the way from Pioneer Square in Seattle to Skagway and beyond, following the trail of the gold seekers. **Sitka National Historic Park** is the place to see totem poles.

The remote **Pribilof Islands** in the Bering Sea is a seal and otter reserve. **Clarence Rhode Wildlife Refuge,** to the northwest of Bethel, encompasses one of the world's largest waterfowl breeding grounds. Nunivak Island, site of **Nunivak National Wildlife Refuge,** is noted for its herd of reindeer and musk-ox.

Camping   The **Alaska Department of Natural Resources,** Division of Parks (Box 7001, Anchorage 99510), can give you information on camping in state parks and campgrounds. Modest fees, typically $5–$8, may be charged at some campgrounds. Many of them offer facilities such as boat-launching ramps. Space may be scarce and your stay limited in the more popular areas such as Eagle River and Bird Creek in the Chugach district, and Fort Abercrombie on Kodiak Island.

Camping in the Chugach or Tongass national forests will probably include a $5–$7 fee. The **Fish and Wildlife Service** maintains primitive campgrounds in the Kenai National Wildlife Refuge; you can't make reservations, but information is available from the Refuge Manager (Box 2139, Soldotna 99669).

The **Bureau of Land Management** (701 C St., Box 13, Anchorage 99513) operates about 25 free camping areas; contact them for details.

National park campgrounds in Canada usually have a nightly fee of $5 to $8.

Dining

The key to dining in Alaska is informality. It is virtually impossible to find a restaurant here where formal attire is required. In most restaurants, appropriate attire simply means a clean shirt and pants for men, and a pair of pants or comfortable skirt or dress for women.

Most menus will emphasize fresh seafood in season. Because the prime seasons vary so much among the seafood selections, your best bet is to go with a local recommendation if you're looking for a good salmon, halibut, shrimp, or crab dinner. Keep in mind that off-season seafood is probably fresh from the kitchen freezer and will not be quite as good as it would have been if it were served the day it was caught. Some menus will also boast frontier specialties, including reindeer, moose, and bear. Let your sense of adventure be your guide—some of these dishes are quite tasty, but these are not "must" experiences.

Lodging

Lodging can mean almost anything in Alaska. Although rustic is the easiest to find, the range covers high-rise hotels to fishing and hunting camps.

Hotels and Motels You'll find some familiar chain names scattered across the state, like Days Inn, Great Western, Hilton, Holiday Inn, and Sheraton; they will be of similar quality to the chain's other U.S. properties. Westmark Hotels is a regional chain with hotels in Anchorage, Fairbanks, Juneau, Kenai, Kodiak, Sitka, and Valdez in Alaska; Beaver Creek and Whitehorse in Canada's Yukon Territory.

Wilderness Lodges The preferred choice of the fishing and get-away-from-it-all crowd, these lodges typically provide homey accommodations in the middle of typically breathtaking Alaskan wilderness (*see* Chapter 4 for a listing by region).

Bed-and-Breakfasts The **Alaska Bed & Breakfast Association** (Box 21890, Juneau 99802, tel. 907/586–2959 or 800/627–0382) serves the Southeast region. Try **Alaska Private Lodgings** (4631 Caravelle Drive, Anchorage 99502, tel. 907/248–2292) in the South Central region.

Youth Hostels The **Alaska Council of American Youth Hostels** (Box 9-1461, Anchorage 99509, tel. 907/276–3635) has general information on the state's 13 hostels. Or contact the National Offices (AYH, 1332 I St. NW, Suite 800, Washington, DC 20005). The hostels in Anchorage and Juneau are open year-round. Those in Delta Junction, Haines, Ketchikan, Mt. Alyeska, Moose Pass, Sheep Mountain Lodge, Sitka, Soldotna, Tok, Fairbanks, and near Willow offer summer service only, for the most part. Travelers, not always in their youth, may stay for as little as $10 a night.

Credit Cards

The following credit card abbreviations are used: AE, American Express; DC, Diners Club; D, Discover; MC, MasterCard; V, Visa.

2 Portraits of Alaska

Alaska

By James
Michener

*In this excerpt
from* Alaska,
*Michener traces
the transfer of
Alaska from
Russian to
(unwilling)
American hands
and tells of a
scornful U.S.
Congress, which
condemned its
new northern
"icebox" to rueful
neglect.*

The transfer of Alaska from Russia to the United States formed one of those unbelievable incidents of history, because by 1867, Russia was nervously eager to get rid of it, while the United States, still recovering from the Civil War and immersed in the impending impeachment of President Johnson, refused to accept it on any terms.

At this impasse an extraordinary man monopolized center stage. He was not a Russian, a fact which would become important more than a century later, but a *soi-disant* baron of dubious background, half Austrian, half Italian, and a charmer who was picked up in 1841 for temporary duty representing Russia in the United States and who lingered there till 1868. In that time Edouard de Stoeckl, parading himself as a nobleman, although no one could say for sure how or when or even if he had earned his title, became such an ardent friend of America that he married an American heiress and took upon himself the task of acting as marriage broker between Russia, which he called his homeland, and the United States, his adopted residence.

He faced a most difficult task, for when the United States showed hesitancy about accepting Alaska, support for the sale withered in Russia, and later when Russia wanted to sell, half a dozen of the most influential American politicians, led by Secretary of State William Seward of New York, looked far into the future and saw the desirability of acquiring Alaska to serve as America's arctic bastion, yet the hardheaded businessmen in the Senate, the House, and the general public opposed the purchase with all the scorn they could summon. "Seward's Icebox" and "Seward's Folly" were two of the gentler jibes. Some critics accused Seward of being in the pay of the Russians; others accused de Stoeckl of buying votes in the House. One sharp satirist claimed that Alaska contained nothing but polar bears and Eskimos, and many protested that America should not accept this useless, frozen domain even if Russia wanted to give it away.

Many pointed out that Alaska had no wealth of any kind, not even reindeer, which proliferated in other northern areas, and experts affirmed that an arctic area like this could not possibly have any minerals or other deposits of value. On and on went the abuse of this unknown and somewhat terrifying land, and the castigations would have been comical had they not influenced American thinking and behavior and condemned Alaska to decades of neglect.

But an ingenious man like Baron de Stoeckl was not easily diverted from his main target, and with Seward's unflinching support and admirable statesmanship, the sale squeaked by with a favorable margin of one vote. By such a narrow margin did the United States come close to losing one of her potentially valuable acquisitions, but of course, had one viewed Alaska from the vantage point of frozen Fort Nulato in 1867, with the thermometer at minus-fifty-seven and about to be attacked by hostile Athapaskans, the purchase at more than $7,000,000 would have seemed a poor bargain.

Now the comedy intensified, became burlesque, for although the U.S. Senate had bought the place, the U.S. House refused to appropriate the money to pay for it, and for many tense months the sale hung in the balance. When a favorable vote was finally taken, it was almost negated by the discovery that Baron de Stoeckl had disposed of $125,000 in cash for which he refused to give an accounting. Widely suspected of having bribed congressmen to vote for land that was obviously worthless, the baron waited until the sale was completed, then quietly slipped out of the country, his life's ambition having been achieved.

One congressman with a keen sense of history, economics and geopolitics said of the whole affair: "If we were so eager to show Russia our appreciation for the help she gave us during the Civil War, why didn't we give her the seven million and tell her to keep her damned colony? It'll never be of any use to us."

So the sale was completed and the scene of the comedy moved to San Francisco, where a fiery Northern general named Jefferson C. Davis—no relative of the president of the Confederacy—was informed that Alaska was now American property and that he, Davis, was in command of the icebergs, the polar bears and the Indians. A short-tempered man who during the Civil War had gunned down a Northern general to whom he had taken a dislike—the other general died, and Davis was forgiven on the grounds that he, Davis, did have a short temper—he had spent the postwar years chasing Indians on the Plains, and he accepted his job in Alaska under the impression that his duty there would be to continue chasing Indians.

On 18 September 1867, the steamer *John L. Stevens* sailed from San Francisco bearing the two hundred and fifty soldiers who were to govern Alaska for the ensuing decades. One who left that day wrote a dismal account:

As we marched in battle gear to our waiting ship, no maidens stood on the corners to throw roses at us and no enthusiastic crowds gathered to cheer us on our way. The public was so disgusted with our purchase of Alaska that they showed only contempt as we passed. One man shouted directly at me: "Give it back to Russia!"

When the Stevens *reached Sitka a holy mess developed. The Russians follow a calendar which is eleven days behind ours, so everything was confused. Also, in Alaska they keep the Moscow day, which is one ahead of ours. You figure that out. At any rate, when we arrived the Russian commander said: "You're here early. This is still Russia and no foreign troops can land till the American commissioners arrive," and we poor soldiers have had to stay in our stinking ship's quarters ten days looking at a volcano off our port side, which I can see as I write. I don't like volcanoes and I certainly don't like Alaska.*

Finally, the ship bearing the American commissioners came into the sound, and now the troops were permitted, belatedly, to land; they were a grumbling unhappy lot, but soon they were engaged in the formality of transfer, which to everyone's surprise took place that very afternoon.

It was not a well-managed affair. Prince Maksutov, who could have handled it beautifully, was prevented from doing so by the presence of a stuffy minor official sent from Russia to represent the tsar, while Arkady Voronov, who knew more about the Russian holdings than anyone else, was not allowed to participate at all. There was, however, a certain formality that pleased the few people who climbed the 80 steps to Baranov's Castle, where the Russian flag streamed from a 90-foot pole made from a Sitka spruce. There were cannon salutes from the bay and a proper ceremony for the lowering of one flag and the raising of another, but a painfully silly mishap marred the ritual, as explained by Praskovia Voronova in a letter home:

Although we had already signified our intention of becoming American citizens, Arkady, as you would expect, wanted the farewell Russian performance carried out with proper dignity, as would befit the honor of a great empire. He rehearsed our Russian soldiers with great care in the lowering of our flag and I helped mend torn uniforms and supervised the polishing of shoes. I must say that our troops looked pipe-clay neat when Arkady and I were finished.

Alas, it came to naught. For when one of our most reliable men pulled the halyards to lower our glorious flag, a sudden gust of wind whipped it about the flagpole, fastening it so tightly that nothing could be done to dislodge it. The poor man with the rope looked woefully at Arkady, who indicated with his hands that he should give it a good tug. He obeyed, but succeeded only in ripping off the bunting which decorated the flag and tightening the flag even more securely to the pole. It was obvious that no amount of pulling was going to loosen that flag, and I almost broke into cheers, thinking it to be an omen that the sale would not take effect.

At this point Arkady left me, swearing under his breath, and I heard him tell two of his men: "Get that damned thing down. Now!" They had no idea of how this could be done, and I am humiliated to confess that it was an American

*sailor who called out: "rig up a bosun's chair!" I couldn't
see how this was done, but pretty soon a man was clamber-
ing up the pole like a monkey on a rope, and he broke our
flag loose, tearing it further in his haste.*

*Freed at last, it fell ignominiously earthward, where it
landed on the heads of our men, who failed to catch it in
their hands, and then it became mixed up in their bayonets.
I was mortified. Arkady continued to swear, something he
rarely does, Prince Maksutoy looked straight ahead as if
there were no flag and no pole, and his pretty wife fainted.*

*I wept. Arkady and I are determined to remain here in
Sitka, as it is now to be called, and to be the best citizens we
can be of our new nation. He is staying because his mother
and father had such close associations with these islands,
and I shall stay because I have grown to love Alaska and its
enormous potential, and when you come to visit us next
year I believe you will see a city twice this size and twice as
prosperous, for they assure us that when America assumes
control, it will pour millions of dollars in here to make this
a major possession.*

It was not premature for Praskovia and the other Russians who were selecting American citizenship to an-
nounce their choice, because in the days before the
transfer, Prince Maksutov had assembled the heads of families and explained in glowing terms the Russian-American
treaty which would govern such matters. Standing in his
crisp white officer's uniform and smiling warmly, he was
obviously proud of the work his committee had done: "Both
countries deserve commendation for the excellent rules
they've agreed to. Great statesmanship, really." When a
young teacher from the local college, one Maxim Luzhin,
asked for details, Maksutov patiently explained: "I helped
draft the regulations, so I can assure you that you'll be fully
protected, however you choose."

"For example?" Luzhin pressed, and the prince said: "If you
want to go back to Russia, you can do so anytime within
three years. We'll provide free transportation to your home
district. If you elect to remain here and become Americans,
your new government promises you full citizenship automatically, no restraints because you're Russian, and complete freedom of religion." Smiling at people who trusted
him, he told them honestly: "Not often in life do you get two
choices, each one excellent. Choose as you wish. You can't
go wrong."

So when the Voronovs participated in the transfer ceremo-
nies they did so as American citizens, but their transition
into their new homeland was a rude one, for no sooner had
the American flag risen to the top of the pole on that first
day than General Davis issued a startling order: "All Russians on the hill to vacate their quarters before sunset!" and
a major directed his soldiers to occupy the buildings.

Arkady went to the major, and in a quiet, respectful voice, explained: "My wife and I have elected American citizenship. Our home is up there," and he pointed to their quarters atop the castle.

"You're Russian, aren't you?" the major growled. "Out by sunset. I'm taking those rooms."

When Voronov, burning with indignation, informed his wife of the order, she laughed: "The prince and princess have been tossed out of their quarters, too. General Davis wants their rooms."

"I can't believe it."

"Look at the servants," and Arkady saw the Maksutov possessions being toted down the hill.

The Voronovs moved their goods into a small cottage near the cathedral, where they watched as their Russian friends made agonizing choices. Those who had enjoyed their life in Sitka longed to remain, willing like the Voronovs to trust their fate to American generosity, but friends in Russia applied such strong pressure for them to return home that most decided to sail on whatever steamer arrived to carry them to Petropavlovsk.

"What will happen to them when they get to Russia?" Praskovia asked, and Arkady replied: "I wouldn't like to guess." But now distraught neighbors, unable to decide for themselves, came to the Voronov cottage, asking Arkady what to do, and usually he advised: "Go home." And if a husband and wife differed in their choice, he invariably counseled a return to Russia: "There you know what your neighbors are going to do."

This repeated recommendation that people who harbored doubts should go back to Russia had a surprising effect on him, for although he had started with a firm resolve to stay in Alaska, his constant projection of himself into the minds and conditions of others revealed how insecure in his choice he was. One evening as he and Praskovia walked home from a meeting with the Maksutovs, who were reconciled to returning home and perhaps even eager to do so, Arkady said without warning: "Praska, are we doing the right thing?" and she temporized, wishing to know the full range of his doubts: "What do you mean, Arkady?" and he revealed his uncertainty: "It's a fearful decision, really. The rest of our lives. We don't know Russia anymore, we've been away so long. And we don't know America, because we can't predict how they'll behave 10 years from now . . . or even now, for that matter. This General Davis? I wonder if he has any concept of what Alaska is. I wonder if he's very bright."

"I'm certainly not impressed with his first decisions," Praskovia said, "but he may get better." She encouraged her husband to spread out all his fears, and as he ventilated them she saw that they were nothing more than the sensible alternatives that any people their age should consider when making a decision of such gravity: "Go on, what's your greatest fear?" and he said gravely: "That it's the last big choice we'll ever make. Not for me really. I was never attached to Russia, you know. I'm from the islands. But you . . . " and he looked at her with the great love which had always been the mark of Voronov men. His great-grandfather and his grandfather, both in Irkutsk, had enjoyed the good fortune of loving their wives. His father Vasili, had found in the islands a love with his Aleut bride that few men know, and he had been the same. From the first moment he saw Praskovia during his student days in the capital he had loved only her, and now he feared that he might be behaving as his father had done when he surrendered Sofia Kuchovskaya in order to accept soaring promotion in the church. He was thinking of himself and not of his wife, and very quietly he said, "I'm an island man. I'm forcing you into a cruel choice."

She did not laugh, or even smile at his ingenuousness, but she did take him by the arm and lead him toward the cathedral, where they entered together to find rude chairs in the back among the shadows, and there she informed him as to her vision of the future: "Arkady, you're 66. I'm 58. How many years are we gambling on this thing? Not many. An error, if we make one, won't be the wastage of an entire life." Before he could respond, she said with great force: "At Nulato, watching the Yukon sweep past, feeling the immense cold, getting to know those sled dogs and seeing how Father Fyodor was greeted in the villages . . . " She smiled and squeezed his hand: "I made my choice then, whether Alaska remained Russian or not. This is my home. I want to be here to witness the conclusion of our great adventure." Before he could speak, she concluded: "Arkady, I do believe that if you elected to go home to Russia, I might stay here by myself." Then she added in a confidential whisper: "Truth is, but don't tell the prince, I actually prefer their American name Sitka to the Russian name New Archangel."

After that revealing moment, Arkady stopped advising anyone what to do, nor did he volunteer any information as to what Praskovia and he would do when the first ship sailed, the one that would take Prince Maksutov and his wife away. Instead, the Voronovs bought a somewhat larger house that was being vacated by a family heading home, and in it they began accumulating those comfortable odds and ends that would mean so much to them when Sitka became a totally American city. "It's to be a wonderful new life," Praskovia said, but Arkady, who was witnessing each day the inability of the Americans to govern their new possession, had additional reasons for apprehension.

As Christmas approached in that fateful year 1867, the Maksutovs held a farewell dinner party to thank those trusted friends who had worked so hard for Russia but who now elected to become American citizens. "I cannot challenge your decisions," he said gently, "but I pray you will serve your new homeland honorably." He explained that although he must remain two more weeks to complete the transfer, his wife would be sailing on the morrow. And then nature pulled a cruel trick. During these weeks of departure Sitka's normal fog and gloom had established a mood proper for farewell, but on the final day the mists lifted, revealing Sitka in its refulgent grandeur: There stood the noble volcano, the rim of snow-clad mountains, the myriad green islands, the green onion dome of the Orthodox cathedral, the trim neatness of the most congenial port in Russian America.

"Oh, Praska!" the princess cried as she embraced her friend. "We're throwing away the most beautiful town in the Russian Empire," and it was in bitterness that she made her departure.

Two weeks later the Voronovs formed an honor guard for Prince Maksutov as he marched in dignity down the hill to where a small boat waited to ferry him to his waiting ship: "I leave Alaska in the hands of you Voronovs. You know it better than anyone else." From atop the hill, General Davis, now ruling from Baranov's Castle, ordered a salute to be fired, and as the echoes reverberated through the mountains and valleys of Sitka, the Russian Empire in Alaska came to an end.

The United States assumed responsibility for Alaska on 18 October 1867, and by early January 1868 it was apparent to the Voronovs and the Luzhins that no sensible form of government—indeed, none at all, sensible or ridiculous—was going to be installed. General Davis and his soldiers were supposed to be in charge, but only a part of the blame could be placed on them.

The fault lay with the American Congress, which, remembering the irresponsible oratory opposing the purchase of Alaska, had claimed that the area was worthless and populated by no one meriting serious attention. So, incredible as it would seem to later historians, America refused to give Alaska any form of government. It refused even to give it a proper name: In 1867 it was called the Military District of Alaska; in 1868, the Department of Alaska; in 1877, the Customs District of Alaska; and in 1884, simply the District of Alaska. From the first day of ownership it should have been designated the Territory of Alaska, but that would have presupposed eventual statehood, and orators opposing the suggestion ranted: "That icebox will never have enough population to warrant statehood," so the area was initially denied the step-by-step learning experience of first being an unorganized territory with judges and sheriffs, then an organized one with its own legislature and emerging government, and finally a full-fledged state.

Why were normal rights denied the area? Because businessmen, saloon keepers, trappers, miners and fishermen demanded a free hand in garnering the riches of Alaska and feared that any form of local self-government might pass laws restricting them. And especially because Alaska was then and would remain America's blind spot. No matter what happened here—what riches were uncovered, what triumphs achieved—the American people and their government would not believe. For generations this treasure would be left to float adrift in icy seas, like an abandoned ship whose planking slowly rotted.

By mid-January, Arkady Voronov began to fear that a kind of creeping paralysis had engulfed Sitka and the rest of Alaska, but he did not appreciate the depth of the confusion until he talked with the young teacher Maxim Luzhin: "Arkady, you can't imagine the situation! An enthusiastic businessman from California came north on the ship that brought the troops. He wants to move here and open some kind of trading business. But he can't buy land for a home and office because there is no land law. And he can't start his business because there is no business law. If he settles here, he can't leave his property to his children, for there is no office to legalize wills or enforce them."

When the two Russians looked into other impediments, they were told: "You can't call upon the sheriff to protect your rights, because there is no sheriff, no jail and no court to appeal to for redress, for there is no court, which is understandable, because there is no real judge."

Together the two men climbed the hill to inform General Davis of the concern the Russians had for their safety amid such chaos, and when they met him at ease in his quarters, they were struck by how handsome and military he looked. Tall, lean, carefully erect, with a heavy black beard, a voluminous mustache and a romantic wealth of dark hair which covered much of his forehead, he looked a born ruler of men, but when he spoke the illusion was shattered: "I'd like to enforce the law, but there is no law. And I can't make guesses about it because no one knows what Congress will do." When they asked what form the new government would probably take, he said: "Legally, I think we're a customs district, so I guess when a customs officer arrives, he'll be in charge."

Despite the perspicacity of their questioning, they could elicit no substantial explanations from the general, and they left the meeting both confused and disheartened, so they were not surprised when, upon the arrival of a passenger ship, well over half the local Russians decided to leave Alaska and head back to Siberia. When General Davis saw the huge number departing, he tried ineffectively to entice them to remain, but they'd had enough of American vacillations and would not listen.

Voronov and Luzhin, better able than Davis to estimate the high quality of those who were fleeing Sitka, consoled each other and their wives with the hopeful thought: "Those of us who are staying will have extra work to do . . . and extra opportunities to do it," and each of the four was determined to be the best possible American citizen.

The rest of the Russian story is quickly and sadly told. After the first contingent of émigrés fled, the undisciplined American troops, with no clear mission to occupy them or any stern leader to keep them under control, began to run wild, and Voronov, like the other Russians who had stayed behind, became appalled at what was happening.

Aleut women who had worked as servants of Russian families transferred their duties to the barracks where the soldiers were billeted, and before the week was out three cases of the ugliest kind of rape were reported. When nothing was done to discipline the men, they went outside the palisade and raped two Tlingit women, whose husbands promptly killed a soldier in retaliation, but he was not one of the rapists.

This particular case was resolved by paying the aggrieved husbands 25 American dollars each and sending the mother of the dead soldier a medal and the news that her son had died bravely in action against the enemy.

But now the violence extended to Russian families, who began locking and barring their doors, and two of the men complained bitterly to General Davis, but nothing happened. However, Voronov assured his wife: "This madness will stop."

It didn't. When a gang of drunken soldiers staggered down to a nearby village and assaulted three women, the Tlingits retaliated with a series of hammering counterblows, which General Davis interpreted as a dangerous insurrection against American rule. Dispatching a gunboat to the offending village, he ordered the place to be chastised; it was totally destroyed, with heavy loss of Tlingit life.

This resulted in the rupture of contact between the occupation force and the Tlingits, which meant that little fresh food made its way into the town. Tempers ran high, and one afternoon, as Praskovia returned from a visit with distraught Russian neighbors, she saw something that sent her screaming for her husband.

When the Voronovs and the Luzhins reached the front door of their cathedral they saw that in the sanctuary, at the iconostasis and throughout the main body of the cathedral, everything breakable had been smashed, paint was smeared over the walls, and the pulpit was destroyed. The cathedral was a wreck; it would take thousands of rubles to restore it, and even at that cost the icons hallowed by time could not be replaced. When General Davis was informed of the sacrilege, he shrugged his shoulders and absolved his men of any blame: "No doubt some angry Tlingits sneaked in when we weren't looking."

That night those Russians with administrative or mercantile experience met at the Voronovs' to discuss what could be done to protect their rights and perhaps their lives, and the consensus was that because General Davis would not assume responsibility for his troops, the only practical thing to do was to appeal to the captain of the first foreign ship putting into Sitka, and Arkady volunteered for the assignment.

I t was a French ship, and the captain was a man well versed in maritime tradition. After listening to Voronov's recitation of complaints, he fumed: "No self-respecting general allows his troops to rape," and he marched directly to the castle and made a formal protest. Davis was outraged at this interference, and his assistant, who took note of Voronov's name in the Frenchman's recitation, warned the Frenchman that if there was any further intervention from him, "the cannon up here will know what to do."

That night, perhaps by accident, perhaps by design, three soldiers went to Voronov's house, while he was known to be absent at a protest meeting, and tried to rape Praskovia, who fought them off vigorously and ran from the house screaming for help. Before she could make good her escape, one of the men grabbed her, dragged her back into the house, and started stripping off her clothes.

Neighbors alerted Voronov, who came running home in time to find his wife practically naked in their bedroom, fighting and scratching and gouging at the three men, who were laughing maniacally. When they saw that three big Russians were crowding in behind the enraged husband, they beat a planned retreat through a back window, smashing it and as much kitchenware as they could.

The other Russians wanted to chase the soldiers, but Voronov would not allow this. Instead, he gathered his wife's clothes, helped her dress, and then packed in three bags everything they could possibly salvage from their new house. In the dark of night he led Praskovia, the Luzhins, and their children down to the shore, where he signaled the French ship, in vain. Throwing off his shoes and jacket, he entered the cold water and swam out, shouting as he approached the ship: "Captain Rulon, we seek asylum!"

In the darkness the Voronovs and Luzhins fled Sitka.

Coming into the Country

By John McPhee

McPhee is the author of a dozen books and contributor to magazines such as The New Yorker, Time, the Saturday Evening Post and the Atlantic Monthly.

With a clannish sense of place characteristic of the bush, people in the region of the upper Yukon refer to their part of Alaska as "the country." A stranger appearing among them is said to have "come into the country."

Donna Kneeland came into the country in April 1975. Energetically, she undertook to learn, and before long she had an enviable reputation for certain of her skills, notably her way with fur. Knowledgeable people can look at a pelt and say that Donna tanned it. In part to save money, she hopes to give up commercial chemicals and use instead the brains of animals—to "Indian tan," as she puts it—and she has found a teacher or two among the Indian women of the region, a few of whom remember how it was done. The fur is mainly for sale, and it is the principal source of support for her and her companion, whose name is Dick Cook. (He is not related to Earl Cook, of the Capital Site Selection Committee.) A marten might bring $50. Lynx, about $300. Wolf, $250. They live in a cabin half a dozen miles up a tributary stream, at least 40 and perhaps 60 miles from the point on the border meridian where the Yukon River leaves Yukon Territory and flows on into Alaska. The numbers are deliberately vague, because Cook and Kneeland do not want people to know exactly where the cabin is. Their nearest neighbors, a couple who also live by hunting and trapping, are something like 20 miles from them. To pick up supplies, they travel a good bit farther than that. They make a journey of a couple of days, by canoe or dog team, to Eagle, a bush community not far from the Canadian boundary whose population has expanded in recent years and now exceeds a hundred. For three-quarters of a century, Eagle has been an incorporated Alaskan city, and it is the largest sign of human material progress in 20,000 square miles of rugged, riverine land. From big bluffs above the Yukon— 500, 1,000, 1,500 feet high—the country reaches back in mountains, which, locally, are styled as hills. The Tanana Hills. The tops of the hills are much the same height as New Hampshire's Mt. Washington, Maine's Mt. Katahdin, and North Carolina's Mt. Mitchell. Pebble-clear streams trellis the mountains, descending toward the opaque, glacier-fed Yukon, and each tributary drainage is suitable terrain for a trapper or two, and for miners where there is gold.

For Donna Kneeland, as many as five months have gone by without a visit to Eagle, and much of the time she is alone in the cabin, while her man is out on the trail. She cooks and cans things. She grinds wheat berries and bakes bread. She breaks damp skins with an old gun barrel and works them with a metal scraper. A roommate she once had at the

University of Alaska went off to "the other states" and left
her a $150 Canadian Pioneer parka. She has never worn it,
because—although her cabin is in the coldest part of Alaska—winter temperatures have yet to go low enough to
make her feel a need to put it on. "We've had some cool
weather," she admits. "I don't know how cold, exactly. Our
thermometer only goes to 58." When she goes out at such
temperatures to saw or to split the wood she survives on—
with the air at 60 and more below zero—she wears a down
sweater. It is all she needs as long as her limbs are active.
Her copy of *The Joy of Cooking* previously belonged to a
trapper's wife who froze to death. Donna's father, a state
policeman, was sent in to collect the corpse.

Donna is something rare among Alaskans—a white
who is Alaska-born. She was born in Juneau, and as
her father was biennially transferred from post to
post, she grew up all over Alaska—Barrow, Tok, Fairbanks. In girlhood summers, she worked in a mining camp
at Livengood, cooking for the crew. At the university,
which is in Fairbanks, she majored in anthropology. In
1974, she fell in love with a student from the University of
Alberta, and she went off to Edmonton to be with him.
Edmonton is Canada's fourth-largest city and is the size of
Nashville. "In Edmonton, every place I went I could see
nothing but civilization. I never felt I could ever get out. I
wanted to see something with no civilization in it. I wanted
to see even two or three miles of just nothing. I missed this
very much. In a big city, I can't find my way out of a paper
bag. I was scared to death of the traffic. I was in many ways
unhappy. One day I thought, I know what I want to do—I
want to go live in the woods. I left the same day for Alaska."

In Alaska, where "the woods" are wildernesses beyond the
general understanding of the word, one does not prudently
just wander off—as Donna's whole life had taught her. She
may have lived in various pinpoints of Alaskan civilization,
but she had never lived out on her own. She went to Fairbanks first. She took a job—white dress and all—as a dental assistant. She asked around about trappers who came to
town. She went to a meeting of the Interior Alaska Trappers Association and studied the membership with
assessive eyes. When the time came for a choice, she would
probably have no difficulty, for she was a beautiful young
woman, 28 at the time, with a criterion figure, dark-blond
hair, and slate-blue, striking eyes.

Richard Okey Cook came into the country in 1964, and put
up a log lean-to not far from the site where he would build
his present cabin. Trained in aspects of geophysics, he did
some free-lance prospecting that first summer near the
head of the Seventymile River, which goes into the Yukon a
few bends below Eagle. His larger purpose, though, was to
stay in the country and to change himself thoroughly "from
a professional into a bum"—to learn to trap, to handle dogs

and sleds, to net fish in quantities sufficient to feed the dogs. "And that isn't easy," he is quick to say, claiming that to lower his income and raise his independence he has worked twice as hard as most people. Born and brought up in Ohio, he was a real estate appraiser there before he left for Alaska. He had also been to the Colorado School of Mines and had run potentiometer surveys for Kennecott Copper in Arizona. Like many Alaskans, he came north to repudiate one kind of life and to try another. "I wanted to get away from paying taxes to support something I didn't believe in, to get away from big business, to get away from a place where you can't be sure of anything you hear or anything you read. Doctors rip you off down there. There's not an honest lawyer in the Lower Forty-eight. The only honest people left are in jail." Toward those who had held power over him in various situations his reactions had sometimes been emphatic. He took a poke at his high school principal, in Lyndhurst, Ohio, and was expelled from school. In the marine corps, he became a corporal twice and a private first class three times. His demotions resulted from fistfights— on several occasions with sergeants, once with a lieutenant. Now he has tens of thousands of acres around him and no authorities ordinarily proximitous enough to threaten him—except nature, which he regards as God. While he was assembling his wilderness dexterity, he spent much of the year in Eagle, and he became, for a while, its mayor. A single face, a single vote, counts for a lot in Alaska, and especially in the bush.

The traplines Cook has established for himself are along several streams, across the divides between their headwaters and on both banks of the Yukon— upward of a hundred miles in all, in several loops. He runs them mainly in November and December. He does not use a snow machine, as many trappers in Alaska do. He says, "The two worst things that ever happened to this country are the airplane and the snow machine." His traplines traverse steep terrain, rocky gullies—places where he could not use a machine anyway. To get through, he requires sleds and dogs. Generally, he has to camp out at least one night to complete a circuit. If the temperature is colder than 30 below, he stays in his cabin and waits for the snap to pass. As soon as the air warms up, he hits the trail. He has built lean-tos in a few places, but often enough he sleeps where he gets tired—under an orange canvas tarp. It is 10 feet by 10, and weighs 2½ pounds, and is all the shelter he needs at, say, 20 below zero. Picking out a tree, he ties one corner of the tarp to the trunk, as high as he can reach. He stakes down the far corner, then stakes down the two sides. Sometimes, he will loft the center by tying a cord to a branch above. He builds a lasting fire between the tree and himself, gets into his sleeping bag, and drifts away. Most nights are calm. Snow is light in the upper Yukon. The tarp's configuration is not so much for protection as to reflect the heat of the fire. He could make a closed tent with the tarp, if necessary. His ground cloth, or bed pad, laid out on the snow beneath him, is the hide of a caribou.

He carries dried chum salmon for his dogs, and his own food is dried moose or bear meat and pinole—ground parched corn, to which he adds brown sugar. In the Algonquin language, pinole was "rockahominy." "It kept Daniel Boone and Davy Crockett going. It keeps me going, too." He carries no flour. "Flour will go rancid on you unless you buy white flour, but you can't live and work on that. I had a friend who died of a heart attack from eating that crap. It's not news that the American peo-ple are killing themselves with white flour, white sugar, and soda pop. If you get out and trap 30 miles a day behind dogs, you can damned well tell what lets you work and what doesn't." From a supplier in Seattle he orders hundred-pound sacks of corn, pinto beans, unground wheat. He buys cases of vinegar, tomato paste, and tea. Forty pounds of butter in one-pound cans. A hundred pounds of dried milk, 65 of dried fruit. Twenty-five pounds of cashews. Twenty-five pounds of oats. A 40-pound can of peanut butter. He carries it all down the Yukon from Eagle by sled or canoe. He uses a couple of moose a year, and a few bear, which are easier to handle in summer. "A moose has too much meat. The waste up here you wouldn't believe. Hunters that come through here leave a third of the moose. Indians don't waste, but with rifles they are overexcitable. They shoot into herds of caribou and wound some. I utilize everything, though. Stomach. Intestines. Head. I feed the carcasses of wolverine, marten, and fox to the dogs. Lynx is another matter. It's exceptionally good, something like chicken or pork."

With no trouble at all, Dick Cook remembers where every trap is on his lines. He uses several hundred traps. His annual food cost is somewhere under a thousand dollars. He uses less than a hundred gallons of fuel—for his chain saws, his small outboards, his gasoline lamps. The furs bring him a little more than his basic needs—about fifteen hundred dollars a year. He plants a big garden. He says, "One of the points I live by is not to make any more money than is absolutely necessary." His prospecting activity has in recent years fallen toward nil. He says he now looks for rocks not for the money but "just for the joy of it—a lot of things fall apart if you are not after money, and prospecting is one of them."

In winter on the trail, he wears a hooded cotton sweatshirt, no hat. He does use an earband. He has a low opinion of wool. "First off, it's too expensive. Second off, you don't have the moisture problem up here you have in the States." He wears Sears's thermal long johns under cotton overalls, and his feet are kept warm by Indian-made mukluks with Bean's felt insoles and a pair of wool socks. He rarely puts on his parka. "You have to worry up here more about overdressing than about underdressing. The problem is getting overheated." Gradually, his clothes have become rags, with so many shreds, holes, and rips that they seem to cling to him only through loyalty. Everything is patched, and loose bits flap as he walks. His red chamois-cloth shirt has holes in the front, the back, and the sides. His green overalls are torn open at both knees. Half a leg is gone from his corduroy pants. His khaki down jacket is quilted with patches and has a long rip under one arm. His hooded sweatshirt hangs from him in tatters, spreads over him like the thrums of a mop. "I'll tell you one thing about this country," he says. "This country is hard on clothes."

Cook is somewhat below the threshold of slender. He is fatless. His figure is a little stooped, unprepossessing, but his legs and arms are strong beyond the mere requirements of the athlete. He looks like a scarecrow made of cables. All his features are feral—his chin, his nose, his dark eyes. His hair, which is nearly black, has gone far from his forehead. His scalp is bare all the way back to, more or less, his north pole. The growth beyond— dense, streaked with gray—cantilevers to the sides in unbarbered profusion, so that his own hair appears to be a parka ruff. His voice is soft, gentle—his words polite. When he is being pedagogical, the voice goes up several registers, and becomes hortative and sharp. He is not infrequently pedagogical.

A decade and more can bring deep seniority in Alaska. People arrive steadily. And people go. They go from Anchorage and Fairbanks—let alone the more exacting wild. Some, of course, are interested only in a year or two's work, then to return with saved high wages to the Lower Forty-eight. Others, though, mean to adapt to Alaska, hoping to find a sense of frontier, a fresh and different kind of life. They come continually to Eagle, and to Circle, the next settlement below Eagle down the Yukon. The two communities are about 160 river miles apart, and in all the land between them live perhaps 30 people. The state of New Jersey, where I happen to live, could fit between Eagle and Circle. New Jersey has 7½ million people. Small wonder that the Alaskan wild has at least a conceptual appeal to certain people from a place like New Jersey. Beyond Circle are the vast savannas of the Yukon Flats—another world. Upstream from Circle are the bluffs, the mountains, the steep-falling streams—the country. Eagle and Circle are connected only by river, but each of them is reachable, about half the year, over narrow gravel roads (built for gold mines) that twist through the forest and are chipped out of cliffsides in high mountain passes. If you get into your car in Hackensack, Circle is about as far north as you can go on North America's network of roads. Eagle, with its montane setting, seems to attract more people who intend to stay. In they come—young people in ones and twos—from all over the Lower Forty-eight. With general trapping catalogues under their arms, they walk around wondering what to do next. The climate and the raw Alaskan wild will quickly sort them out. Some will not flinch. Others will go back. Others will stay on but will never get past the clustered cabins and gravel streets of Eagle. These young people, for the most part, are half Cook's age. He is in his middle 40s. He is their exemplar—the one who has done it and stuck. So the newcomers turn to him, when he is in town, as sage and mentor. He tells them that it's a big but hungry country out there, good enough for trapping, maybe, but not for too much trapping, and they are to stay the hell off his traplines. He does not otherwise discourage people. He wants to help them. If, in effect, they are wearing a skin and carrying a stone-headed club, he suggests that technology, while it can be kept at a distance, is inescapable. "The question," he will say, "is how far do you want to go? I buy wheat. I use axes, knives, I have windows. There's a few things we've been trained to need and can't give up. You can't forget the culture you were raised in. You have to satisfy needs created in you. Almost everyone needs music, for instance. Cabins may be out of food, but they've all got books in them. Indian trappers used deadfalls once—propped-up logs. I wouldn't want to live without my rifle and steel traps. I don't want to have to live on a bow and arrow and a deadfall. Somewhere, you have to make some sort of compromise. There is a line that has to be drawn. Most people feel around for it. Those that try to be too Spartan generally back off. Those who want to be too luxurious end up in Eagle—or in Fairbanks, or New York. So far as I know, people who have tried to get away from technology completely have always failed. Meanwhile, what this place has to offer is wilderness that is nowhere else."

A favorite aphorism of Cook's is that a farmer can learn to live in a city in six months, but a city person in a lifetime cannot learn to live on a farm. He says of newcomers, "A lot of them say they're going to 'live off the land.' They go hungry. They have ideas about everything—on arrival. And they've got no problems. But they're diving off too high a bridge. Soon they run into problems, so they come visiting. They have too much gear, and their sleeping bags are too heavy to carry around. They are wondering where to get meat, where and how to catch fish, how to protect their gear from bears. You can't tell them directly. If you tell them to do something, they do the opposite. But there are ways to let them know."

Cook seems to deserve his reputation. In all the terrain that is more or less focused on the post office at Eagle, he is the most experienced, the best person to be sought out by anyone determined to live much beyond the outermost tip of the set society. He knows the woods, the animals, sleds, traps, furs, dogs, frozen rivers, and swift water. He is the sachem figure. And he had long since achieved this status when a day arrived in which a tooth began to give him great pain.

He lay down in his cabin and waited for the nuisance to pass.
But the pain increased and was apparently not going to go
away. It became so intense he could barely stand it. He was
a couple of hundred miles from the most accessible dentist.
So he took a pair of channel-lock pliers and wrapped them
with tape, put the pliers into his mouth, and clamped them
over the hostile tooth. He levered it, worked it awhile, and
passed out. When he came to, he picked up the pliers and
went back to work on the tooth. It wouldn't give. He passed
out again. Each time he attacked the tooth with the pliers,
he passed out. Finally, his hand would not move. He could
not make his arm lift the pliers toward his mouth. So he set
them down, left the cabin, and—by dogsled and mail
plane—headed for the dentist, in Fairbanks.

Native Alaskans

By Stanton H.
Patty

I t is an old joke, simple, but filled with a somewhat bitter irony. In 1728, the history books say, Alaska was discovered by Vitus Bering, a Dane serving in the Russian Navy. "But," native Alaskans reply with a wink, "we knew it was there all the time."

The history of Alaska's native peoples—Eskimos, Indians, and Aleuts—is not unlike that of aboriginal people throughout Central and North America. After holding domain over their land for thousands of years, their elaborate societies were besieged by a rapid onslaught of white settlers. Unable to stem the tide, they were forced into retreat.

Bering died on his journey home, but survivors returned to Russia with a rich booty of sea otter furs, sparking a stampede that would crush the traditional lifestyles of Alaska's native peoples. The way was open for eager Russian fur traders who plundered Aleut territory along the Aleutian Islands.

Records indicate that the native population of the Aleutian chain dropped from perhaps 20,000 to about 2,500 in the first 50 years of Russian rule. Diseases took a heavy toll, but the more ruthless among the Russian frontiersmen were also responsible—killing Aleut leaders to discourage native uprisings. Stories of brutality are common. One trader, Feodor Solovief, reportedly tied together 12 Aleuts and fired a musket ball through them to see how far it would penetrate. It stopped in the body of the ninth man.

In 1867, when the United States purchased Alaska, the natives were classified in the Treaty of Cession as "uncivilized tribes." To early tourists, they were little more than "those charming folk you take pictures of in their quaint villages."

Early missionaries and government teachers in Southeast Alaska ordered Indian totem poles destroyed, mistakenly believing them to be pagan symbols. Important works of art were lost. The totems of the Tlingit and Haida Indians were—and still are—nothing more than the decorative record of outstanding events in the life of a family or clan.

The plight of the natives improved little as Alaska grew more prosperous by exploiting its great natural resources. A painful split between traditional and modern living developed—public health experts call it "a syndrome of grief." Under increasing pressure from this clash of cultures, alcoholism has grown to epidemic levels, and the suicide rate of Alaskan natives climbed to twice that of Indians living on reservations in the continental United States. Still, by the 1960s, native groups were making major strides toward claiming overdue political clout. In 1966, native leaders from across the state gathered and organized the present Alaska Foundation of Natives. It was a fragile coalition of differing cultures, but the meeting was a significant move. With 16% of the state's population, a unified native voice was suddenly a political force to be reckoned with.

At the same time, Eskimo leaders founded the *Tundra Times* and selected Howard Rock, a quiet, articulate man from Point Hope village, as its editor. Rock, whose background was in art rather than journalism, quickly prodded natives to press their aboriginal land claims.

"The natives are reticent by nature, and time was passing them by," the Eskimo editor said. "At first, it was kind of discouraging. Nothing happened. And then, one by one, the native leaders started speaking up."

The *Tundra Times* helped file the first suit for native land claims. More lawsuits followed, and soon the whole state was tied up in litigation. Oil companies, hungry to build a pipeline from the newly discovered giant oil field at Prudhoe Bay to Valdez, on Alaska's southern coast, soon realized there was no chance of getting federal construction permits until the native land claims were settled.

In 1971, the natives won a spectacular settlement in Congress: 40 million acres of land and almost $1 billion in cash.

The settlement has not been a cure-all for the many problems of Alaska's natives. Poverty is still widespread, as little of the land-claims money (allocated mostly to 13 regional, for-profit native corporations by Congress) has trickled down to the village level. But the settlement has given many a sense of dignity and purpose. Several villages in the Arctic have voted themselves "dry" (prohibiting alcohol) to combat drinking problems. A new cadre of bright native leaders is taking charge to help its people.

Today, the fundamental issue is whether the natives will be allowed by the larger Alaskan society to pursue their own future, says Byron Mallott, chief operating officer of Sealaska Corp., the regional native corporation for Southeast Alaska.

"In one way, Alaska is truly the last frontier," Mallott says. "Will the final chapter of the total and unremitting decimation of our nation's native American people be written in Alaska—or will, with the benefit of the lesson of history, Alaska be the place where native peoples finally are able to become a part of the overall society with their pride, strength, and ethnicity intact?"

There are, he adds, few guideposts to suggest the answer.

Most of Alaska's natives still reside in widely scattered communities spread across the half-million square miles of

Alaska. Unlike the Indians of the lower 48 states, the Alaskan natives have never been restricted to reservations. Many villages remain isolated, the preference of traditional villagers; others have plunged into modern life with mixed results.

The different native peoples tend to group in well-defined regions. Here is a brief look at the different native cultures and where you will find them.

Eskimos. Most of Alaska's more than 40,000 Eskimos are found in scattered settlements along the Bering Sea and Arctic Ocean coasts, the deltas of the lower Yukon and Kuskokwim rivers in western Alaska, and on remote islands in the Bering Sea such as St. Lawrence, Nunivak, and Little Diomede. Principal Arctic and sub-Arctic Eskimo communities include Barrow, Kotzebue, Nome, Gambell, Savoonga, Point Hope, Wainwright, and Shishmaref.

T he Eskimos are divided into two linguistic groups: the Inupiaq of the Far North and the Yup'ik, who reside mostly along the coastal regions of the west. The Yup'ik share the same dialect as the Eskimos of Siberia. Both groups are famed for their hunting and fishing skills. They are also noted craftsmen, carving animals and creating jewelry from native materials.

Don't go to Alaska expecting to see igloos, nose-rubbing for kisses, or wife-swapping among the Eskimos. These stereotypes have no basis in fact and are quite offensive to Alaskan Eskimos. Igloos, for instance, belong to the culture of Canada's Inuit people. Alaska's Eskimos never built them, although they sometimes do improvise walls of ice or snow blocks for windbreaks on winter hunting trips. The only igloo you're likely to see in Alaska these days is the occasional imitation fashioned for tourist promotions.

Indians. Alaska has four major Indian cultures: Tlingit, Haida, Athapaskan, and Tsimshian.

Once among North America's most powerful tribes, the Tlingits (pronounced "Klink-its") are found mostly throughout coastal Southeast Alaska. They number about 13,000 and are found in cities such as Juneau, Ketchikan, and Sitka, and in villages from Hoonah, near Juneau, to Klukwan, near Haines.

The Tlingits developed a highly sophisticated culture and fought hard against Russian incursions. Social status among early Tlingits depended on elaborate feasts called potlatches. Heads of families and clans vied in giving away vast quantities of valuable goods, their generosity so extravagant at times that the hosts fell into a form of ancient bankruptcy. There are still potlatches for important occasions, such as funerals, but they are greatly scaled down from earlier times.

Haidas are also found mainly in Southeast Alaska, as well as in British Columbia. They number only about 1,000 in Alaska. Their principal community is Hydaburg on Prince of Wales Island, near Ketchikan. The Queen Charlotte Islands of British Columbia are another vital center of Haida culture.

Historically, the Haidas were far-ranging voyagers and traders. Some historians credit the artistic Haidas with originating totem carving among Alaska's natives.

Most of Alaska's 7,000 or so Athabaskan Indians are found in the villages of Alaska's vast interior, including Fort Yukon, Stevens Village, Beaver, Chalkyitsik, and Minto, near Fairbanks. Other Athabaskans are scattered from the Kenai Peninsula–Cook Inlet area, near Anchorage, to the Copper River area near Cordova.

Linguistically, the Athapaskans are related to the Navajos and Apaches of the American Southwest. They were driven out of Canada by warring Cree Indians more than 700 years ago.

The ancestral home of the Tsimshian (pronounced "Simp-shee-ann") Indians was British Columbia, but Tsimshian historians say their forebears roamed through much of Southeastern Alaska fishing, hunting, and trading long before the arrival of the white man. The 1,000 or so Tsimshians of Alaska settled in 1887 on Annette Island, near Ketchikan, when a dissident Church of England lay missionary, William Duncan, led them out of British Columbia to escape religious persecution. The town of Metlakatla on Annette Island is their principal community. Their artwork includes a variety of wood carvings, from totems to ceremonial masks.

Aleuts. With their villages on the Aleutian Islands, curving between Siberia and Alaska like broken beads, the Aleuts (pronounced "Al-ee-oots") were first in the path of early explorers and ruthless fur traders.

There are about 7,000 Aleuts in Alaska today, their principal communities being Dutch Harbor/Unalaska, Akutan, Nikolski, and Atka in the Aleutians, and St. Paul and St. George in the Pribilof Islands. Grass basketry, classed by museums as some of the best in the world, is the principal art of the Aleuts. Finely woven baskets from Attu, at the tip of the Aleutian chain—where villages were destroyed in American-Japanese combat during World War II and never rebuilt—are difficult-to-obtain treasures.

Recently, Alaska's native peoples have become more enterprising in the tourist business. No longer content to play the role of "quaint" camera subjects and letting out-of-state tour operators have all the business, they are now starting to take charge of tours in their communities.

In Kotzebue, a major Arctic gathering point, the Eskimo-owned NANA Development Corp. has created a tour company, known as Tour Arctic, to conduct all excursions there. NANA (North Alaska Natives Association) also owns and operates the $3-million Museum of the Arctic in Kotzebue, one of Alaska's top-rated museums.

In the tiny Bering Sea village of Gambell on remote St. Lawrence Island, about 150 air miles southwest of Nome, residents have formed Alaska Village Tours Inc. to organize and conduct tours of their village, only 40 miles from the Siberian coast. The one-day tours depart from Nome in small-plane flights to Gambell, There the Eskimos prepare lunch and guide visitors through the ancient village. Traditional dancing is presented, and elders tell of whale hunts and how walrus ivory is carved into art objects.

3 Cruising in Alaska

By Mary Ann Hemphill

A freelance travel writer, Mary Ann Hemphill specializes in cruising. Her work has appeared in newspapers and magazines throughout the country, including the Miami Herald, Dallas Times Herald, *and* Chicago Tribune.

At first glance, the notoriously luxurious, lazy cruise seems an incongruous way to tour raw and rugged Alaska. The image seems too refined, the ships too far removed from the grand spectacle. But a closer look reveals that most of Alaska's prime attractions—glaciers, snow-capped mountains, spirited small towns—are arrayed along the water. Often the only roads leading to them are the water routes through the Inside Passage, from Ketchikan to Skagway, and along the Gulf of Alaska.

The narrow Inside Passage is walled by an ever-changing panorama of lush evergreen slopes, jagged mountains, countless waterfalls, granite fjords, and massive glaciers. Wildlife is abundant. Cruise along this marine highway and you're apt to see killer whales, cavorting porpoises, soaring eagles, and jumping salmon. One sniff of the crisp air on deck and you'll know you're not too far removed; you're so close to the spruce and hemlock forests you can smell the trees. Cruises along the gulf encounter the Columbia Glacier, which stands taller than a 20-story building and sheds up to 14 million tons of icebergs every day. From port towns, passengers journey overland to Anchorage, jumping-off point for a variety of excursions and land tours.

There are important distinctions between cruising Alaska and cruising tropical destinations. Although there are sunny days, you can't count on sitting by the pool developing a deep tan. The weather is capricious; it can be warm one day, cold and drizzly the next. There are no fun-filled party ships with a cargo of merrymakers on this route. Many ships have gala evenings, but if you want ports with glamorous, sophisticated nightlife, you'll have to cruise elsewhere.

Like other cruises, Alaska cruises are a relaxing way to travel. There is no driving from town to town, packing and unpacking. Your meals and most of your activities are paid for up front. You're free to simply sit back and watch the passing parade of glorious scenery.

Although the scenery is spectacular, some potential cruisers are apprehensive about boredom. Not to worry. A wealth of shipboard activities and frequent port calls keep boredom at bay.

A look at any ship's daily paper reveals a full range of activities, from classics such as bingo, bridge tournaments, and deck games to more contemporary pursuits such as computer classes, stress-management seminars, and financial planning lectures. Alaska cruises are particularly noted for offering seminars and lectures by a variety of experts to enhance your understanding of the land unfolding around you. Then there's always the option of curling up with a hefty book that you never have time for at home, or chatting with new acquaintances. Evening entertainment can be a revue, a cabaret, a first-run film, dancing, or perhaps a shot at the casino.

Port calls are almost a daily event. Ashore, adventures such as flightseeing with bush pilots, river rafting expeditions, and hikes across glaciers are easily arranged. Tours through ports and nearby towns reveal the influence of Alaska's many cultures: Native Indian, Russian traders, and gold rush pioneers. You can—and should—reserve these shore excursions in advance with your cruise line or directly from local suppliers (*see* Shore Excursions, below).

In keeping with today's emphasis on physical fitness and good nutrition, most ships have upgraded their fitness facilities from a lone stationary bicycle to slick gyms with all the equipment, instruction, and classes needed to counteract over-indulgence in the dining room. Food is still plentiful, but menus have been lightened, and there is usually a selection of salt-free, low-fat, and low-cholesterol items.

Alaska has traditionally attracted older cruisers, although this pattern is changing. More active options ashore and more contemporary on-board amenities now regularly draw passengers in their 40s and 50s. Families are another growing segment of the Alaska cruise market. Most ships carry youth counselors in the summer to entertain kids with their own activities—don't be surprised to see a group of young cruisers flying kites off the stern. Ashore, kids like Alaska's casual frontier atmosphere and variety of active excursions.

A voyage along the Inside Passage was along the traditional cruise route. Then, in 1983, when the demand for permits to cruise Glacier Bay National Monument exceeded the number allowed by the National Park Service, some lines turned to the Gulf of Alaska as an alternative. The new route, along the South Central coast, was a huge success. Several lines have added the Gulf route to their Inside Passage route. Instead of a round-trip starting and ending in Vancouver, the Gulf route is a one-way voyage between Anchorage and Vancouver (or other southern ports).

The advantages are many. Instead of returning over waters you've already cruised, you get to see new scenery, more glaciers, and an even more rugged side of Alaska. The gulf cruises begin or end in Anchorage's ports, Whittier and Seward. From here, excursions take in Denali National Park and Mt. McKinley, the very accessible Portage Glacier, Valdez and its terminus for the trans-Alaska pipeline, and Anchorage itself.

Cruise Tours

The increasingly popular one-way cruise itinerary makes a good deal of sense. Glorious as the coastal scenery is, cruising takes visitors to only a small portion of this vast and varied state. To flesh out their cruises and gain a broader perspective of Alaska, more and more travelers are combining a land tour with the sea portion of their vacation.

Unlike shore excursions, which almost always last less than a full day, the land portions of cruise tours tend to last several days. A land tour may venture north across the Arctic Circle to Prudhoe Bay or into the Canadian Rockies. There are tours exploring Gold Rush Country and the exotic Eskimo culture of the Arctic. Other tours wind through Denali National Park to view wildlife or trek to the remote Pribilof Islands to visit a colony of seabirds and fur-seal herds (*see* General-Interest Tours in Before You Go, Chapter 1). Last year **Holland America Line-Westours** introduced trips that combined an Alaska cruise with a trip to the Soviet Far East and rides on the Trans-Siberian Railroad. **Princess Tours** will offer a similar program this year and is adding a new series of adventure tours and "ecotours," which focus on the environment.

Most cruise lines and their affiliated tour companies offer both independent and escorted tours. Independent tours allow maximum flexibility. You have a preplanned itinerary with confirmed hotel reservations and transportation arrangements, but you're free to follow your interests and whims in each town. Tour company representatives are usually available to help out should you need assistance.

Escorted tours are more organized. You travel with a group, led by a tour director. Activities are preplanned, and typically prepaid, so you have a good idea of how much your trip will cost you (not counting incidentals) before departing.

Modes of tour transportation range from plane to bus, rail to ferry. Major cruise tour operators include travel on private, glass dome-top railway cars in most of their packages. Running between Anchorage, Denali National Park, and Fairbanks, the **McKinley Explorer** (operated by Holland America Line-Westours) and the **Princess's Midnight Sun Express Ultra Dome,** railways offer a comfortable ride with unobstructed views of the passing surroundings and wildlife (*see* Getting Around Alaska in Before You Go).

In addition to full-fledged cruise tours, many cruise lines have pre- or post-cruise packages lasting one to three days. Hotel accommodations and some sightseeing in port cities are usually included.

Of the conventional cruise ship fleet, only the *Song of Flower, Sun Viking,* and *Universe,* do not currently offer cruise tour packages. The small ships *Discovery, Sea Lion, Sea Bird, Society Explorer,* and *Stephanie Anne* do not include these options. If you would like to add a land tour to one of these cruises, contact an independent tour operator (*see* General-Interest Tours in Before You Go, Chapter 1).

When to Go

Cruise season runs from early May to late September; demand peaks from late June through August. Although Alaskan weather never carries any guarantees, sunshine and warm days are apt to be most plentiful from mid-June through August. The Gulf of Alaska can get rough any time of year, but it's generally calmer in the summer. During these weeks, twilight lingers long into the short night.

Peak season means peak rates. The further away from the most popular months you go, the lower the rates. Expect to pay in the neighborhood of $100 to $150 per person less for a cruise in the "value" seasons—just before and just after peak season. Cruises during the May and late September low seasons are usually another $100 or so less than value seasons, or $200 or so less than peak.

According to experienced Alaska travelers, there are plenty of other advantages in addition to the lower fares. Many cite spring as their favorite time. It's a season when wildflowers are abundant. You're apt to see more wildlife along the shore, because the animals have not yet gone up to higher elevations. Fall brings the splendor of autumn hues, the first snowfalls in the mountains. The animals have returned to low ground, and shorter days bring the possibility of seeing the Northern Lights. Temperatures along the cruise routes in May, June, and September are in the 50s and 60s. July and August averages are in the 60s and 70s, with occasional days in the 80s.

Availability of ships and particular cabins is greater in the shoulder season. The ports are almost completely empty of tourists during the low seasons, but crowding is never really a problem in peak season either. The cruise ships follow a staggered schedule of calls during peak season, as each port has limited dock space, buses, guides, and flightseeing planes.

Packing Tips

What to pack? Daytime wear aboard ship and in port is casual. Weather conditions on deck vary; be prepared for bathing suit days by the pool or to bundle up against wind and chill. Alaska's fickle weather requires you to dress in layers.

You'll definitely want a sweater and a lightweight, water-repellent, wind-resistant jacket, hat, and gloves. Comfortable walking shoes, with rubber soles, are a must.

Evening dress varies with your ship. There are general guidelines in the ship profile section. Women should take along a dressy sweater or shawl; shipboard air-conditioning can be cooler than a glacial breeze.

A pair of binoculars are great for spotting wildlife and for getting close-up views of the glacier's craggy faces. Don't forget sunscreen; and pack more film than you think you'll need—you'll probably use it.

Cruise Costs

Cruising Alaska is not about to make anybody's list of budget vacations. It's not outrageously expensive, but it will cost more than the average North American vacation. Fares for a standard outside cabin in peak season average $199–$590 per person, per day, based on double occupancy (*see* The Cruise Fleet, below).

Then come the extra costs, like airfare to the port city (some lines offer free or discounted fares). Shore excursions can be a substantial expense. The best in Alaska are not cheap. Expect to pay, per person, at least $100 for most flightseeing excursions, $45 to more than $150 for river rafting (depending on the length of the trip), and $20 for salmon bakes. Skimp too much on your excursion budget and you'll end up depriving yourself of an important part of the Alaska experience.

Tipping is another extra. It's customary to tip your room steward, waiter, and busboy at the end of the cruise. The average tip, per person, per day, is $6 to $9. Each ship offers guidelines; or, you can ask for recommendations at the reception desk. As you would on land, tip bartenders, deck stewards, and the wine steward as you use their services; 15% is the norm. Maître d'hotels and headwaiters should be tipped according to special services rendered on your request, beyond their expected duties.

Other out-of-pocket expenses include your drinks, flings in the casino, laundry (some ships have complimentary self-service laundry rooms), shopping, and any meals you have ashore.

Purchasing trip-cancellation insurance is a good idea. Most cruise lines impose penalties if you cancel your reservations—the severity of the penalty often depends on how far in advance of the departure date you cancel.

Shopping carefully can save you money. Alaska is a competitive market, and various discounts abound. Many cruise lines offer discounts on shoulder-season cruises, usually late May to mid-June, and again from late August to the end of the season in September. Some lines offer early-booking fare reductions for reserving well in advance, typically requiring a deposit by the end of January. A third or fourth person (including children) sharing a stateroom with two full-fare adults pays substantially less. Group discounts are also available for parties traveling together; policies on the minimum group size vary.

As the season draws closer, check with various travel agents—including those specializing in cruises—and watch the ads in travel sections for last-minute discounts.

Single travelers should be aware that there are few single cabins on most ships; taking a double cabin for yourself will cost more than the advertised per person rates (which are based on two people sharing a room). Some cruise lines will find singles roommates of the same sex so that each can travel at the regular per person, double occupancy rate.

Because scenery is the prime attraction of an Alaska cruise, this is not the time to save money by booking an inside cabin. Twilight lasts long into the night, and at all times you will want to see as much of the passing show as possible. Don't cheat yourself of a porthole peek.

The Cruise Fleet

The best way to make sure your cruise is shipshape is to choose carefully the ship you're going to make your bon voyage on.

More than two dozen vessels—small yachts, expedition vessels, and cruise ships—will be cruising Alaska's waterways in 1992. Passenger capacity will range from 10 on the *Stephanie Anne* to 1,590 on the *Regal Princess*.

This year's newest ship is Princess Cruises' *Regal Princess*. Noted architect Renzo Piano, known for his controversial design of the Pompidou Center in Paris, created a streamlined hull whose lines resemble a dolphin moving through the water.

Royal Cruise line spent $20 million converting the former *Royal Viking Sea* into the *Royal Odyssey*, which has retained its spaciousness and single-seating dining. In addition, it now features many excellent programs that make this ship a favorite with the senior market.

This will be the *Daphne*'s last Alaska season. In the fall the ship will join Prestige Cruises, a joint Costa-Soviet venture.

With only two ships, the luxury fleet is the smallest it's been in years. Longtime Alaska cruiser, the *Royal Viking Sky*, has been retired, and after two summers in Alaska, the *Crystal Harmony* is spending summer 1992 in Europe.

The small ship fleet, which booked quickly last year, continues to offer the most diverse cruise styles. Noted for their focus on

Cruise Chart

● Port is visited on every cruise
○ Port is only visited on some cruises

CLASS / SHIP	NIGHTS	ROUTE	Inside Passage	Davidson & Rainbow Glaciers (cruise)	Admiralty Island	Agate Beach	Anan Creek	Elfin Cove (cruise)	Endicott Arm (cruise)	Ford's Terror
Standard										
Daphne	7	round-trip from Vancouver	●	●					●	
Regent Sea	7	between Vancouver and Whittier	●						●	
Regent Star	7	between Vancouver and Whittier	●							
Sun Viking	7	round-trip from Vancouver	●							
SS Universe	14	round-trip from Vancouver	●							
Premium										
Dawn Princess	7	between Vancouver and Whittier	●							
Fair Princess	7	between Vancouver and Whittier	●							
Island Princess	7	between Vancouver and Whittier	●							
Nieuw Amsterdam	7	round-trip from Vancouver	●							
Noordam	7	round-trip from Vancouver	●							
Pacific Princess	7	between Vancouver and Whittier	●							
Regal Princess	7	round-trip from Vancouver	●							
Rotterdam	7	between Vancouver and Seward	●							
Royal Odyssey	7	round-trip from Vancouver	●							
	7	between Vancouver and Anchorage	●							
	10	Vancouver to San Francisco	●							
	12	round-trip from San Francisco	●							
Sky Princess	10	round-trip from San Francisco	●							
Westerdam	7	round-trip from Vancouver	●							
Luxury										
Sagafjord	11	Vancouver to Anchorage	●						●	
	10	Anchorage to Vancouver	●						●	
Song of Flower	7	between Vancouver and Whittier	●							
	7	round-trip from Vancouver	●							
Small Ships										
Discovery	6	round-trip from Cordova								
Executive Explorer	7	between Glacier Bay Lodge & Ketchikan	●							
	2	round-trip from Glacier Bay Lodge								
Sea Bird	11	between Sitka and Prince Rupert	●		●		●	●		
Sea Lion	11	between Sitka and Prince Rupert	●		●	●	●			
Society Explorer	10	between Prince Rupert and Kodiak	●							
	14	Vancouver to Juneau	●							
	14	Kodiak Island to Vancouver	●							
Spirit of Alaska	7	between Seattle and Juneau	●							
Spirit of Glacier Bay	2,3	round-trip from Juneau								
Stephanie Anne	7	round-trip from Ketchikan	●				●			●

| Glacier Bay | Haines | Homer | Juneau | Ketchikan | Le Conte Bay (cruise) | Misty Fjords (cruise) | Petersburg | Point Adolphus (cruise) | Sitka | Skagway | Snow Passage | Taku Harbor | Tracy Arm (cruise) | Wrangell | **Gulf of Alaska** | College Fjord (cruise) | Columbia Glacier (cr.) | Hubbard Glacier/ Yakutat Bay (cruise) | Icy Bay | Katmai National Park | Kenai Fjords National Monument (cruise) | Kodiak Island | Seward | Valdez | **Prince William Snd.** | **British Columbia** | Hartley Bay | Prince Rupert | Queen Charlotte Islands | Victoria | Vancouver |

Alaska's natural wonders, their ability to wander through mazes of waterways that are inaccessible to the large ships, and the camaraderie quickly developed among passengers, these ships offer excellent alternatives for those who want to see Alaska's coastline in a less structured manner. Many offer landings on remote beaches, in and out of tiny coves.

Clipper Cruises has charted the *Society Explorer* for a series of in-depth, cultural and natural-history cruises, operated under the line's new division, Clipper Adventure Cruises. The cruises featuring the Kodiak Islands and the islands of British Columbia add a welcome, imaginative addition to Alaska itineraries.

InnerAsia Expeditions has retired the original *Discovery*, replacing it with an extensively refurbished, 122-foot *Discovery* that will ply Prince William Sound.

Check with your travel agent for other additions to the Alaska fleet. World conditions, such as the Persian Gulf War, which caused several ships to head to Alaska instead of Europe, can cause changes in cruise lines' schedules and itineraries.

Cruise ships sport distinctive personalities, and not every ship will be right for every passenger. Use the same personal, subjective considerations when selecting a vessel as you would when selecting a shipmate; the best marriage is a ship whose amenities are compatible with your lifestyle. Would you prefer the wide range of facilities and activities a large ship can offer, or the camaraderie of a smaller one? Do you enjoy dressing for dinner, or is your style more casual, relaxed? Do you want to visit well-known ports? Or do you prefer to travel off the beaten track?

Practical considerations, such as price, desired length of the cruise, the ports that appeal to you, and the cruise tour options available should also be weighed when choosing a ship.

The following profiles will introduce you to the Alaskan fleet. You can contact the cruise lines directly for brochures and information, though some will accept reservations only from travel agents. Be sure the agent you work with is familiar with more than his or her favorite ship or cruise line and takes your budget and lifestyle into account.

The ships are divided into three categories, defined both by price and ambience: standard, premium, and luxury. Price ranges listed in each category are computed on a per person, per day, double occupancy basis for an outside cabin during peak season—the most standard accommodation to use for comparison. There are lower fares for inside cabins and higher ones for the best accommodations, ranging up to a penthouse with private veranda.

Although there is some overlap in price range, on-board amenities (such as the level of service and, cuisine, sophistication, amount of activities) further determine a ship's category.

For standard ships, peak season fares may run from $200 to $340, per person, per day, for an outside double cabin. You can expect good food, but nothing extraordinary. Most of these ships are older vessels, lacking some of the facilities of newer ships. Menus are not as extensive as on more luxurious ships, and dress is often more casual.

The premium category is the core of the Alaska-bound fleet. Peak season fares for a standard outside double range from $260 to $500 per person. These are highly experienced cruise lines, consistently good with regard to itineraries, food, and entertainment. Waiters are more likely to be of one nationality, such as Italian, which adds a distinctive flair to the dining room.

The hours and selections for room service also increase on premium ships. Menu choices are more varied and of higher quality. Featured dishes may be prepared at table side. Evenings are dressier; the ambience is similar to that of a good restaurant. There are usually several formal nights.

The luxury ships purvey the finest and freshest cuisine, have single-seating dining, and offer special ordering. They have the highest ratio of crew to passengers, creating a high level of personalized service. Passengers tend to be experienced, more sophisticated cruisers and are older than those vacationing on other ships. Evenings are dressy, with many formal nights. The rates keep the number of families down. The average outside double cabin during peak season costs $320–$590 per person.

Unless otherwise noted, all ships have stabilizers, passenger elevators, cabins with private bath, telephone, radio, individually controlled air-conditioning, and at least one swimming pool. Public rooms include a dining room, bars, lounges, theater for lectures and movies, a casino, shops selling sundries, local crafts, local and cruise souvenirs, and some duty-free items.

Because the days are so long and the scenery is such an important part of an Alaska cruise, you'll want a ship that allows you as much and as comfortable a view as possible. A forward observation deck is important in places like Glacier Bay; we've noted ships that don't have full walk-around promenades. A forward observation lounge, with large windows, will be appreciated in inclement weather and during twilight viewing hours. Good views from the dining room will enhance your meals.

When it comes to dress, casual is the byword for all ships by day and in port. There are substantial differences at night, however. The level of dressiness is designated in each ship profile. Here are the guidelines:

Formal. Suit and tie are required for men at dinner; cocktail dresses or trouser suits for women. On formal nights, men should plan to don a dinner jacket or tuxedo and women to wear a semiformal evening gown or elegant cocktail dress.

Informal. Sports jackets with slacks, preferably a tie, or a suit and tie, are what men are expected to wear at dinner. Nice dresses or pant suits are appropriate for women. On the few formal evenings, a dark suit with tie or dinner jacket are required for men; long or short evening gowns or dressy outfits for women.

Casual. Jacket and tie is only for special evenings, when women's attire ranges from dressy slacks to cocktail dresses. Some women use the occasion to wear a long dress.

Very casual. Leave your jacket and tie at home. This is the style aboard most of the small ships.

Standard

Standard outside double cabin, per person per day: $200–$340.

Daphne. Both the ship and the cabins are spacious, but there is no forward observation lounge. Some cabins offer double beds and private balconies, and all have a bath and shower. Good service, warm atmosphere, an emphasis on Italian cuisine, and the comfort of the ship make this a good value. *Costa Cruise Lines, World Trade Center, 80 S.W. 8th St., Miami, FL 33130, tel. 800/462–6782. Built 1955; refurbished 1989. Accommodates 420 passengers. Liberian registry; Italian officers and European and Filipino staff. Additional facilities: piazetta, gelateria, gymnasium, sauna, massage. Dress: informal.*

Regent Sea. Classic in appearance, 95% of the cabins are outside and spacious. There is a glass-enclosed promenade available for comfortable sightseeing, and a naturalist is onboard for Alaska cruises. *Regency Cruises, 260 Madison Ave., New York, NY 10016, tel. 212/972–4499. Built 1957; refurbished 1985 and 1987. Accommodates 729 passengers. Bahamian registry; European officers and staff. Additional facilities: outdoor pool, health and fitness center, whirlpools, sauna, massage. Cabin amenities: 24-hr. room service, some double beds. Dress: informal.*

Regent Star. Most of the cabins are outside and spacious. Glass-enclosed and open promenades make sightseeing comfortable in any weather, and a naturalist is onboard for Alaska cruises. *Regency Cruises, 260 Madison Ave., New York, NY 10016, tel. 212/972–4499. Built 1957; refurbished 1987. Accommodates 950 passengers. Bahamian registry; Greek officers and European staff. Additional facilities: indoor and outdoor pools, 2 whirlpools, gym, sauna, massage. Cabin amenities: 24-hr. room service, some beds convertible to doubles. Dress: informal.*

Sun Viking. This smaller, more intimate ship brings Royal Caribbean's consistently high-quality service to Alaska. The Viking Crown Lounge, cantilevered off the funnel, gives passengers a unique high vantage view of the passing scenery. Cabins are compact. *Royal Caribbean Cruise Line, 1050 Caribbean Way, Miami, FL 33132, tel. 305/539–6000. Built 1972; refurbished 1988. Accommodates 724 passengers. Norwegian registry; Scandinavian officers and international staff. Additional facilities: gym, sauna, massage, fitness program. Cabin amenities: Some cabins with double beds, 24-hr. room service. Dress: informal.*

Universe. This ship offers a cruise with a difference, emphasizing the experience of Alaska itself. So extensive is the on-board program by experts in history, art, geology, marine life, music, and geography that college credit can be earned during the cruise. Its itinerary is extensive, incorporating long port stays and an excellent array of shore excursions. The ship is functional in appearance, and its cabins are devoid of radios or telephones. This is not a glitzy cruise with Las Vegas-type revues or gambling. Evening entertainment is by noted classical artists. It's comfortable and a good value. Views are easy to enjoy, even in bad weather, from a glass-enclosed promenade deck; that's compensation for the fact that the dining room offers no view and the ship lacks a forward observation lounge. On selected voyages, carefully screened gentlemen hosts provide companionship for unescorted women. And, thanks to its Asian crew, menu choices include oriental specialties. *World Explorer Cruises, 555 Montgomery St., San Francisco, CA 94111, tel. 415/391–9262 or 800/854–3835. Built 1953; refurbished 1991. Accommodates 550 passengers. Liberian registry; Chinese officers and Filipino and Chinese staff. Additional facilities: 12,000-volume library, fitness center, massage, complimentary self-service laundry, youth center. Dress: casual.*

Premium

Standard outside double cabin, per person per day: $260–$500.

Fair Princess and *Dawn Princess*. These classically styled ships, which use a lot of wood, offer spacious cabins with abundant storage space, but not much noise insulation between units. Despite actual space, the vessels can seem crowded at times. As for the menu, the Italian ambience influences the specialties. No views are afforded from dining room windows. *Princess Cruises, 10100 Santa Monica Blvd., Los Angeles, CA 90067, tel. 213/553–1770. Built 1957/1958, refurbished 1989. Accommodates 890 passengers. Liberian registry; Italian officers and Italian and Portuguese staff. Additional facilities: gymnasium, sauna, pizzeria, 3 swimming pools, youth and teen centers, complimentary launderettes. Cabin amenities: upper berths, 24-hr. room service, TVs in suites and minisuites. Dress: informal.*

Island Princess and *Pacific Princess*. The smallest of the Princess ships, these "original Love Boats" boast old liner appeal, and convey a warm intimacy. Dining rooms don't offer any views, but two forward lounges have lots of windows. Standard cabins are on the small side. Retractable glass roofs over the pools allow for swimming on inclement days. *Princess Cruises, 10100 Santa Monica Blvd., Los Angeles, CA 90067, tel. 213/ 553–1770. Island Princess built 1972; refurbished 1984. Pacific Princess built 1971; refurbished 1984. Each accommodates 610 passengers. British registry; British officers; Italian dining room staff and British room stewards. Additional facilities: gymnasium, sauna, massage, 2 swimming pools, fitness program, pizzeria. Cabin amenities: 24-hr. room service. Dress: informal.*

Regal Princess. The newest ship in the Princess fleet features a sleek innovative hull design by Renzo Piano. The 13,000 square foot, forward Dome entertainment area combines observation/ conversation areas, casino, dance floor, and bar. Although the ship is spacious, a very small forward observation area and only partial promenade limit forward views of the scenery. There's a ⅙-mile tractioned outdoor running track, and the ship carries an impressive contemporary art collection valued at $1 million. Cabins are quite spacious, and suites and minisuites offer balconies and tubs. *Princess Cruises, 10100 Santa Monica Blvd., Los Angeles, CA 90067, tel. 213/553–1770. Built 1991. Accommodates 1,590 passengers. Italian registry; Italian officers and primarily European staff. Additional facilities: 2 pools, 1 with in-pool bar, 4 whirlpools, health and beauty center with sauna, massage, complimentary laundry, pizzeria, wine bar, demitasse and patisserie bar. Cabin amenities: color TV, twin beds convertible to a queen, picture windows, safe, refrigerator, walk-in closet, 24-hr. room service. Dress: informal.*

Sky Princess. This ship combines an old liner atmosphere with modern touches such as a forward observation lounge with large windows, one of the biggest showrooms afloat, and a notable contemporary art collection. Cabins are spacious. Suites have verandas and bathtubs. *Princess Cruises, 10100 Santa Monica Blvd., Los Angeles, CA 90067, tel. 213/553–1770. Built 1984; refurbished 1989. Accommodates 1,200 passengers. British registry; British officers; European hotel staff. Additional facilities: health and beauty center, massage, sauna, fitness program, whirlpool spa, 3 pools, children's facilities, jogging track, paddle tennis court, pizzeria, complimentary launderettes. Cabin amenities: 24-hr. room service, safe, television. Dress: informal.*

Nieuw Amsterdam and Noordam. These twin ships are immaculately maintained and carry aboard a multimillion-dollar collection of 17th- and 18th-century antiques tracing the story of Dutch maritime explorations. Outside state rooms are spacious. Features include a Fitness Program. Tipping is not required, but passengers tend to tip anyway, about half the amount given on other lines. *Holland America Line Westours, 300 Elliott Ave. W, Seattle, WA 98119, tel. 206/281–3535.* Nieuw Amsterdam *built 1983.* Noordam *built 1984. Each accommodates 1,214 passengers. Netherlands Antilles registry; Dutch officers and Indonesian and Filipino staff. Additional facilities: tennis practice courts, children's video game room, youth activity counselor, gymnasium, saunas, massage, whirlpool, complimentary ice cream bar, complimentary launderettes, 2 pools. Cabin amenities: closed-circuit TV, some king- or queen-size beds, 24-hr. room service. Dress: informal.*

Rotterdam. This beautiful, classic liner, with three decades of worldwide cruising experience, received a $15 million renovation in 1989. Unfortunately, no views are possible from the dining room and there's no forward observation lounge, but open and glass-enclosed promenades offer comfortable sightseeing in all weather conditions. Because this is an older ship, cabins come in all sizes and shapes. Inexpensive inside cabins are quite small. Tipping is not required, but passengers tend to tip anyway. The ship features the Passport to Fitness Program. *Holland America Line Westours, 300 Elliott Ave. W, Seattle, WA 98119, tel. 206/281–3535. Built 1958; refurbished 1989. Accommodates 1,075 passengers. Netherlands Antilles registry; Dutch officers and Indonesian and Filipino staff. Additional facilities: tennis practice courts, children's video game room, youth activity center, gymnasium, massage, 1 inside and 1 outside pool. Cabin amenities: 24-hr. room service. Dress: informal.*

Westerdam. This is Holland America's newest and largest ship. Cabins are spacious. There's no forward observation lounge, but floor-to-ceiling windows in many public rooms afford good views of passing scenery. There's an on-board collection of 17th- and 18th-century treasures from around the world. One of the two pools has a retractable glass dome for open-air swimming in warm weather. The Passport to Fitness Program is featured. Tipping is not required, but passengers tend to tip anyway. *Holland America Line Westours, 300 Elliott Ave. W,*

Seattle, WA 98119, tel. 206/281–3535. Built 1986; redesigned and lengthened, 1990. Accommodates 1,494 passengers. Bahamian registry; Dutch officers and Indonesian and Filipino staff. Additional facilities: children's video game room, youth activity center, 2 whirlpools, complimentary launderettes. Cabin amenities: 24-hr. room service, TV. Dress: informal.

Royal Odyssey. Twenty million dollars was spent last year to transform the former *Royal Viking Sea* into the *Royal Odyssey*. The many changes include totally refurbished cabins, the addition of three outdoor whirlpools, and the installation of new sound and lighting systems in the lounges. The ship has retained its spaciousness and single-seating dining. With a "Host Program" for single travelers, a "New Beginnings" motivational lecture series, and an alternative low-fat, low-cholesterol dining program, the ship appeals to more mature cruisers. A forward observation lounge, large windows in the dining room, and a full promenade deck offer excellent views of the passing scenery. Penthouse suites have private verandas and the services of a private butler. *Royal Cruise Line, One Maritime Plaza, Suite 1400, San Francisco, CA 94111, tel. 415/956–7200. Built 1973; refurbished 1991. Accommodates 765 passengers. Bahamian registry; Greek officers and staff. Additional facilities: gymnasium, sauna and massage, fitness program, swimming pool, paddle tennis court, outdoor grill, full-service deli. Cabin amenities: closed–circuit color TV, 24–hr. room service; some have refrigerators, hair dryers, picture windows, and bathtubs. Dress: informal.*

Luxury

Standard outside double cabin, per person per day: $320–$590.

Sagafjord. A very mature group, many of them loyal repeaters, is drawn to this spacious ship, responding to its classic liner ambience, highly rated cuisine, and excellent service. It's consistently one of the best. Other pluses include single-seating dining, a large number of tables for two, and the Golden Door Spa at Sea. *Cunard, 555 Fifth Ave., New York, NY 10017, tel. 800/221–4770. Built 1965; refurbished 1983. Accommodates 589 passengers. Bahamian registry; Norwegian officers and European staff. Additional facilities: massage, sauna, indoor/outdoor nightclub, 1 outdoor and 1 indoor pool, large dining room windows, complimentary launderettes. Cabin amenities: 24-hr. room service, robes, some private terraces. Dress: formal.*

Song of Flower. This ship carries only 172 passengers but is included in the cruise ship fleet because its on-board lifestyle and facilities are those of a luxurious cruise ship, not a small ship. Although the vessel is Japanese-owned, the onboard lifestyle is designed for the North American market. High-level, personalized service; outstanding cuisine; open seating; single-seating dining are some of the features. All cabins are outside and very spacious. Rooms are equipped with refrigerators stocked on a complimentary basis. Fares include tips and all drinks. *Seven Seas Cruises, North America, 555 W. Hastings St., Suite 2300, Vancouver, B.C. V6B4-N5, Canada, tel. 800/661–5541. Built 1976: totally gutted and rebuilt as Explorer Starship in 1986: refurbished 1989. Accommodates 172 passengers. Norwegian registry; Norwegian officers and European staff.*

Additional facilities: Health and fitness center, whirlpool, sauna, water-sports equipment, excursion boat, tuxedo and formal gown rental service. Cabin amenities: TV/VCR, some cabins with tubs and queen-size beds, some verandas. Dress: formal.

The Small Ships

Standard outside double cabin, per person per day: $225–$389.

The small-ship fleet presents diverse cruise opportunities. Carrying 10 to 100 passengers, these ships offer unique and personalized travel experiences.

Size is the factor that sets this fleet apart—both in facilities and lifestyle—from conventional cruise ships.

Because they are small, these ships do not have swimming pools, casinos, beauty salons, fitness centers, elevators, medical staff or facilities, elevators, telephones, televisions, or radios in the cabins. Onboard lifestyle is more casual, and meals are served in a single seating, often family style. The exceptions are the *Discovery,* with a small pool, fitness center, sauna, and hospital, and the *Spirit of Alaska,* with a bit of fitness equipment.

The small ships' size enables them to sail to passages and ports that are inaccessible to the larger vessels. Shore excursions include hikes, fishing, and wildlife observations. The emphasis of these cruises is on Alaska—the beauty, the wildlife, the delicate environment—not on shipboard life.

Most of these ships carry U.S. registry, allowing them to begin and end their cruises in Alaska or Seattle.

Discovery. This yacht-style cruising vessel offers an itinerary that focuses on natural history in Prince William Sound. Instead of port calls, there are clam digs, hikes in a rain forest and on a glacier, and observations of bears feeding and salmon spawning. This is expedition cruising, a learning and participatory experience that is enhanced by an on-board naturalist. Cabins are small, with private baths, and you make your own bed. *InnerAsia Expeditions, Inc., 2627 Lombard St., San Francisco, CA 94123, tel. 415/922–0448 or 800/777–8183. Built 1962; scheduled to be rebuilt 1992. Accommodates 20 passengers. U.S. registry; American officers and crew. Additional facilities: Jet skiffs. Dress: very casual.*

Executive Explorer. In addition to Inside Passage cruises, this catamaran makes three-day, in-depth cruises of both arms of Glacier Bay. The vessel has a low spaciousness ratio, but that might not be a concern since most of the daytime is spent ashore or on deck watching the sights. The two public rooms, the dining room and the lounge, have viewing windows. All the cabins are outside. Bow-landing ability allows passengers to go ashore in Glacier Bay. *Glacier Bay Tours & Cruises, 520 Pike St., Suite 1610, Seattle, WA 98101, tel. 800/451–5952 (U.S. and Canada). Built 1986. Accommodates 49 passengers. U.S. registry; American officers and staff. Cabin amenities: TV/VCR, minirefrigerator. Dress: casual.*

Sea Bird and Sea Lion. These small draft ships have the freedom to sail through narrow straits and visit out-of-the-way areas, such as Elfin cove, that are inaccessible to the larger ships. The boats forego visits to the standard port calls at larger, busy towns, and instead make stops to visit smaller towns such as Petersburg, zodiac raft landings, wildlife searches, and beachcombing on Agate Beach and barbecues in Tracy Arm. All cabins are outside staterooms, but Category 1 rooms have only a high port light. *Special Expeditions, 720 Fifth Ave., New York, NY 10019, tel. 212/765–7740. Both built 1982;* Sea Lion *refurbished 1989,* Sea Bird *refurbished 1990. Each accommodates 70 passengers. U.S. registry; American officers and staff. Dress: casual.*

Society Explorer. Clipper has chartered this—the world's first true expedition ship—for a series of in-depth, cultural, and natural history–oriented cruises, including some very innovative Alaska itineraries. On-board naturalists will enhance explorations of Alaska's wilderness. All cabins are outside. This is the only vessel in the small ship fleet with a pool (albeit small) and hospital facilities. *Clipper Adventure Cruises, 7711 Bonhomme Ave., St. Louis, MO 63105, tel. 314/727–2929. Built 1969; refurbished 1985. Accommodates 98 passengers. Liberian registry; German officers; international staff; American cruise and catering staff. Additional facilities: Small pool and fitness center with sauna, beauty salon, library, movie theater/lecture room, laboratory, hospital. Dress: casual.*

Spirit of Alaska. This ship offers casual, close-up viewing of the Inside Passage, including both the east and west arms of Glacier Bay National Park. A forward lounge area with wraparound windows provides good views. *Alaska Sightseeing Tours/TravAlaska, Suite 700, 4th & Battery Bldg., Seattle, WA 98121, tel. 206/441–8687 or 800/426–7702. Built 1980; refurbished 1991. Accommodates 82 passengers. U.S. registry; American officers and crew. Additional facilities: Rowing machine, stairstep machine. Cabin amenities: All outside cabins with either windows or high port lights, some with double or queen-size beds. Dress: very casual.*

Spirit of Glacier Bay. If you're doing the ferry/car route through Alaska, here's a way to cruise Glacier Bay on a two-night route from Juneau. The ship's small size allows a close-up look at the glaciers and inlets along both arms of Glacier Bay. *Alaska Sightseeing Tours/TravAlaska, 4th & Battery Bldg., Suite 700, Seattle, WA 98121, tel. 206/441–8687 or 800/426–7702. Built 1971; refurbished 1990. Accommodates 49 passengers. U.S. registry; American officers and crew. Cabin amenities: All outside cabins with either windows or high port lights, some queen-size beds. Dress: very casual.*

Stephanie Anne. Here's an opportunity to sail out-of-the-way passages while making yourself at home on a custom yacht. Skiffs and saltwater fishing gear are carried on board. A bear observatory, a sea lion rookery, and whale-watching are part of the itinerary. There are five double state rooms (one has a private bath, the remaining four share two baths). All meals are served family style. *Bendixen Yacht Cruises, 818 West Argand, Seattle, WA 98119, tel. 206/285–5999. Built 1980; refurbished 1991. Accommodates 10 passengers. U.S. registry; American officers and crew. Dress: very casual.*

Salen Linblad's high-tech expedition vessel, the **Frontier Spirit,** explored Alaska in 1991, but at press time her schedule for summer, 1992, was not yet established. The same situation applies to the ***Corinthian,*** a 200-foot, 65-passenger yacht. Check with your travel agent for information on these vessels.

Itineraries

When heading to Alaska via ship, the home port you're likely to leave behind will be Vancouver, B.C., thanks to a federal law preventing foreign vessels (which most of the Alaska-bound ships are) from using U.S. ports like Seattle as a home base. One-way cruises typically run between Vancouver and Whittier or Seward, the ports for Anchorage. A few cruises get underway in San Francisco, usually making calls in British Columbia en route to Alaska.

Alaska cruises range from seven to 14 days; seven-day voyages are the most popular. While some seven-day cruises sail just the Inside Passage, the best itineraries proceed from the passage north to include the Gulf of Alaska. The least attractive itinerary is a seven-day Inside Passage–only cruise that doesn't include Glacier Bay. Unless you will be cruising by the mighty glaciers of the gulf route, don't give up Glacier Bay.

Longer cruises take you to more ports, often spending more time in each port. The length of time in port is listed in each cruise line's brochure. By comparing the length of port calls to this chapter's list of shore excursion possibilities, you can determine if enough time is allotted to get in all the sights and activities that interest you. Generally, ports with a lengthy list of options require a full-day visit. Juneau, for example, has more than a dozen options, and you'll want a full day and an evening there to enjoy several of them.

For more diverse itineraries and calls at less-frequented ports, consider the small ship fleet.

Shore Excursions

Be sure to grab a bit of the frontier spirit during your Alaska cruise. With the exception of Anchorage, ports are small and easily walked in a short time, leaving you with plenty of opportunity to enjoy a variety of unusual shore excursions.

Among the many options available, there are some "musts." Try flightseeing—it's the only way you'll grasp the expanse and grandeur of the land. Go to an evening salmon feast, where you'll savor freshly caught fish cooked over an open fire in a natural setting. And experience an outdoor adventure—you don't have to be athletically inclined to raft down a river or paddle across a lake.

Before your cruise, you'll receive a booklet describing the shore excursions offered by your cruise line. Some lines let you book excursions in advance; all sell them on board during the cruise. If you cancel your excursion, you may incur penalties, the amount varying with the number of days remaining until the tour. There are, of course, no cancellation penalties for flightseeing excursions called off because of weather conditions.

Because of the specialized nature of these trips, many have limited capacity and are sold on a first come, first serve basis.

The cost of a shore excursion can add up quickly, but you can save yourself a considerable amount of money by making many of your own arrangements, thus avoiding the cruise line mark-ups. All it takes is a bit of time and a few phone calls or stamps.

Request brochures on all sightseeing and flightseeing options and a city map from tourist information offices. You can make reservations in advance, or in the case of a basic sightseeing tour, sign on when you hit port. Once in port, stop by the tourist information offices (*see* Important Addresses and Numbers in Chapter 7) for details.

Unless you require wheelchair-accessible facilities, there's no need to book a sightseeing tour of the ports. With the exception of Anchorage, all are small and easily seen by walking. *See* walking tours in Chapter 7, and ask the staff members at visitors bureaus to help you plot your route on a map.

If you prefer guided tours, they are readily available in port. Last summer, tours of Juneau were sold dockside for $9; the ship's shore excursion, similar in content, was $16.

Not all the excursions listed below are offered by all of the cruise lines. If a particular trip intrigues you, check with your travel agent or cruise line to see if it's available on your cruise or check with the local visitors bureau.

Although advance arrangements are always a good idea, you can sometimes pick up an excursion after you reach port. Flightseeing operations are commonly located near the docks, for example. You might find space available and the cost should be about the same as the cruise line would charge. The "Alaska 1992 Official Vacation Planner" from the Alaska Division of Tourism (Box E–101, Juneau 99811, tel. 907/465-2010) has an extensive list of companies offering outings to local attractions and such memorable activities as windsurfing near Anchorage.

Alaska Travel Adventures (9085 Glacier Hwy., Suite 204, Juneau 99801, tel. 907/789–0052) operates many of the adventure-type excursions. The firm also arranges custom trips for groups—extended river expeditions to van tours—with at least 90 days notice. Minimum group size depends on the type of trip.

You'll usually have time to do more than one trip while ashore. The number depends on the length of the excursion and the length of the port call. All shore excursion brochures tell how long the trips take and often note which trips conflict with others. There are usually several departures for flightseeing trips, so you can arrange one that will allow you time for a second excursion.

Holland America Line Westours has two packages that include shore excursions at a lower cost than if they were purchased separately. The "Adventure Cruise," for a $200 add-on rate, includes canoeing on a lake near Ketchikan, rafting down the Mendenhall River, and a motorized raft trip in Sitka. The "Explorer Cruise," $275 add-on, includes salmon fishing in Ketchikan, a helicopter flight to the Mendenhall Glacier, and a covered-yacht cruise among the wilderness islands around Sitka.

There are reduced children's fares for some shore excursions. If there is no children's rate listed, ask if there is a special fare.

Although the following excursions have been categorized, expect some overlap. Just about any trip you take will offer scenery, and narrated tours can be counted on to cover some historical background. To get the most value for your money, pick the excursions that are unique to Alaska. Flying low over a glacier and landing on an ice field for a closer look is a truer Alaskan experience than a gold-rush revue. In general, the adventure category offers the most exciting and, unusual tours. Don't let the "adventure" scare you—most of these trips are enjoyable to travelers of all ages and require no special physical prowess.

Anchorage

A mix of big city and frontier life, Anchorage is a base for a variety of land tours.

Adventure **Glacier Expedition:** Flightseeing over Anchorage, through the mountains of Chugach State Park, and over six glaciers, landing on one for a picnic of Alaskan hors d'oeuvres.

Cultural **Alaska's Bread Basket:** A look at the fertile countryside of the Matanuska Valley and a tour of the University of Alaska's demonstration garden in Palmer. The tour includes stops at the Musk Ox Farm and Iditarod Sled Dog Headquarters and lunch at a family farm. This is a side of Alaska that many travelers miss.

Anchorage City Tour: Highlights of the city, with stops at a float-plane base and the Anchorage Museum of History and Art.

Haines

A small coastal community, Haines was originally settled by the Tlingit Indians. Known for good fishing and, in the fall, lots of bald eagles.

Adventure **Chilkat River Float:** Rafting through the Chilkat Bald Eagle Preserve reveals some eagles and—if you're lucky—perhaps a moose or a bear. A smooth, rather long trip with no white water, but little wildlife.

Glacier Bay Flightseeing: A low-altitude flight over Glacier Bay offers panoramic views and excellent photo opportunities.

Cultural **The Chilkat Dancers:** Sightseeing drive through town, stopping at Fort William H. Seward and including a dance performance by the Chilkat Dancers, noted for their vivid tribal masks.

Haines Cultural and Natural Wonders Tour: This begins with a narrated tour of Fort Seward, followed by time in Haines to browse through local artisans' shops and tour the Sheldon Museum and Cultural Center and the Alaskan Indian Arts Center. The trip concludes with a drive through the countryside and a nature walk.

Dining with a Difference **Chilkat Dancers and Salmon Bake:** Combines the narrated tour of Haines and Fort Seward and a Chilkat Dancers's performance with a dinner of salmon grilled over an open fire.

Chilkat Lake Boat Tour: A cruise on the lake offers views of forests, mountains, waterfalls, and wildlife.

Scenic **Valley of the Eagles:** This bus tour journeys through the Chilkat Valley, where large numbers of eagles remain in the summer. Each bus has a spotting scope for observing wildlife, and the tour includes short walks on the beach and through a rain forest and sometimes concludes with a salmon bake.

Homer

This is an isolated artist's colony and fishing community.

Adventure **River of Ice:** Helicopter flightseeing over, and landing on, Droshin Glacier. Great photo opportunities.

Scenic **Gull Island Bird Rookery:** This trip to a sea bird rookery is popular with bird-watchers and photographers.

Homer Sightseeing: The tour includes a ride down the 4½-mile Homer Spit for a look at the local fishing industry, a saloon, then on to the Pratt Museum and a photo stop.

Juneau

This is Alaska's capital, where old and new mix in a frontier atmosphere. The setting is beautiful, and the town has a glacier in its backyard.

Although Juneau itself is easy to see by foot, it's recommended that you take advantage of the great array of shore excursions offered here—the finest variety of any port. You'll probably have time to take more than just one excursion here.

Adventure **Charter Fishing:** Fish for salmon or halibut, and view wildlife along the way. Trips include all fishing gear and bait, with four to six fishermen per boat. Fish will be cleaned, and arrangements can be made to have your catch frozen or smoked and shipped home. A Princess Cruise chef will cook it for your table.

Glacier Bay Flightseeing: A low-altitude flight over Glacier Bay offering a panoramic view. Excellent photo opportunities.

Goldpanning and Gold Mine Tour: Pan for gold with a prospector guide and tour the entrance area of the Alaska-Juneau mine. Great for kids.

Helicopter Glacier Tour: A flight over Mendenhall Glacier, or other glaciers, with a landing on a field of ice for a walk on the glacier. Special boots and, if needed, rain gear are provided. One of the best.

Juneau Ice Cap Adventure: A float-plane flight over glaciers to the stark beauty of the Juneau Ice Field—1,500 miles of solid ice.

Mendenhall Glacier Float Trip: A rafting trip down the Mendenhall River, with some stretches of gentle rapids. Experienced oarsmen row the rafts; rubber rain boots, protective clothing, and life jackets are provided. Minimum age is nine years—and kids love this one. An excellent first rafting experience for those in good health. Great fun.

Dining with a **Gold Creek Salmon Bake:** An all-you-can-eat outdoor meal, featuring
Difference turing Alaska king salmon barbecued over an open alderwood fire. After dinner, walk in the woods, explore an abandoned mine, or pan for gold. Gets high reviews.

Taku Glacier Lodge Wilderness Salmon Bake: Fly over the Juneau Ice Field to Taku Glacier Lodge. Dine on outstanding barbecued salmon, then explore the virgin rain forest or enjoy the rustic lodge. There's a large mosquito population here; repellent is available. Expensive, but consistently gets rave reviews as one of the finest experiences ashore.

Entertainment   *Lady Lou Review:* A musical comedy by a cast of eight, inspired by the poetry of Robert Service.

Scenic   **Juneau and Mendenhall Glacier Tour:** A visit to the "drive-in" glacier, just 13 miles from downtown Juneau, and a narrated city tour.

Juneau City/Gastineau Hatchery Tour: Drive through Juneau, then cross the Gastineau Channel to Douglas for a briefing on commercial fishing and a look at spawning salmon swimming up Alaska's largest fish ladder.

Skagway Fly/Cruise Tour: A chance to get to the Gold Rush Country while your ship is in Juneau. Includes a visit to Mendenhall Glacier, a narrated cruise up the Lynn Canal, a tour of Skagway, dinner, and a return flight to Juneau.

Ketchikan

This is the salmon capital of Alaska. Ketchikan is also known for its authentic native totem poles.

Adventure   **Flightseeing, Misty Fjords:** Aerial views of granite cliffs rising 4,000 feet from the sea, waterfalls, rain forests, and wildlife are afforded from your plane window. Landing on a high, wilderness lake is included.

Kayaking Adventure: After learning the basic strokes of kayaking in the boat harbor, paddle up to Creek Street and on to Pennock Island to observe bald eagles and visit a rain forest. Dress in layers, bring rain gear, and wear rubber boots or old tennis shoes.

Mountain Lake Canoe Adventure: You and your guide paddle across a mountain lake in oversize canoes (fast, stable, easy to maneuver) and watch for eagles roosting in the trees. Good outdoor experience. Some lines include a guided nature hike in this excursion.

Sportfishing: Try for Alaska King and Silver salmon or halibut along the Inside Passage. All equipment is provided; you buy your license on board. Group size is limited. Fish will be cleaned, and arrangements can be made to have your catch frozen or smoked and shipped home.

Cultural   **Champagne and Caviar:** A brief city tour precedes a thorough tour of a seafood processing facility. The trip winds up with a stop at a hillside lodge for a bit of champagne and caviar.

Saxman Totem Village: A visit to an Indian village featuring over 20 totem poles. The inhabitants still practice traditional arts; you'll learn much about the Tlingit culture. A visit here sometimes includes a tour of Ketchikan.

Dining with a   **Salmon Falls Resort Tour:** A comprehensive trip combines
Difference   flightseeing over Misty Fjords, the landing on a wilderness lake, seafood buffet lunch at the resort, a nature walk through

its tidepools and rain forest, then a tour of Totem Bight State Park.

Scenic **Historical Waterfront Cruise:** A cruise around the harbor, viewing fishing boats and crews at work. A tour of a processing plant is included. Another shore excursion covers the same attractions on a walking tour.

Totem & Town Tour: Ketchikan's history is related during an excursion past Creek Street, boat harbors, working canneries, and a pulp mill. Visit Totem Bight State Park, a salmon hatchery, and the city's new Totem Heritage Center.

Petersburg

This village, the "Halibut Capital of Alaska," retains its Norwegian cultural heritage.

Adventure **Le Conte Glacier Flightseeing:** View the Stikine ice field, fish spawning, and Le Conte Glacier among others.

Scenic **"Little Norway" Tour:** View downtown, then cross Mitkof Island for scenic views.

Seward

This tiny town, nestled against the mountains, is the port for Anchorage.

Adventure **Harding Ice Field by Helicopter:** Fly over the Harding Ice Field and the Kenai Fjords to view calving glaciers, then land near the face of Bear Glacier.

Kenai Canyon Rafting: Experience white-water rafting through a remote section of the Kenai River, which includes shooting some rapids. Also, hike in the Kenai National Wildlife Refuge, a great outdoor adventure.

Kenai River Float Trip: A two-hour float trip, good for wildlife spotting, follows a salmon bake on the riverbanks. Sometimes the raft trip is extended to four hours. Some lines add a salmon bake.

McKinley Flightseeing: After a stop at Portage Glacier, continue on to Anchorage for a flight over Denali National Park and view the wildlife on Mt. McKinley's slopes.

Seward Flightseeing Tour: This tour features a helicopter flight above mountains, glaciers, valleys, then a landing on Ellsworth Glacier.

Cultural **Alaska Dogsled Show:** Seward is Mile 0 of the dog team gold rush trail, which is used today for the 1,150-mile Iditarod Trail International Sled Dog Race. Visit a sled-dog lot for a demonstration by a race veteran.

Anchorage Overland Tour: This all-day trip makes the long bus ride—part of it along beautiful Turnagain Arm, including a stop at Portage Glacier—to Anchorage, where there's a brief orientation tour, then free time. Additional stops are included in some ships' tours.

Scenic **Kenai Fjords Floatseeing:** Spend the day boating in Kenai Fjords National Park and observing the abundance of wildlife and sea birds. View glaciers, eagles' nests, sea lion colonies, and thousands of puffins.

Portage Glacier: The drive along Turnagain Arm to Portage Glacier is one of Alaska's most beautiful. The tour sometimes includes a cruise across the lake on the MV *Ptarmigan* for a close-up view of the glacier.

Resurrection Bay: There are many outstanding sights on this half-day trip: hanging glaciers, sea bird colonies, seals, sea otters, and an occasional black bear or moose.

Seward and Exit Glacier: National park rangers provide information on the glacier and fjords, part of the Kenai Fjords National Park. Some trips include a stop at an Alaskan husky dog training center.

Sitka

For the 126 years that the czars ruled Alaska, Sitka was the capital. Vestiges of the Russian fur trading empire are still evident. Good walkers can do the town on foot.

Adventure **Catamaran Wildlife and Raft Adventure:** First a catamaran trip tours Sitka's islands, then your group transfers to motorized rafts for a closer look at wildlife, which is sometimes scarce. You may have to wait on the catamaran for your turn on the raft. The catamaran trip is also available without the raft portion, but you'll see more scenery than wildlife.

Fishing Tour: Try for the salmon, halibut, and red snapper that are abundant in these waters. All equipment is provided; you buy your license on board. Your catch can be frozen and shipped home.

Cultural **Sitka Drive:** This tour of Sitka, which Clipper offers as a walking tour, includes stops at the Sheldon Jackson Museum, Castle Hill, Sitka National Historic Park, and St. Michael's Cathedral. Sometimes you can see a performance by the New Archangel Dancers, local women who've mastered the intricate timing and athletic feats required for their traditional style of dance. Some excursions include the Raptor Rehabilitation Center (*see* below).

Visit to an Eagle Hospital: Visit the Alaska Raptor Rehabilitation Center, where medical professionals and volunteers feed, care for, and rehabilitate birds of prey before releasing them back into the wild. This is an outstanding experience.

Scenic **Silver Bay Cruise:** A two-hour voyage through wilderness to Silver Bay, passing mine entrances, nesting eagles, and some wildlife. Most of this is a continuation of what you see from your ship.

Skagway

This was the gateway to the Klondike, and the town's wooden sidewalks and false-front buildings stir up memories of gold-rush fever. Historical lore and tales of the town's characters and escapades are part of all the excursions.

Adventure **Chilkoot Bald Eagles Preserve Flightseeing and Float Trip:** Glide over ice fields and Glacier Bay on a one-hour flight, then land in Haines. From an 18-foot inflatable raft, watch for bald eagles and perhaps other wildlife perched in the trees. This tour involves no white water. Unique combination tour.

Glacier Bay Flightseeing: A low-altitude flight over Glacier Bay offering a panoramic view. Excellent photo opportunities. As there are so many other worthwhile tours in Juneau, Skagway is probably a better spot from which to take this trip.

Glacier Flightseeing and Fishing Adventure: Fly from Skagway over the "Valley of the Eagles." Then enjoy an afternoon of freshwater fishing for trout or salmon; rubber boots and rain gear are provided. The return flight to Skagway includes a half-hour of flightseeing, followed by a city tour on the way back to the ship. A good range of activities on one trip.

Nature Tour & Glacier Flightseeing: Fly over the fjord, glaciers, and an ice field to Haines, where you'll join an expedition bus to the Chilkat Bald Eagle Preserve. Scopes aid in sighting eagles, brown bear, and other wildlife. Sometimes the return is by· van.

Skagway Gold Rush Helicopter Tour: Fly over the prospectors' rugged Chilkoot Gold Rush Trail into a remote mountain valley for a landing on a glacier. Special boots are provided for walking on the glacier.

White Pass and Yukon Route Railroad: The 20-mile trip on the narrow-gauge railway, built to serve the Yukon gold fields, goes past the Trail of '98, edges granite cliffs, and rolls past rivers and canyons. Some of the vintage cars are more than 50 years old. A must for railroad buffs; great for kids. One of Alaska's best excursions.

Cultural   **Skagway's Gold Rush Days Revisited:** Visit Chilkoot Trailhead and walk the trail. A city tour is included. Variations include a stop in the Arctic Brotherhood Hall for a show, a trip to Liarsville's Tent City for a campfire gathering and gold panning, or a performance of the Soapy Smith Show.

Haines Flightseeing and Chilkat Dancers: A glacier flightseeing trip, stopping in Haines for a dance performance by the Chilkat Dancers, noted for their vivid tribal masks.

Skagway Streetcar Excursion: Drive through town to the Gold Rush Cemetery and Reid Falls in a vintage auto. Historical lore is your companion along the way. Some tours add gold panning, a stop at Liarsville Tent City, or the "Days of '98" show.

Entertainment   *Soapy Smith and the Days of '98:* This long-running dramatization of gold-rush history features cancan dancers, honky-tonk piano, and melodrama focusing on con artist Soapy Smith.

Madame Jan's Gold Panning Camp: Pan for gold at the foot of the Gateway Trail, gather around the camp fire for tales of gold rush fever, browse through Madame's antiques collection.

Scenic   **Burro Creek and Historical Cruise Tour:** Cruise on the *Glacier Queen* to Smuggler's Cove Long Bay, walk through Burro Creek homestead, and visit a salmon hatchery. A historical tour of Skagway is sometimes included.

Gateways to Gold—Skagway/Dyea: Stop at Dyea, a former departure point for gold seekers headed to the Klondike, then walk up the Chilkoot Trail and ride along the Klondike Highway.

Yukon Territory Adventure: Follow the trail of the miners bound for Dawson City to Carcross and Lake Bennett. Lunch at the newly completed Frontierland Theme Park and Museum of Yukon Natural History.

Valdez

Valdez is the terminus for the 800-mile trans-Alaska pipeline. Surrounded by alpine scenery and spectacular waterfalls, Valdez has been called the "Switzerland of Alaska." The town can be walked, but there's not a whole lot to see.

Adventure **Columbia Glacier Helicopter Flightseeing:** The 55-minute flight over the huge Columbia Glacier includes a landing near the face of Shoup Glacier and aerial views of Valdez Bay, the pipeline terminus, and the old Valdez site.

Keystone River Rafting: This 1½-hour raft trip goes down the Lowe River, through a scenic canyon, and past waterfalls and spawning salmon. Narrated motor-coach trip to and from the ship.

Cultural **Pipeline Story:** A tour of the pipeline terminus, and tales of how the pipeline was built. Very worthwhile, and the only way to get into this high-security area.

Scenic **Thompson Pass and Worthington Glacier:** This sightseeing tour of the area around Valdez includes a few photo stops and a visit to a walk-up glacier.

Whittier

A fishing and boating center, Whittier is one of the ports used for Anchorage.

Cultural **Anchorage City Tour:** This tour includes highlights of the city, such as Lake Hood, which is a huge seaplane base; the Anchorage Museum of History and Art; and the Alaska Aviation Heritage Museum.

Scenic **Portage Glacier Cruise/Tour:** The drive along Turnagain Arm to Portage Glacier is one of Alaska's most beautiful. Board the MV *Ptarmigan* for a cruise on Portage Lake to the face of the glacier.

Wrangell

This small island community is one of the oldest towns in Alaska and the only one to have been governed under three flags—Imperial Russian, British, and American.

Adventure **Stikine Wilderness Flightseeing:** View the Stikine ice field, spawning, among others, Le Conte Glacier, the southernmost tidal glacier in Alaska, and the fastest receding one.

Cultural **City Tour:** Indian history at Shakes Island, the Wrangell Museum, Petroglyph Beach, and sometimes, a seafood bake.

4 Parks, Wilderness Areas, and Wildlife Refuges

By Peggy Wayburn

Ms. Wayburn is
the author of
"Adventuring in
Alaska", the
Sierra Club's
guide to the state.

In the Aleut language, the word "Alaska" means "The Great Land"—an appropriate name for the 49th of the United States, the one with more land in national parks, wilderness areas, and national wildlife refuges than all the other states combined.

These are lands on a prodigious scale. Three great mountain ranges sweep through Alaska: One is the highest coastal range in the world; another culminates in the highest point on the North American continent (Mt. McKinley, 20,380 feet); the third lies north of and roughly defines the Arctic Circle. In between the mountains there are rugged canyons, broad treeless valleys, softly rolling hills, flower-filled meadows, limpid lakes, blue-iced glaciers, hanging waterfalls, deep-shadowed rain forests, and spacious tundras. Adding to this wealth is some 40,000 miles of spectacular tidal coastline.

Protected by its relative inaccessibility, Alaska's wilderness has until recently been little touched. In 1980, the U.S. Congress seized a rare opportunity and set aside in protected status more than 100 million acres of Alaska's public land, almost one third of the state. The combined National Forest Service wilderness areas, state of Alaska parklands, and the new national parks, national preserves, and wildlife refuges are a treasure house of public lands, offering incomparable Arctic and sub-Arctic adventuring.

There are many ways to enjoy Alaska's wilderness. If you're a strong hiker and like to backpack, you can travel in virtually any part of the state. If you don't want a strenuous outing, you can be spot-packed in to a lovely lake where you can take day hikes and enjoy the scene at a slower pace. Running Alaska's wild rivers—in a kayak, canoe, or rubber raft—provides another wonderful way to see and experience the state's bush country. Traveling on the waterways gives a sense of closeness to the landscape that is hard to come by any other way, and it offers perhaps the best opportunity to see Alaska's wildlife.

There is a sense of challenge and adventure in traveling through Alaska's wilderness areas. The terrain is rugged, demanding both care and strength; good sturdy footwear and dependable equipment are essential. Tundra travel is often delightful—especially in higher alpine country—but it can require the skill of a ballet dancer if the ground is tufted with tussocks (clumps of tough grass making little hillocks). There are likely to be insects to contend with almost anywhere you go during the summer months—mosquitoes, no-see-ums (which can invade all but the finest tent netting) and white-sox flies.

The weather, too, must be reckoned with on any outdoor journey in Alaska. Although Alaska is not a land of perpetual ice and snow—the state is 97% snow-free during summer—it is a place of climatic extremes. Summer days can bring heat in the 90s and make down sleeping bags feel like ovens. Temperatures in the fall and the spring frequently drop below freezing, and winters bring weather so frigid that a glass of water tossed out a window can turn to ice before it hits the ground. In many parts of the state, rain comes unpredictably and all too frequently. Wild winds—the kind that can wrestle a freestanding tent out of your hands and send it tumbling over the tundra—are apt to race out of the mountains with no notice. The trick to a successful trip is careful preparation with a good dash of flexibility.

During the summer months it stays light all night throughout Alaska, and you won't need a flashlight; a sleep shade may be more to the point to simulate darkness. Not only plants, but animals and people in Alaska have adapted to the long hours of daylight, and travelers do well to adapt to them, too. If you're traveling with a local, you may find yourself canoeing down a river at 1 AM with the sun still shining as you look, at long last, for a place to make camp.

Wilderness adventurers in Alaska should be prepared to coexist with the animals that make their home in the vastness of Alaska's wild places. Your chances of spotting bear, moose, caribou, or wolf are good if you keep a low profile and treat the animals with respect. Most of them will be more anxious than you are to avoid a close encounter, but some of the larger animals will hold their ground if you venture into their territory. Moose, common in many parts of the state, are usually peaceful and anxious to leave as soon as they see you; but if a mother moose feels challenged, she will go to great lengths to protect her young and can inflict major damage with her hoofs. Bears are wonderful subjects for photographs, but nobody needs to tangle with them. They are likely to move away before you get too close, but your best bet is to keep your distance; a long lens is a lot cheaper than a hospital stay. If you should surprise a bear and be confronted by it, try not to panic; back away slowly. If a bear should charge you, drop to the ground, cover your head with your arms, and "play dead."

While traveling alone through the wilderness may be a romantic idea, think twice about it in Alaska—especially on a first visit. The country is enormous. If you get rained in or lost it can get very lonely fast. Bear experts believe there's safety in numbers in a bear encounter. And it's simply more fun to share a special experience. Going with a guide offers many advantages. Guides offer expert advice and often special opportunities for photographers, river runners, and birders, and they take the hassle out of organizing an extensive outing into the bush. Having a guide may add to the expense of an Alaska outing, but is usually well worth it.

Staying in a wilderness lodge also adds to the expense, but it is the most comfortable way to experience the Alaska bush. There is a happy choice of accommodations available, and many of the lodges offer not only fabulous fishing but also local hikes and nature programs for photographers and bird-watchers. Lodge proprietors are usually true Alaskans who have pioneered in bush living and developed ingenious ways to meet its challenges, making them exceptional attractions in themselves.

Most of Alaska's wild places can be reached only by air, but don't consider that a drawback. Small planes have played a legendary part in the state's history; bush pilots (less romantically known as air-taxi pilots these days) have helped explore Alaska and been responsible for many dramatic rescue missions. Be aware that small planes cannot transport more than a limited amount of gear and that they cannot fly safely in poor weather. Your drop-off flight, as well as your pickup, is therefore subject to delays. Delays are sometimes counted in days, not hours. Seasoned Alaska trekkers carry extra rations to be prepared for waiting for their air taxis.

Parks and Wilderness Areas

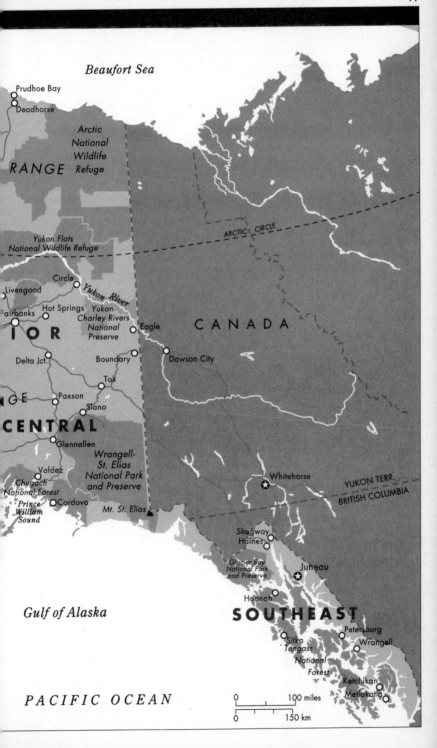

Beaufort Sea

Prudhoe Bay
Deadhorse

Arctic
National
Wildlife
RANGE   Refuge

Yukon Flats
National Wildlife Refuge

ARCTIC CIRCLE

Circle
Livengood   Yukon River
Fairbanks   Hot Springs   Yukon-
            Charley Rivers   Eagle   CANADA
            National
            Preserve
Delta Jct.   Boundary   Dawson City
I O R   Tok
G E   Paxson
        Slano
C E N T R A L
        Glennallen
            Wrangell-
            St. Elias
            National Park
        Valdez   and Preserve
Chygach
National Forest   Whitehorse   YUKON TERR.
Prince   Cordova   Mt. St. Elias   BRITISH COLUMBIA
William
Sound

                                    Skagway
                                    Haines
                            Glacier Bay
                            National Park
                            and Preserve   Juneau

                            Hoonah
Gulf of Alaska   S O U T H E A S T

                                            Petersburg
                            Sitka   Wrangell
                            Tongass
                            National
                            Forest
                                        Ketchikan
PACIFIC OCEAN   Metlakatla

                0   100 miles
                0   150 km

Although you can expect a true wilderness experience in most of the parks and protected areas in Alaska, it is worth noting that the better known and more popular ones—such as Glacier Bay National Park and Preserve and Denali National Park and Preserve—are visited more frequently. Some wild places are actually overcrowded and overused. If you want to get away from it all, it's a good idea to check your options. Parks off the beaten track can be as exceptional as the more accessible Denali, and they can be enjoyed in solitude.

Essential Information

Important Addresses and Numbers

The centers listed below can show you videos of different aspects of the Alaskan scene, as well as offer detailed information about both state and federal public lands and recreational opportunities. They can also supply the names of guides, lodges, and air-taxi operators. You can visit them in Alaska or write ahead.

Alaska State Park Information (Box 107001, Anchorage 99510, tel. 907/762–2617, fax 907–762–2535).
Anchorage Alaska Public Lands Information Center (C St. and 4th Ave., Anchorage 99501, tel. 907/271–2737).
Fairbanks Alaska Public Lands Information Center (250 Cushman St., Fairbanks 99701, tel. 907/451–7352; fax 907/452–7286).
Forest Service Information Center (Centennial Hall, 101 Egan Dr., Juneau 99801, tel. 907/586–8751).
Tok Alaska Public Lands Information Center (Box 359, Tok 99780, tel. 907/883–5667 or 883–5666; fax 907/883–5668).

In addition to the local tour operators listed in each regional section of this chapter, there are some outfits headquartered outside of Alaska that conduct good tours throughout the state. Notable are: **Questers Tours and Travel, Worldwide Nature Tours** (257 Park Ave. S, New York, NY 10010, tel. 212/673–3120) and the **National Outdoor Leadership School** (Box AA, Lander, WY 82520, tel. 307/332–6973).

Southeast Alaska

Southeast Alaska is a world of its own. Separated from the rest of the state geographically, its terrain is very different from the main body of Alaska. It's a land not only of high, snowy mountains but also of deep, shadowed forests and many islands at the edge of the sea. This is a place where bald eagles soar overhead, where whales and porpoises wheel through waterways, and where salmon crowd the streams. You can walk on a glacier and look over one of the continent's last great ice fields. Alaska "blue days," with their luminous, clear skies, have special meaning here because of their relative infrequency and extraordinary beauty.

Because roads in Southeast (referred to by Alaskans with a capital *S*) are pretty limited, plan to get around by ferry or small plane. The state ferry system, which travels the Inside Passage (Marine Highway), provides not only good transportation between the Southeast villages but also some excellent opportunities for outdoor adventuring. Anything you can carry on, including a kayak or a bicycle, goes free on the ferries, and you have unlimited stopovers along your route. You can take your kayak with you and start a trip at Sitka, for example, and make a takeout at Pelican, timing your travels to coincide with the ferry schedule (the smaller villages, such as Pelican, are served only once or twice weekly). If you have your bike along and want to lay over in Ketchikan and ride to a campsite for an overnight, you can pick up the ferry a day or two later to continue your Southeast travels. *For ferry information: Alaska Division of Marine Transportation, Box R, Juneau 99811, tel. 800/ 642–0066. For reservations: tel. 206/623–1970 in Seattle, 907/ 465–3941 in Juneau, 907/272–7116 in Anchorage.*

If you like to travel on foot, there are interesting but somewhat limited opportunities in Southeast. When traveling on foot in the backcountry, expect steep, grassy, and slippery mountain sides; muddy, potholed trails that become streams when it's raining; and heavy underbrush. The dense forests are beautiful, but try to stay away from the devil's club, which glows golden in the understory. It is heavily armored with nasty stinging thorns. Trails through the forested land are difficult to maintain since the ground stays soggy most of the time and the brush grows back quickly and thickly after it is cut. Virtually all of the backcountry in Southeast (excluding Glacier Bay National Park and Preserve) is part of the 16.7-million-acre **Tongass National Forest,** administered by the U.S. Forest Service. The service doesn't consider trail maintenance a top priority, but it is mindful of recreation as one of the uses of its lands. It's worth checking with the rangers at the Forest Service Centennial Hall Information Center in Juneau (*see* Important Addresses and Numbers, above) for the latest information on the condition of backcountry trails.

Probably the best—and certainly the most accessible—hiking is out of the larger communities in Southeast. There are numerous day hikes you can take out of **Juneau** that will give you some wonderful views of the surrounding countryside. (Ask at Centennial Hall for the forest service booklet on local trails.) There are also good day hikes out of **Sitka, Haines,** and **Ketchikan;** you can ask about these at the local visitor centers. Keep in mind that backcountry trail warnings also apply to these trails, especially in wet weather, and that all of these trails will, following Southeastern terrain, go up. If you want pleasant, more relaxing strolls, you'll find them through the streets of most Southeast communities, all of which include at least some waterfront.

If you're a strong and experienced backpacker and like a challenge, you might want to hike the highly scenic, historic **Chilkoot Trail** from Skagway to Canada's Lake Bennett. For this 33-mile trip, you should allow at least four days. The National Park Service (Box 517, Skagway 99840, tel. 907/983–2921) has detailed information about this route of the gold-rush sourdoughs and a very helpful publication, *The Chilkoot Trail Guide.* Remember to expect steep slopes and muddy, potholed trails along with exhilarating vistas over a very different country in Canada when you get to the summit. You can return to Skagway—a delightful historic Gold Rush town—on the White Pass & Yukon Railroad. (You may want to take this spectacular train ride even if you don't hike the Chilkoot.) *For information contact the White Pass & Yukon Route, Box 435, Skagway 99840, tel. 800/343–7373 or 907/983–2217, fax 907/983–2658.*

You can also hike in **Glacier Bay National Park and Preserve,** although these parklands, like the rest of Southeast, are notable primarily for their lovely waterways. Once above the willows and alders, the going is pleasant. Check with the National Park Service in Bartlett Cove (Box 140, Gustavus 99826, tel. 907/697–2230) or at Centennial Hall for particulars.

Ketchikan, Sitka, and Juneau all serve as gateways into the dozen watery wilderness areas in Southeast, including the national monuments at **Misty Fjords** and **Admiralty Island.** If you want to travel by small boat, you can either transport your boat to one of these communities or rent one on arrival. (You can also rent boats at Bartlett Cove in Glacier Bay.) Travel on the Southeast waters can be almost a mystical experience with the greens of the forest reflected in waters as still as black mirrors. You may find yourself in the company of a whale, or see a bear fishing for salmon along the shore, or pull in your own salmon for an evening meal. Paddling in sight of the ice-blue face of a tidewater glacier, you may hear the great primeval sound of an avalanche of ice. White waterfalls make lace over sheer, deep gray-black cliffs. The raucous conversation of ravens may ring out while a bald eagle feeds its young in the top of an ancient spruce tree. Your paddle may encounter a yellow-gold water lily in a lake and seem to drip diamonds when you lift it out of the clear water.

Traveling in small boats in Southeast waters requires both care and skill. Although this country looks deceptively mild, it is wilderness, and the weather (brewed in the Gulf of Alaska) can change the scene completely, and with remarkable speed. Many Southeast waters are frigid and you may paddle among floating icebergs, with the occasional passenger seal perched on top. Floating icebergs can be treacherous; don't try to leap onto one to have your picture taken, as they can easily roll. Stay well back, at least a quarter of a mile, from the faces of glaciers; they can calve icebergs unexpectedly (and spectacularly). Tides and currents must be observed with caution. The tides at Juneau are as much as 26 feet, and throughout the Southeast you can lose your boat and equipment if you park them below the high tide mark. The currents are unbelievably strong and can have you spending hours trying to cross a narrow stretch of water; they can also take you where you may not want to go. Consider traveling with an experienced, professional guide.

There are numerous guides and outfits that conduct small boat outings in the Southeast. You might also consider taking a ferry ride to some of the more remote villages in Southeast. Although not as intimate as a small boat, a ferry provides some wonderful views and a good sense of the country. The Forest Service keeps a comprehensive list of up-to-date facilities in Southeast communities; the rangers who travel on cruise ships and the larger ferries usually have this information.

However you travel, be prepared for rain. Rain is what makes the Southeast a beautiful green world, with lush forests, grasses, and muskegs. Waterproof clothing is essential, and, if you spend much time here, you will benefit from a pair of knee-high rubber boots (known as "Southeast sneakers" or "dancing

shoes"); you can usually find a pair for sale in the larger Southeast towns. Although the climate is milder here than elsewhere
in Alaska, it can get cold, and you'll want warm clothing: Down
jackets (and sleeping bags) have the disadvantage of getting
soggy when they are wet; wool and some of the newer synthet-
ics are the materials of choice.

Tongass National Forest has some 130 wilderness cabins that
can be rented very reasonably; most have eight bunks and good
wood stoves but, of course, no electricity or running water.
Those located on lakes usually have their own skiffs. Most of
these cabins require an air taxi; all are available on a first come,
first serve basis and require advance reservations. *For information, write Cabin Information, Tongass National Forest,
3031 Tongass Ave., Ketchikan 99901, tel. 907/225-2148.*

Tour Operators and Outfitters

Out of Juneau **Alaska Discovery** (369 S. Franklin St., Juneau 99801, tel. 907/
586-1911) conducts guided tours and offers small-boat rentals
by the hour, the day, or longer.
Alaska Travel Adventures (9085 Glacier Hwy., Suite 204, Juneau 99801, tel. 907/789-0052; fax 907/789-1749) conducts half-
day raft trips, lake canoe trips, and marine wildlife tours.
Alaska Up Close (c/o Judy Shuler, Box 32666, Juneau 99803, tel.
907/789-9544) is for birders and nature lovers.

Out of Glacier Bay **Glacier Bay Sea Kayaks** (Box 26, Gustavus 99826, tel. 907/697-
2257).

Out of Angoon **K.J. Metcalf** (Box 10, Angoon 99820, tel. 907/788-3111) has an
intimate knowledge of Admiralty Island National Monument.

Out of Sitka **Larry Edwards** (Box 2158, Sitka 99835, tel. 907/747-8996).

Out of Ketchikan **Outdoor Alaska** (c/o Dale Pihlmann, Box 7814, Ketchikan
99901, tel. 907/225-6044 or 225-3498) will carry your canoe,
kayak, or raft as well as lead your trip.

Wilderness Lodges

Admiralty Island **Thayer Lake Lodge** (c/o Bob Nelson, Box 5416, Ketchikan
99901, tel. 907/225-3343) is a beautiful, small, and reasonably
priced wilderness lodge.

Ketchikan The **Ketchikan Chamber of Commerce** (Box 5957, Ketchikan
99901, tel. 907/225-3184) has information on Bell Island Hot
Spring, Clover Pass Resorts, Misty Fjords Resort, Salmon
Falls Resort, Yes Bay Lodge, and others.

Other Important Addresses and Numbers

Southeast Alaska Tourism Council (Box 20710 Juneau 99802,
tel. 907/586-4777; fax 907/463-4961) offers brochures and information about easy trips in Southeast.
Ketchikan Chamber of Commerce (Box 5957, Ketchikan 99901,
tel. 907/225-3184).
Misty Fjords National Monument (3031 Tongass Ave., Ketchikan 99901, tel. 907/225-2148).
Admiralty Island National Monument (Angoon Community
Center, Angoon 99820, tel. 907/788-3166).

South Central Alaska

Anchorage is the gateway to some of Alaska's most spectacular parks and wilderness areas. The city lies at the convergence of two of Alaska's most magnificent mountain systems. To the east of the city and sweeping on to its southwest are the **Chugach-Kenai-Kodiak Mountains,** a young, active, and impressively rugged range notable for its immense relief. There are near-mile-high valley walls and peaks rising thousands of feet directly from the sea. Across Cook Inlet to the southwest march high volcanic peaks of the **Alaska Range,** part of the Pacific Ocean's great Ring of Fire, but snowcapped nonetheless. Farther north in the Alaska Range, and visible on clear days, shimmers **Mt. McKinley,** with **Mt. Foraker** at its shoulder, the towering giants of the North American continent.

Nature lovers can rejoice at the meeting of these two ranges, for it brings together a wide sampling of Alaska's flora and fauna. The Chugach Mountains are a place where both Dall sheep (which roam the Interior and Arctic but not the Southeast) and mountain goats (found in Southeast but not in the Interior or Arctic) dance their way around the heights. Tree species mingle here, too, offering you the chance of seeing the three different varieties of spruce that grow in Alaska—Sitka spruce (from Southeast, here reaching its northernmost and westernmost limits), black spruce (which doesn't grow in Southeast) and white spruce (a tree of the Alaska Peninsula and the Interior). Larch, birch, and aspen here turn golden in the crisp days of late summer and early autumn.

You'll also see a wide variety of wildflowers, everything from the shy blossoms of the wet forest to the blue-violet lupine that colors the low meadows. Fireweed splashes the roadside rose-red, and you may see wild iris, potentilla, anemone, paint brush, wild geranium, dwarf dogwood, harebell, bluebell, and even polemonium in places you would least expect to find them. These flowers bloom intensely in their brief growing season, taking full advantage of the long summer days.

The natural scene in Alaska's South Central country is not only beautiful, but much of it is easily accessible. A short drive from the Anchorage airport, trailheads lead into **Chugach State Park,** where you can hike for a day or a week. Or, you can head south down the **Kenai Peninsula** for a trek on the **Harding Icefield** (one of the continent's greatest, with 300 square miles of ice and snow), or take a canoe trip through the waters of the **Kenai Moose Refuge.** If you don't mind a few stretches of primitive road, you can drive to the edge of the **Wrangells,** considered by many to be Alaska's grandest mountains. Just north of Anchorage, **Denali State Park** has good hiking trails.

If you want more of a wilderness experience in South Central Alaska, Anchorage serves as a good takeoff point. It's a major hub for small plane travel. Planes that are either amphibious or on floats are the aircraft of choice in South Central (as well as Southeast) Alaska because of the many waterways suitable for landing. Anchorage's Lake Spenard is, in fact, the busiest float-plane terminal in the United States. The Alaska Public Lands Information Center (605 W. 4th Ave., Anchorage 99501, tel. 907/271–2737) can refer you to an air-taxi operator.

Even if you have only a little time to explore in and around Anchorage, you can enjoy a stroll along the city's well laid out 17-mile trail system, which follows the Cook Inlet waterfront. Check at the Log Cabin Visitor's Information Center (F St. and 4th Ave. in Anchorage, tel. 907/274–4118) for trail maps.

Keep in mind that most Alaskans love the outdoors and use their accessible countryside accordingly. Don't expect a solitary promenade through the mountains near Anchorage or a solo run on any of the nearby waterways. In good weather a great many people will turn out to enjoy the readily reached natural scene.

Chugach State Park is Alaska's most accessible wilderness. There are five points of entrance and a good interpretive visitor center at **Eagle River Valley**, less than an hour north of Anchorage (tel. 907/694–2108). There is an extensive trail system as well as several easy-to-follow cross-country routes. The views from high perches in this park are heady. Nearly a half million acres in size, the park rises from the coast to more than 8,000 feet. You can look down on the city of Anchorage, observe the great tides in Cook Inlet, or delineate the grand procession of snowy peaks going down the Alaska Peninsula. Many of the trails are historic, blazed by early miners who usually found the easiest passes. They are suitable for day hikes or week-long backpacks. The mountains have names like Williwaw Peak, Temptation Peak, Mt. Magnificent, The Wedge, The Ramp, and Mt. Rumble. There are blue lakes, glaciers, and waterfalls, as well as one-of-a-kind subalpine birch woodlands in spectacular countryside. Berrying is great in season (late summer). Camping facilities are available, and park officials put on enlightening weekend programs during the summer. For information, call Alaska State Parks (tel. 907/762–2617).

The Kenai Peninsula

This is a glacier-shaped landscape with a remarkable variety of geographical features: an outwash plain with many lakes and clear rivers; a vast ice field (the Harding) with numerous active glaciers; a continuation of the Chugach Mountains (here subsiding in height as they head for the Pacific Ocean); and a spectacular coastline. The Kenai Peninsula offers just about every kind of outdoor recreation you'll find in Alaska—canoeing, kayaking, hiking, snowmobiling, cross-country and downhill skiing (Alyeska, south of Anchorage, has the most developed skiing facility in the state), bird-watching, glacier exploring, horseback riding, fishing (the Russian River is wall-to-wall fishermen when the salmon are running, and with good reason), sailing, camping, beachcombing, or just sitting in the sun (the climate around Homer is one of Alaska's best). Not surprisingly, this is a mecca for Alaskan outdoors people.

Chugach National Forest, adjoining Chugach State Park on its southeast boundary, extends over nearly 6 million acres to embrace the major part of the Kenai Peninsula as well as Prince William Sound. This national forest has an excellent interpretive center, the **Begich-Boggs Visitor Center** (named for two U.S. congressmen who disappeared on a small-plane journey out of Anchorage in 1972), and a splendid view of the photogenic Portage Glacier. The visitors center is located off the Seward Highway, 50 miles southeast of Anchorage.

The Chugach National Forest maintains a number of campgrounds and recreational cabins that are available for a modest charge; about half of these are on the Kenai Peninsula, with several on Prince William Sound. Most require a fly-in, although a few can be reached by car or on foot. Forest service cabins have a seven-day limit (from May to September, the limit for the hike-in cabins is three days) and can be reserved up to six months in advance. *Chugach National Forest Cabin Registrations, 201 E. 9th Ave., Suite 206, Anchorage 99501, tel. 907/271–2599 (recorded information only).*

Picture postcard pretty Seward is the gateway for the 670,000-acre **Kenai Fjords National Park** (Box 1727, Seward 99664, tel. 907/224–3874). This is a spectacular coastal parkland with sheer, dark, slate cliffs rising from the sea, ribboned with white waterfalls or tufted with deep-green spruce. Kenai Fjords offers a rare opportunity to see blue-iced tidewater glaciers as well as some remarkable ocean wildlife up close. If you take a day-trip on a tour boat out of Seward, you can be pretty sure of seeing sea otters (you might surprise one sleeping afloat on its back), crowds of Steller sea lions lazing on the rocky shelves along the shore, a porpoise or two, bald eagles soaring overhead, and tens of thousands of seabirds. It is noteworthy that the coming of a national park to Seward (established in 1980 by the Alaska National Interest Lands Conservation Act) has made enthusiastic naturalists out of the people living there; you can expect excellent interpretive comments from your tour guide. (*See* Tour Operators and Outfitters, below.)

The U.S. Fish and Wildlife Service administers nearly 2 million acres on the Kenai Peninsula in one of its prime wildlife refuges. **The Kenai National Wildlife Refuge** takes in most of the Harding Icefield as well as two large and very scenic lakes, Skilak and Tustemena. The refuge is not only the finest moose habitat in the region, but it is great for canoeing and kayaking. The fish and wildlife service maintains a canoe system, campgrounds, and four free cabin-shelters. Two of the cabin-shelters are fly-ins; you can hike or canoe to the other two. For information (including canoe rentals), contact the Alaska Public Lands Information Center in Anchorage (*see* Important Addresses and Numbers, above).

When the weather is good, the **Lake Clark National Park and Preserve** on the Alaska Peninsula is idyllic. The parklands stretch from the coast to the heights of two grand volcanoes— Mt. Iliamna and Mt. Redoubt, both topping out above 10,000 feet. The country in between holds glaciers, waterfalls, and turquoise-stained lakes. The river running is superb—watch out for getting sunburned in good weather. You can make your way through dark forests of spruce, travel through open stands of birches and balsam poplars, or find your way over the high tundra. The animal life is profuse. Look for bear, moose, Dall sheep, wolves, wolverine, foxes, beaver, and mink on land; seals, sea otter, and white whales offshore. Wildflowers embroider the meadows and tundra in the spring, and wild roses border the forests.

Given the splendid choice of waterways, one of the best ways to enjoy this country is to run a river. Ask the **National Park Service** (2525 Gambell St., Anchorage 99503, tel. 907/257–2696) or the **Alaska Public Lands Information Center** (605 W. 4th Ave., Anchorage 99501, tel. 907/271–2737) for more information.

Plan your visit for the end of June or for July, when the insects may be less plentiful. Or, consider an early September trip, when the fall colors should be flaming.

In a land of many grand and spectacularly beautiful mountains, the **Wrangell–Saint Elias Range** has been singled out by many Alaskans as the finest of them all. As one Alaskan author put it, no other area of Alaska can surpass it for "sheer mountainousness." This is an extraordinary, compact cluster of immense volcanic peaks, located in the southeastern part of the main body of Alaska. Covering an area some 100 miles by 70 miles, the Wrangells tower above the 2,500-foot-high Copper River Plateau, and the peaks of mounts Jarvis, Drum, Blackburn, Sanford, and Wrangell rise 15,000 to 16,000 feet. The white-iced spire of Mt. Saint Elias reaches over 18,000 feet, the third-tallest mountain on the North American continent and crown of the planet's highest coastal range.

The geology of the Wrangell–Saint Elias Range is richly diverse, with an unusually varied assortment of colorful rocks. Although some of the mighty volcanoes in the range are quiescent, others, including Mt. Wrangell, are still very much alive. Some Alaskan bush pilots can recall being showered with volcanic dust in this region not many decades ago.

The Wrangells are frequently wreathed in snow-filled clouds, their massive height making a giant wall that contains the great storms brewed in the Gulf of Alaska. As a consequence, they bear some of the continent's largest ice fields, with more than 100 glaciers radiating from them. One of these glaciers, the **Malaspina,** is 1,500 square miles in size—larger than the state of Rhode Island. This glacier has an incredible pattern of black and white stripes made by the other glaciers that coalesce to form it. Look for it on the coast north of Yakutat if you fly between Juneau and Anchorage.

Rising through many life zones, the Wrangells have an exceptional array of flora, with everything from coastal rain forests to high alpine tundra. They also support a wealth of typical Alaskan wildlife. Birders can add species such as trumpeter swans to their lists if they travel the **Copper River,** one of the two mighty rivers that drain the Wrangells; the other is the 2,300-mile-long Yukon.

To protect this superb region, Congress established the **Wrangell–Saint Elias National Park** (8.1 million acres) **and Preserve** (1.1 million acres) in the Alaska National Interest Lands Conservation Act of 1980. Canada has set aside some 6.6 million adjacent acres in the **Kluane National Park and Game Sanctuary,** thus protecting almost 16 million acres of this prime scenic wild land.

The Wrangell–Saint Elias National Park and Preserve are undeveloped wilderness parklands on a grand scale. You can expect adventures here to be equally grand, but you need to prepare for them. Weather is frequently rough here, with fierce storms and high winds. Trails blazed by prospectors in times past can be demanding and are generally unmaintained. Rivers, many of them braided and milky with glacial silt, can pose barriers for travelers on foot, especially when storms engorge them. The same rivers, though, can provide exciting runs. Mountains offer unequaled challenges to climbers; many of the continent's grandest summits can be reached here, and there are still unclimbed peaks. **The Saint Elias Alpine Guides** (Box 111241, Anchorage, 99511, tel. 907/277–6867) conduct an ascent of one unclimbed peak every summer.

From June through September, it is usually possible to reach the Wrangells from the north on a jeep road via Slana to the ghost town of Nabesna. A recently upgraded road travels the old railroad grade, built when the Kennecott Copper Mine was operating, from Chitina on the Copper River to the gold-mining town of McCarthy in the central part of the range. You have to leave your vehicle (be sure to lock it!) and cross the Kennicott River on a cable tram to actually enter the town. McCarthy has a small airstrip, and it is possible to catch the mail plane into it.

Tour Operators and Outfitters

Sanctuary Travel Services (3701 E. Tudor Rd., Anchorage 99507, tel. 907/561–1212 or 800/247–3149) is a knowledgeable travel agency in Anchorage that can help you plan a backcountry adventure with or without a guide. This travel agency will donate 20% of its commission from your travel bookings to the environmental group of your choice.
Alaska Association of Mountain Wilderness Guides (Box 141061, Anchorage 99514, tel. 907/276–6634).
Kenai Fjords Tours Inc., (Box 1889, Seward 99664, tel. 907/224–8068; fax 907/224–8934), based in Seward, runs excellent seasonal day boat trips in the Kenai Fjords National Park.

Wilderness Lodges

Koksetna Camp (Box 69, Iliamna 99606, tel. 907/781–2227). Owners Chuck and Sara Hornberger offer a comfortable wilderness experience with fine food and excellent fishing in the Lake Clark region.
Kennicott Glacier Lodge (Box 103940, Anchorage 99510, tel. 907/258–2350) is a spectacular location outside McCarthy.

Other Important Addresses and Numbers

The **Alaska Public Lands Information Center** (Box 359, Tok 99780, tel. 907/883–5667; fax 907/883–5668) has the names of guides, air-taxi pilots, and accommodations in the Wrangell–Saint Elias National Park.

Wrangell-Saint Elias National Park and Preserve (Box 29, Glennallen, AK 99588, tel. 907/822–5235).

In McCarthy, there is a wilderness lodge (Kennicott Glacier, *see* above), a hotel (McCarthy Lodge, McCarthy 99588, tel. 907/333–5402 or 376-1154), and an obliging taxi guide service (inquire at the hotel) as well as a charming bed-and-breakfast run by Saint Elias Alpine Guides (*see* text, above).

The Interior

The Alaska Range rises more than 20,000 feet—the "great wall" dividing Interior Alaska from the South Central region. Its grandest member, **Mt. McKinley** (known among natives as Denali, "the High One" in the Athabascan language), rises 18,000 sky-filling feet from base to peak, the highest uplift of any mountain in the world. (Although Mt. Everest reaches more than 29,000 feet above sea level, it rises only 11,000 feet from the Tibetan Plateau.)

This tumultuous landscape was formed by the head-on collision of two tectonic plates. Between them, in the Denali fault system, lies the largest crack in the crust of the North American continent. As high as it is, this barrier between South Central and the Interior Plateau gathers colder weather, and it bears a fine glacial system. These ice-capped mountains give a good idea of the way things were over a large part of the continent during the ice ages. Flying in a small plane over the black-striped glaciers of the Alaska Range can be a dazzling experience.

Below the high snowy reaches of the Alaska Range, the lower foothills—many of them are 14,000 feet high themselves—are often stained with color, evidence of their ancient, restless geological past. Polychrome Pass in Denali National Park is aptly named; it commands a vista of rose, orange, soft brown, and gray-shaded slopes fingered by meadows of green alpine tundra. This is fine hiking country, but in many other parts of the park the ground is tufted with slippery tussocks, and even the most nimble-footed will be forced into balancing acts.

Below the tundra, the trees of the taiga take over: dark spiky spruce, paper birch, aspen, and, in the wetter places, cottonwood. The soft green leaves of the deciduous trees turn silver in the summer breezes and shine golden in the autumn. Among and around the trees, fireweed paints the landscape deep rose. The meadows are blue with lupine in the spring, summer brings succulent berries, and fall touches the berry leaves with pure crimson. Winter turns this world frigid, white, and crisp with ice.

Fairbanks is the principal gateway to the Interior parks, as well as an immediate takeoff point for many wilderness preserves in the fringe areas. It is possible to fly commercially from Fairbanks to **Kotzebue, Bettles,** and **Kaktovik,** where air taxis serve the Arctic parks (*see* Chapter 10). From Fairbanks you can also drive directly to the Yukon-Charley National Preserve.

There's a two-mile nature walk through a migratory waterfowl refuge administered by the Alaska Department of Fish and Game a short distance from downtown Fairbanks. You can get information about this and other local hiking areas (there are several administered by the Bureau of Land Management nearby) at the **Fairbanks Alaska Public Lands Information Center** (250 Cushman St., Fairbanks 99701, tel. 907/451–7352).

To read of a pleasant historical stroll you can take around Fairbanks, pick up a copy of **"Ghosts of the Goldrush,"** a good interpretive booklet, at the log cabin Visitor's Center on First Avenue on the banks of the Chena River.

Fairbanks has two very helpful sporting goods stores that supply both information and equipment, particularly if you're interested in river running. Try **Beaver Sports** (3480 College Rd., tel. 907/479–2494) or **Clem's Backpacking and Sporting Goods Store** (315 Wendell St., tel. 907/456–6314).

The more than 6-million-acre **Denali National Park and Preserve** is the most accessible of the large national parks in Alaska. It's possible to reach it by car over a good two-lane road from Fairbanks to Anchorage. A park road runs from park headquarters to Wonder Lake, with a half dozen campgrounds along the way: Riley Creek, at the park entrance; Savage River, at Mile 12; Sanctuary River, at Mile 22; Teklanika River at Mile 28; Igloo Creek, at Mile 33; Wonder Lake at Mile 85 (tent camping only). The National Park Service runs a free, scheduled shuttle bus along the park road, which is not open to private vehicles beyond Savage River (except to access campgrounds at Sanctuary and Teklanika). To go beyond Teklanika you must use the shuttle bus.

Tour buses to Denali run regularly out of both Fairbanks and Anchorage. The **Alaska Railroad** is perhaps a more pleasant way to reach the park, with daily service during the summer from Fairbanks and Anchorage. It offers classy service and spectacular views of Mt. McKinley in clear weather. *For information, contact the Alaska Railroad, Box 107500, Anchorage 99510, tel. 800/544–0552 or 907/265–2623.*

Denali National Park is one of the best and easiest places to see wildlife in the world. While providing transportation into the park, the park service shuttle-bus drivers point out sheep finding their way along dizzying slopes, grizzlies frequenting streams and willows, the moose that prefer Wonder Lake, and the odd wolf or caribou that may dart across the road. A privately operated tourist bus goes to the **Toklat River Eielson Visitor Center** (Mile 53 on the park road). Both bus services get early morning (wee hours) starts to take advantage of the best wildlife viewing hours.

Bear in mind that, as one park lover put it, "This ain't no zoo." You might hit an off day and have few viewings—enjoy the surroundings anyway. Under any circumstances, don't feed the animals or birds (a mew gull may try to share your lunch at Eielson Center).

Both day hikes and backpacking can be excellent in Denali. You can plan your itinerary with park officials and utilize the shuttle bus for your transportation to and from a roadhead. Climbing the great mountain may be every mountaineer's dream, but too many visitors have left a real litter problem on its slopes. If you feel you must, talk to the park service people about procuring a guide for this Himalaya-class expedition.

Denali's rivers are silt-laden, racing glacial streams—not wonderful for running. There are, however, commercially run raft trips down the **Nenana River,** which you take from near the park entrance (*see* Participant Sports in Chapter 8).

A bustling tourist industry has grown up around the eastern entrance to Denali, with numerous motels and restaurants. Inside the entrance is the **Denali National Park Hotel,** well-run and heavily visited. The same owners operate another, very elegant hotel adjacent to the park entrance, the **McKinley Chalet Resort.** *Information on both hotels: 825 W. 8th Ave., Anchorage 99501, tel. 907/276–2734; fax 907/258–3668.*

Camp Denali is a wonderful place to stay. Located in the center of the park, this wilderness lodge has excellent food and charming cabins (with running stream water). Hosts Wally and Jerri Cole offer an outstanding naturalist program stressing wilderness values. If Mt. McKinley is visible, you'll have a superlative view from here. The Coles or their staff meet the train on Mondays, Wednesdays, and Fridays from early June to early September. Wildlife watching is provided from the camp vehicle en route to the facilities. Write ahead for reservations. *For information, contact Camp Denali, Box 67, Denali National Park 99755, tel. 907/683–2302 in winter or 907/683–2290 in summer.*

For information and help in planning outings in Denali National Park, write to the Denali National Park Superintendent (Box 9, Denali Park 99755, tel. 907/683–2686 or 907/683–2294).

Yukon-Charley National Preserve The Yukon is one of the world's great rivers. (Only four rivers in the Americas have a greater capacity: the Amazon, the Saint Lawrence, the Mississippi, and the Missouri.) Twenty miles wide in places, it runs for 2,300 miles, from Canada to the Bering Sea, and along the way it gathers its waters from as far away as Southeast Alaska to north of the Arctic Circle. It travels through some of the most beautiful country of the Interior Plateau, a unique area that escaped glaciation all through the ice ages and so became a place of refuge for many plant and animal species. The river also has a firm place in history, having served as the pathway for countless people as they moved through the North American continent. And it served as a principal gateway to the gold fields in Canada, discovered at the turn of the century.

The 126-mile area of the **Yukon River** running between the small towns of Eagle and Circle (former gold-rush metropolises) have been protected in the 2.5-million acre **Yukon-Charley National Preserve,** established in 1980. As its name suggests, this parkland also covers the pristine watershed of the **Charley River,** a crystalline white-water stream flowing out of the Yukon-Tanana uplands. This waterway provides fine river running. You can put in a raft or a kayak (via small plane) at the headwaters of the Charley and travel 88 miles down this joyful, bouncing river. Along the way, you'll pass old miners' cabins being reclaimed by the land, and you may see peregrine falcons in midflight or a Dall sheep skipping nimbly along the steep cliffs rimming the river.

In great contrast to the Charley, the Yukon is dark with mud and glacial silt, and it is an inexorably powerful stream. Only one bridge has been able to withstand its stormy moods, that built for the trans-Alaska pipeline north of Fairbanks. The river's muddy waters surge deep, and to travel on it in a small boat is a humbling, if magnificent, experience. You can drive to **Eagle** (via the Taylor Highway off the Alaska Highway) and to **Circle** (via the Steese Highway), and it is thus possible to arrange for a ground transportation shuttle at either end of a river trip. There are accommodations and grocery stores at Eagle and you can rent a raft there; Circle has an old hot-springs resort with lots of character. Both towns have residents who are mindful of their history. Eagle has restored many of its historic buildings and during the summer months offers guided walking tours through the town and the adjacent **Fort Egbert.**

The **National Park Service** (Box 64, Eagle 99738, tel. 907/547–2233) has a ranger station in Eagle that provides excellent in-depth information about the Yukon-Charley National Preserve and about how best to enjoy and protect it. Despite its rough appearance, this is fragile country.

Tour Operators and Outfitters

Alaska Denali Guiding (Box 326, Talkeetna 99676, tel. 907/733–2649).

Other Important Addresses and Numbers

Fairbanks Alaska Public Lands Information Center (250 Cushman St., Fairbanks 99701, tel. 907/451–7352; fax 907/452–7286).

Tok Alaska Public Lands Information Center (Box 359, Tok, AK 99780, tel. 907/883–5667 or 907/883–5666; fax 907/883–5668).

The Fringe Areas of Alaska

As the Alaska Range separates South Central from the Interior, the Brooks Range cuts the northern Arctic region off from the rest of the state. This is a mountain range so grand that it contains many mountain systems—the Davidson, Romanzof, Franklin, Shublik, Sadlerochit, Philip Smith, Endicott, Schwatka, DeLong, and Baird.

The 18-million-acre **Arctic National Wildlife Refuge** is administered by the U.S. Department of Fish and Wildlife for its wilderness and wildlife values. Both are exceptional. The spine of mountains that runs east–west through the refuge is softly colored with tans, rosy browns, and dark slate blue. Although it wears no glaciers, it can be dusted white with snow at almost any season. The vast sweeps of Arctic tundra, bright with yellow Arctic poppies in the summer, stretch into seemingly infinite distances. Permafrost has worked over this land for centuries and fragmented it into giant polygons that make a fascinating pattern when viewed from the air. Thousands of lakes and ponds dot the Arctic slope.

This refuge is home to one of the greatest remaining groups of caribou in the world, the **Porcupine Caribou Herd.** The herd, numbering 250,000, is unmindful of international boundaries and migrates back and forth across Arctic lands into Canada. Fortunately, Canada has set aside a sanctuary on its side of the border to accommodate the animals' almost ritual movements.

This is a place to experience true wilderness—and to walk with care, for it is fragile here. You can expect harsh, frigid weather virtually any month of the year. Many of the rivers are runnable, and there are lakes suitable for base camps. A Kaktovik air taxi can drop you off and pick you up. The hiking can be invigorating. While it is a myth that Alaska is a frozen snow-covered wasteland, the stories about the mosquitoes here unfortunately are true. In June and July they can be ferocious in the refuge. However, as U.S. Fish and Wildlife officials put it: "If you're going to enjoy the wilds, don't let mosquitoes or anything else dictate the time of your visit." You could be lucky and have insect-free, absolutely glorious blue days.

The Arctic National Wildlife Refuge lies wholly within the Arctic Circle and includes the only stretch of Arctic shoreline presently set aside for protection. As of this writing, whether or not this wilderness will remain inviolate is being considered in Congress. Despite the lesson of the 1989 oil spill that fouled Prince William Sound, pressures to open the refuge to oil drilling continue.

For all refuge information, contact the Alaska Public Lands Information Center (250 Cushman St., Fairbanks 99701, tel. 907/451–7352).

The **Gates of the Arctic National Park and Preserve** include more than 8.4 million acres in the center of the Brooks Range. This is parkland on a scale suited to the country; it includes the Endicott Mountains to the east and the Schwatka Mountains to the southwest, with the Arrigetch Peaks in between. "Arrigetch" is an Eskimo word meaning "fingers of a hand outstretched," which aptly describes the immensely steep and smooth granite peaks that reach into the sky. To the north lies a sampling of the Arctic foothills, with their colorful tilted sediments and pale-green tundra. Lovely lakes are cupped in the mountains and in the tundra, as well. The "gates" that guard this Arctic wilderness, Boreal Mountain and Frigid Crags, were so named by the intrepid Arctic explorer, Robert Marshall, in the 1930s. The Gates of the Arctic Park and Preserve lie entirely north of the Arctic Circle; they were designated an International Biosphere Reserve by the United Nations in 1984.

Treeline occurs almost precisely along the continental divide, which winds through the center of this parkland. To the south are stands of white spruce in the lower canyons, and black spruce tip drunkenly in the wet meadows (which may also have slippery, ankle-grabbing tussocks of cotton grass that make the going rough); to the north, only cottonwoods can survive the Arctic winds and darkness, and there are few of them. Throughout, however, the willows thrive and the alders reach 20 to 25 feet.

This is not easy country to get around in. Hiking may entail those troublesome tussocks, and the trails have lots of ups and downs. One of the best ways to travel through the park is on one of the large, south-flowing rivers such as the **John, Koyukuk, Kobuk,** or **Alatna.** Some of these waterways have drawbacks, though, because their lower stretches may be extravagantly looped and winding, with the wind forever seeming to blow upstream.

Expert mountaineers find great challenge in this part of the world, and some of the peaks have actually become overcrowded with climbers. If you have alpine ambitions, it's a good idea to check with the park service people before launching your expedition.

The village of **Bettles** is the gateway to Gates of the Arctic. You can fly into it commercially and charter an air taxi out. Check with the small ranger station there for the names of guides, outfitters, canoe rentals, and air-taxi service. *National Park Service, Box 74680, Fairbanks 99707, tel. 907/456–0281.*

Gathering its waters from the rock-spired heart of the Brooks Range, the **Noatak River** travels through more than 425 miles of wilderness on its way to Kotzebue Sound. Its course runs westward for more than 300 miles of the distance and then makes an unexpected turn southward. Along the way, the river courses between two softly rounded mountain ranges, the DeLongs to the north and the Bairds to the south.

This is a generally clear Arctic river with bottle-green waters and a series of white-water rapids that mark the moraines of ancient glaciers. River runners call it a class II stream, but like all Arctic waterways, it can be more or less a "rock garden" in dry seasons and can turn into a formidable torrent when it's stormy. The water can rise as much as five feet in a few hours.

The Noatak is recommended for long, unhurried trips. It is possible to put into the headwaters at **Pingo Lake** (reached by air taxi) and exit (again by air taxi) a week later, but many visitors spend a month on this river, ending their trip at the Eskimo village of **Noatak.** There is good camping in the tundra and nice hiking in the **Poktovik Mountains** and the **Igichuk Hills.** Birding can be exceptional: horned grebes, gyrfalcon, golden eagles, parasitic jaegers, owls, terns, and loons are among the species you may see.

The 6.5-million-acre **Noatak National Preserve,** established in 1980, takes in much of the basin of the river. This is the largest mountain-ringed river basin that is still relatively wild (part of it is a designated National Wild River) in the United States. Lying adjacent to the Gates of the Arctic National Park and Preserve, this, too, is an International Biosphere Reserve. *For more detailed information, contact the National Park Service, Box 1029, Kotzebue 99752, tel. 907/442–3890 or 907/442–3573.*

Kobuk Valley National Park is another parkland lying entirely north of the Arctic Circle. Here the Arctic tundra encounts abcdefegh about akberk is also notable for its two inland deserts—the **Great Kobuk Sand Dunes** and the **Little Kobuk Sand Dunes**—two Arctic areas with the characteristics of an African Sahara, including temperatures that rise above 100 shimmering degrees. Both sets of dunes are accessible by foot from the Kobuk River (which makes a nice run; you put in at Walker Lake in the Gates of the Arctic and take out at the village of Kiana).

The Kobuk Valley is also rich in archaeological treasures; sections of it lay open to the Bering land bridge that linked North America to Russia during the ice ages. Early settlers found their way to this continent across this bridge of land, which was probably about 900 miles wide but now lies under the Bering Sea. Traces of their prehistoric travel thousands of years ago abound in such spots as Onion Portage on the Kobuk River. This particular archaeological site is considered the most important yet discovered in the Arctic.

In addition to the Kobuk River, the Kobuk Valley National Park contains three smaller rivers that make for delightful running: the **Ambler,** the **Squirrel,** and the **Salmon.** All are brilliantly clear streams accessible by wheeled plane, and all offer a good week's worth of pleasure, if the weather cooperates. The 125-mile-long Kobuk River calls for at least one portage (unless you're an expert small-boater) and has wide meanders. It may also have upstream winds in its lower section. You can expect to see caribou, grizzly bear, red fox (which may pose for you to photograph them), beaver, muskrat, moose, waterfowl, shorebirds, and songbirds along these rivers. The rivers also carry an abundant supply of salmon and sheefish. Eskimos here continue to use the Kobuk Valley National Park for subsistence, as they have since prehistoric times.

Kobuk Valley National Park is, like most of the Alaska parks, undeveloped wilderness. It's a good place for backpacking and spot-camping. Its gateway is Kotzebue, where the National Park Service has a visitor center. The villages of **Kobuk** and **Kiana** both provide more immediate takeoff points and have air service. *National Park Service, Box 1029, Kotzebue 99752, tel. 907/442–3890 or 907/442–3573.*

Lying only 10 miles northwest of Kotzebue, 560,000-acre **Cape Krusenstern National Monument** has been set aside for its important cultural and archaeological values. This is a coastal parkland with an extraordinary series of beach ridges built up by storms over a period of at least 5,000 years. Almost every ridge (there are 113) contains artifacts of different human occupants—representing every known Eskimo culture in North America. The present Eskimo occupants, whose culture dates back some 1,400 years, use the fish, seal, caribou, and birds of this region for food and raw materials much as their ancestors did. They are also closely involved in the archaeological digs that are taking place in the park, unearthing part of their own history.

Cape Krusenstern National Monument is a starkly beautiful Arctic land shaped by ice, wind, and sea. Its low, rolling, gray-white hills scalloped with light-green tundra are not inviting for ordinary recreation. The monument's other values—human and historical—are paramount. It should be experienced as something of a marvelous living museum. It is possible to camp in the park, but be mindful, as are the native people when they rig their big white canvas tents for summer fishing, that any tent pitched along the shore is subject to those winds.

Check with the U.S. Park Service in Kotzebue regarding the hiring of a local guide who can interpret this unusual scene. The area is accessible by air taxi and by boat from Kotzebue. *National Park Service, Box 1029, Kotzebue 99752, tel. 907/442–3890 or 907/442–3573.*

The frozen ash and lavas of the 2.8-million-acre **Bering Land Bridge National Preserve** lie between Nome and Kotzebue immediately south of the Arctic Circle. This volcanic landscape is unique; the Imuruk lava flow is the northernmost flow of major size in the United States, and the paired maars (clear volcanic lakes) are a geological rarity.

Of equal interest are the paleontological features of this preserve. Sealed into the permafrosted land are flora and fauna—bits of twigs and leaves, tiny insects, small mammals, even remnants of woolly mammoths—that flourished here when the Bering land bridge linked North America to what is now Russia. It is thought that early settlers wandered here through this treeless place of lava and tundra thousands of years ago, but the traces they left are faint. Stacked slabs of volcanic rock are piled on many of the crests of craters in cairns that have no known meaning. These people may have been following the woolly mammoths or the musk-oxen (whose descendents still occupy this terrain); or they may have stopped to admire the many flowers that star the tundra. There are a remarkable 250 species of flowering plants in this seemingly barren region. Almost certainly, they paused at the sight of the tens of thousands of migrating birds—121 species, including ducks, geese, swans, sandhill cranes, shorebirds, and songbirds—that come here from all over the world in spring, and they probably lingered to listen to the haunting call of loons on the many clear lakes and lagoons.

The Bering Land Bridge National Preserve has no developed facilities, although the Park Service has talked of establishing primitive camp areas for hikers and backpackers. Access is generally by air taxi out of Kotzebue or Nome. There is a road north of Nome that goes within walking distance of the parkland. The Serpentine Hot Springs, accessible only by air taxi, lies on the southeast side of the preserve. It's known for its body-soothing properties as well as for the unique flora and fauna around it. *If you are interested in visiting this unusual parkland, contact the National Park Service in Nome, Box 220, Nome 99762, tel. 907/443-2522.*

The **Wood-Tikchik State Park** (1.4 million acres), located 300 air miles west of Anchorage, has two spectacular sets of lakes with six lakes in each set. These lake systems lie adjacent to one another; each set drains a different watershed and empties into a different river. This is superb country for canoeing, fishing (the salmon make solid red pools at the mouths of lakeside streams), wilderness rambling, or simply enjoying the scenery. **Dillingham** is the town of entrance. You can also go from Dillingham by boat or by air to view the display of walrus on Round and Walrus islands. For further information on Wood-Tikchik, contact one of the Alaska Public Lands Information Centers (*see* Important Names and Addresses, above).

For an extraordinary perspective on the awesome power of volcanoes, visit the **Katmai National Park and Preserve.** In the **Valley of the Ten Thousand Smokes** you can see a moonlike landscape formed about 80 years ago by an eruption so vast that it was heard in Juneau, 750 miles away. It showered ash and heavy sulphuric fumes that reached Vancouver, B.C., and enveloped closer areas in darkness. A 300- to 700-foot-deep layer of ash and pumice was dumped over 40 square miles at the foot of Mt. Katmai. Steam spouted in thousands of fountains from the smothered streams and springs beneath the ash and gave the name to the valley (*see* Exploring the Fringe Areas in Chapter 10). Although the steaming has virtually stopped, an eerie sense of earth forces at work remains, and several nearby volcanoes still smoulder.

Katmai is one of the best places to see salmon migrating in season and to view brown bears as they lumber their way through the wilds. **King Salmon** is the point of entrance; you can fly there commercially from Anchorage. The National Park Service in King Salmon provides a popular campground at **Brooks River.** Reservations are necessary, and stays are limited due to demand. *Contact the National Park Service, Box 7, King Salmon 99613, tel. 907/246-3305.*

Another extraordinary living volcano rises to the south of Katmai—**Aniakchak,** which has one of the largest calderas in the world, with a diameter averaging six miles across, and small Surprise Lake within it. Although Aniakchak erupted as recently as 1931, the immense explosion that left it with its enormous crater occurred before history was written. Since the area is not glaciated, geologists place the blow-up after the last

Ice Age. It was, literally, a world-shaking event. Marking the volcano's significance, Congress established the 138,000- acre **Aniakchak National Monument,** with an adjacent 376,000-acre National Preserve, in 1980.

This is wild and forbidding country, with a climate that brews mist, clouds, and winds of great force much of the year. Although the **Aniakchak River** (which drains Surprise Lake) is floatable and exciting in its upper stretch, it is short, and reaching it can be something of an expedition. The best way to enjoy Aniakchak is to wait for a clear day and fly to it in a small plane able to land you on the caldera floor or on Surprise Lake—in either case, an unforgettable experience. Camping is permitted anywhere in the monument and preserve. Aniakchak is administered by the National Park Service out of King Salmon (Box 7, King Salmon 99613, tel. 907/246–3305).

Wilderness Lodges

Katmai   **Brooks Lodge** (Katmailand, Inc., 4700 Aircraft Dr., Anchorage 99502, tel. 800/544–0551, fax 907/243–0649). Located on Lake Naknek where the Brooks River flows in, it offers comfortable accommodations, including cabins, and makes good headquarters for adventuring. Katmailand also operates more remote facilities such as Grosvenor Lodge and Kulik Lodge.

5 Wildlife Viewing and Recreational Fishing

Wildlife Viewing

By Peggy Wayburn Although the March 1989 oil spill damaged extensive stretches of its coast, Alaska remains one of the greatest places to see wildlife in its own spectacular habitat.

Alaska is one of the few places in the world where it is possible to view wildlife in its natural state. The state is unique among the 50 United States because of its vast resource of protected wilderness, which is rich in wildlife and fish (*see* Chapter 4). And Alaska's wild beauty adds a powerful dimension to any wildlife viewing experience.

Alaska's 375 million acres support nearly a thousand species of animals—mammals, birds, and fish. And among these species there is incredible variety. The 105 different mammals range from whales to shrews. (Alaska's shrews are the smallest of North America's land mammals, weighing 0.1 ounce.) The more than 400 species of birds include everything from hummingbirds to bald eagles, including species found nowhere else in North America. Among the 430 different kinds of fish, there are some weighing close to 500 pounds (halibut) and others that are only 16 ounces (Dolly Varden)—both greatly prized by anglers; and there are five different kinds of salmon (*see* Recreational Fishing, below).

The most prodigious numbers of animals can be seen during periods of migration. And the state is strategically located for creatures that migrate vast distance. Some birds, for instance, fly from the southern tip of South America to nest and rear their young on sandbars in Alaska's wild rivers. Others travel from parts of Asia to enjoy an Alaskan summer. Sea mammals congregate in great numbers in the waters of Prince William Sound (some perished in the 1989 oil spill) and the Bering Sea. Tens of thousands of caribou move between Canada and Alaska across the Arctic slope. Anadramous fish by the millions swim up Alaska's rivers, returning unerringly to the place where they were born.

Spotting bear, moose, and other large mammals can be a highlight of a visit to Alaska. Bears live in virtually every part of the state and, though often solitary, it is not unusual to see a mother bear with cubs (keep a safe distance). Moose abound in the wetter country of Southeast, South Central, and Interior Alaska. Caribou wander over the tundra country of the Arctic, sub-Arctic and even South Central, although there are fewer in this part of the state. The mountains of Southeast and South Central harbor wild goats, while the mountains of the Interior and the Arctic are home to Dall sheep, which sometimes come down to the streams in the summer. Wolves and lynx, though not so easily seen, live in many parts of the Interior and, if you're lucky, a wolf may dash across the road in front of you, or a smaller mammal, such as the Arctic fox, may watch you if you're rafting or even when you're traveling on wheels.

Important Addresses and Numbers

Alaska Department of Fish and Game (Box 3–2000, Juneau 99802, tel. 907/465–4112; fax 907/586–6595).
Alaska Division of Tourism (Box E–701, Juneau 99811, tel. 907/465–2010, fax 907/586–8399).

Anchorage Alaska Public Lands Information Center (C St. and 4th Ave., Anchorage 99501, tel. 907/271–2737).

Anchorage Audubon Society (Box 1161, Anchorage 99510, tel. 907/248–2473, bird report recording).

Fairbanks Alaska Public Lands Information Center (250 Cushman St., Fairbanks 99701, tel. 907/451–7352).

Forest Service Information Center (Centennial Hall, 101 Egan Dr., Juneau 99801, tel. 907/586–8751).

Tok Alaska Public Lands Information Center (Box 359, Tok 99780, tel. 907/883–5667).

U.S. Fish and Wildlife Service (1011 E. Tudor Rd., Anchorage 99503, tel. 907/786–3487 or 786–3486; fax 907/562–2297).

Wildlife Viewing Tips

From the Roadside   Bears, moose, caribou, and many species of birds can be watched from your car. Keep in mind, however, that Alaska's road system is limited and many of the roads are unpaved and, at times, full of chuck holes. There are highly scenic roads out of Haines, Skagway, Tok, Fairbanks, and Anchorage, however, as well as down the Kenai Peninsula. For the latest information about roads and road conditions, request a copy of *The Milepost* from Alaska Northwest Books (130 2nd Ave. South, Edmonds, WA 98020 or tel. 206/774–4111). The book is $14.95 plus postage.

One of the best roads for wildlife viewing extends into **Denali National Park,** but the better part of it can be reached by bus only; it is closed to private vehicles beyond the Savage River. The same is true of the northern section of the Dalton Highway, which pierces the Brooks Range; it is closed to all but commercial vehicles north of Atigan Pass.

From the Water   The **Alaska Marine Highway**—the route plied by Alaska's state ferries—passes through waters rich with fish, sea mammals, and birds. Throughout the Southeast, ferries often provide sightings of whales and virtually always of bald eagles. Contact Alaska Marine Highway (Box R, Juneau, AK 99811, tel. 907/465–3941 or 800/642–0066; fax 907/465–2476) for information. The 1989 oil spill did not impact ferry routes. Kenai Fjords National Park, a mecca for those interested in sea mammals and seabirds, was affected, but there remain excellent tour boat opportunities. Contact Kenai Fjords National Park (Box 1727, Seward, AK 99664, tel. 907/224–3874) for current conditions in this area. Smaller boats and touring vessels are found in such places as **Glacier Bay National Park.** Glacier Bay is an especially good place to spot humpback whales, puffins, seals, shorebirds, and perhaps a black or brown bear. Write Glacier Bay National Park (Box 140, Gustavus, AK 99826, tel. 907/697–2230) for further information.

Guides to Wildlife Viewing

The following can add immeasurably to the comfort, safety, and success of your wildlife viewing.

Dress for Alaskan Weather   Wildlife viewers and birders need to pay special attention to the weather and their clothing since they may be standing still for long periods. The most beautiful "blue day" can disintegrate into rain in a matter of minutes. Winds can sweep down with no notice and the thermometer can plummet suddenly. In the Arctic, you can encounter snow flurries in June or July, or any month, for that matter. To keep warm and dry, dress in layers, being sure your outer layer is waterproof as well as windproof. Buy the best raingear you can afford. Bring along a warm hat and gloves. Wool is an excellent insulater as are manmade fabrics. Silk long underwear is warm and lightweight.

Carry a good tent. For trips into the bush, bring the best freestanding tent you can afford. You may need it while you wait out a storm or awaiting your air-taxi pilot. A tent with tight mesh may prove to be your best—or only—haven against Alaska's insects. Also be sure to have along at least one day's extra food with you.

Know What You're Looking For Have some idea of the habitat the wildlife you seek thrives in. A good primer on the various Alaskan animals and their habitats is the March/April 1991 issue of *Alaska's Wildlife*, which lists the best times and locations for seeing specific animals. Contact the Alaska Department of Fish and Game (Box 3–2000, Juneau, AK 99802, tel. 907/465–4286). This bimonthly publication costs $4, plus $1 postage and handling, and is published by ADF&G. Season and time of day are critical. For example, you may want to view during twilight, which during summer in certain parts of Alaska can last all night. Interestingly, winter may be the best time to look for wolves because they stand out against the snow (not true for Arctic fox, which turn white in winter). You may only have a few hours out of the day during which you can look, and in parts of Alaska, there won't be any daylight at all during the winter months.

Know How to Look The first rule is to **keep a good distance,** especially with animals that can be dangerous, e.g., bears and moose. Whether you're on foot or in a vehicle, don't get too close. A pair of good binoculars or a scope are well worth the extra weight. **Move slowly,** stop often, look, and listen. The exception is when you see a bear; you may want to let the animal know you're there. Avoid startling an animal and risking a dangerous confrontation, especially with a mother bear with cubs or a mother moose with calf (*see* Bear Facts, below).

Be prepared to wait. Patience often pays off with unexpected dividends when you see a creature you weren't seeking. If the animal should be disturbed, limit your viewing time and leave as quietly as possible. If you're an enthusiastic birder or animal watcher, be prepared to hike over some rough terrain—Alaska is full of it—to reach the best viewing vantage. And, **respect and protect** both the animal you're watching and its habitat. Limit your use of plastic containers, and never leave them behind. The less evidence of your visit, the more the next person will appreciate it.

Some Don'ts The first is **don't disturb or surprise the animals,** which also applies to birds' eggs, the young, the nests, and such things as beaver dams. It's best to let the animal discover your presence quietly, if at all, by keeping still or moving slowly (except when viewing bears or moose). **Don't chase or harrass the animals.** The willful act of harrassing an animal is punishable in Alaska by a $1,000 fine. This includes flushing birds from their nests and purposely frightening animals with loud noises. **Don't use a tape recorder** to call a bird or to attract other animals if you're in bear country, as you might call an angry bear. And, finally,

don't feed the animals, as any creature that comes to depend upon humans for food almost always comes to a sorry end.

Some Caveats There are a few hazards to keep in mind. Alaska's waters, even its wild rivers, often carry **giardia** (intestinal parasites) that can cause diarrhea. Boil or filter your drinking water in the bush. The fox you admire may be carrying **rabies.** Therefore, never try to get too close to or touch a fox. (If you're traveling with pets, keep them leashed.) **Keep your hat on** if you are in territory where Arctic terns or pomerine jaegers nest. Both species are highly protective of their nests and young, and they are skillful dive-bombers. Occasionally, they connect with human heads and the results can be painful.

If time is short, decide what you want to see, and pick a place where you'll be likely to see it. For example, you can be reasonably certain of seeing and photographing bears in the following places:

Pack Creek, on Admiralty Island in Southeast. Fly (air charter) or take a boat out of Juneau to see brown bears fishing for spawning salmon—pink, chum, and silver. If you time your visit to coincide with the salmon runs (the summer months) you will almost surely see bald eagles and flocks of gulls, too. Primitive camping is available. Check with the ADF&G (Alaska Division of Wildlife Conservation, tel. 907/747-5449) before setting up your trip. This is such a popular spot that you will have to take your chances in a drawing.

The **McNeil River State Game Sanctuary,** on the Alaska Peninsula in Southwest Alaska. Photographic opportunities are good here, especially if you want to get a picture of a brown bear. Peak season, when the local salmon are running, is July 1–August 25. As with Pack Creek, you'll have to fly in and take your chances with Lady Luck! The ADF&G has strict viewing limits here, and your stay will have to be determined by a lottery drawing in May. For these particulars, contact ADF&G (333 Raspberry Rd., Anchorage, AK 99518, tel. 907/267-2180).

The U.S. Fish & Wildlife Service is conducting bear viewings at **Kodiak National Wildlife Refuge** by lottery. Call 907/487-2600 for details.

Katmai National Park, also on the Alaska Peninsula, has an abundance of bears. From mid- to late summer, when the salmon are running up Brooks River, the animals concentrate around Brooks River Falls at Brooks Camp, resulting in a great view of bears as they fish, and the spectacle of hundreds of salmon leaping the falls. The photographic opportunities are excellent. There is a viewing platform, a public campground (expect to have bears around), and Katmailand, a privately run lodge with cabins. The best way to get here is by air from King Salmon. The Katmai National Park and Preserve (Box 7, King Salmon, AK 99613, tel. 907/246-3305) has further information. *Note: the eastern shores of Katmai National Park were tainted by the 1989 oil spill. Check with park officials to see which parts of the park have been affected.*

You can't be absolutely sure you'll spot a bear in **Denali National Park,** but your chances are good and you can do it from the comfort and safety of a wildlife-viewing bus. Accommodations and camping facilities are available. See your travel agent or contact Denali National Park (Box 9, McKinley Park, AK 99975, tel. 907/683–2294).

Marine Animals There are two primary spots for spotting marine mammals. The first is **Round Island** out of Dillingham in the Southwest, where bull walruses by the thousand haul out during the summer, providing a sight unique in the world. This Alaska State Game sanctuary can be visited by permit only. For details, contact the ADF&G (Box 1030, Dillingham, AK 99576, tel. 907/ 842–1013). Access is by floatplane or, when seas are calm, by boat. Expect rain, winds, and being weathered in. Rubber boots are essential as are a windproof tent and plenty of food. It's easier to visit the **Pribilof Islands**—where about 80 percent of the world's northern fur seals and 191 species of birds can be seen—but you also may encounter fog. Tours to the Pribilofs leave from Anchorage. Contact the Alaska Maritime National Wildlife Refuge (Box 3069, Homer, AK 99603–3069, tel. 907/ 265–6546) for information.

Caribou The migrations of caribou across Alaska's North Slope are wonderful to watch, but they are not always easy to time. The caribou move to their own timetable. The U.S. Department of Fish and Wildlife (1011 East Tudor Rd., Anchorage, AK 99503, tel. 907/786–3487) will have the best guess as to where you should be when. Or you can settle for seeing one or a few caribou in places such as Denali National Park (*see* Parks, Wilderness Areas, and Wildlife Refuges in Chapter 4).

Bear Facts Bears, which are among the greatest animals to view in Alaska, can also be dangerous. The free ADF&G booklet, *The Bears and You*, gives excellent advice on minimizing confrontation. Write to Box 3–2000, Juneau, AK 99802. Always make noise as you walk through bear country. Some people tie bells to their boots or onto their packs, or bang tin cups with spoons, or use a whistle. (Avoid whistling to yourself; the bears may think you're another wild animal.) Steer clear of obvious bear habitats—along streams when the salmon are running, through brush and berry patches, and bear paths down to streams, across ridges, through woods. Stay upwind so that the bear can smell you, and keep a clean camp. Never leave food lying around or try to feed a bear. Be especially vigilant about getting close to a mother with cubs (the same goes for moose with calves), and never get between a mother and her young. Carry binoculars, or a scope, or a long lens if you want to take a close-up picture. Should you stumble across a bear, keep calm and back slowly away; never imitate the bear's gestures. If a close encounter is unavoidable, drop prone, cover your head with your arms, and "play dead." If you're familiar with firearms, you may want to carry a large-caliber gun. (Note, however, that guns are prohibited in some national parks.)

Bird-watching

With more than 400 species, Alaska is one of the prime places in the world for bird-watchers. You can be thrilled by the sight of the sun darkened by shorebirds and waterfowl above the Copper River Delta in spring, or watch a congregation of thousands of bald eagles in the Chilkat Valley out of Haines in winter. Or you can witness the huge number of Steller's eiders that gather along the Alaska Peninsula in autumn.

You can write to ADF&G to get a comprehensive bird checklist and for information about obtaining checklists for Southeast, South Coastal, Central, Southwestern, and Western Alaska. Another good source (and very handy for a backpack) is *A Guide to the Birds of Alaska,* a field guide by R. H. Armstrong, published by Alaska Northwest Books. The book is $16.95 and is available through major bookstores.

For information on birding trips in Alaska, contact the **Alaska Public Lands Information Center** in Anchorage (for Central and South Central Alaska), or the center in Tok or Fairbanks (for Interior, Western, and Arctic Alaska). For trips in the Southeast, contact the **U.S. Forest Service Information Center** in Juneau (*see* Important Addresses and Numbers, above). The **National Audubon Society** has five branches in Alaska, including ones in Juneau, Anchorage, and Fairbanks. The Anchorage "hotline" number (tel. 907/248–2473) provides the latest information on trips, meetings, and unusual sightings in this part of the state. The free **Alaska Vacation Planner** has birding opportunities as well as phone numbers of Chambers of Commerce throughout the state. Contact the Alaska Division of Tourism (Box E-701, Juneau, AK 99811, tel. 907/465–2010).

Tour Operators

The following offer birding opportunities in Alaska.

Alaska Up Close (c/o Judy Shuler, Box 32666, Juneau 99803, tel. 907/789–9544) retraces John Muir's steps in Southeast.
Alaska Wild Wings (Goose Cove Lodge, Box 325, Cordova 99574, tel. 907/424–5111) also has sea otter viewings.
Wings (c/o Will Russell, Box 31930, Tucson, AZ 86751, tel. 602/749–1967) offers tours throughout Alaska, Barrow to Pribilofs.
Field Guides, Inc. (c/o Bret Whitney, Box 160723, Austin, TX 78746, tel. 512/327–4953).
Wilderness Birding Adventures (Box 10-3747, Anchorage 99510, tel. 907/694–7442) includes the historic landmark area in Nome.

Bird-watching Tips

If your time in Alaska is limited and you want easily accessible birding on your own, try the following sure bets. In **Anchorage:** walk around Potter Marsh, Westchester Lagoon, or along the Coastal Trail for shorebirds and waterfowl. In **Juneau:** visit the Mendenhall Wetlands State Game Refuge, next to the airport, for ducks, geese, and swans among others (there are trails and interpretive signs). In **Fairbanks:** head for Creamer's Field Migratory Waterfowl Refuge on College Road; if you're lucky, your visit might coincide with that of the sandhill cranes that gather in the adjacent fields in spring and summer. Otherwise, if you're there in mid-April to mid-May, look for spectacular shows of ducks and geese.

If your time is more flexible and you want a sure bet, travel to **Haines** in November or December to see bald eagles. (You can go by ferry from Juneau.) Write to the Chilkat Eagle Preserve (400 Willoughby St., Juneau, AK 99811, tel. 907/465–4653) for particulars. In the summer, consider rafting almost any Alaskan river with the near certainty of seeing nesting shorebirds, Arctic terns, and merganser mothers swimming ahead of you trailed by chicks. Or take the plunge and look into taking a trip to **Attu:** it's a great place if you're compiling a lifetime list.

Tips for the Photographer

Alaska is one of the premier spots for bird and wildlife photography because of the combination of abundant birds and animals and spectacular scenery. Exceptional photo opportunities abound during migrations of birds and caribou.

Many professional photographers use ASA 64 color film under all conditions, though you may want to pack a roll or two of higher-speed film for action shots. You'll need to take into account the extraordinary qualities of Alaska's slanting light (the sun is never directly overhead and there are long shadows). Be mindful of Alaska's weather when choosing equipment. Keep your camera dry; some people slip their cameras into plastic bags. It's all too easy to put your camera down in the tundra and not be able to find it, so tie a bright orange ribbon onto your camera, or mark it obviously with orange tape. Bring the longest lens you can afford; a wide-angle lens may embrace the scenery but can be inadequate for many animal pictures. (The exceptions may be birds in flight or the elusive caribou.) Film—though available in the cities, bush villages and lodges—tends to be expensive, so carry plenty. And be sure to pack extra batteries for your camera. A tripod is useful for almost any Alaskan photography, and it's essential for wildlife.

Recreational Fishing

Alaska counts its species of fish in the hundreds, its miles of shoreline in the tens of thousands, its lakes and streams in the hundreds of thousands. On top of that it has some of the world's great rivers. Despite the oil spill of spring 1989, much of Alaska remains a superb place for fishing. Indeed, fish have played—and continue to play—a major role in the state's economic livelihood. Many Native peoples as well as certain animals subsist on fish, and many Alaskans fish for both income and pleasure.

The choices and opportunities available to recreational fisherman are equal to those of several states. For comparison, a fishing trip to the Pacific Northwest would involve a choice between Washington, Oregon, and Northern California. The Alaska-bound fisherman must decide among Southeast, South Central, Southwest, Northwest, the Interior, and the Arctic—each of these regions encompassing hundreds of square miles.

Important Addresses and Numbers

The **Alaska Department of Fish and Game** is *the* source for information about fishing in Alaska. The ADF&G publishes up-to-date fishing information and can supply the names of local fishing guides, air-taxi pilots, and charter operators. It also writes rules, sets limits, stocks lakes, and runs an ambitious hatchery program. (One out of every five salmon taken in Alaska is hatchery-produced.) ADF&G strives to provide a diverse range of fishing, including trophy-size angling, throughout the state. The following is a list of ADF&G offices in Alaska.

Anchorage (tel. 907/267–2218); **Cordova** (tel. 907/424–3212); **Delta Junction** (tel. 907/895–4632); **Dillingham** (tel. 907/842–

2427); **Fairbanks** (tel. 907/456–4359); **Glennallen** (tel. 907/822–3309); **Haines** (tel. 907/766–2625); **Homer** (tel. 907/235–8191); **Juneau** (tel. 907/465–4286; for fishing licenses, 907/465–2376; for publications call collect, 907/562–4286); **Ketchikan** (tel. 907/225–2859); **King Salmon** (tel. 907/246–3340); **Kodiak** (tel. 907/486–4791); **Kotzebue** (tel. 907/442–3420); **McGrath** (tel. 907/524–3323); **Nome** (tel. 907/443–5167); **Palmer** (tel. 907/745–5016); **Petersburg** (tel. 907/772–3801); **Seward** (tel. 907/224–3017); **Sitka** (tel. 907/747–5355); **Soldotna** (tel. 907/262–9368); **Tok** (tel. 907/883–2971); **Wrangell** (tel. 907/874–3822); **Yakutat** (tel. 907/784–3222).

Also based out of Alaska is the U.S. Fish & Wildlife Service (1011 E. Tudor Rd., Anchorage, AK 99503, tel. 907/786–3487, 907/786–3486, or 907/786–3309; fax 907/562–2297).

Another good source of detailed information for the fisherman is the free *Alaska Vacation Planner*, which is published yearly by the Division of Tourism (*see* Important Addresses and Numbers in Wildlife Viewing, above). It contains the names of numerous fishing lodges, charter operators, air-taxi pilots, and wilderness guides, as well as chambers of commerce (many are fonts of knowledge) and federal and state land agencies.

Planning a Fishing Expedition

The first step is to write away for the ADF&G publications *Recreational Fishing Guide, Alaska Sport Fishing Predictions*, and the current *Sport Fishing Regulations*. The guide is $5; the other two are free. These booklets provide a good overview of the remarkable opportunities available for fishing in Alaska, as well as the state's limitations on the sport. You can buy a fishing license from ADF&G or you can obtain one from a sporting goods store, a charter boat operator, or a fishing lodge. Seasonal licenses for residents are $10; for nonresidents, year-round licenses are $50, 14-day are $30, 3-day are $15, 1-day are $10.

Step two is to identify the fish you're going after, and whether you'll be fishing for sport (catch and release) or to fill your freezer. Trophy-fishermen can get information from ADF&G about its requirements for a certificate; you'll find this in the *Recreational Fishing Guide*. ADF&G has recently started a trophy program for catch-and-release anglers. It is wise to check with a taxidermist regarding requirements for mountings before you set out. The chart below will give you a start.

Note: Several of these species in the chart, such as Dolly Varden and northern pike, are seasonal, and you have to be at a particular place at a particular time to find them. Others, including the prized king salmon or chinook, can be fished year-round.

Catch-and-release fishing has been gaining in popularity in Alaska. Most recreational anglers use a barbless hook for the pure sport of it, and as pressures on Alaskan fisheries increase ADF&G is requiring catch and release in the more popular and sensitive spots. Over two dozen locations with brook trout populations were recently regulated.

The final, and most critical decision, will be how you'll go fishing on your Alaskan expedition. None of your options will be cheap. The least expensive way to go is under your own power—by car, on a bike, or on foot, which entails either a trip by ferry or by plane (or both) or a long drive up the Alaska Highway through Canada. This auto trip is not easy. (The Alaska Highway is not recommended for bikers, either; flying gravel is a hazard in places.) Airfares tend to be steep. The Alaska State Ferry is the least costly choice, particularly if you're on foot. (You can carry a bicycle on board free.) And you can fish from the ferries.

Alaska Top Fish and Their Sources

Species	Common Name	Where Found
Arctic Char (F)	Dolly Varden	SC, SW, NW, I, A
Arctic Grayling (F)	Grayling	SE, SC, SW, NW, I, A
Brook Trout (F)	Brookies	SE
Burbot (F)	Ling Cod	SC, SW, NW, I, A
Chinook Salmon (F,S)	King Salmon	SE, SC, SW, NW, I, A
Chum Salmon (F,S)	Dog Salmon	SE, SC, SW, NW, I, A
Coho Salmon (F,S)	Silver Salmon	SC, SW, NW, I, A
Cutthroat Trout (F,S)	Cutthroat	SE, SC
Dolly Varden (F,S)	Dollies	SE, SC, SW, NW, I, A
Lake Trout (F)	Lakers	SE, SC, SW, NW, I, A
Northern Pike (F)	Northerns, Hammerhandles	SE, SC, SW, NW, I, A
Pacific Halibut (S)	Halibut	SE, SC, SW
Pink Salmon (F,S)	Humpies	SE, SC, SW
Rainbow Smelt (F,S)	Smelt	SE, SC, SW
Rainbow Trout (F)	Rainbows	SE, SC, SW, NW, I, A
Sheefish (F)	Shee, Inconnu	NW, I, A
Sockeye Salmon (F,S)	Red Salmon	SE, SC, SW
Steelhead (F)	Steelies	SE, SC, SW

(F) = *Freshwater*
(S) = *Saltwater*
(F,S) = *Freshwater and Saltwater*

NW = *Northwest*
I = *Interior*
A = *Arctic*
SE = *Southeast*
SC = *Southcentral*
SW = *Southwest*

By Car If you choose to drive, you can fish from the roadside, as some Interior and Kenai Peninsula rivers and lakes are accessible by car. Or you can fish from docks in Haines or other Southeast ports, or from the shore. (Both dockside and shore fishing can be great for children.) The truly ambitious can strap a boat onto their car.

By Boat Chartering or renting a boat with an optional guide works well if you want to stay in a hotel—in Ketchikan or King Salmon, for instance—and choose your time to fish. (Many hotels will freeze your catch and arrange for packing it to send home.) Guided fishing boats can be chartered for one day or several, in which case you will overnight in nearby coves or bays and sleep and eat on board. Southeast charter boats have a six-line limit, so there are no "party boats" jammed with fishermen. Charters usually provide the essentials: bait, lures, rods and reels, rain gear (although you'll probably want to bring your own), coffee, lunch or complete meals. Be sure to check what comes with your package. Southeast charters can also arrange crabbing, stream fishing, beach combing, diving, photography, or sightseeing trips. Many charters also sell Alaskan fishing licenses. Day charter fares start at well over $100 per day and go up from there; multiple-day trips cost $300–$450 a day. Knowledgeable Alaskans suggest that you visit the dock when charter boats return and quiz the captain and the fishermen about the day's activities to assess the caliber of services provided.

By Air Taxi Another option is to stay in a hotel in a nearby town such as Dillingham and fly in to fish by the day or week. You can hire a guide or be flown in solo to a good spot. The local ADF&G or the chamber of commerce can provide a list of guides and current air-taxi rates.

From a Fishing Lodge To practically guarantee a successful fishing trip stay at a fishing lodge, most of which are reached by air-taxi. The advantages are plenty: Lodges are strategically located; operators know the best fishing holes and take you to them—on foot, by boat, or by small plane—every day, weather permitting. Many lodge operators even pilot their own planes. Everything is provided and some lodges are sumptuous, with superb food, hot tubs, saunas, excellent guides, and a fleet of small planes. Expect to pay dearly for all the amenities and attention: from a rock-bottom minimum of $300 up to $575 a day. Begin to make inquiries and reservations a year in advance. It's a good idea to be prepared for weather contingencies and for the possibility that you may be weathered in overnight. Even the best and most experienced lodge operator has been caught with a party of fishermen when a typical Alaskan storm moved in. The seasoned fisherman always packs warm clothes, extra food, and good rain gear.

Fishing Tips Know the species you want to catch and the best suitable tackle. You may have ursine competition, especially if you're fishing salmon streams (*see* Bear Facts, in Wildlife Viewing, above). Treat the fishing spot you choose with respect, as others may want to use it. Know the official limits or practice catch and release. Bring insecticide and perhaps a head net. Be mindful of the flighty weather; buy the best rain gear you can afford and always have it with you.

If time is a consideration but cost is not, pick a getaway into the region of your choice and call the local ADF&G for details about your options. Both Juneau and Ketchikan (Southeast) are accessible by commercial flights, and offer salmon, halibut, steelhead, and cutthroat, as well as Dungeness crab and clams. Further north, Yakutat (Southeast), also served by commercial airlines, is great for salmon—kings, humpies, reds, and silvers—and for native steelhead (there are two runs a year). Accommodations in the Southeast are limited and you'll need to make plans months in advance. Both Homer and Seward (South Central) are good choices for fishing halibut; check with ADF&G about current conditions. Both towns are accessible by car and air.

Anchorage is the primary gateway to Southwest Alaska via Iliamna or King Salmon, both served by scheduled air flights. Southwest Alaska has one of the great salmon populations of the world as well as numerous species of sport fish. Commercial air service to Dillingham access the Wood River–Tikchik areas (also Southwest) and more exceptional angling possibilities. Nome (Northwest) provides access to fishing for salmon, Dolly Varden, and Arctic char, from the road, while Kotzebue is the launching point for trips north of the Arctic Circle for sheefish and northern pike. Fairbanks, Delta Junction, and Tok provide access to the Interior, in particular the Tanana River, one of Alaska's finest fishing streams with at least ten species, incuding king and pink salmon.

6 Anchorage

By Howard C. Weaver and Barbara Hodgin

Born and raised in Anchorage, Howard Weaver is the managing editor of the Anchorage Daily News. *A series written by Weaver earned the* Daily News *a Pulitzer Prize in 1976. Barbara Hodgin is the owner and manager of Anchorage-based Rosebud Publishing.*

A local newspaper columnist once dubbed it "a city too obviously on the make to ever be accepted in polite society." Rural neighbors snicker at its "citified" ways. It's not a historic gold-rush town or an old Russian outpost. Despite it all, slowly, grudgingly, Anchorage is gaining some respect. Amidst the wild countryside that bundles around it on all sides, Anchorage is growing into a vigorous, spirited, cosmopolitan city—by far Alaska's largest and most sophisticated.

Anchorage's youth has a lot to do with its struggle for recognition. As recently as 75 years ago, there was no Anchorage. Its population has an average age of just over 28 years old and an aggressive style that makes Anchorage the Yuppie of Alaskan cities. Rather than earn its keep through the oil, fishing, or timber industries that fuel the state's economy, Anchorage hustles its living as the government, banking, transportation, and communications hub those businesses depend on.

The relative affluence of this white-collar city (with a sprinkling of olive drab from nearby military bases) attracts fine restaurants and pricey shops, first-rate repertory theater and world-class sporting events. Flashy modern towers stab into the skyline. Traffic from the city's busy international airport, served by more than 15 airlines representing a dozen countries, lends Anchorage a more cosmopolitan air than a city of 225,000 might expect.

Even with such modern amenities, Anchorage has not lost touch with Alaska's frontier spirit. Dog-sled races are still among the most popular events held here, and moose occasionally roam along city bike trails.

Anchorage residents are almost all immigrants, and the fact that they have chosen to make Anchorage their home seems to have given them a bigger stake in local events. Ferocious political battles and dedicated community activism are trademarks of the city. Residents describe local politics as their "second favorite indoor sport."

Although representing less than 5% of the population, Native Alaskan Indians, Eskimos, and Aleuts add, through their influence, an important cultural dimension to the city. A growing oriental population is also having an impact. Among Anchorage's cable TV channels is one devoted entirely to Korean programming; well-stocked oriental food stores and authentic restaurants are increasingly familiar sights.

Anchorage got its start with the construction of the federally built Alaska Railroad (completed in 1917); traces of the city's railroad heritage remain today. Once the tracks were laid, the town grew because its pioneer forefathers actively sought growth by hook and—not infrequently—by crook. City fathers, many of whom are still alive, delight in telling how they tricked a visiting U.S. congressman into dedicating the site for a federal hospital that had not been approved.

Boom and bust periods followed major events: an influx of military bases during World War II; a massive build-up of Arctic missile-warning stations during the Cold War; and most recently, the biggest bonanza of all, the discovery of oil at Prudhoe Bay and the construction of the trans-Alaska pipeline. Not surprisingly, Anchorage positioned itself as the perfect home for the new pipeline administrators and support industries, and it attracts a large share of the state's oil tax dollars.

These days, Anchorage residents are no longer alone in singing their city's praises. The U.S. Olympic Committee has endorsed Anchorage as the American candidate city for future Winter Olympic Games. The city has responded by hosting numerous international sporting events and lobbying enthusiastically for the games. Whether the Olympics qualifies as "polite society" is debatable, but being a serious contender for such a prestigious event marks something of an arrival for Anchorage.

Essential Information

Arriving and Departing

By Plane Anchorage International Airport is six miles from downtown Anchorage on International Airport Road. It is served by **Delta, United, Northwest,** and **Alaska** airlines (*see* Arriving and Departing in Chapter 1). Anchorage is also served by international carriers from Europe and the Orient: **China Airlines, British Airways, Air France, Korean Airlines, KLM, Sabena, Iberia, Lufthansa,** and **SAS.** Several intrastate carriers serve Anchorage, including **Markair, Reeve Aleutian Airways, Southcentral Air,** and **ERA.** Charter airplanes and helicopters serve the area from Lake Hood, which is adjacent to Anchorage International Airport. There are also air taxis and air-charter operations at Merrill Field, two miles east of downtown on 5th Avenue.

Between the Airport and Center City The municipality operates hourly People Mover buses from the lower level of the terminal to downtown Anchorage. The downtown bus terminal at 6th Avenue and G Street is close to the Westmark Hotel but at least four blocks from all other major hotels. The first bus leaves the airport at 7:21 AM, and the last bus leaves at 5:50 PM for downtown. Buses from the downtown bus terminal leave hourly until the last bus at 5:13 PM. The fare is 80¢. Call People Mover (tel. 907/343–6543) for more information.

Taxis line up at the lower level of the airport terminal outside the baggage claim area. **Alaska Cab, Checker Cab,** and **Yellow Cab** all line up here; you'll get whichever cab is next in line. All charge between $10 and $15, including tip, for the ride to downtown hotels.

Some of the larger hotels have airport limousine service; inquire when making reservations.

By Car There is only one road into Anchorage from the north, and only one road out on the south. The Glenn Highway enters Anchorage from the north and becomes 5th Avenue near Merrill Field; this route will lead you directly into downtown. Gambell Street leads out of town to the south, turning into the Seward Highway at 36th Avenue.

By Bus **Gray Line of Alaska** (300- Elliott Ave. W, Seattle, WA 98119, tel. 800/544–2206) covers much of the state; **Alaska Sightseeing Tours** (543 W. 4th Ave., Anchorage 99501, tel. 907/276–1305 or 800/426–7702) connects with the State Ferry System at Haines.

By Train The **Alaska Railroad** runs between Anchorage and Fairbanks via Denali National Park and Preserve daily, May to September (*see* Getting around Alaska in Chapter 1).

By Boat Cruise ships sailing the Gulf of Alaska and the Alaska Marine ferries call in Seward or Whittier, a short train ride from Anchorage (*see* Chapter 3). The **Alaska Marine Highway's** South Central route connects Kodiak, Port Lions, Homer, Seldovia, Seward, Valdez, Cordova, and Whittier. *Alaska Marine Hwy. Information, Box R, Juneau 99811, tel. 907/465–3941 or 800/642–0066.*

Getting Around

On Foot Downtown Anchorage is about 15 blocks square. It is possible to see most of the major downtown points of interest on foot. Hotels and restaurants are all within a 10-minute walk of one another.

By Bus The municipal People Mover bus system covers the whole Anchorage bowl. It is not convenient for short downtown trips but can be used for visits to outlying areas. The central bus depot is located at 6th Avenue and G Street. Schedules and information are available there. The fare is 80¢. A red double-decker London bus runs on a loop downtown during summer months. The loop also goes out Spenard Road to hotels in the airport area and to the University Center shopping mall. This bus is free; a schedule is available at the Log Cabin Information Center at 4th Avenue and G Street and at hotels.

By Taxi Prices for taxis start at $2 for pickup and $1.50 for each mile. Most people in Anchorage telephone for a cab; it is not common to hail one. Allow 20 minutes for arrival of the cab during morning and evening rush hours. The main cab companies are Alaska Cab (tel. 907/563–5353), Checker Cab (tel. 907/276–1234), and Yellow Cab (tel. 907/272–2422).

By Car Downtown Anchorage is hard to get lost in—it was laid out by the Army Corps of Engineers in nice square blocks. Streets running west to east are numbered. North–south streets run in alphabetical order, using letters (A,B,C, etc.) west of A Street, and Alaska place names (Barrow, Cordova, Denali, Eagle, etc.) east of it.

By Recreational Vehicle Many visitors to Alaska bring their RV or rent one on arrival. Parking downtown on weekdays is challenging for an RV. A big parking lot on 3rd Avenue between C and E streets is a good place to park and walk. Parking is not a problem in other parts of town.

By Bicycle Anchorage has more than 125 miles of bicycle trails and many streets have marked bike lanes. In the evening, downtown streets are uncrowded and safe for cyclists. Bikes are available for rental from **Big Boy Toys** (6511 Brayton, tel. 907/349–1425); **America Rents** (3600 Arctic Blvd., tel. 907/563–3600); and the **Clarion Hotel** (on Spenard Rd. at Lake Hood, tel. 907/243–2300). The Clarion bikes cost $5 for two hours, $10 for four hours, and $15 all day. The 6th & B (tel. 907/279–5293) bed-and-breakfast also rents bikes.

Important Addresses and Numbers

Tourist Information The Anchorage Convention and Visitors Bureau operates the Log Cabin Information Center at 4th Avenue and F Street (tel. 907/274–3531). The Information Center itself is a log cabin with a sod roof like old-timers built in the bush, festooned with huge hanging baskets of fuchsias, begonias, and geraniums, which thrive in the long Arctic daylight. Volunteer staff answer questions and distribute literature daily from 7:30 AM to 7 PM in summer, 8:30 AM to 6 PM in May and September, and 9 AM to 4 PM in winter. There is also an information center at the airport in the main terminal building on the lower level among the baggage claim areas. For a telephone recording of daily events citywide, call 907/276–3200.

Tourist information by mail. The Anchorage Convention and Visitors Bureau will send information to visitors planning a trip to Anchorage. Write to ACVB (201 E. 3rd Avenue, Anchorage 99501).

Emergencies Dial 911 for **police** and **ambulance** in an emergency. **Poison Control Center,** tel. 907/261–3193. TTY/TDD emergency for deaf callers (machine only), tel. 907/276–7232.

Doctor **Providence Hospital** (3200 Providence Dr., tel. 907/562–2211) and **Humana Hospital** (2801 DeBarr Rd., tel. 907/264–1131) both have emergency rooms. Each hospital also operates a physician referral service (tel. 907/562–3737 at Providence, tel. 907/264–1722 at Humana).

The Anchorage **Neighborhood Health Center and Dental Clinic** (1217 E. 10th Ave., tel. 907/258–7888) also offers services; charges are based on ability to pay. It's open weekdays and Saturday mornings; walk-in patients are taken, but expect to wait at least an hour. **First Care Primary and Family Medical Clinic** (3710 Woodland Dr., tel. 907/248–1122) offers minor emergency care on a walk-in basis. Hours are 9 to 9 on weekdays, 10 to 9 on weekends.

Pharmacy There is no 24-hour pharmacy in Anchorage. The **Rexall Drug Store** (415 W. 5th Ave., tel. 907/277–2567) is open weekdays from 9 to 7, Saturdays from 9 to 6, and Sundays from 11 to 5. The **Carr's** grocery store pharmacy (1340 Gambell St., tel. 907/272–4574), a mile from downtown, is open weekdays from 9 to 9, Saturdays from 9 to 7, and Sundays 10 to 7.

Laundry A coin-operated laundromat, which also offers dry cleaning and drop-off laundry service, is located at 6th Avenue and Fairbanks Street.

Guided Tours

Orientation Tours **Alaska Sightseeing** (543 W. 4th Ave., tel. 907/276–1305) and **Gray Line of Alaska** (547 W. 4th Ave., tel. 907/277–5581) offer bus tours of the city and environs. The Alaska Sightseeing route takes three hours and costs $22 for adults, $11 for children. Grey Line's city tour takes 3½ hours, with a $21 price tag for adults, $10.50 for children. Grey Line has service counters in the Hilton, Captain Cook, and Westmark hotels. Both outfits offer extended tours that include Turnagain Arm and views of the Portage Glacier.

Alaskans hosting family and friends from "outside" will usually try to figure out how to get their guests up in an airplane. This perspective gives both a sense of the size of Alaska and a view of how wilderness surrounds Anchorage on all sides. Any air-taxi company can arrange for a flightseeing trip over Anchorage and environs. The fee will be determined by the length of time you are airborne and the size of the airplane. Airplanes generally rent for between $150 and $200 an hour and can carry two to six people. Air taxis are located at Merrill Field and at Lake Hood near International Airport.

Talkeetna Air Taxi (tel. 907/733–2218) can take up to four people in a Heliocourier aircraft from Anchorage to Mt. McKinley. If weather permits, it lands on the Ruth Glacier, in a spectacular alpine amphitheater high on the mountain. The three-hour trip costs $600 total, regardless of the number of passengers. They will also assist you in setting up a shared trip with other groups of passengers in order to keep down the cost per person.

Special-Interest Tours **ERA Helicopters** (tel. 907/248–4422 or 800/843–1947) offers a 45-minute trip over Anchorage and the Chugach Mountains. The trip is available May through September and costs $155 per person.

The local chapter of the **Audubon Society** offers referrals to local birders who will advise you on the best bird-watching spots; with proper enthusiasm and encouragement you might be able to entice these experts into giving you a private tour. The referral service line is 907/276–7034.

Wilderness Birding Adventures (Box 10-3747, Anchorage 99510, tel. 907/694–7442) offers guided boat or hiking tours to view wilderness wildlife.

Walking Tours A guided walking tour of historic downtown buildings is available from **Anchorage Historic Properties** (tel. 907/564–0338). The tour—popular with locals—costs $2 per person and must be booked in advance.

Exploring Anchorage

Numbers in the margin correspond to points of interest on the Anchorage map.

The official Anchorage city limits extend considerably into the surrounding countryside. An old mining camp named Girdwood—now home to the Alyeska Ski Resort—is within the city's boundaries despite the fact that it's 40 miles south of city center. The municipality also stretches more than 20 miles to the north.

Downtown Anchorage was laid out with military precision by the Army Corps of Engineers; streets and avenues run exactly east–west and north–south, with numbers in the first direction and letters of the alphabet in the other. The only aberration is the absence of a "J" street—a concession, some say, to the city's early Swedish settlers, who had difficulty pronouncing the letter. It's tough to get lost in the regular grid of downtown Anchorage.

A downtown tour can easily be done on foot. The walking tour suggested here covers a variety of sites: museums, parks, historic buildings, and shops. It should take three to four hours, longer if you really browse. The second tour covers a much wider stretch of territory. Having a car is necessary for most of the stops. Some of the closer-in spots included, such as Earthquake Park, can be reached on foot (or bike) if you don't mind a sizable hike; the Anchorage Zoo, about seven miles from city center, is served by the city's People Mover bus system (*see* Getting Around, above).

❶ Start at the **Log Cabin Visitor Information Center** at the corner of 4th Avenue and F Street. A marker out front shows the mileage to various world cities. Fourth Avenue sustained heavy damage in the 1964 earthquake. The businesses on this block of 4th Avenue withstood the destruction, but those one block east, where the McDonald's restaurant now stands, fell into the ground as the earth under them slid away toward Ship Creek.

❷ The **Old City Hall** is next door to the visitor center to the east. It was built in 1936. The marble sculpture in front of the building is a monument to William Seward, the secretary of state who engineered the purchase of Alaska from Russia.

Opposite the visitor center, you can get an audiovisual introduction to Anchorage and the rest of Alaska through *Anchorage Gateway to Alaska*, a multi-image projection film. The 52-minute show features images of the city and the state, from the early gold rush days to the oil spill in Prince William Sound. *Anchorage Gateway to Alaska, 519 W. 4th Ave., tel 907/333–2582. Shows presented June 1 - Sept. 30, hourly 10-6. Admission: $6 adults, $5 seniors, $3 children to age 12.*

❸ Kitty-corner from the visitor center at 4th Avenue and F Street is the **Alaska Public Lands Information Center.** The center has displays about Alaska's national parks, forests, and wildlife refuges. The center shows daily films highlighting different parts of the state. There's a trip-planning computer for public use.

Take F Street north (downhill) to 2nd Avenue. The houses in this neighborhood are original town-site homes built by the Alaska Engineering Commission, which built the Alaska Railroad in the early 20th century. A plaque in front of each house reveals a bit of its history.

❹ Turn east on 2nd Avenue and head 1½ blocks to the Eisenhower Statehood monument and the stairway leading downhill to the **Alaska Railroad depot.** Outside are totem poles and a locomotive built in 1907. A monument in front of the depot relates the history of the railroad.

❺ Just north of the depot, **Ship Creek** tumbles into Cook Inlet. Salmon run up this creek all summer; it's easy to watch them from a viewing platform. It is closed to fishing except for 10 days during the summer. Return uphill and head back west on 2nd Avenue.

If you enter the coastal trail from 2nd Avenue, west of Christianson Drive, Mount Susitna (known locally as the Sleeping Lady) is the prominent low mountain to the northwest. To her north, Mount McKinley is often visible. On the left is Captain Cook Park, a cantilevered viewing platform above the trail.

❻
❼ The **Oscar Anderson house** is right next to the trail at the north end of **Elderberry Park.** It was Anchorage's first permanent frame house, built in 1915 by tent city butcher Oscar Anderson.

Tours are free. The park is also a good place to watch for whales off the coastline.

8 Take 5th Avenue uphill from the park and continue east to H Street. **The Imaginarium** (725 5th Ave.) is a fun stop for kids and adults; it's an experiential science museum with a great museum shop.

9 The new **Performing Arts Center** at Fifth Avenue and G Street occupies a full block. This is one of several major civic buildings planned during the oil boom of the late 1970s and early 1980s. Call ahead (tel. 907/343–1948) to find out what's on.

10 The **Egan Convention Center,** across 5th Avenue from the Performing Arts Center, was also built during the boom days. The lobby has a beaded curtain, which evokes the northern lights, and several modern native Alaskan sculptures. During the oil boom, public buildings were required to set aside 2% of their total cost for public art.

11 Across the street at 5th Avenue and E Street, the **Kimball Building** houses two shops operated by Anchorage old-timers. Kimball's Dry Goods has been in this location for over 60 years. Next door, the Gold Pan sells coffee, tea, Russian goods, and native art and artifacts.

12 The **Anchorage Museum of History and Art** occupies the whole block at 6th Avenue and A Street. The museum's entrance is on 7th Avenue. The museum houses a fine collection of historic and contemporary Alaskan art, displays on Alaskan history (second floor), and a special section for children.

Head back downtown on A Street to 5th Avenue. Turn left and go three blocks to D Street. One block down on the left, the **13** white-turreted **Wendler Building** is embraced by a newer brick building. The Wendler was moved to this site from its original home at 4th Avenue and I Street. It was built in 1915 and has housed a popular restaurant, and, for a time, a ladies-only bar. On the 4th Avenue side, you can watch native Alaskan carvers at work through the front windows, making items of wood, horn, ivory, woven reeds, and leather.

Driving Tour **Earthquake Park** vividly demonstrates the power of the devas-
14 tating 1964 earthquake, which sent most of this neighborhood sliding into Cook Inlet. A short walk down the coastal trail through the woods takes you to the inlet's shore. In the woods, mounds of earth and pools of standing water are the new landscape left by the earthquake; in some places along the beach, remains of foundations of some destroyed houses are still visible. Recent visitors have noted that the park is not as well-maintained as it once was. *Follow Northern Lights Blvd. 2 mi west of Minnesota Dr. to get to the park.*

15 Continue west on Northern Lights Boulevard 1.7 miles to **Point Woronzof,** a large parking area on the right side of the road. From this vantage point, there are good views of Cook Inlet, Mt. Susitna, the Alaska Range, and Mt. McKinley, especially on a day when a temperature inversion acts as a lens to make the mountains appear larger than life. Fire Island stands between Point Woronzof and the Kenai Peninsula.

Retrace your route on Northern Lights Boulevard, and turn right after 1.8 miles on Aircraft Drive into the Lake Hood float-plane base. Turn left on unmarked Lakeshore Drive at six-

Anchorage

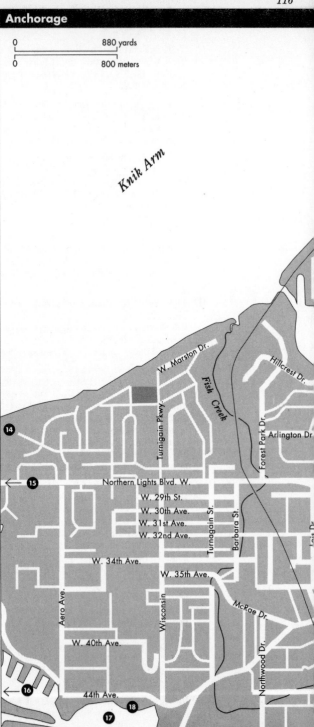

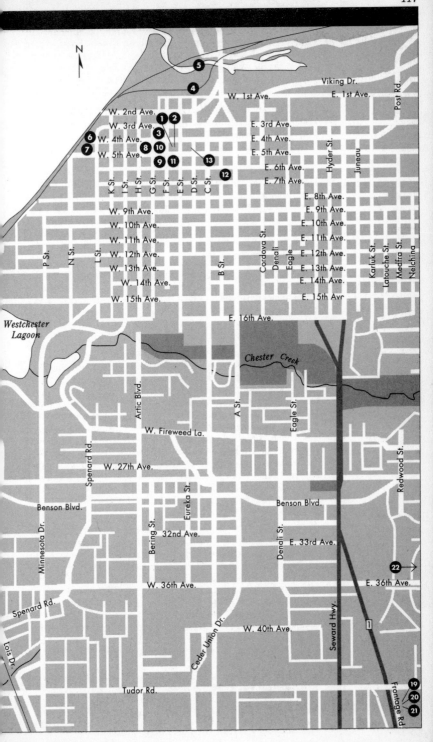

tenths of a mile. Go one short block and turn left again. Go another two-tenths of a mile and turn left again, winding around
(16) (17) (18) **Lake Hood** and **Lake Spenard** to **Spenard Beach.** Float planes bound for bush lakes take off here all day long. Hardy Alaskans sunbathe and swim here in summer. Take Spenard Road right to International Rd., turn left to Minnesota Drive, then turn right and travel for 3 miles to the New Seward Hwy.

Head south of downtown on the Seward Highway and you will
(19) reach **Potter Marsh** in about 10 miles. This is the home of the **Potter Point** game refuge. Canada geese and other migratory birds make their home here in the summer. Elevated boardwalks are provided so that visitors can get near the birds without disturbing them. Two miles farther south on the Seward
(20) Highway is the **Potter Point Section House,** an old railroad service building preserved by the Chugach State Park and operated as a museum and state park information center. Staff at the section house can provide up to date information about trails and where to view wildlife in Chugach State Park. *Call Alaska State Parks, tel. 907/765–4565, or the Alaska Public Lands Information Center, tel. 907/271–2737, for hours and directions.*

(21) The **Alaska Zoo** is about six miles south of downtown via the Seward Highway, and two miles east (left) on O'Malley Road. The zoo has polar bears, musk-oxen, seals, brown bears, and a variety of Alaska birds. *Tel. 907/346–3242. Admission: $4 adults, $3 senior citizens and teens 13–18, $1.50 children 3–12, children under 3 free. Open daily 9–6.*

(22) **Chugach State Park** encompasses all of the mountains to the east of Anchorage, from Eklutna on the north to the Kenai Peninsula on the south. Trails from two to 30 miles in length take hikers and mountain bikers into this accessible wilderness. Bear and moose roam the park and occasionally enter hillside neighborhoods. Alaskans know that the way to avoid close encounters with these dangerous-if-provoked animals is to make noise, so hikers sing, carry a bell, or converse loudly when hiking in areas where vegetation limits visibility. Thousands of Alaskans use these trails annually without incident by using common sense and by viewing wildlife close up only through a telephoto lens. Maps of trails are available from the State Division of Parks (3601 C St., Suite 1280, Anchorage 99508, tel. 907/694–2108).

Trailheads in the park are at the top of O'Malley, Huffman, and DeArmoun roads and, to the north of town, at Arctic Valley Road (six miles out) and Eagle River Road (13 miles out). Eagle River Road leads 10 miles into the mountains from the bedroom community of Eagle River. The **Eagle River Visitor Center** at the end of the road has wildlife displays, wildlife spotting telescopes, and park rangers to answer questions—rangers also lead day hikes and offer nature programs. The Dew Mound trail behind the visitor center is an easy walk to the river. The trail continues on from there to join the Crow Pass Trail, which leads to Girdwood, 40 miles south of Anchorage. *Tel. 907/694–2108. Open Fri.–Mon. 11–7.*

Anchorage for Free

Music The Friends of the Library offers open-air concerts in summer every Wednesday at noon on the plaza at the Loussac Library at 36th Avenue and Denali Street (tel. 907/261–2975). The concerts range from jazz to barbershop.

Films The Loussac Library and the Anchorage Museum of History and Art (7th Ave. and A St., tel. 907/343–6173) both offer films. Call for listings. The Alaska Public Lands Information Center (4th Ave. and F St.) offers daily video presentations on topics about Alaska. Lunchtime films are popular with downtown workers. The ARCO Theater offers films and slide presentations on industry and art in the ARCO building (7th Ave. and G St., tel. 907/263–4545). Call ahead for the schedule.

Gardens Anchorage residents love gardening. The summer is short but intense, and local neighborhoods offer a chance to see people's flower and vegetable beds over their fences. The South Addition, the neighborhood just across the park strip from downtown, is an older neighborhood with established perennials and shrubs. Cooperative Extension agent Wayne Vandre can refer you to areas that have plants of special interest to you (tel. 907/279–5582). The municipal greenhouse raises plants for public gardens around the city and operates a greenhouse with plants not native to Alaska. You can visit the greenhouse at Russian Jack Springs Park on DeBarr Road. (Tel. 907/333–8610 for hours. The greenhouse is sometimes closed to the public because it is a popular place for weddings.)

Scenic Walks The **Tony Knowles Coastal Trail** is a 10-mile paved bike and pedestrian trail that follows the coastline from downtown Anchorage to Kincaid Park, beyond the airport. There is access to the trail on the waterfront at the ends of 2nd, 5th, and 9th avenues, and at Westchester Lagoon. A connecting bicycle and pedestrian trail that runs from Westchester Lagoon to the mountains through the Chester Creek greenbelt can be approached from the lagoon; from A, C, and E streets; and from a stairway at 16th Avenue and H Street. This trail runs roughly where 17th Street should be. The trail is shared by bicycles, runners, and walkers, so it's important to keep to the right and keep your ears open.

What to See and Do with Children

The **Imaginarium** (725 W. 5th Ave., tel. 907/276–3179) is an experiential science museum/fun house for children. They can learn how eyeglasses correct vision, stand inside a giant soap bubble, and make giant drawings with a swinging pendulum. The gift shop sells educational toys.

The **Alaska Zoo** (4731 O'Malley Rd., tel. 907/346–3242), is open daily in the summer from 9 AM to 6 PM. It includes a petting zoo. The most popular residents are Binky the polar bear and Annabelle the elephant. The Department of Fish and Game sometimes brings orphaned animals here for rearing; these animal babies are very popular with local children.

The **Ship Creek Salmon Overlook** and **Westchester Lagoon** are both good places to take children to see ducks and geese. Do not feed the birds, because feeding can discourage them from migrating south for the winter. The best spot on Westchester Lagoon is approached by taking L Street south to the Hillcrest off ramp. Turn left at the top of the hill on Hillcrest. Go left four blocks to Spenard Road and turn left. At the bottom of the hill on the left is a parking area next to the lagoon where hundreds of ducks gather. Return to downtown on Spenard Road. **Potter Marsh** at the south end of town on the Seward Highway has Canada geese nesting in summer. Do not feed these wild birds.

Children enjoy the railroad train engines parked at the Alaska Railroad depot at 2nd Avenue and E Street and at 9th Avenue and E Street on the park strip.

Chuck E. Cheese (308 E. Northern Lights Blvd.) is a pizza parlor that caters to children, with electronic games and waiters costumed as animals.

The **Loussac Library** and the **Anchorage Museum of History and Art** both feature special displays and events for children (*see* Anchorage for Free, above).

Off the Beaten Track

The lower stretch of the **Eagle River** contains icy, heart-pounding white-water rapids. Shooting these rapids will undoubtedly put some thrill in your trip. Alaska Whitewater (tel. 907/337–7238) offers guided runs along the river. The cost is $89 per person, and children under 13 are not permitted. Transportation can be provided from downtown hotels, and wet suits are provided.

During the summer, white beluga whales roll offshore in the **Cook Inlet.** Head out to Kincaid Park along the coastal trail that starts at Westchester Lagoon (at the end of 15th Ave.), and you might be lucky enough to share a moment with them. The trip from Westchester Lagoon to Kincaid is about nine miles.

Twenty-six miles north of Anchorage on the Glenn Highway is a small native community called the **Eklutna Indian Village.** Residents often sit on old sofas along the highway to watch and wave at passersby. Traditional Russian Orthodox crosses and above-ground grave houses peacefully coexist with colorful native spirit houses, an intriguing mix of cultures.

On the south side of Anchorage is **Turnagain Arm,** where explorer Captain Cook searched for the Northwest Passage. Local lore has it that the arm is so named because Cook entered it repeatedly, only to be turned back by the huge tides, forcing him to turn around again. The tide is so powerful, it sometimes rushes up the arm as a tidal bore—a wall of water that goes up an inlet. Check the weather table in the newspaper for the time and size of the tides, pick a spot along Turnagain Arm between Beluga Point and Girdwood, and imagine the battle between man and nature. Across the arm from Beluga Point, you should also be able to see the buildings of the little gold-mining town of Hope.

The **Reeve Picture Museum** is tucked into the south wall of the Anchorage 5th Avenue shopping mall, across from Nordstrom's (6th Ave. and D St.). Housed in this unlikely setting are hundreds of black-and-white photos of pioneer Alaskan aviators, including Bob Reeve, the glacier pilot and founder of Reeve Aleutian Airways.

The **northern lights** (aurora borealis) are best viewed in late fall and early spring. They are most active when there are solar disturbances, and the lights are usually seen in the sky to the north of Anchorage. City light interferes with viewing the aurora; drive north out of town and pull over at a wayside, drive up to Chugach State Park, or try Government Hill just across the C Street bridge from downtown, if the lights at the port are not illuminated.

Shopping

Native Alaskan handicrafts of all kinds are sold at many of the gift shops downtown. To make sure you are getting the real thing, check for the official polar bear symbol—most Alaskan-made products display it. A hand symbol indicates an article was handcrafted locally by native artisans.

Tlingit and Haida Indian traditional arts and crafts include totem poles, button blankets, wood carvings, and silver jewelry. Athapaskan Indian craftsmen are known for their beadwork, which adorns slippers, headbands, and jewelry. Eskimo handicrafts include ivory, soapstone, and whale baleen baskets. Aleut grass baskets are so fine and tightly woven that some hold water.

Art The **Stonington Gallery** (415 F St., tel. 907/272–1489) carries better known Alaskan artists, both native and non-native. Nancy Stonington is an Alaskan watercolorist. Originals, prints, jewelry, and sculpture are available.

Artique (314 G St., tel. 907/277–1663) carries paintings, prints, and jewelry by Alaskan artists. Both Artique and Stonington can package for shipping.

Books The **Book Cache** (436 W. 5th Ave., tel. 907/277–2723) carries a large Alaska selection up front near the door. There are guides to hikes and wildflowers, historical treatises, explanations of Alaskan place names, and illustrated Alaska books for children. Two diverging views of Alaska by modern authors are *Coming into the Country* by John McPhee (*see* excerpt in Chapter 2) and *Going to Extremes* by Joe McGinness.

Cyrano's (413 D St., tel. 907/274–2599) bookstore has coffee and books on Alaska upstairs and an intelligently chosen selection of mostly paperback books downstairs. This is a bookstore made for browsing, with a chair for those who forget themselves. It's a good spot for a late-night coffee on weekends, when the downstairs turns into a cabaret.

Fur Fur buyers can find merchants on 4th Avenue between A Street and C Street and on 5th and 6th avenues downtown. Not all furs sold in Alaska come from Alaska; ask the furrier to explain the origin of the item. Major department stores in Anchorage also carry furs. During the Fur Rendezvous in February, raw furs can be bought at auction.

Oomingmak (6th Ave. and H St., tel. 907/272–9225), the muskox producers' cooperative, sells items made of qiviut, or muskox fur. Scarves, snoods, and vests are knitted in traditional patterns. The light-brown qiviut is warm, lacy, and light.

Gift Ideas Three local outlets have locally made goods of high quality. The **Alaska Native Arts and Crafts Association** (333 W. 4th Ave., tel.

907/274–2932) sells items from all native groups and carries the best known native carvers, silversmiths, and beadworkers, as well as unknown, but high-quality, artists. The **Anchorage Museum of History and Art** gift shop (7th Ave. and A St., tel. 907/343–6173) carries a small selection of native arts and crafts. The best buys on Native Alaskan artists' work can be had at the **Alaska Native Medical Center** gift shop (3rd Ave. and Gambell St., tel. 907/279–6661). Hours are irregular, but the shop is usually open from 10 AM to 2 PM.

The **Gold Pan** (6th Ave. and F St., tel. 907/272–3626) is an old-fashioned store selling coffee, tea, candy, and imported goods from Russia. Ivory and a small selection of Native Alaskan artifacts are also available. There's always a pot of coffee on, and you can catch up on local gossip at the counter.

Frozen seafood and smoked fish packed for shipping are available from **10th and M Seafoods** (1020 M St., tel. 907/272–3474). You can carry your purchases on your flight back or ship them. Give them a day's lead time to pack your order.

The Imaginarium (725 W. 5th Ave., tel. 907/276–3179) is a good spot to look for educational toys for a child waiting at home.

Shopping Malls Large shopping malls are located at 36th Avenue and the Seward Highway, at the Glenn Highway and Airport Heights Road, and at Dimond Boulevard, half a mile east of the Seward Highway.

Opening and Closing Times

Shops Most Anchorage stores are open from 10 to 9 in the summer. They keep shorter hours in winter.

Banks Weekdays 10–6.

Bars Typically open 8–2.

Restaurants Generally open from 11 to 11. Those serving breakfast open earlier. Long daylight in summer keeps people out until all hours, and the merchants respond accordingly.

Participant Sports

Canoeing/Kayaking Local lakes and lagoons, such as Westchester Lagoon, Goose Lake, and Jewel Lake, offer good boating. Some are stocked with fish as well. Rental boats are available from **Adventures and Delights** (36th Ave. and C St., tel. 907/276–8282) and from **Recreational Equipment Inc.** (2710 Spenard Rd., tel. 907/272–4565).

Fishing Local lakes are stocked with trout. You must have a valid Alaska sportfishing license to fish. Jewel Lake in south Anchorage, Mirror and Fire lakes near Eagle River, and lakes in Chugach State Park all hold fish. Call the **Alaska Department of Fish and Game** (tel. 907/267–2218) for information. Ship Creek downtown is open for fishing on Tuesdays and Wednesdays for five weeks during the summer. Dip-netting season for hooligan along Turnagain Arm and in the mouth of the Twentymile River runs from April 1 through May 31.

Golf Three golf courses are open to the public. **Russian Jack Springs** (tel. 907/333–8338) and the course at **O'Malley Road** (tel. 907/522–3363) are run by the city. Russian Jack has nine holes and no greens. O'Malley has 18 holes and greens. Golf carts and clubs are available for rental. **Moose Run** (tel. 907/428–0056), off the Glenn Highway at Arctic Valley Road, is open to the general public. It has 18 holes and greens. Carts and clubs are available.

Jogging/Biking The coastal trail and other bike trails in Anchorage are used by runners, bikers, skaters, rollerskiers, and walkers. The trail from Westchester Lagoon at the end of 15th Avenue runs two miles to Earthquake Park and another seven miles out to Kincaid Park.

Competitions among amateurs are held for both runners and bikers throughout the summer. Check the newspapers for listings. In addition, the **Municipal Parks and Recreation Department** (620 E. 10th Ave., Anchorage, AK 99501, tel. 907/343–4474) publishes a runner's calendar every summer; it's available for $1.

The **Alaska Women's Run** in early June attracted more than 3,000 participants in 1990—the third-largest women's run in the country. Women of all abilities run this race, many pushing baby carriages. The **Mayor's Midnight Sun Marathon** is also run in June.

Skating **Ben Boeke** ice arena (tel. 907/274–2767) offers open skating. The University of Alaska also has an ice rink open to the public during lunch hour (tel. 907/277–7571). Most public schools and parks also have outdoor skating rinks.

Skiing **Aleyska Ski Resort** (tel. 907/783–2222) at Girdwood, 40 miles south of the city, is a full-service resort with a lodge, condominiums, restaurants, four lifts, and a vertical drop of 2,000 feet. The mountain offers runs for beginners to experts. **Alyeska Property Rental** (tel. 907/783–2155) can set you up in a privately owned cabin or condo fully equipped with bedding and cooking gear. **Arctic Valley** is smaller, but closer; call 907/349–SNOW for conditions and information. Cross-country skiing is also very popular; locals ski **Girdwood Valley** or use the bicycle trails and **Chugach State Park** hiking trails for skiing in winter. Rental skis are available from **Recreational Equipment Inc.** (2710 Spenard Rd., tel. 907/272–4565).

Tennis The park strip at 9th Avenue and C Street has several tennis courts. The **Alaska Club** (5201 E. Tudor Rd., tel. 907/337–9550) honors IRSA (International Racquet Sports Association) cards. The club has a pool, weight room, and racquetball and squash courts. The **Alaska Athletic Club** (630 E. Tudor Rd., tel. 907/562–2460) rents racquetball courts to nonmembers for $10 per person, per hour.

White-Water Rafting Several commercial river runners work in the Anchorage area. **Alaska Whitewater** (tel. 907/337–7238) runs Eagle River (*see* Off the Beaten Track, above). Other companies run rivers farther out of town, offering transportation to and from Anchorage. Check with the Log Cabin Information Center for listings.

Windsurfing **Gary King Sporting Goods** (tel. 907/272–5401) offers windsurfing lessons on Westchester Lagoon. Experienced windsurfers can try the lagoon or Twentymile River, 40 miles south of town on the Seward Highway. Dry suits are a must.

Spectator Sports

Basketball   The University of Alaska hosts the **Great Alaska Shootout** in Anchorage in November. Top NCAA basketball teams from around the country use the shootout as a tune-up for the collegiate season.

Dog-Sled Races   World Championship races are run the second week in February, with three consecutive 25-mile heats through downtown Anchorage, out into the foothills, and back. People line the route with cups of coffee in hand to cheer on their favorite mushers. Some watch the start of the race, then disappear into a warm bar to wait for the mushers to return to 4th Avenue. The races are part of the annual **Fur Rendezvous**, the fourth-largest festival in the United States; pick up a guide to events from the festival office (737 W. 5th Ave., Anchorage 99501, tel. 907/277–8615).

In March, mushers and their dogs compete in the 1,049-mile **Iditarod Trail Sled Dog Race.** The race commemorates the delivery of serum to Nome by dog mushers during the diphtheria epidemic of 1925. The race leaves downtown Anchorage and winds through the Alaska range, across the Interior of Alaska, out to the Bering Sea coast, and on to Nome.

Ice Hockey   The University of Alaska at Anchorage has a Division I NCAA hockey team that draws at least 2,000 loyal fans most weekends at the **Sullivan Arena** (tel. 907/279–2596).

Skiing   In Anchorage's bid to host a future winter Olympics, **Aleyska Ski Resort** (tel. 907/783–2222) has gone out of its way to land major ski competitions like a World Cup giant slalom and the U.S. National Alpine Championships. Check with the resort for a schedule of upcoming races and events.

Dining

Anchorage is a cosmopolitan city with substantial native Alaskan and Asian populations. It is illegal to sell most native Alaskan foods that are hunted for subsistence purposes. You can, however, sample seafood, fiddlehead ferns, and reindeer in local restaurants. Japanese, Korean, and Thai restaurants are common.

This list is divided into restaurants that are within walking distance of downtown hotels and those that require a car trip. Anchorage is a casual city, and you will be welcome in any restaurant in anything but a bathing suit or fishing waders. You might be more comfortable in the more expensive restaurants in a sport coat, but it's very much a personal choice. Anchorage restaurants do not allow you to bring in your own bottle for decanting.

Highly recommended restaurants are indicated with a star ★.

Category	Cost*
Very Expensive	over $40
Expensive	$25–$40

| Moderate | $10–$25 |
| Inexpensive | under $10 |

per person, without drinks or tip

Downtown
American

Elevation 92. This restaurant features mostly intimate booths, all with a view of the inlet. The bar serves ample hors d'oeuvres that could make a meal (oysters in a number of permutations, including Rockefeller, sashimi, and nachos) and champagne by the glass. The restaurant serves seafood, pasta, steaks; try the Halibut Olympia, a favorite local recipe in which halibut filets are baked in a mayonnaise sauce on a bed of onions. *1007 W. 3rd Ave., tel. 907/279–1578. Reservations for dinner are advised. AE, DC, MC, V. No lunch weekends. Expensive.*

Continental

The Crow's Nest. Elegant cuisine is the order of the day, along with the best view in Anchorage—every table has a window of its own. The presentation is elegant but not too fussy, with plenty of starched napery and with brass and hardwood gleaming in the evening light. Local seafood is always on the menu, frequently grilled with julienned vegetables and chanterelles or enoki mushrooms. The lobster bisque is presented with a puff pastry lid in individual ramekins. Tableside flambée dishes are always available; the Chateaubriand for two is carved at table side. A Sunday brunch is available 10 AM to 2 PM. *On top of the Hotel Captain Cook, 5th Ave. and K St., tel. 907/276–6000. Reservations advised. Open 5 PM–11 PM; closed Mon. AE, DC, D, MC, V. Very Expensive.*

The Top of the World. Views from this restaurant atop the Anchorage Hilton look mostly north toward Mt. McKinley. Not all tables have windows, but those away from windows are elevated. Some curvaceous upholstered booths are available; they're a little like those at a Las Vegas dinner show. Etched glass panels flank the entryway. There's an outdoor rooftop bar for views of the sunset. More interesting seasonal additions to the menu have included spicy duck sausage, fiddlehead ferns, miniature vegetables, and white-chocolate mousse. *Anchorage Westward Hilton at 3rd Ave. and E. St., tel. 907/265–7111. Reservations advised. AE, DC, D, MC, V. Sunday brunch 10 AM–2 PM; dinner daily 6 PM–11 PM. Very Expensive.*

Deli

The Downtown Deli. The food is classic delicatessen fare, such as pastrami sandwiches and chopped chicken liver. Lunch and dinner includes Alaska touches, like grilled halibut and salmon. The chicken soup comes with optional kreplach, matzo ball, or noodles; it's dark and rich. Breakfasts range from omelets to blintzes. Wooden booths offer privacy; if you don't want it, sit out front at the sidewalk tables. Locals bring their Sunday newspaper and linger over coffee here. Service is efficient and cheery. *525 W. 4th Ave., tel. 907/276–7116. AE, D, MC, V. Open 6 AM–10 PM. Inexpensive.*

Fried Chicken

The Lucky Wishbone. This old Anchorage restaurant serves great fried chicken. Lots of old-timers are regulars here. It's got brightly lit formica tables, and the waitresses never seem to have a bad day. An all-white-meat order comes with just the good part of the breast, only the wishbone and no ribs. There is a no-smoking policy here. *1033 E. 5th Ave., tel. 907/272–3454. Cash or checks only. Open 10 AM–midnight; closed Sun. Inexpensive.*

Dining

Club Paris, **19**
Crow's Nest, **11**
Double Musky, **28**
Downtown Deli, **18**
Elevation 92, **10**
Garden of Eatin', **3**
Hogg Brothers'
Cafe, **4**
Kumagoro, **14**
Lucky Wishbone, **26**
Maharajah, **16**
Marx Brothers'
Cafe, **22**
Mexico in Alaska, **29**
Sack's Cafe, **15**
Simon and Seafort's
Saloon and Grill, **8**
Sourdough Mining
Company, **27**
Thai Cuisine, **13**
Top of the World, **21**

Lodging

Anchorage Hilton, **17**
Anchorage Hotel, **20**
Anchorage
International Hostel, **6**
Best Western Barratt
Inn, **2**
Clarion Hotel
Anchorage, **1**
Days Inn, **24**
Holiday Inn, **23**
Hotel Captain
Cook, **12**
Inlet Towers, **5**
Sheraton
Anchorage, **25**
Voyager Hotel, **7**
Westmark Hotel, **9**

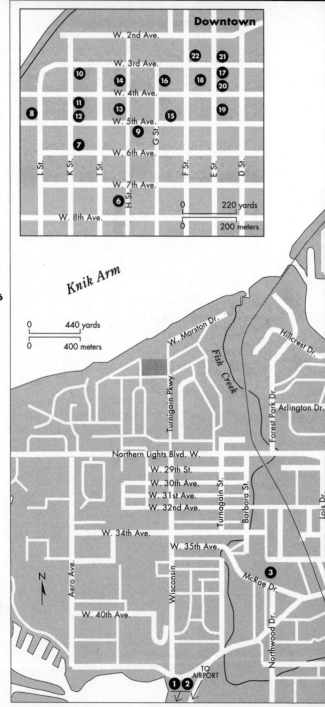

SEE DETAIL
MAP
AT LEFT

W. 2nd Ave.
W. 3rd Ave.
W. 4th Ave.
W. 5th Ave.

Viking Dr.
W. 1st Ave.
E. 1st Ave.
E. 3rd Ave.
E. 4th Ave.
E. 5th Ave.
E. 6th Ave.
E. 7th Ave.

Post Rd.
Hyder St.
Juneau

23
24
25
26

K St.
I St.
H St.
G St.
F St.
E St.
D St.

W. 9th Ave.
W. 10th Ave.
W. 11th Ave.
W. 12th Ave.
W. 13th Ave.
W. 14th Ave.
W. 15th Ave.

E. 8th Ave.
E. 9th Ave.
E. 10th Ave.
E. 11th Ave.
E. 12th Ave.
E. 13th Ave.
E. 14th Ave.
E. 15th Ave.

Karluk St.
Latouche St.
Medfra St.
Nelchina

C St.
B St.

Cordova St.
Denali
Eagle

P St.
N St.
L St.

5

*Westchester
Lagoon*

E. 16th Ave.

Chester Creek

Artic Blvd.

A St.

Eagle St.

Redwood St.

4

W. Fireweed La.

Spenard Rd.

W. 27th Ave.

Benson Blvd.

Minnesota Dr.

Bering St.
Eureka St.

32nd Ave.

Benson Blvd.

Denali St.
E. 33rd Ave.

W. 36th Ave.

E. 36th Ave.

Spenard Rd.

Dr.

W. 40th Ave.

Seward Hwy.

1

Tudor Rd.

Frontage Rd.

27 **28** **29**

Japanese **Kumagoro.** Japan Air Lines crew members always seem to be here, which says a lot about the restaurant's authentic presentation. There is a sleek new sushi bar. A Japanese-style breakfast is offered; it's salmon teriyaki, fried eggs, seaweed, pickles, and rice. The best items on the menu are the salmon teriyaki and the teriyaki steak dinner, a mound of steak strips grilled and brought still hissing to your table. They come with miso soup and salad. The house dressing of rice vinegar and oil is subtly flavored with ginger. Very inexpensive noodle soups are available. The Shabu Shabu dinner is a boiling stock pot brought to your table in which you cook meats and vegetables. *533 W. 4th Ave., tel. 907/272–9905. AE, MC, V. Open 9 AM–10 PM. Moderate.*

Nouvelle American **The Marx Brothers' Cafe.** The little frame house on the bluff
★ was built in 1916 and refurbished by the three "Marx Brothers"—Jack Amon, Van Hale, and Ken Brown. These are tight quarters, but locals love the chance to run into friends and talk food and wine with the owners. Chef Jack Amon's *melitzanosalata* appetizer is an Anchorage favorite—it's an eggplant spread served up with Greek olives and pita bread. The seafood mousse is a light pâté of smoked sturgeon, smoked salmon, and Maine lobster. Grilled local seafood and wild game are usually available; the caramelized rack of lamb is another favorite. Van Hale makes a garlic-rich, not-too-tart Caesar salad at table side. The wine list is extensive. *327 W. 3rd Ave., tel. 907/278–2133. Reservations recommended. AE, DC, MC, V. Open 6 PM with seatings for dinner until 9:30 PM; closed Sun. Expensive.*

Sack's Cafe. A cool modern cafe offering light new American food. They use trendy ingredients like chevre (goat cheese) and interesting combinations of ethnic cuisines, like pasta with a Mexican mole sauce. Their salads are large enough for a light meal. Desserts include a decadent chocolate gateau. *625 W. 5th Ave., tel. 907/276–3546. AE, MC, V. Open 11–9 and Sun. brunch 11 AM–2:30 PM. Moderate.*

Seafood **Simon and Seafort's Saloon and Grill.** The high ceilings and big windows overlooking Cook Inlet light up the brass-and-wood interior. Waitresses in long black dresses and frilly white aprons add a Gay '90s flavor. The attraction here is seafood. Fish is blackened, grilled, fried, or treated any way you like it. Try the grilled halibut with ginger lime butter. The menu also offers beef and pasta. For dessert or as a late night snack in the bar, try the brandy ice. It's vanilla ice cream whipped up with brandy. *420 L St., tel. 907/274–3502. Reservations recommended. AE, MC, V. Lunch 11:15 AM–2:30 PM; dinner 5 PM–10 PM. Closed Sun. lunch. Moderate.*

Steak **The Club Paris.** It's dark and smoky up front in the bar, where old-time Anchorage folks have met for a drink and a chat for decades. The restaurant in back serves big, tender, flavorful steaks of all kinds. No vegetables here except huge baked potatoes with optional cheddar cheese sauce. There's halibut and fried prawns on the menu, but the real attraction is the beef. If you forget to make reservations, have a drink up front in the bar area and order the hors d'oeuvres tray; it's a sampler of steak, cheese, and prawns and could be a meal for two people. *417 W. 5th Ave., tel. 907/277–6332. Reservations should be made early in the day. AE, DC, D, MC, V. Open 11:30 AM–2:30 PM and 5 PM on. Moderate.*

Thai **Thai Cuisine.** Lines formed for dinner every night when the restaurant opened in 1987. Things have calmed down, but Anchorage still loves this airy white restaurant. Seating is on benches and white lawn chairs, and Thai paper umbrellas sway overhead. If you are new to Thai food, stick to dishes with no more than one star on the menu; more stars will be too spicy. Try the Pad Thai, a noodle mélange with egg, chicken, shrimp, and peanuts. The kang kew warn is boneless chicken stewed in coconut milk. Appetizers include beef satay (skewered grilled beef) with peanut sauce and corn cakes with hot sweet dipping sauce. Thai iced tea is bright red, served with lots of sweet cream. *444 H St., tel. 907/277–8424. Reservations not needed. AE, MC, V. Open Mon.–Sat. 11 AM–10 PM and Sun. 5 PM–10 PM. Moderate.*

Greater Anchorage **Sourdough Mining Company.** They offer up barbecued baby
American back ribs, chicken, and pork. This is a fun place to take kids because it looks like the inside of an old mining-camp mess hall. Big fans revolve overhead and big tables sit end to end. The corn fritters are served hot with honey butter. It's located right off the Seward Highway on Juneau Street and International Airport Road. There's no off ramp there, so take the Tudor Road off ramp and cross Tudor onto the frontage road to get there. *Juneau St. and International Airport Rd., tel. 907/563–2272. Reservations accepted but not necessary. AE, DC, D, MC, V. Open weekdays 11 AM–11 PM, Sat. noon–11, Sun. 10–11. Moderate.*

The Hogg Brothers' Cafe. This is a funky little lunch counter with a few tables squeezed in. Loud rock music is the cook's favorite, and it had better be yours, too. It's run by aging hippies, and all the help are relatives or friends. The breakfast menu includes El Breakfast de Roberta—scrambled eggs on English muffins surrounded by home fries, all topped with onions, green chilies, and cheese sauce. The burgers are ample. A few tables are available in the back of the bar next door. *2421 Spenard Rd., tel. 907/276–9649. No reservations and no credit cards. Open 8–4. Inexpensive.*

Cajun **The Double Musky.** This is one of the best restaurants in Alas-
★ ka. Make that the West Coast. Many Anchorage residents take the 40-mile drive down just for dinner. The restaurant is casual, with wooden floors and walls draped with souvenirs from trips to Mardi Gras. Outside, huge Sitka spruce are framed by the windows. The food is mostly Cajun, like blackened salmon and boneless chicken breasts with Cajun sausage stuffing and white sauce. The steaks are huge and tender. The béarnaise sauce is smooth and redolent of tarragon. The appetizers are extensive—try the coconut batter fried salmon with plum sauce. The biggest attraction, though, is the Double Musky pie. It's chocolate, it's got pecans, it's gooey, and it's out of this world. *Located in Girdwood: Exit the Glacier Hwy. (heading towards the Alyeska ski area) on Crow Creek Rd., turn left on Crow Creek Rd.—the restaurant is a half-mile ahead on the left-hand side; tel. 907/783–2822. No reservations. MC, V. No checks. Open Tues.–Thurs. 5 PM–10 PM and Fri.–Sun. 4 PM–10 PM; closed Mon. Expensive.*

Mexican **Mexico in Alaska.** The best Mexican food in town is served here; this is ungreasy, subtle fare. Owner Maria Elena Ball makes everyone her friend, particularly young children; for them, the à la carte side of the menu is a good choice. The *chilaquiles* is a tortilla casserole with chocolate mole sauce. Her *entremesa de queso* is a platter of melted cheese with chilies served with homemade tortilla chips. *7305 Old Seward Hwy., tel. 907/349-1528. No reservations necessary. AE, MC, V. Open weekends 11 AM–10 PM; Sat. noon–10 PM; Sun. 4 PM–9 PM. Inexpensive.*

Steak **The Garden of Eatin'.** Opened in 1951 in the quonset hut it still occupies, this restaurant is popular with Anchorage old-timers. The inside is painted a trendy peach, and somebody's mother-crocheted curtains hang in every window. The beef here is excellent—tender, moist, and carefully handled. Entrees come with mounds of fries or real mashed potatoes. This is real home-cooked food. *2502 McRae St., tel. 907/248-3663. AE, MC, V. Open 6 PM–10 PM; closed Sun. and Mon. Moderate.*

Lodging

Most hotels in Anchorage are located either downtown or near the airport. In summer, advance reservations are a must for the major hotels. The selections offered here vary in price, but all offer good value in their price range. All hotels are subject to an additional 8% hotel tax. Hotels in downtown and the airport area (known as Spenard) are listed in descending order by price.

The most highly recommended properties are indicated by a star ★.

Category	Cost*
Very Expensive	over $140
Expensive	$90–$140
Moderate	$60–$90
Inexpensive	under $60

per double room

Downtown
Very Expensive
Anchorage Hilton. The Hilton's ample lobby is decorated in soft pink and green throughout, with big chandeliers that look like glacier ice. The reception desk is paneled with brass and jade. Its old tower withstood the 1964 earthquake, and both towers were renovated extensively in 1987. Rooms looking north and east have the best views. *500 W. 3rd Ave., 99501, tel. 907/272-7411 or 800/327-0329. 500 rooms. Facilities: roof-level pool, athletic club with exercise equipment, sauna, Jacuzzi, 2 restaurants. AE, DC, D, MC, V.*

★ **Hotel Captain Cook.** This hotel takes up a full city block. Its three towers were built from 1964 to 1978. The decor recalls Captain Cook's voyages in the South Pacific. Teak paneling lines most public area walls. Rooms have teak furniture and muted taupe, maroon, and burnt-orange furnishings. *5th Ave. and K St., 99501, tel. 907/276-6000 or 800/843-1950. 564 rooms. Facilities: boutiques, gift shops, barber shop, hair salon, 4 restaurants, full athletic club with pool, racquetball courts, weight-training equipment, saunas, steam rooms. AE, DC, D, MC, V.*

Sheraton Anchorage. The Sheraton sits on a full city block on the east side of downtown. The glass-canopied lobby boasts a jade staircase and acres of cream-color marble that is edged with brass. Guest rooms are subdued dark green and burnt orange. Tlingit Indian art prints hang in most rooms. The furniture is teak with brass corners. The hotel is about 7 blocks from downtown attractions and 3 blocks from the museum. *401 E. 5th Ave., 99501, tel. 907/276–8700 or 800/325–3535. 375 rooms. Facilities: 2 restaurants, lounge, 24-hr room service, athletic club with sauna, steam, and exercise equipment. AE, DC, D, MC, V.*

Westmark Hotel. The Westmark is a 14-story hotel built in 1971 and renovated in 1987. The lobby has parquet floors, pink-and-teal area rugs, and the same glacial chandeliers as the Hilton. The rooms are calm colonial blue, with dark teak furniture and chintz bedspreads. *720 W. 5th Ave., 99501, tel. 907/274–6631 or 800/544–0970. Facilities: coffee shop, 24-hr room service, penthouse cocktail lounge and restaurant, balconies on every room. AE, DC, D, MC, V.*

Expensive **Anchorage Hotel.** The little Anchorage Hotel building has been around since 1916, and it is called "the only hotel in Anchorage with charm" by experienced travelers. It was remodeled and reopened in 1988. The lobby has a calm Victorian feel, with pink and gray furniture, creamy white walls, and lace curtains. Coffee and pastries are served here every morning. The original sinks and tubs and window casements were restored. Upstairs hallways are lined with old photos of Anchorage. Third-floor suites cost $10 more than rooms, but each comes with a sitting area and wet bar. Senior citizens get a 10% discount. Rear rooms look at the alley. *330 E St., 99501, tel. 907/272–4553 or 800/544–0988. Facilities: near downtown restaurants and shopping. AE, DC, MC, V.*

Days Inn. The Days Inn is an aluminum-skinned boxy building, with Spartan but spacious rooms. The lobby is a small tiled room with area rugs. Rooms on the first floor along Cordova Street will be noisy. *321 E. 5th Ave., 99501, tel. 907/276–7226 or 800/325–2525. 116 rooms. Facilities: exercise room, 24-hr restaurant, courtesy van, 24-hr room service, nonsmoking rooms. AE, DC, D, MC, V.*

Holiday Inn. The Holiday Inn offers predictable style and service. It's a good place to stay during the Fur Rendezvous; ask for a room on the 4th Avenue side and watch the sled-dog races from your window. All other times of the year, these rooms are the least desirable because of the noise of 4th Avenue late nighters. The rooms are mauve, coral, and deep green. *239 W. 4th Ave., 99501, tel. 907/279–8671 or 800/465–4329. 252 rooms. Facilities: restaurant open 6 AM–11 PM, bar, indoor swimming pool. AE, DC, D, MC, V.*

★ **Quality Inns Tower Suites.** This 14-story building in a residential area offers apartment suites for very reasonable rates. Two couples can stay here for the price of one in a downtown hotel room. The building was built in 1952 and renovated in 1987. Corner rooms have expansive views. There's a little grocery right across the street. *1200 L St., 99501, tel. 907/276–0110 or 800/544–0786. 140 suites. Facilities: sauna, weight-training room, laundromat, beauty salon. Near bike trails and Westchester Lagoon. AE, DC, D, MC, V.*

The Voyager Hotel. This small hotel catering to business travelers offers a good value. It's four stories high, and all the rooms are the same: queen-size beds and a sofa bed that turns into a double bed. Upstairs, east-side rooms have views of the inlet. Full kitchens, hair dryers, and cable TV in every room. Dark plum carpets, floral bedspreads. *501 K St., 99501, tel. 907/277–9501. Facilities: restaurant (serves dinner only). AE, DC, D, MC, V.*

Inexpensive **Anchorage International Hostel.** The hostel is downtown on H Street, a block and a half from the bus depot. It's a cinder-block building, with the Alaska Center for the Environment next door. Guests share a kitchen and household chores. Laundry facilities are available. The furniture is hand-me-downs. Reservations are not necessary, except for the three private double rooms. Other rooms for two couples are also available. Families could share a six-bed room. Other rooms are dormitory-style. *700 H St., 99501, tel. 907/276–3635. Accommodates 80 guests. Facilities: kitchen, laundromat, locked storage area. No credit cards or out-of-town checks. Traveler's checks accepted.*

Spenard/Airport **Clarion Hotel Anchorage.** The Clarion sits on Lake Hood, the
Very Expensive world's largest float-plane base. You can watch the planes come
★ and go from the restaurant. The lobby resembles a gentleman's hunting and fishing lodge with its stone fireplace and trophy heads and mounted fish on every wall. Rooms have conservative rosewood furnishings, teal rugs, and cloud-print bedspreads. Nonsmoking and special rooms for handicapped persons are available. The handicapped-access rooms have wider doors and lower fixtures. *4800 Spenard Rd., 99517, tel. 907/243–2300 or 800/544–0784. 248 rooms. Facilities: 24-hr room service, exercise room with Lifecycles and Jacuzzi, bar, gift shop, laundry and valet services, airport shuttle. On red double-decker bus route. Bicycles available for rental. AE, DC, D, MC, V.*

Expensive **Best Western Barratt Inn.** The Barratt, near Lake Hood, has four buildings: the older buildings (no. 1 and no. 2) offer traditional motel decor, in pleasant pastels with outdoor walkways; buildings no. 3 and no. 4 across the street are newer and more high-tech. The old buildings were renovated in 1988. Avoid rooms next to noisy Spenard Road. *4616 Spenard Rd., 99503, tel. 907/243–3131 and 800/221–7550. 210 rooms. Facilities: restaurant, washers and dryers, hair dryer in each room. Courtesy van to airport and downtown. On red double-decker bus route. AE, DC, D, MC, V.*

Bed-and-Breakfast **Alaska Private Lodgings** (4631 Caravelle Dr., Anchorage 99502, tel. 907/248–2292) has 43 properties in Anchorage and other parts of the state. Prices range from $50 to $150 for a double room with breakfast. Some homes have fireplaces in the room. Urban and rural locations are available. Advance reservations are recommended.

The Arts

The lobby box office of the **Performing Arts Center** (tel. 907/343–1948) sells tickets to a variety of productions and is a good all-around source of information. Hours are weekdays 10 AM–5 PM during the winter—the height of the cultural season. For recorded information on cultural events of the week, call 907/276–ARTS.

Theater Call the new downtown Performing Arts Center for a schedule of current productions and for ticket reservations. Community and student productions from the **Theater Guild, University of**

Anchorage Theater, and the **Anchorage Community Theater** can be energetic and winning. See the local newspapers for reviews.

Opera **The Anchorage Opera** produces two or three operas during its September-to-March season. The Performing Arts Center box office sells tickets.

Nightlife

Anchorage does not shut down when it gets dark. Bars here—and throughout Alaska—open early (as in "AM") and close at 2 AM.

Bars and **Chilkoot Charlie's** (2435 Spenard Rd., tel. 907/272–1010). A
Nightclubs huge timber building with sawdust floors, very loud music, and rowdy customers. This place is where younger Alaskans go to get crazy. Not for the faint of heart.

Club Paris (417 W. 5th Ave., tel. 907/277–6332). Lots of old-timers favor this dark, smoky bar. Once the classiest place in downtown Anchorage, with its Paris mural behind the bar and French street lamps hanging behind the bar. The glamour has gone, but the faithful have not. They play mostly swing on the jukebox, and the bartender knows how to mix a martini.

Fletcher's (5th Ave. and K St., tel. 907/276–6000). The Captain Cook's bar is decorated in leaded glass and dark wood to resemble an English pub. Like those of the other hotel bars (e.g., the Hilton and Sheraton), the atmosphere is discreet and genteel.

Pioneer Club (739 W. 4th Ave., tel. 907/276–9354). A linoleum and fluorescent hall with pool tables. Not much to look at, but the folks are friendly, the prices affordable, and the spirit genuinely Alaskan. The building rolled through the big 1964 earthquake; most of its patrons did, too.

Simon and Seafort's (420 L St., tel. 907/274–3502). The "in" place for the 30-something crowd. The views of Cook Inlet are fine and you can watch local lawyers trying to hustle one another. The high ceilings, wood wainscoting, and brass fixtures lend a Gay '90s look to the place. There is a special Scotch menu and an extensive selection of imported beers.

Once an old Irish bar, **F Street Station** (325 F St., tel. 907/272–5196) now caters to the yuppie crowd.

Comedy **Fly by Night Club.** Mr. Whitekeys is the proprietor of this self-proclaimed "sleazy Spenard nightclub." Every summer he produces a revue called the Whale Fat Follies, with tacky Alaska jokes, accomplished singing, and the boogie-woogie piano of Mr. Whitekeys himself. Locals and tourists alike vie for tickets, and line up on stand-by at the door if they can't get reservations. It's a good idea to reserve several days in advance. *3300 Spenard Rd., tel. 907/279–7726. Open Tues.–Sat. at 8 PM.*

Live Music Most of the bigger hotels have rock bands playing in at least one of their bars. The **Fly by Night Club** (3300 Spenard Rd., tel. 907/279–7726) serves up rock, boogie, Cajun, jazz, and blues on nights when the Whale Fat Follies isn't playing. **Chilkoot Charlie's** (2435 Spenard Rd., tel. 907/272–1010) is the place to go for pounding rock.

Midnight Express (2610 Spenard Rd., tel. 907/279–1861). Your best bet for good local rock bands.

7 Southeast Alaska

By Mike Miller

Updated by
Barbara Hodgin

Southeast, as Alaskans call the region, stretches below the state like the tail of a kite. It is a world of massive glaciers, fjords, and snowcapped peaks. Thousands of islands are blanketed with lush stands of spruce, hemlock, and cedar. Bays, coves, lakes of all sizes, and swift, icy rivers provide some of the continent's best fishing grounds—and scenery as majestic and unspoiled as any in North America.

Like anywhere else, the region has its drawbacks. For one thing, it rains a lot. If you plan to spend a week or more here, you can count on showers during at least a few of those days. Loyal Southeasterners simply throw on a light slicker and shrug off the rain. Their attitude is philosophical: without the rain, there would be no forests, no lakes, and no streams running with world-class salmon and trout, no healthy populations of brown and black bear, moose, deer, mountain goat, and wolves.

Another disadvantage—or advantage, depending on your point of view—is an almost total lack of connecting roads between the area's communities. To fill this void, Alaskans created the Marine Highway System of fast, frequent passenger and vehicle ferries. The ships, complete with staterooms, observation decks, cocktail lounges, and heated, glass-enclosed solariums, connect Seattle and Prince Rupert, B.C., with Southeast's Ketchikan, Wrangell, Petersburg, Sitka, Juneau, Haines, and Skagway. Smaller Bush Route vessels connect more remote towns and villages.

Beyond the ferries, there are the big cruise ships that ply Southeast waters, about 20 or so of them during the height of the summer. Regular jet service also provides access from the lower 48 states and from mainland Alaska to the north. Closer to the lower 48 states than any other Alaskan region, Southeast is therefore the least costly to reach.

The native peoples you'll meet in the Southeast coastal region are Tlingit, Haida, and Tsimshian (pronounced KLIN-git, HY-da, and SIM-see-EN) Indians. These peoples, like their coastal neighbors in British Columbia, continue a culture rich in totemic art forms, including deeply carved poles, masks, baskets, and ceremonial objects.

There are, by the way, only a few Alaskan Eskimos in the region, and those who do live here are relative newcomers, as are other immigrants of European, Filipino, and African descent.

Southeast Alaska is a busy and bustling region; it's a place of commercial fishermen, loggers, pulp-mill workers, government civil servants, modern-day miners, merchants, and white-collar professionals. It's a region vastly different from South Central or Interior Alaska, just as those regions differ dramatically from Alaska's Arctic or Canada's Yukon.

Because of its location, you might find Southeast a logical place to begin your Alaskan odyssey.

Essential Information

Getting Around

By Plane **Alaska Airlines** (tel. 800/426–0333) operates several flights daily from Seattle and dozens of other Pacific Coast and southwestern cities to Ketchikan, Wrangell, Petersburg, Sitka, Glacier Bay, and Juneau. The carrier connects Juneau to the north with Yakutat, Cordova, Anchorage, Fairbanks, Nome, Kotzebue, and Prudhoe Bay. **Delta Airlines** (tel. 800/241–4141) has at least one flight daily from Seattle to Juneau and from Juneau to Fairbanks.

By Car Only Skagway and Haines, in the northern Panhandle, and tiny little Hyder, just across the border from Stewart, B.C., are accessible by conventional highway. To reach Skagway or Haines, take the Alaska Highway to the Canadian Yukon's Whitehorse or Haines Junction, respectively, then drive the Klondike Highway or Haines Highway southwest to the Alaska Panhandle. You can reach Hyder on British Columbia's Cassiar Highway, which can be reached, in turn, from Highway 16 just north of Prince Rupert.

By Ferry From the south, the **Alaska Marine Highway System** (tel. 800/642–0066) operates stateroom-equipped vehicle and passenger ferries from Bellingham, WA, and from Prince Rupert, B.C. The vessels call at Ketchikan, Wrangell, Petersburg, Juneau, Haines, and Skagway, and they connect with smaller vessels serving Bush communities. One of the smaller ferries also operates between Hyder and Ketchikan. In the summer, staterooms on the ferries are always sold out before sailing time; reserve months in advance. Early reservations are also highly recommended for vehicle space.

BC Ferries (1112 Fort St., Victoria, B.C., Canada V8V 4V2, tel. 604/669–1211) operates similar passenger and vehicle ferries from Vancouver Island, B.C., to Prince Rupert.

By Train At present, Southeast Alaska's only railroad, the **White Pass and Yukon Route** (tel. 800/343–7373), operates round-trip summer sightseeing excursions between Skagway and the White Pass summit and Fraser, B.C., a mountain-climbing, cliff-hanging route of 28 miles each way. Bus connections are available at Fraser to Whitehorse, Yukon.

By Bus Year-round service between Whitehorse and Anchorage (including Fairbanks) is available from **Alaska Direct Bus Lines** (Box 501, Anchorage, 99510, tel. 907/277–6652 or 800/328–9730). Service to and from Minneapolis is also available most of the year. For Minneapolis information call 612/228–1009 or 800/328–9730. **Gray Line of Alaska** (tel. 800/544–2206) offers summertime connections from these same cities to Anchorage, Fairbanks, and other stops en route. **Alaska-Yukon Motorcoaches** (tel. 800/637–3334) offers similar seasonal service between Haines and Anchorage. Though it's a long ride, you can travel **Canadian Greyhound** (tel. 604/662–3222) from Vancouver or Edmonton to Whitehorse and make connections there with Gray Line buses to Southeast Alaska.

By Cruise Ship Southeast waters attract cruise ships varying in size from 65 feet, with capacity for a few dozen passengers, to nearly 800 feet, with beds for more than a thousand (*see* Chapter 3 for itineraries, costs, and a review of the fleet).

Scenic Drives   The descent (or ascent, depending on which direction you're traveling) from the high, craggy Canadian mountain country to the Southeast Alaska coast makes both the **Klondike Highway** into Skagway or the **Haines Highway** to Haines especially memorable traveling. At the top of the respective passes, vegetation is sparse and pockets of snow are often present, even in summertime. The scenery is stark, with mountains and major features silhouetted sharply against frequently blue skies. As you near the saltwater coast of the Panhandle, the forest cover becomes tall, thick, and evergreen. Both drives are worth an excursion, even if you don't intend to drive any farther than the Canadian border and return. (*See* Car Rentals in Chapter 1 if you need to rent a vehicle.)

Every city, town, and village in Southeast Alaska has one or more waterfront drives that take in hustling, bustling dock scenes and tranquil bays and beaches, and they also offer the possibility of seeing wildlife. Inquire at local information centers.

Guided Tours

Alaska Sightseeing Tours (tel. 800/367–3334) and **Bendixen Yacht Cruises** (tel. 206/285–5999) offer cruises through the Panhandle in vessels small enough to visit secluded coves and bays such as the iceberg-clogged waters of LeConte Bay near Petersburg.

Yacht charters—for sightseeing, fishing, (limited) whale watching, and simply cruising—are available in every community in Southeast Alaska for trips that range from a half-day around one community to more than a week around the whole Panhandle. Only a few are listed below. Contact visitor information offices for additional names, addresses, and phone numbers.

Haines   **Alaska Nature Tours** (907/766–2876) conducts bird-watching and natural history tours to the Bald Eagle Preserve.
Alaska Rafting and Wildlife Tours (tel. 907/766–3195) packages float trips through the Chilkat Bald Eagle Preserve, home of the largest concentration of bald eagles in the world. Tours include viewing of brown bears, wolves, and other wildlife.
Alaska Sightseeing Tours (tel. 907/766–2435 or 800/637–3334). Visitors travel by motor coach to historic Fort Seward, the Alaska Indian Arts Center, Sheldon Museum, and the bald eagle viewing grounds.
Haines Street Car Company (tel. 907/766–2819) offers city tours of Haines, Fort Seward, Chilkoot and Chilkat state parks, and the Chilkat Bald Eagle Preserve. It also provides bus service between the state ferry terminal and town.

Juneau   **Alaska Discovery Tours** (tel. 907/586–1911) offers guided Southeast Alaska wilderness trips by kayak or canoe in Glacier Bay, Yakutat, and Admiralty Island.
Alaska Rainforest Treks (tel. 907/463–3466) schedules daily, escorted hikes on trails around Juneau. Terrain includes mountains, glaciers, forests, and ocean shores. Food and rain gear provided.
Alaska Travel Adventures (tel. 907/789–0052) packages a half-

day guided raft trip (there's *almost* white water) down the Mendenhall River; includes mid-trip snack of Alaska smoked salmon, reindeer sausage, cheeses, apple cider, and an alcoholic brew called Mendenhall Madness.

Alaska Sightseeing Tours (tel. 907/586–6300 or 800/637–3334) and **Gray Line of Alaska** (tel. 907/586–3773 or 800/544–2206) both offer motor-coach sightseeing tours of Juneau, Mendenhall Glacier, and other points of interest.

Alaska Up Close (tel. 907/789–9544) provides custom sightseeing tours in small vans, specializing in natural history and fine art.

Juneau Carriage Company (tel. 907/586–2121) offers Southeast Alaska's newest horse-drawn carriage tour, 45 minutes through and around downtown Juneau's historic district.

Phillips Cruises & Tours (tel. 907/276–8023 or 800/544–0529) schedules daily six-hour cruises from Juneau to the twin glaciers at Tracy Arm fjord. Also offers nightly dinner cruise in waters around Alaska's capital city.

Ptarmigan Ptransport and Ptours (tel. 907/789–5179) has sightseeing tours to Juneau, neighboring Douglas, and Mendenhall Glacier in a bright red double-decker bus.

Temsco Helicopters (tel. 907/789–9501) pioneered helicopter sightseeing over Mendenhall Glacier with an actual touchdown and a chance to romp on the glacier. **Era Helicopters** (tel. 907/586–2030) offers a similar quality experience.

Ketchikan **Alaska Sightseeing Tours** (tel. 907/225–2740 or 800/637–3334) offers sightseeing motor coach tours of downtown Ketchikan, Totem Bight State Historical Park, and Totem Heritage Center. Boat tours of Misty Fjords and the Inside Passage are also available.

Gray Line of Alaska (tel. 907/225–5930 or 800/544–2206) offers a city tour comparable to the above, plus a day tour to nearby Annette Island and the Tsimshian Indian community of Metlakatla.

Captain Ted Pratt (Bar Harbor, Box 9419, Ketchikan 99901, tel. 907/225–0055) schedules tours throughout the Panhandle aboard the 70-foot *Midnight Sun*, surely one of the most luxurious cruise yachts in Southeast Alaska. (Would you believe a *wood-burning fireplace* in the main lounge?)

Outdoor Alaska (tel. 907/225–6044) provides cruise or cruise-fly day-long excursions from downtown Ketchikan to Misty Fjords National Monument, a wilderness of steep-walled fjords, mountains, and islands. Harbor cruises of the Ketchikan waterfront are also available.

Petersburg **LeConte Cruises** (Box 913, Petersburg, 99833, tel. 907/772–4790) offers yacht tours for sightseeing, photography, and fishing.

Pacific Wing, Inc. (tel. 907/772–9258) gets high marks from locals for its flightseeing tours over LeConte Glacier.

Sitka **Alaska Travel Adventures** (tel. 907/789–0052) operates boat and motorized Zodiac raft excursions to a seal rookery and bird refuge; en route, see porpoises, sea lions, and (if you're lucky) whales.

Baidarka Boats (tel. 907/747–8996) rents sea kayaks and offers guided custom trips in the island-dotted waters around Sitka.

Prewitt Enterprises (tel. 907/747–8443) meets state ferries and provides short city tours while vessels are in port; stops at Sitka National Historical Park, Sheldon Jackson Museum, and downtown shopping area. Also offers more inclusive three-hour sightseeing tours that visit St. Michael's Cathedral, Old Sitka, Castle Hill, and old Russian cemetery.

Skagway **Alaska Sightseeing Tours** (tel. 907/983–2828 or 800/637–3334) and **Gray Line of Alaska** (tel. 907/983–2241 or 800/544–2206) provide motor-coach tours through Skagway's historic district, Gold-rush Cemetery (where frontier "bad guy" Soapy Smith lies buried), and the trailhead of the Chilkoot Trail to the Yukon gold fields.

Gold Rush Tours (tel. 907/983–2289) provides a spectacular drive across the Canadian border to a picnic in the world's smallest desert. This is no joke—there really is a tiny desert a few miles north of Carcross, Yukon.

Skagway Hack (tel. 907/983–2472) offers horse-drawn transportation through the historic district of Klondike National Historical Park, also trailhead or waterfront tours.

Wrangell **Aqua Sports** (tel. 907/874–3811) specializes in waterborne glacier tours, river running, photo excursions, and fishing.

TH Charters (tel. 907/874–3455) provides a fast-pace jet-boat ride into the Stikine River wilderness country to Shakes Glacier, Shakes Hot Springs, and other historic and natural attractions.

Important Addresses and Numbers

Tourist Information **Southeast Alaska Tourism Council** (Box 710, Juneau 99802, tel. 907/586–4777).

Gustavus Visitors Association (Box 167, Gustavus 99826, tel. 907/697–2358).

Glacier Bay National Park and Preserve (Gustavus 99826, tel. 907/697–2230).

Haines/Fort Seward Visitor Information Center (2nd Ave. near Willard St., tel. 907/766–2202). Open June–August, 8 AM–8 PM daily; winter hours posted.

Juneau Convention and Visitors Bureau (76 Egan Dr., Suite 140, Juneau 99801, tel. 907/586–1737) and **Davis Log Cabin Information Center** (134 3rd Ave., tel. 907/586–2201). Information also available at the kiosk on the cruise ship dock, downtown at Marine Park.

Ketchikan Visitors Bureau (131 Front St., Ketchikan 99901, tel. 907/225–6166). Open daily May 15–September 30, 8–5; weekdays in winter 8–5.

Petersburg Chamber of Commerce Visitor Center (221 Harbor Way, Box 649, Petersburg 99833, tel. 907/772–3646). Located downtown in the Harbormaster building overlooking the boat harbor.

Sitka Convention and Visitors Bureau (Box 1226, Sitka 99835, tel. 907/747–5940). Open weekdays 8–5 and when cruise ships are in port. **The Greater Sitka Chamber of Commerce** (Box 638, Sitka 99835, tel. 907/747–7816). Open weekdays 9–5. Both are located in the Centennial Building on Harbor Drive downtown.

Skagway Convention and Visitors Bureau (City Hall, 7th Ave. and Spring St., Box 415, Skagway 99840, tel. 907/983–2854). Open 8:30–noon and 1–5.

The Klondike Gold Rush National Historical Park visitor center (2nd Ave. and Broadway, Skagway 99840, tel. 907/983–2921)—which has lots of information on the city as well—is housed in the old White Pass and Yukon Route railroad terminal downtown. Open 8:30–noon, 1–5.

Wrangell Convention and Visitors Bureau (Box 1078, Wrangell 99929, tel. 907/874–3800). Located at the Wrangell Museum, 122 2nd Street, a block and a half up the hill from the ferry terminal. Open May 15–September 15, Monday–Saturday, 1–4 and for an hour whenever a cruise ship or ferry is in port; in winter, open Tuesday evenings 7–9, and Wednesday 1:30–4. **Chamber of Commerce Visitors Center** (Box 49, Wrangell 99929, tel. 907/874–3901) in the A-frame on the waterfront next to City Hall. Open when cruise ships or ferries are in port, and at other posted times during the summer.

Emergencies
Police and Ambulance

In Haines/Fort Seward, Juneau, Ketchikan, Petersburg and Sitka, dial 911. Gustavus EMS (tel. 907/697–2222). Skagway: Police (tel. 907/983–2301), Ambulance (tel. 907/983–2300). Wrangell: Police (tel. 907/874–3304), Ambulance, Fire Department (tel. 907/874–2000).

Doctor and Dentist

Haines/Fort Seward Health Clinic, next to the Visitors Information Center, tel. 907/766–2521. Pharmacy needs also cared for.
Juneau: Bartlett Memorial Hospital, 3260 Hospital Drive, located just off the Egan Expressway, about four miles north of downtown, tel. 907/586–2611.
Ketchikan General Hospital, 3100 Tongass Avenue, in the north end of the city business district, tel. 907/225–5171.
Petersburg General Hospital, located downtown at 1st Street and Fram Street, tel. 907/772–4291.
Sitka Community Hospital, 209 Moller Drive, north of downtown, tel. 907/747–3241.
Skagway Health Clinic, on 11th Avenue between State Street and Broadway, tel. 907/983–2225.
Wrangell Hospital, on the airport road, next to the elementary school, tel. 907/874–3356.

Pharmacy

Juneau: Juneau Drug Co., 202 Front Street, downtown, across from McDonald's, tel. 907/586–1233. **Ron's Apothecary,** 9101 Mendenhall Mall Road, located about 10 miles north of downtown in Mendenhall Valley, next to the Super Bear market, tel. 907/789–0458; after-hours emergencies, 907/789–9522.
Ketchikan: Race Pharmacy/Downtown, 300 Front Street, tel. 907/225–5171. **Race Pharmacy,** 2300 Tongass Avenue, across from the Plaza Portwest shopping mall, tel. 907/225–4151. After hours, call the hospital.
Petersburg: Rexall Drugs (tel. 907/772–3265). After hours, call the hospital.
Sitka: White's Pharmacy, 705 Halibut Point Road, tel. 907/747–5755. **Harry Race Drug,** 106 Lincoln Street, tel. 907/747–8666.
Wrangell: Wrangell Drug, Front Street, tel. 907/874–3422.

Exploring Southeast Alaska

Orientation

The Southeast Panhandle stretches some 500 miles from Yakutat at its northernmost to Ketchikan and Metlakatla at the southern end. At its widest the region measures only some 140 miles, and in the upper Panhandle just south of Yakutat it's a skinny 30 miles across. Most of the Panhandle consists of a sliver of mainland buffered by offshore islands.

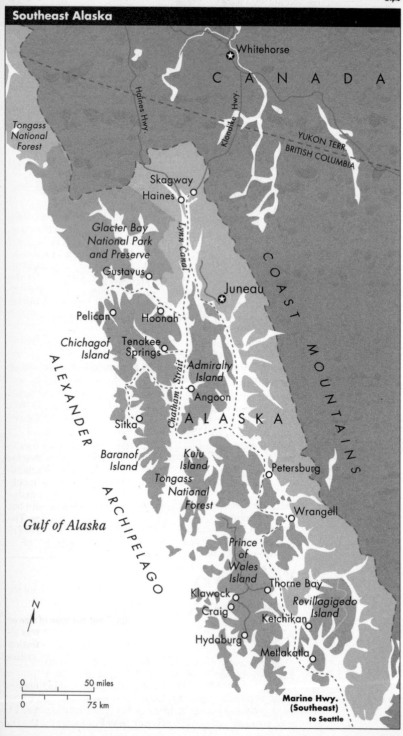

Southeast Alaska

Whitehorse

C A N A D A

Haines Hwy.

Klondike Hwy.

Tongass National Forest

YUKON TERR
BRITISH COLUMBIA

Skagway
Haines

Lynn Canal

Glacier Bay National Park and Preserve

Juneau

Gustavus

C
O
A
S
T

M
O
U
N
T
A
I
N
S

Pelican

Hoonah

Chichagof Island

Tenakee Springs

Chatham Strait

Admiralty Island

Angoon

A L A S K A

Sitka

Baranof Island

Kuiu Island

Tongass National Forest

Petersburg

A
L
E
X
A
N
D
E
R

Gulf of Alaska

A
R
C
H
I
P
E
L
A
G
O

Wrangell

Prince of Wales Island

Thorne Bay

Klawock

Revillagigedo Island

Craig

Ketchikan

Hydaburg

Metlakatla

N

0   50 miles
0   75 km

Marine Hwy. (Southeast) to Seattle

There are, in fact, more than a thousand islands up and down the Panhandle coast—most of them mountainous with lush covers of timber. Collectively they constitute the Alexander Archipelago. On the mainland to the east of the U.S.–Canadian border lies British Columbia.

You can get to and around the area by ship or by plane, but forget the highway. The roadways that exist in these parts run at most a few dozen miles out from towns and villages, then they dead-end.

Not surprisingly, most of the communities of the region are located on islands rather than on the mainland. The principal exceptions are Juneau, Haines, Skagway, and the Indian village of Klukwan. Island outposts include Ketchikan, Wrangell, Petersburg, Sitka, Metlakatla, and a number of other towns, Indian villages, and logging camps.

If shipboard sightseeing is your pleasure, more than two dozen cruise ships and state ferries await your booking. The usual (though not the only) pattern is for cruising visitors to board ship at Vancouver, B.C., or San Francisco, then to set sail on an itinerary that typically includes Ketchikan, Juneau, Skagway, and Sitka. Other itineraries go to Glacier Bay as well. Cruise ship travel includes a mix of sailing and port visits, which can vary from a few hours to a full day. The state ferries (southern ports of origin: Bellingham, WA or Prince Rupert, B.C.) rarely spend much time in the cities where they call, but you can get off one ship, spend a day or more ashore, then catch another vessel heading north or south to your next destination.

Don't overlook the region's alternative means of travel. Small float planes, some carrying five or fewer passengers, and yachts sleeping a half dozen or so ply the routes from the larger population centers to tiny settlements and even more remote sites where there are no permanent residents at all (unless you count bears).

If you're interested in fishing you have a number of options to choose from (or mix). There are saltwater salmon charter boats, salmon fishing lodges (some near the larger communities, others remote and accessible by float plane), fly-in mountain lake lodges where the fishing is for trout and char, and—bargain hunters take special note—more than 150 remote but weather-tight cabins operated by the U.S. Forest Service. The USFS rents these units for the absurdly reasonable rate of $15 per night per group (*see* Off the Beaten Track, below).

Ketchikan

Numbers in the margin correspond to points of interest on the Ketchikan map.

Alaskans call Ketchikan "the First City," not because of size or population, but because in the days before air travel it was always the first Alaskan port of call for northbound steamship passengers. For many travelers today—arriving by air, cruise ship, or ferry—the tradition continues.

Ketchikan is perched on a large mountainous island underneath 3,000-foot Deer Mountain. The island's name is a jaw breaker, Revillagigedo (Alaskans just say "Revilla"), named by English mariner George Vancouver, who was exploring the Inside Passage in 1793. He often named things for his crew and friends; in this case it was named after the viceroy of Mexico.

The site at the mouth of Ketchikan Creek was a summer fish camp for the Tlingit Indians until white miners and fishermen came to settle in the town in 1885. Gold discoveries just before the turn of the century brought more immigrants, and valuable timber and commercial fishing resources spurred new industries. By the 1930s the town bragged it was the "Salmon Canning Capital of the World."

Today Ketchikan ranks fourth among Alaskan cities in size (7,600 residents in the city proper, 5,000 in the borough, or county). Fishing and timber are still the mainstays of Ketchikan's economy, although tourism is certainly helping out.

It's an easy town to sightsee in and enjoy. **Alaska Sightseeing Tours** (tel. 907/225–2740) and **Gray Line of Alaska** (tel. 907/225–5930) offer city tours by motor coach that take in points of interest, including totem parks both within the city and out in the borough. **Royal Hyway Tours** offers similar excursions, but only for passengers aboard ships of their parent company, Princess Cruises.

There's a lot to be seen in downtown Ketchikan on foot. The

❶ best place to begin is at the **Ketchikan Visitors Bureau** on the dock, where you can pick up a free historic walking tour map. From there head up Mission Street, past the Sub–Post Office located in the Trading Post (the main post office is inconveniently located several miles south, near the ferry terminal), to

❷ Bawden Street and **St. John's Church and Seaman's Center.** The 1903 church structure is the oldest remaining house of worship in Ketchikan, its interior formed from red cedar cut in the native-operated sawmill in nearby Saxman. The Seaman's Center, next door to the church, was built in 1904 as a hospital. It later housed the *Alaska Sportsman Magazine* (now *Alaska Magazine*), which began publication in Ketchikan in 1936.

❸ At Dock St., your tour passes the ***Ketchikan Daily News*** build-
❹ ing, then jogs east to the **Tongass Historical Museum and Totem Pole.** Plan to spend a half hour or so here browsing among Indian artifacts and pioneer relics of the early mining and fishing era. Among exhibits: a big and brilliantly polished lens out of Tree Point Lighthouse, the bullet-riddled skull of a notorious and fearsome old brown bear called Old Groaner, Indian ceremonial objects, and a Chilkat blanket. There's even a 14-foot model of a typical Alaskan salmon fishing seine vessel. *Museum admission: $1.50 Mon.–Sat.; free on Sun. Open Mon.–Sat. 8–5, Sun. 9–4.*

❺ Continuing north, then east on Park Street, you can see **Grant Street Trestle,** constructed in 1908. At one time virtually all of Ketchikan's walkways and streets were wooden trestles. This is the last remaining example of the city's early road system.
❻ Get out your camera and set it for fast speed at the **Salmon Falls, Fish Ladder,** and **Salmon Carving** just off Park Street. When the salmon start running in mid-summer and later, thousands will literally leap the falls (or take the easier ladder route) to spawn in Ketchikan Creek's waters farther upstream.
❼ Many can be seen in the creek feeding the falls. At **City Park** you can see small ponds that were once holding areas for the first hatchery that operated in the area, from 1923 to 1928. The
❽ modern **Deer Mountain Hatchery** now disperses tens of thou-

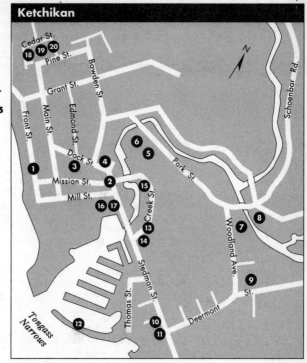

Ketchikan

9 sands of salmon annually into local waters, much to the satisfaction of local sport and commercial fishermen. Also at the park is the **Totem Heritage Center and Nature Path.** Definitely plan to spend some time in the center viewing authentic ancient examples of the carver's art. *Admission: $1.50. Open Mon.–Sat. 8–5, Sun. 9–4.*

10 Continuing south to Deermount Street and then west on Stedman Street, you pass the **Ketchikan Indian Corporation** site of a former Bureau of Indian Affairs school, and a colorful **11** wall mural called *Return of the Eagle.* It was created by 21 native artists on the walls of the Robertson Building of the Ketchikan campus, University of Alaska–Southeast.

12 Next comes **Thomas Street** and **Thomas Basin.** The street was constructed in 1913 to be part of New England Fish Company's cannery here; Thomas Basin is a major, and picture-worthy, harbor. One of four harbors in Ketchikan, it is "home port" to a wide variety of pleasure and work boats.

13 Now your tour takes you to **Creek Street.** Formerly this was Ketchikan's infamous red-light district; today its small, quaint houses, built on stilts over the creek waters, have been restored as trendy shops. The street's most famous brothel, **14** **Dolly's House,** has been preserved as a museum, complete with furnishings, beds, and a short history of the life and times of Ketchikan's best-known madam. *Admission: $2. Open when cruise ships are in port.*

Farther up Creek Street, there's more good salmon viewing in **15** season at the **Creek Street Footbridge.** Head south to Mill Street

⑯ and see the **Federal Building/U.S. Forest Service** and historic
⑰ **Knox Bros. Clock,** a large outdoor timepiece. It's one of three
that once served the city's downtown business district.

If you're into steep street climbing, head up Main Street past
⑱ the Ketchikan Fire Department to the **Kyan Totem Pole,** a replica of a 1913 original that once stood near St. John's Church.
Local legend says "Rub its tummy, you'll surely have money"
⑲ within 24 hours. Nearby is the **Monrean House,** a 1904 struc
⑳ ture on the National Register of Historic Places, and a **scenic
lookout** that looks down on City Float and the waters of
Tongass Narrows.

Ketchikan's two most famous totem parks (there are more totems in Ketchikan than anywhere else in the world) are, respectively, **Totem Bight State Historical Park,** 10 miles north on
North Tongass Highway, and the park at **Saxman Indian Village,** two miles south on South Tongass Highway. The poles at
both parks are, for the most part, half-century-old authentic
replicas of even older totems brought in from outlying villages
as part of a federal government works/cultural project during
the 1930s.

Totem Bight, with its many totems and hand-hewn Indian tribal house, sits on a particularly scenic spit of land facing the
waters of Tongass Narrows.

Most cruises include a tour of Saxman Village (named for a missionary who helped Indians settle there before 1900), which has
recently added new totems to their collection, as well as a new,
large tribal house believed to be the largest in the world.
There's also a carver's shed nearby where new totems and totemic art objects are created, and a stand-up theater where a
multimedia presentation tells the story of Southeast Alaska's
Indian peoples. Finally, there's a gift shop at the park. Ask the
sales clerk to differentiate for you the authentic handcrafted
items on sale there and the mass-produced, but cheaper, curios
and souvenirs.

Out the highway in either direction, you won't go far before you
run out of road. The North Tongass Highway ends about 18
miles from downtown, at Settler's Cove Campground. The
South Tongass Highway terminates at a power plant. Side
roads soon terminate at campgrounds and trailheads, viewpoints, lakes, boat-launching ramps, or private property.

If you're a tough hiker, the three-mile trail from downtown to
the top of **Deer Mountain** will repay your effort with a spectacular panorama of the city below (facing the water), and the wilderness behind. **Ward Cove Recreation Area,** about six miles
north of town, offers easier hiking beside lakes and streams and
beneath towering spruce and hemlock trees.

Wrangell

*Numbers in the margin correspond to points of interest on the
Wrangell map.*

Next up the line is Wrangell, located on an island near the
mouth of the fast-flowing Stikine River. A small, unassuming
timber and fishing community, the town has had three flags
flown over it since the arrival of the Russian traders. Known as
Redoubt St. Dionysius as part of Russian America, the town

was renamed Fort Stikine after the British took it over. The name was changed to Wrangell when the Americans bought it.

Tourism is much less structured in Wrangell than in the larger cities of the Panhandle—a plus in the minds of many visitors. This is a do-it-yourself touring town. There are no motor-coach excursions. To get the most out of a visit here you should mingle with the locals at cafes, bars, and shops.

The big tourist ships don't come here, but the town welcomes state ferries, the cruise yacht *Sheltered Seas,* and numerous other small craft that pull into port to sample the city's "real Alaskan hospitality."

You can see a lot in Wrangell on foot, and a good place to start

❶ your tour is the A-frame **Chamber of Commerce Visitor Information Center** close to the docks at Front Street and Outer

❷ Drive. It's near **City Hall** and its very tall totem pole. The visitor center is open when cruise ships and the ferries are in port and at other times throughout the summer (tel. 907/874–3901). If you need information and the A-frame is closed, drop by the City Museum (122 2nd St.). The Wrangell Convention and Visitors Bureau is located there. *Bureau open summer, Mon.–Sat. 1–4 PM, and whenever cruise ships or ferries are in port.*

❸ **KikSadi Indian Park,** a "pocket park" of Alaska greenery and impressive totem poles at St. Michael's and Front Street, is a pleasant place to stroll through.

On your way to Wrangell's number one attraction—Chief

❹ Shakes Island—stop at **Chief Shakes gravesite,** uphill from Hansen's Boat Shop on Case Avenue. Buried here is Shakes V, one of a number of local chiefs to bear that name. He led the local Tlingits during the first half of the 19th century. Two killer-whale totems mark the chief's burial place.

❺ On **Shakes Island,** reached by a footbridge off the harbor dock, you can see some of the finest totem poles in Alaska, as well as a tribal house constructed in the 1930s as a replica of the original, which housed many of the various Shakes and their peoples. The interior, which contains six house totems, two of them more than 100 years old, is unfortunately not open very often. It is scheduled for viewing when ships are in port or by appointment. *Tel. 907/874–3503 or 907/874–3747. A donation of $1 is requested.*

After your visit to the island, wander out to the end of the dock

❻ ❼ for the view and picture taking at the **seaplane float** and **boat harbor.**

❽ North and west from the A-frame info center are the **cruise ship**

❾ **dock;** the **public library,** with its small collection of ancient petroglyphs (more about these curious rock carvings later), and

❿ the **Wrangell City Museum** (2nd St. and Bevier St., tel. 907/874–3770). Since its construction in 1906, the museum building has served as a library, a morgue, a doctor's office, and city hall. Now it contains a historical collection that varies from totem fragments, petroglyphs, and other Indian artifacts to a bootlegger's still and even a vintage 1800's linotype and presses.

⓫ Beyond the **state ferry terminal** lies another museum, called

⓬ **"Our Collections"** by its owners, Bolly and Elva Bigelow. It's located in a barnlike building on the water side of Evergreen

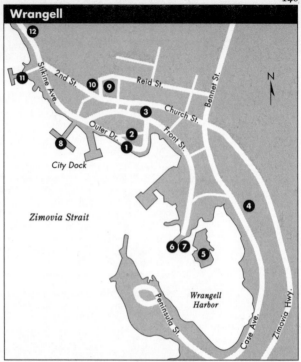

Wrangell

Avenue. To some, the gathering that comprises the collection is less a museum and more a garage sale waiting to happen. Still, large numbers of viewers seem quite taken by the literally thousands of unrelated collectibles (clocks, animal traps, waffle irons, tools, etc.) that the Bigelows have gathered in half a century of Alaska living. *Tel. 907/847–3646. Call before setting out to visit.*

A five-minute walk beyond the Bigelows' brings you (at low tides only) to **Petroglyph Beach,** one of the more curious sights in Southeast Alaska. Here, scattered among other rocks, are three dozen or more large stones bearing designs and pictures chiseled by unknown, ancient artists. No one knows why the rocks were etched the way they are. Perhaps they were boundary markers or messages; possibly they were just primitive doodling. Study them and draw your own conclusions.

If you want a unique souvenir of your Wrangell visit, go to **Norris Gifts** on Front Street and buy rice paper and crayon-rubbing supplies. The staff or the people at the city museum will demonstrate the proper rubbing technique for recording your own copy of the petroglyph designs. Do not, of course, attempt to move any of the petroglyph stones.

There are other stones in Wrangell that you can take with you. These are natural garnets, gathered at Garnet Ledge, facing the Stikine River. The semiprecious gems are sold on the streets for 50¢ or a dollar.

A lot of recreation, for both locals and visitors, centers around boating on the Stikine River. (*See* Guided Tours, above, for the names of operators that offer trips by speedy jet boat and other craft through the Stikine wilderness.)

Petersburg

Numbers in the margin correspond to points of interest on the Petersburg map.

Getting to Petersburg is an experience, whether you take the "high road" by air or the "low road" by sea.

Alaska Airlines claims the shortest jet flight in the world from takeoff at Wrangell to landing at Petersburg. The schedule calls for 20 minutes of flying, but it's usually more like 10.

At sea level, ferries and smaller cruisers squeak through Wrangell Narrows with the aid of more than 50 buoys and range markers along the 22-mile crossing. At times the water channel seems too incredibly narrow for ships to pass through, making for a breathtaking—though safe—trip.

At first sight of Petersburg you may think you're in the old country. Neat, white, Scandinavian-style homes and storefronts with steep roofs and bright-colored swirls of leaf and flower designs (called "rosemaling") and row upon row of sturdy fishing vessels in the harbor invoke the spirit of Norway. No wonder. This prosperous fishing community was founded by Norwegian Peter Buschmann in 1897.

You may occasionally even hear some Norwegian spoken, especially during the Little Norway Festival held here each year on the weekend closest to May 17. If you're in town during the festival, be sure to partake in one of the fish feeds that highlight the Norwegian Independence Day celebration. You won't find better beer-batter halibut and folk dancing without going to Norway itself.

Petersburg, like Wrangell, is a destination for travelers who prefer not to be hand-held, or spoon-fed information by a tour guide. On your own, sample the brew at **Kito's Kave** bar on Sing Lee Alley (in the afternoon if you don't like your music in the high-decibel range) and examine the outrageous wall decor there, which varies from Mexican painting on black velvet to mounted Alaska king salmon and two stuffed sailfish from a tropical fishing expedition. Wander, at high tide, to **Hammer Slough** for one of Southeast's most popular picture-taking opportunities—houses and buildings on high stilts reflected perfectly in still slough waters. Or simply wander down Nordic Drive, the city's main shopping street, and window-shop the imported Norwegian wool sweaters or metal Viking helmets, complete with horns.

One of the most pleasant things to do in Petersburg is to simply wander among the fishing vessels tied up at dockside. This is one of Alaska's busiest, most prosperous fishing communities and the variety of seacraft is enormous. You'll see small trollers, big halibut vessels, and no small number of sleek pleasure craft as well. Wander, too, around the fish processing structures. There are no tours inside these facilities but even from the outside, watching shrimp, salmon, or halibut coming ashore, you'll get a real appreciation for this vibrant industry and the hardworking people who engage in it.

❶ From the **visitor center** overlooking the city harbor there are great viewing and picture-taking vantage points. Out Nordic **❷** Drive to **Sandy Beach** where there's frequently good eagle viewing and access to one of Petersburg's favorite picnic and recreation locales.

❸ Heading north up the hill brings you to the **Clausen Museum** and the bronze "Fisk" (Norwegian for "fish") sculpture at Second and Fram streets. The monument, featuring literally scores of separately sculpted salmon, halibut, and herring, celebrates the bounty of the sea. It was created in 1967 as part of Petersburg's celebration of the 100th anniversary of the Alaska Purchase from Russia.

The museum—not surprisingly in this busiest of Southeast Alaska's commercial fishing ports—devotes a lot of its space to fishing and processing. There's an old "iron chink" used in the early days for gutting and cleaning fish, as well as displays that illustrate how the several types of fishing boats do their thing. A 126.5-pound king salmon, the largest ever caught when it came out of a fish trap on Prince of Wales Island in 1939, is on exhibit, as is the world's largest chum salmon—a 36-pounder. Indian history and artifacts are included, as is an old Indian canoe.

❹ ❺ ❻ Three pioneer churches—**Catholic, Lutheran,** and **Presbyterian**—are located nearby at Dolphin and 3rd streets, Excel and 5th streets., and on Haugen Street between 2nd and 3rd streets, respectively. Of the three, the half-century-old Lutheran edifice is the oldest. It is said that young boys wheelbarrowed fill from elsewhere in the city for landscaping around the foundation. Their compensation? Ice cream cones. The enticement was so successful that after three years of ice cream rewards, it was necessary to bring in a bulldozer to scrape off the excess dirt.

The large, white, barnlike structure on stilts that stands in **❼** Hammer Slough off Indian Street is the **Sons of Norway Hall,** an organization devoted to keeping alive the traditions and culture of the old country. North of the hall, from the Nordic Drive **❽** bridge, is the high-tide **Hammer Slough** reflecting pool so favored by local and visiting photographers.

Petersburg's other attractions are located south of the city along the Mitkof Highway, where you pass seafood processing plants and the state ferry terminal (at Mile .8) en route to the **❾** **Frank Heintzleman Nursery** at Mile 8.6 (named for a much-loved former territorial governor); the **Fall's Creek fish ladder** at Mile 10.8, where coho and pink salmon migrate upstream in late summer and fall; and the **Crystal Lake State Hatchery/Blind Slough Recreation Area** at Mile 17.5, where more than 60,000 pounds of salmon and trout are produced each year.

Petersburg's biggest attraction lies about 25 miles east of town but is accessible only by water or air. **LeConte Glacier** is the continent's southernmost tidewater glacier and one of its most active, often calving off so many icebergs that the lake at its face is carpeted wall-to-wall with floating bergs. Ferries and cruise ships pass it at a distance. Sightseeing yachts, charter vessels, and flightseeing tours are available. For a list of operators, contact the Visitors Bureau.

Catholic church, **4**
Clausen Museum, **3**
Frank Heintzleman
Nursery, **9**
Hammer Slough, **8**
Lutheran church, **5**
Presbyterian church, **6**
Sandy Beach, **2**
Sons of Norway Hall, **7**
Visitor center, **1**

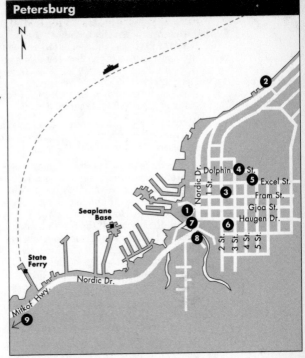

Petersburg

Sitka

Numbers in the margin correspond to points of interest on the Sitka map.

For centuries before the Russians came at the end of the 18th century, Sitka was the ancestral home of the Tlingit Indian nation. Unfortunately for the Tlingits, Russian Territorial Governor Alexander Baranov (often spelled Baranof, as the island is now spelled) came to covet the Sitka site for its beauty, mild climate, and economic potential. In the island's massive timbered forests he saw raw materials for shipbuilding; its location offered trading routes as far east as Hawaii and the Orient, and as far south as California.

In 1799 Baranof negotiated with the local chief to build a wooden fort and trading post some six miles north of the present town. He called the outpost St. Archangel Michael and shortly after moved a large number of his Russian and Aleut fur hunters there from their former base on Kodiak Island.

The Indians soon took exception to the ambitions of their new neighbors, and in 1802 they attacked Baranov's people, burned his buildings, and assumed they were done with the troublesome outsiders.

Fortunately for Baranov, he was away at Kodiak at the time. He returned in 1804 with a formidable force including shipboard cannons, attacked the Indians at their fort near Indian River (site of the present-day 105-acre **Sitka National Historical Park**), and drove them to the other side of the island.

Under Baranov and succeeding managers, the Russian-American Company and the town prospered until, in the middle of the 19th century, it could be called "the Paris of the Pacific." Besides the fur trade, the community contained a major shipbuilding and repair facility, boasted saw mills and forges, had a salmon saltery, and even initiated an ice industry. The Russians shipped blocks of ice from nearby Swan Lake to the booming San Francisco market. Baranov shifted the capital of Russian America to Sitka from Kodiak.

Amenities of the town included schools, a library, a hospital, and the crown jewel of the Russian Orthodox Church in Russian America—St. Michael's Cathedral.

❶ A good place to begin a tour of modern-day Sitka is at the Sitka Visitors Bureau headquarters, located in the **Centennial Building** on Harbor Drive. A big Tlingit Indian war canoe rests nearby, while inside the building you'll find a museum, auditorium, art gallery, and lots of advice on what to see and how to see it. The staff will know if the colorfully costumed New Archangel Russian Dancers are performing, whether concerts or recitals are on tap for the annual Sitka Summer Music Festival, or if logging competitions or the community's annual salmon derby is scheduled soon.

In the Centennial Building there's also an accurate model of New Archangel, as the Russians called their colony. It shows where the Russians built boats, milled their flour, and cut ice for shipment to gold-rush–booming San Francisco bars.

❷ For photo taking, atmosphere, and outdoor orientation, you would do well to stop at **Castle Hill.** It overlooks Crescent Bay, the John O'Connel Bridge to Japonski Island, and no small number of other islands, isles, and rocks in the nearby waters. A path and steps beside the post office will take you to the top. For years after Sitka's founding, a succession of residences for Russian managers was located on this lofty promontory. The last one—called Baranof's Castle, though he never lived there—burned in 1894.

Atop the hill now are venerable Russian cannons and the flagpole where, on October 18, 1867, the czarist Russian standard was lowered and the Stars and Stripes of the United States raised. Each Alaska Day (October 18), citizens of Sitka in period costumes reenact the ceremony with the same pomp and ceremony that signified the official transfer of Alaska to the United States.

At this same site, on January 3, 1959, jubilant Alaskans raised the first 49-star American flag, signifying Alaskan statehood.

❸ The large four-level red-roof structure with the imposing 14-foot statue in front is the **Sitka State Pioneers' Home,** built in 1934 and the first of several state-run retirement homes and medical-care facilities for Alaska's senior citizens. The statue, symbolizing Alaska's frontier sourdough spirit, was modeled by an authentic pioneer, William "Skagway Bill" Fonda. It portrays a determined prospector with pack, pick, rifle, and supplies on his back headed for the gold country.

Across the street in **Totem Square** you'll find three old anchors discovered in local waters and believed to be 19th-century British in origin. Look on the totem pole in the park for the double-headed eagle of czarist Russia carved into the cedar.

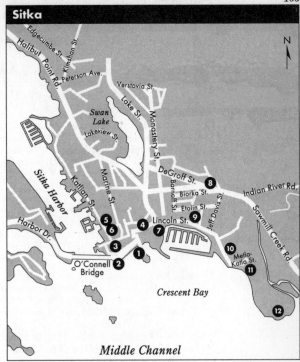

④ St. Michael's Cathedral, in the middle of Lincoln Street, had its origins in a log-built, frame-covered structure erected between 1844 and 1848. In 1966 the church was totally destroyed in a fire that swept through the downtown business district. As the fire engulfed the building, local townspeople risked their lives and rushed inside to rescue the cathedral's precious icons, religious objects, vestments, and other treasures brought to the church from Russia.

Using original measurements and blueprints, an almost exact replica of onion-domed St. Michael's was built and dedicated in 1976. Today, visitors can see numerous icons, among them the much-prized Our Lady of Sitka (also known as the Sitka Madonna) and the Christ Pantocrator (Christ the Judge) on either side of the doors of the interior altar screen. Among other objects to be viewed: ornate gospel books, chalices, crucifixes, much-used silver-gilt wedding crowns dating back to 1866, and an altar cloth said to have been worked by Princess Maksoutoff, who lies buried in the Russian cemetery nearby. This is an active church, so visitors should respect the services and privacy of worshipers. *A $1 donation is requested. Open June 1–Sept. 30, daily 11–3.*

⑤ ⑥ North of the Pioneer Home on the west edge of town are the **Russian blockhouse** and the **Russian cemetery** where Princess Maksoutoff, wife of Alaska's last Russian governor and others are buried. The old headstones and crosses of the Russian Orthodox faith make this a striking sight.

⑦ The **Russian Bishop's House** also stands on Lincoln Street, constructed by the Russian-American Company for Bishop Inno-

cent Veniaminov in 1842. Now restored by the National Park
Service as a unit of Sitka National Historical Park, the structure is one of the few remaining Russian log structures in Alaska. *Admission free. Open daily 8–5.*

8 Farther north and east is the **Sitka National Cemetery** on Sawmill Creek Road, where America's dead from the Civil War and
the Aleutian Campaign of World War II are buried along with
many notable Alaskans.

9
10 Southeast on Lincoln Street lies the campus of **Sheldon Jackson
College,** founded in 1878, and the **Sheldon Jackson Museum.**
The octagonal museum, built in 1895 and now under the juris-
diction of the Alaska State Division of Museums, contains
priceless Indian, Aleut, and Eskimo items collected by Dr.
Sheldon Jackson in the remote regions of Alaska he traveled as
an educator and missionary. Carved masks, Chilkat Indian
blankets, dogsleds, kayaks—even the helmet worn by Chief
Katlean during the 1804 battle between the Sitka Indians and
the Russians—are on display here. Budget at least an hour at
the museum. *Admission: $1 adults, free for students. Open
daily 8–5.*

11 **Sitka National Historical Park's** Visitor Center and totem park
is located at the end of Metlakatla Street, about a half mile from
town. Audiovisual programs and exhibits at the site, plus Indian and Russian artifacts, give an overview of Southeast Alaska
Indian culture, both old and new. Often, contemporary Indian
artists and craftsmen are on hand to demonstrate and interpret
the traditional crafts of the Tlingit people.

A self-guiding trail through the park to the actual site of the
12 **Tlingit Fort** passes by some of the most skillfully carved totems
in the state. Some of the poles are quite old, dating back more
than eight decades. Others are replicas, copies of originals lost
to time and a damp climate. *Admission free. Open June–Sept.
daily 8–5; Oct.–May weekdays 8–5.*

Juneau

*Numbers in the margin correspond to points of interest on the
Juneau map.*

Juneau, like Haines and Skagway to the north, is located on the
North American mainland. Unlike Haines and Skagway, you
can't drive there by conventional highway from the rest of the
United States and Canada. No matter. There are lots of easy
ways to reach Alaska's capital and third-largest city. For one,
there's the Alaska Marine Highway ferry system, which provides near daily arrivals and departures in the summer. For another, virtually every cruise ship plying Southeast waters calls
at Juneau. And two jet airlines—Alaska and Delta—provide
several flights daily into Juneau International Airport from
other points in Alaska and the other U.S. states.

Juneau owes its origins to two colorful sourdoughs, Joe Juneau
and Dick Harris, and to a Tlingit chief named Kowee. The chief
led the two white men to rich reserves of gold, both in the outwash of the stream that now runs through the middle of town
and in quartz rock formations back in the gulches and valleys.

That was 1880, and shortly after the discovery a modest stampede resulted in the formation of first a camp, then a town, then

finally the movement of the Alaska district government (such as it was) to the area in 1906. Thus Juneau became the capital of Alaska, a title the community still retains.

For 60 years or so after Juneau's founding, gold remained the mainstay of the local economy. In its heyday, the AJ (for Alaska Juneau) gold mine was the biggest low-grade ore mine in the world. It was not until World War II, when the government decided it needed Juneau's manpower for the war effort, that the AJ and other mines in the area ceased operations.

After the war, mining failed to start up again, and government—first territorial, then state—became the city's principal employer.

These days, government (state, federal, and local) remains Juneau's number one employer. Tourism, transportation, and trading—even a belated mining revival—provide the other major components of the city's economic picture.

A good place to start a walking tour is the visitor kiosk at ❶ **Marine Park** on the dock where the cruise ships tie up. The park itself is a little gem of benches, shade trees, and shelter, a great place to enjoy an outdoor meal purchased from any of Juneau's several street vendors. The kiosk is staffed from 9 AM to 6PM ❷ daily in the summer months. The **Log Cabin Visitor Center** up Seward Street at 3rd Street operates weekdays 8:30–5 and weekends 10–5.The cabin is a replica of a 19th-century structure that served first as a Presbyterian Church, then as a brewery.

Head east a block from Marine Park to S. Franklin Street. Buildings here and on Front Street are among the older and most interesting structures in the city. Many reflect the architecture of the 1920s and '30s, and some are even older.

The smallish (40 rooms) **Alaskan Hotel** at 167 S. Franklin Street was called "a pocket edition of any of the best hotels on the Pacific Coast" when it opened in 1913. Owners Mike and Bettye Adams have restored the building with period trappings, and it's worth a visit even if you're not looking for lodging. The barroom's massive mirrored oakwood back bar, accented by Tiffany lights and panels, is a particular delight.

Also on S. Franklin Street: **The Alaska Steam Laundry Building,** a 1901 structure with a windowed turret that now houses a coffee house, a film processor, and other stores. Across the street, the equally venerable **Senate Building mall** contains one of the two Juneau Christmas Stores, a children's shop, and a place to buy Russian icons.

Close by are numerous other curio and crafts shops, snack shops, two salmon shops, and the tourist-filled **Red Dog Saloon,** a decades-old institution now housed in new but still frontierish quarters at 159 S. Franklin Street.

After a S. Franklin Street foray, head one block toward the water, then uphill on Seward Street past the Log Cabin Visitor Center. You'll come across 4th Street to an older, obviously governmental building fronted by huge marble pillars. The pillars are of native Southeast Alaska marble, and the building is ❸ the **Alaska State Capitol,** constructed in 1930 to serve the city as federal building, governor's office, post office, and meeting place for the biennial sessions of the Alaska Territorial Legisla-

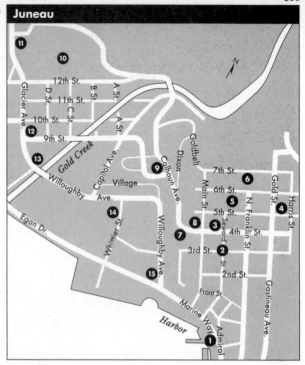

ture. Today the structure still houses the governor's offices and other state agencies, and the state legislature meets there four months each year. *Tel. 907/465–4565. Tours in summer, daily 8:30–5.*

Uphill one block and two blocks to the east stands quaint little
4 St. Nicholas Russian Orthodox Church, constructed in 1894—the oldest original Russian church in Alaska. *326 5th St. A donation is requested. Check the visitor center for hours.*

Directly uphill behind the Capitol Building, between 5th and
5 6th streets, stands the **five-story totem,** one of Juneau's finer to-
6 tems, and at the top of the hill on 7th Street stands **Wickersham House,** the former residence of pioneer judge and delegate to Congress, James Wickersham. The home, constructed in 1899, is now a part of the Alaska state park system. Summer tours operate Sunday–Friday, 10–5. Memorabilia from the judge's travels throughout Alaska range from rare native basketry and ivory carvings to historic photos, 47 faithful diaries (maintained even on treks through snow and blizzards), and a Chickering grand piano that came "round the horn" to Alaska while the Russians yet ruled in these parts. Admission is free.

Back down the hill on 4th Street, you'll pass "the S.O.B."—or
7 State Office Building. There on Fridays at noon you can pack a lunch like the state workers do and listen in the four-story atrium to organ music played on a grand old theater pipe organ, a veteran of the silent-movie era.

Head west from the front of the Capitol Building, then north on
8 Calhoun Avenue past the **City Museum** (with old mining equip-

ment, historic photos, and pioneer artifacts) and another pho-
❾ to-worthy totem, you come shortly to the **Governor's House,** a
three-level colonial style home completed in 1912. There are no
tours through the house, but it's okay to take pictures of the
totem pole on the entrance side of the building—surely the
only one of its kind to grace the walls of a U.S. governor's man-
sion.

If you're still game for walking, head down Calhoun Avenue,
pass the Gold Creek bridge, and keep going until you come to
❿ **Evergreen Cemetery.** A meandering gravel road leads through
the graveyard where many Juneau pioneers (among them Joe
Juneau and Dick Harris) lay buried. At the end of the lane
⓫ you'll come to a monument commemorating the **cremation spot**
⓬ **of Chief Kowee.** Turn left here, walk past the **Federal Building**
⓭ **and Post Office** at 9th and Glacier, pass the **Juneau–Harris**
Monument near Gold Creek, then walk on to Whittier Street,
⓮ where a right turn will take you to the **Alaska State Museum.**
319 Whittier St., Juneau, tel. 907/465-2901. Open May 15–
Sept. 15, weekdays 9–6, weekends 10–6; Sept. 16–May 14,
Tues.–Fri. 10–6. Admission: $1 adults, children and students
free.

This is one of Alaska's top museums. Plan no less than an hour
here, longer if you can spare the time. Whether your tastes run
to natural history exhibits (stuffed brown bears, a replica of a
two-story-high eagle nesting tree), native Alaskan exhibits (a
40-foot walrus hide oomiak whaling boat constructed by Eskimos from St. Laurence Island and a re-created interior of a
Tlingit tribal house), mining exhibits, or contemporary art, the
museum is almost certain to please.

Finally, on Willoughby Avenue at Egan Drive, there's Ju-
⓯ neau's **Centennial Hall**—the meeting place for large conven-
tions in the capital city and the site of an excellent information
center operated by the U.S. Forest Service and the U.S. Park
Service. Movies, slide shows, and information about recreation
in the surrounding Tongass National Forest or in nearby Glacier Bay National Park and Preserve are available here. *Open*
daily in summer 9–6; 8–5 weekdays the rest of the year.

Haines

Numbers in the margin correspond to points of interest on the
Haines map.

Missionary S. Hall Young and John Muir, the famous natural-
ist, picked the site for this town in 1879 as a place to bring
Christianity and education to the native Indians. They could
hardly have picked a more beautiful spot. The town sits on a
heavily wooded peninsula with magnificent views of Portage
Cove and the Coastal Mountain Range. It lies 80 miles north of
Juneau via fjordlike Lynn Canal and 13 water miles south of
Skagway.

Unlike most cities in Southeast Alaska, you can reach Haines
by road (the 152-mile Haines Highway connects at Haines
Junction with the Alaska Highway). It's accessible as well by
state ferry and by scheduled light-plane service from Juneau.

The town has two distinct personalities. On the northern side of
the Haines Highway is the portion of Haines founded by Hall
and Muir. After its missionary beginnings the town served as

the trailhead for the Jack Dalton Trail to the Yukon during the 1897 gold rush to the Klondike. The following year, when gold was discovered in nearby Porcupine (now deserted), the booming community served as a supply center and jumping-off place for those gold fields as well. Today things are quieter; the town's streets are orderly, its homes are well kept, and for the most part it looks a great deal like any other Alaska seacoast community.

South of the highway, the town looks like a military post, which is what it was for nearly half a century.

In 1903 the U.S. Army established a post—**Fort William Henry Seward**—at Portage Cove just south of town. For 17 years (1922–1939) the post (renamed Chilkoot Barracks to avoid confusion with the South Central Alaska city of Seward) was the only military base in the territory. That changed with World War II. Following the war the post closed down.

Right after the war a group of veterans purchased the property from the government. They changed its name to Port Chilkoot and created residences, businesses, and an Indian arts center out of the officers' houses and military buildings that surrounded the old fort's parade ground. Eventually Port Chilkoot merged with the city of Haines. Although the two areas are now officially one municipality, the old military post with its still-existing grass parade grounds is referred to as Fort Seward.

The Haines–Fort Seward community today is recognized for the enormously successful Indian dance and culture center at Fort Seward, as well as for the superb fishing, camping, and outdoor recreation to be found at Chilkoot Lake, Portage Cove, Mosquito Lake, and Chilkat State Park on the shores of Chilkat Inlet. The latter locale, one of the small treasures of the Alaska state park system, features quality views of the Davidson and Rainbow glaciers across the water.

❶ To sightsee the community you can pick up walking-tour maps of both Haines and Fort Seward at the **Visitor Center** on 2nd Avenue. The easiest place to start your tour, however, is at the ❷ **Sheldon Museum and Cultural Center** near the foot of Main Street. This is another Alaskana collection, home grown with personal care by an Alaskan family. Steve Sheldon began assembling Indian artifacts, Russian items, and gold-rush memorabilia, such as Jack Dalton's sawed-off shotgun, in 1924. His daughter, Elisabeth Hakkinen, carries on and is usually on hand to serve Russian tea, to recall the stories behind many of the items on display, and to reminisce about growing up in Haines before World War II. *25 Main St., tel. 907/766–2366. Small admission fee.*

❸ One of the most rewarding hikes in the area is to the north summit of **Mt. Ripinsky,** the prominent peak that rises to 3,610 feet behind the town. Be forewarned: It's a strenuous trek and requires a full day. The **trailhead** lies at the top of Young Street, along a pipeline right-of-way. For other hikes, pick up a copy of "Haines is for Hikers" at the Information Center.

❹ The **Southeast Alaska State Fairgrounds** is probably worth a drive-through if you're a fair buff or interested in things agricultural. If you happen to be in Haines during the annual fair held each August, plan to spend several hours. It's one of sever-

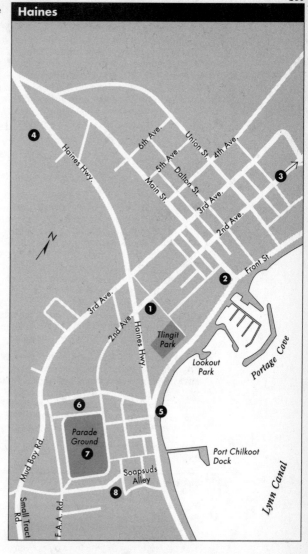

Haines

al official regional fall blowouts staged around the state, and in its homegrown, homespun way it's a real winner.

In addition to the usual collection of barnyard animals (chickens, goats, horses, etc.), the fair offers the finest examples of local culinary arts and the chance to see Indian dances, displays of Indian totemic crafts, lots of hobby crafts, and some surprisingly fine art and photography.

As noted, the Haines Highway roughly divides Haines/Fort Seward. At the base of the highway is **Mile 0**, the starting point of the 152-mile road to the Alaska Highway and the Canadian Yukon. Whether you plan to travel all the way or not, you should spend at least a bit of time on the scenic highway. At about Mile 6 there's a delightful picnic spot near the Chilkat River and an inflowing clear creek; at Mile 9.5 the view of the Takhinsha Mountains across the river is magnificent; and around Mile 19 there is good viewing of the **Alaska Chilkat Bald Eagle Preserve,** where, especially in late fall and early winter, as many as 4,000 of the great birds have been known to assemble. The United States–Canada border lies at Mile 40. If you're traveling on to Canada, stop at Canadian customs and be sure to set your clock ahead one hour, noon in Alaska being 1 PM in this part of Canada. (If you're headed south *from* Canada, check in with U.S. Customs, and of course set your timepiece back an hour.)

The Haines Highway is completely paved on the American side of the border and, except for a few remaining stretches, almost entirely paved in Canada.

Back in town, head for Fort Seward, and don't budget too little time for this unique community. Pull out your Fort Seward walking tour map and wander past the huge, stately, white-columned former commanding officer's home, now a part of the

6 **Halsingland Hotel.** Circle the flat but sloping parade grounds,

7 with its **Indian tribal house** and sourdough log cabin. In the eve-

8 ning, visit the **Chilkat Center for the Arts.** This building once was the army post's recreation hall, but now it's the scene of Chilkat Indian dancing (Mon. and Sat. evenings) or the outrageous "Lust for Dust" historical melodrama (Sun. performances may be at the tribal house; check posted notices.) *Both shows start at 8:30 PM and charge $5.*

Between the Chilkat Center for the Arts and the parade grounds stands the former fort hospital, now being used as a workshop for the craftsmen of **Alaska Indian Arts,** a nonprofit organization dedicated to the revival of Tlingit Indian art forms. You'll see Indian carvers making totems here, metalsmiths working in silver, even weavers making blankets. *Admission free. Open weekdays 9–noon and 1–5.*

The Haines ferry terminal is located 4½ miles northwest of downtown.

Skagway

Numbers in the margin correspond to points of interest on the Skagway map.

Skagway lies 13 miles north of Haines by ferry on the Alaska Marine Highway. If you drive by conventional highway the distance is 359 miles, as it's necessary to cover first the Haines Highway to Haines Junction, Yukon, then a hundred miles of Alaska Highway south to Whitehorse, and then a final hundred south to Skagway on the Klondike Highway. North country folk call this the Golden Horseshoe or Golden Circle tour, because it takes in a lot of gold-rush country in addition to lake, forest, and mountain scenery.

However you get to Skagway, you'll find the town an amazingly preserved living artifact from one of North America's biggest, most storied gold rushes. Most of the downtown district is part of the Klondike Gold Rush National Historical Park, a unit of the national park system dedicated to preserving and interpreting the frenzied stampede that extended to Dawson City in Canada's Yukon. Old false-fronted stores, saloons, and brothels—built to separate gold-rush prospectors from their grub-stakes going north or their gold pokes heading south—have been restored, repainted, and refurnished by the federal government and Skagway's people. When you walk down Broadway today, the scene is not appreciably different from what the prospectors saw in the days of 1898, except that the dust (or mud) of Broadway has been covered with pavement to make your meandering easier.

Actually, there are several units to the National Historical Park. The most southern is at Pioneer Square in Seattle, near the Alaska ferry departure docks. It's an ideal place to look over displays and exhibits and get an advance orientation of what you'll see when you get to Alaska. A closer unit covers the Chilkoot Trail leading from nearby Dyea ("Die-EE") over the Chilkoot Pass to Lake Lindeman.

Skagway had only a single cabin, still standing, when the Yukon gold rush began. At first the argonauts, as they liked to be called, swarmed to Dyea and the Chilkoot Trail, nine miles to the west of Skagway. Skagway and its White Pass trail didn't seem as attractive until a dock was built in town. With that, Skagway mushroomed overnight into the major gateway to the Klondike, supporting a wild mixture of legitimate businessmen, con artists (among the most cunning, Jefferson "Soapy" Smith), stampeders, and curiosity seekers.

Three months after the first boat landed in July 1897, Skagway numbered perhaps 20,000 persons and had well-laid-out streets, hotels, stores, saloons, gambling houses, and dance halls. By spring of 1898, the superintendent of the Northwest Royal Mounted Police in neighboring Canada would label the town "little better than a hell on earth."

A lot of the "hell" ended with a real-life shootout one pleasant July evening in 1898. Good-guy Frank Reid (the surveyor who laid out Skagway's streets so wide and well) faced down bad-guy Soapy Smith on Juneau dock downtown near the present ferry terminal. After a classic exchange of gunfire, Smith lay dead and Reid lay dying. The town built a huge monument at Reid's grave. You can see it in Gold Rush Cemetery and read the inscription on it today: "He gave his life for the honor of Skagway." For Smith, whose tombstone was continually chiseled and stolen by vandals and souvenir seekers, today's grave marker is a simple wooden plank.

One of Soapy Smith's saloons still stands. It's located on 2nd Avenue, and it's open from time to time for tourist visits. No longer, however, are "suckers" invited out back to "see an eagle," then bopped on their heads and rolled for their pokes.

To begin a visit to this storied town, head first to **City Hall** on 7th Avenue. There, on the first floor of a large granite structure built in 1899 to house McCabe Methodist College, the Skagway Convention and Visitors Bureau will give you maps and lots of suggestions for seeing their town. Your first stop should be right upstairs in the City Hall building, where the ❶ **Trail of '98 Museum** is located.

Frank Reid's will is preserved under glass there, as are papers disposing of Soapy Smith's estate. Gambling paraphernalia from the old Board of Trade Saloon is on display along with native artifacts, gold scales, a red-and-black sleigh (one-horse va-

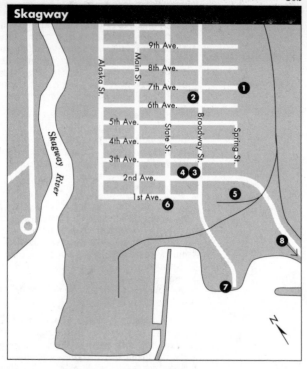

Skagway

riety), a small organ, and a curious blanket made from the skin of duck necks and fortified by pepper bags sewn behind the skin for moth protection.

2 After you've browsed the museum, wander back to Broadway and 6th Avenue to the **Eagles Hall.** Mentally mark this locale and plan to return for the show the locals perform daily called "Skagway in the Days of '98." You'll see cancan dancers, learn a little local history, and watch desperado Soapy Smith sent to his reward. *Posted show hours depend on ship arrivals and departures. Performances are usually at 10 AM and 8 PM.*

3 Farther south on Broadway you come to **Arctic Brotherhood Hall,** the likes of which you'll not see anywhere else in Alaska. The Arctic Brotherhood was a fraternal organization of Alaskan and Yukon pioneers. To decorate the exterior false front of their Skagway lodge building, local members created a mosaic covering out of 20,000 pieces of driftwood and flotsam gathered from local beaches.

4 5 **Soapy's Parlor** is located on 2nd Avenue just west of Broadway, while the former **White Pass and Yukon Route rail depot** is located on the east side of the main thoroughfare. This building, now headquarters and information center for the **Klondike Gold Rush National Historical Park,** contains exhibits, photos, and artifacts from the White Pass and Chilkoot trails. This is of special interest if you plan to take a White Pass train ride, drive the nearby Klondike Highway, or hike the Chilkoot Trail.

Lots of other stops along Broadway and its side streets merit inspection. For children, the **Sweet Tooth Saloon** with its ice cream and sodas is a special favorite. For adults, the 19th-century **Red Onion Saloon** (with its former brothel upstairs) is an interesting and thirst-quenching stop. The **Golden North Hotel,** constructed in 1898 and Alaska's oldest hotel, has been lovingly restored to its gold-rush era milieu. It's worth a stroll through the lobby even if you're not staying there. Curio shops abound, and among the oldest—probably *the* oldest—in all of Alaska is **Kirmse's** (pronounced "KIRM-zees") on Broadway. Visit the shop and see the world's largest, heaviest, and most valuable gold nugget watch chain. On display as well is a companion chain made of the world's tiniest, daintiest little nuggets.

6 At the foot of State Street is the starting place of the **Klondike Highway.** The Klondike often parallels the older White Pass railway route as it travels northwest to Carcross and Whitehorse in the Canadian Yukon. It merges just south of Whitehorse for a short distance with the Alaska Highway, then it heads its own again to its end at Dawson City on the shores of the Klondike River. From start to finish, it covers 435 miles.

Along the way the road climbs steeply through forested coastal mountains with jagged, snow-covered peaks. It passes by big, deep, fish-filled lakes and streams in the Canadian high country, where travelers have at least a chance of seeing mountain goat, moose, black bear, or grizzly.

If you're driving the Klondike Highway north from Skagway you must stop at **Canadian Customs,** Mile 22. If you're traveling south to Skagway, check in at **U.S. Customs,** Mile 6. And remember to change your clock setting at the border. When it's 1 PM in Canada at the border, it's noon in Skagway.

7
8 Just south of Broadway lies the **ferry dock,** a pleasant half-mile walk from town, and somewhat farther south is the **cruise-ship dock** where the big ships land. The mountainside cliff behind the cruise-ship dock, incidentally, is rather incredible, with its scores of advertisements and ships' names brightly painted on the exposed granite face. Most photographed of all the "murals" at the site is a large skull-like rock formation that has been painted white, given appropriate cavities, and named Soapy's Skull.

Two more excursions from Skagway are notable. The first is the previously mentioned **Chilkoot Trail** from Dyea to Lake Lindeman, a trek of 33 miles that includes a climb up Chilkoot Pass at the United States–Canada border. The National Park Service maintains the American side of the pass as part of the Klondike Gold Rush National Historical Park. The trail is good; the forest, mountain, and lake scenery is both scenic and richly historic, and campsites are located strategically along the way to make the several overnights as comfortable as possible.

The Chilkoot is not, however, an easy walk. There are lots of ups and downs before you cross the pass and reach the Canadian high country and rain is a distinct possibility. To return to Skagway, hikers have three choices. They can end their trek at Lake Bennett where a rail motorcar will transport them to Fraser and further rail connections to Skagway, or they can walk a cutoff to Log Cabin on the Klondike Highway. There they can either hitchhike back to town or flag down Gray Line of Alaska's Alaskon Express motor coach heading south to Skagway from Whitehorse. *Tel. 907/983–2241 or 800/544–2206. Fare: $16.*

For the thousands that complete the hike each year, it is the highlight of a trip to the North country. For details, maps, and references contact the National Park Service information center at 2nd Avenue and Broadway.

If you're not a hiker, there's an easier way to follow the second, a prospector's trail to the gold-rush country. You can take the **White Pass and Yukon Route** (WP&YR) narrow-gauge railroad over the "Trail of '98."

This is a premier railroading experience, rated world-class by countless railroad buffs and travelers. The line ceased operations in '82, and many feared the historic gold-rush railroad— which had its start in 1898—would never operate again. Happily, the line's diesel locomotives are once again chugging and towing vintage viewing cars up the steep inclines of the route, hugging the walls of precipitous cliff sides, and exposing thousands of travelers to the view of craggy peaks, plummeting waterfalls, lakes, and forests. It's a summertime operation only.

Two options are available. Twice daily the WP&YR leaves Skagway for a 3-hour round-trip excursion to the White Pass summit. Sights along the way include Bridal Veil Falls, Inspiration Point, and Dead Horse Gulch. The fare is $69. Through service to Whitehorse, Yukon, is offered daily as well—in the form of a train trip to Fraser where motor coach connections are available on to Whitehorse. The one-way fare to Whitehorse is $89. For information call 907/983–2217 or 800/343–7373.

Glacier Bay/Gustavus

Nearly 200 years ago, Captain George Vancouver sailed by Glacier Bay and didn't even know it. The bay at that time, 1794, was hidden behind and beneath a vast glacial wall of ice. The glacier was more than 20 miles across its face and, in places, more than 4,000 feet in depth. It extended more than 100 miles to the St. Elias Mountain Range. Over the next hundred years, due to warming weather and other factors not fully understood even now, the face of the glacial ice has melted and retreated back with amazing speed, exposing nearly 50 miles of fjords, islands, and inlets.

In 1879, about a century after Vancouver's sail-by, one of the earliest white visitors to what is now **Glacier Bay National Park and Preserve** came calling. He was naturalist John Muir, drawn by the flora and fauna that had followed in the wake of glacial withdrawals and fascinated by the vast ice rivers that descended from the mountains to tidewater. Today, the naturalist's namesake glacier, like others in the park, continues to retreat dramatically. Its terminus is now scores of miles farther up bay from the small cabin he built at its face during his time there. (For more on the park, *see* Southeast Alaska in Chapter 4.)

The waterways provide access to no fewer than 16 tidewater glaciers, a dozen of which actively calve icebergs into the bay. The show can be mind-boggling. With a noise that sounds like cannons firing, bergs the size of 10-story office buildings sometimes come crashing from the "snout" of a glacier. The crash sends tons of water and spray skyward, and it propels mini-tidal waves outward from the point of impact. Johns Hopkins Glacier calves so often and with such volume that even the large cruise ships can seldom approach its face closer than two miles.

Companies that offer big-ship visits include Holland America Lines, Princess Cruises, Royal Viking Line, and World Explorer Cruises *(see* Chapter 3). During the several hours that the ships are in the bay, National Park Service naturalists come aboard to explain the comings and goings of the great glaciers, to point out features of the forests and islands and mountains, and to help spot black bears, brown bears, mountain goats, whales, porpoises, and the countless species of birds that call the area home.

Smaller, more intimate, and probably more informative is the day boat *Gold Rush*, which operates daily from the dock at Bartlett Cove, near Glacier Bay Lodge (tel. 800/622–2042). Uniformed Park Service naturalists sail aboard these excursions, too.

At Bartlett Cove, where the glaciers stood and then receded more than two centuries ago, the shore is covered with stands of high-towering spruce and hemlock. This is a climax forest, thick and lush and abounding with the wildlife of Southeast Alaska. As you sail farther into the great bay, the conifers become noticeably smaller, and they are finally replaced by alders and other leafy species, which took root and began growing only a few decades ago. Finally, deep into the bay where the glaciers have withdrawn in very recent years, the shorelines contain only plants and primitive lichens. Given enough time, however, these lands, too, will be covered with the same towering forests which you see at the bay's entrance.

The most adventurous way to see and explore Glacier Bay is up close. Real up close—as in paddling your own kayak through the bay's icy waters and inlets. You can book one of **Alaska Discovery**'s (369 S. Franklin St., Juneau 99801, tel. 907/586–1911) four- or seven-day guided expeditions. Unless you really know what you're doing, you're better off signing on with the guided tours. Alaska Discovery provides safe, seaworthy kayaks, and tents, gear, and food. Their guides are tough, knowledgeable Alaskans, and they've spent enough time in Glacier Bay's wild country to know what's safe and what's not.

Within Glacier Bay Park and Preserve there's only one overnight facility, Glacier Bay Lodge. If it's booked, or too pricey for your budget, don't worry. About a half hour's drive via the 10-mile road that leads out of the park is Gustavus, where additional lodges, inns, and bed-and-breakfast inns abound *(see* Lodging, below).

Gustavus calls itself "the way to Glacier Bay," and for airborne visitors the community is indeed the gateway to the park. The long, paved jet airport, built as a refueling strip during World War II, is one of the best and longest in Southeast Alaska, all the more impressive because facilities at the field are so limited.

Alaska Airlines, which serves Gustavus daily in the summer, has a large, rustic terminal at the site, and from a free telephone on the front porch of the terminal you can call any of the local hostelries for courtesy pickup. Smaller light-aircraft companies that serve the community out of Juneau also have on-site shelters. But aside from these facilities, there's only a small gift shop (the "Puffin Mall," with colorful art offerings and other curios) and a little A-frame where you can sample and purchase tenderly smoked salmon from the Salmon River Smokehouse.

With little in the way of industry or activity at the airport, Gustavus also boasts no "downtown." In fact, Gustavus is not a town. The 150 or so year-round residents there are most emphatic on this point; they regularly vote down incorporation as a city. Instead, Gustavus is a scattering of homes, farmsteads, arts and crafts studios, fishing and guiding charters, and other tiny enterprises peopled by hospitable individualists. It is, in many ways, exemplary of today's version of the frontier spirit in Alaska. For a listing of the 33 firms that make up the Gustavus Visitors Association, write to Box 167, Gustavus 99826.

What to See and Do with Children

Canoe rides in the modern equivalent of an Indian war canoe provide fun and exercise for young people and old at a woodsy lake near Ketchikan. *Alaska Travel Adventures, tel. 907/225–2840. Cost: $49 adults, $30 children.*

Fishing is popular among youngsters from toddlers on up, and no fishing license is required in Alaska for kids under 16. For the best saltwater shoreline, lake, or stream fishing, call the local Alaska Department of Fish and Game office in the city you're visiting. Ask where the hot spots of the moment are to be found. For little children, fishing off one of the region's many docks (life jackets are a must!) can be fun and productive.

Gold panning is fun and sometimes children actually uncover a few flecks of the precious metal in the bottom of their pans. You can buy a pan at almost any Alaska hardware or sporting goods store, or you can look for gold-panning excursions at visitor information centers.

Indian dancing will dazzle the younger set. Masked performers wearing bearskins and brightly designed dance blankets act out the stories of great hunts, fierce battles, and other legends. Among the best known dance groups is the Chilkat Indian Dancers of Fort Seward in Haines. *Performances Mon. and Sat. at 8:30* PM. Admission: $5.

There are **totem pole parks**—featuring the sometimes fearsome countenances of bears, killer whales, great birds, and legendary hunters—at Ketchikan, Wrangell, Sitka, Juneau, and Haines/Fort Seward *(see* Exploring Southeast Alaska, above). Other fine examples of the carver's art can be seen at the Indian villages of Kake, Angoon, and Hoonah *(see* Off the Beaten Track, below). At Kake, you can see a 132.5-foot totem that, when it was carved for the 1970 world's fair in Osaka, Japan, was the tallest in the world.

Kayaking in front of Mendenhall Glacier is sure to create vivid memories for youngsters as well as active adults *(see* Guided Tours, above, for tour operators and outfitters).

Summer sports are a passion in Southeast Alaska, and at Petersburg both young and old visitors are welcome to join in recreational softball or volleyball games. Call the Parks and Recreation Department for details (tel. 907/72–3392).

Off the Beaten Track

Surely one of the world's great travel bargains is the network of 150 or so **wilderness cabins** operated by the U.S. Forest Service alongside remote lakes and streams in the Tongass National Forest of Southeast Alaska. These cabins are weathertight A-frames and Panabodes equipped with bunks for six to eight occupants, tables, stoves, and outdoor privies. The cost: only $15 per night per party. Most are fly-in units, accessible by pontoon-equipped aircraft from virtually any community in the Panhandle. You provide your own sleeping bag, food, and cooking utensils. Don't be surprised if the Forest Service recommends you carry along a 30.06 or larger caliber rifle, in the unlikely event of a bear problem.

If you're a hot-springs or hot-tub enthusiast, **White Sulphur Springs** cabins, out of Sitka, or **Shakes Slough** cabins, accessible from Wrangell or Petersburg, boast these amenities. There's also a hot-springs pool of sorts, big enough for two or three to lounge in, at Bailey Bay, just north of Ketchikan's Revilla Island on the mainland. A 10-minute hike from a landing in a nearby lake or a two-mile trek on an unmaintained but negotiable trail from salt water will bring you to the site. Have your pilot fly over to show you your foot route before you land. Shelter here is a three-sided Adirondack shelter built as a public project during the Depression. *Details and reservation information from the USFS office in each community or call or write: U.S. Forest Service, Box 1628, Juneau 99802, tel. 907/ 586–8806.*

Offbeat, but boasting the ultimate in catered comfort, is the **Waterfall Resort** (Box 6440, Ketchikan, tel. 907/225–9461 or 800/544–5125) on Prince of Wales Island near Ketchikan. At this former commercial salmon cannery you sleep in Cape Cod–style cottages (former cannery workers' cabins, but *they* never had it so good); eat bountiful meals of salmon, halibut steak, and all the trimmings; and fish from your own private cabin cruiser under the tender loving care of your own private fish guide. Pricey, but worth it.

Farther north, **Baranof Wilderness Lodge** (Box 21022, Auke Bay 99824, tel. 907/586–8110) is one of the Panhandle's newer lodge facilities, located at Warm Springs Bay on Baranof Island. Kayaking, canoeing, hiking, and exploring are all options at this facility, as well as fresh- and saltwater fishing. Most popular activity of all is probably hot tubbing, in waters supplied by the warm springs.

One of Southeast Alaska's pioneer lodges is **Thayer Lake Lodge** (in summer, Box 211614, Auke Bay 99821, tel. 907/789–5646; in winter, Box 5416, Ketchikan 99901, tel. 907/789–0944), on Admiralty Island near Juneau. This is a rustic lodge-and-cabins operation that has been satisfying Juneau folk and Alaskan visitors for decades. Bob and Edith Nelson built this resort after World War II on one of the high country lakes in the Admiralty Island wilderness. They did it mostly with their own labor, using native timber for their buildings. Lake fishing is unexcelled for cutthroat and Dolly Varden trout (though they're not overly large). There's also canoeing, hiking, and wildlife photography.

Tenakee Springs is a tiny little fishing, vacation, and retirement community that clings to (in fact hangs out over) the shores of Chichagof Island. The town is accessible from Juneau by air or by the smaller Alaska ferry *LeConte* on an eight-hour run. You certainly won't find any Hiltons here, but there is a cozy Victorian-style lodge on the beachfront, or the local general store can rent you a cabin. With either type of accommodation comes the privilege of partaking in the town's principal pastime—bathing. Tenakee Springs' **bathhouse** is the centerpiece of the community's lifestyle. There is no coed time. Use the baths twice in two days and you'll likely meet three-fourths of the city's population who are of your gender. Use it three times and you'll meet the rest. Between baths you can fish for salmon, halibut, or crab; hike; pick berries; and visit with some of the friendliest townsfolk in the state. For cabin rentals, write Snyder Mercantile (Box 505, Tenakee Springs 99841, tel. 907/736–8001).

Tenakee Inn offers a cozy, beachfront Victorian-style lodge with kitchenettes, private bath, and family-style meals. Also provided are kayaks, bicycles, and skiff. *In summer, Box 54, Tenakee Springs 99841, tel. 907/736–9238; in winter, 167 S. Franklin St., Juneau 99801, tel. 907/586–1000.*

In Sitka, Burgess Bauder rents out his hand-built **Rockwell Lighthouse** (Box 277, Sitka 99835, tel. 907/747-3056) across the sound for $125 a day for a family. The price includes the use of a motorboat to get there.

Finally, if you hanker to know how the Indian village peoples of Southeast Alaska live today, you can fly or take the state ferry *LeConte* to **Kake, Angoon,** or **Hoonah.** You won't find much organized touring in any of these communities, but small, clean hotel accommodations are available (advance reservations strongly suggested), and fishing trips can be arranged by asking around. *In Kake: contact the New Town Inn, Box 222, Kake 99830, tel. 907/785–3472. In Angoon: write or call Kootznahoo Inlet Lodge, Box 134, Angoon 99820, tel. 907/788–3501; or Whalers Cove Lodge, Box 101, Angoon 99820, tel. 788–3123. In Hoonah: contact Totem Lodge, Box 320, Hoonah 99829, tel. 907/945–3636.*

Shopping

Art Galleries Along with the usual array of touristy work by talented but unspectacular artists, Southeast Alaska shops and galleries carry some impressive Alaskan paintings, lithographs, and drawings. Among the best: **Scanlon Gallery,** with locations downtown in Ketchikan (310 Mission St., tel. 907/225–4730) and in the Plaza PortWest, a couple of miles north of downtown. They not only handle major Alaska artists (Byron Birdsall, Rie Munoz, John Fahringer, Nancy Stonington) and local talent (Elizabeth Rose and Dick Miller) but also traditional and contemporary native art, soapstone, bronze, and ivory. In Juneau, knowledgeable locals frequent the **Rie Munoz Gallery** (210 Ferry Way, tel. 907/586–2112) near the cruiseship lightering dock downtown. Ms. Munoz is one of Alaska's favorite artists, creator of a stylized, simple, but colorful design technique that is much-copied but rarely equaled. Other artists' work is also on sale at the Munoz Gallery, including wood-block prints by nationally recognized artist Dale DeArmond. Various books illustrated by Rie Munoz and written by Alaskan children's author Jean Rogers are also available.

Gift Ideas Totem poles, a few inches high to several feet tall, are among the popular Indian-made items available in the Southeast Alaska Panhandle. Other handicrafts from the Tlingit and Haida Indians include wall masks, paddles, dance rattles, baskets, and tapestries with Southeast Alaska Indian designs. You'll find these items at gift shops up and down the coast. If you want to be sure of native Alaskan authenticity, buy items tagged with the state-approved "Authentic Native Handcraft From Alaska" label.

Gold-nugget rings, bracelets, necklaces, and watchbands, though costly, are popular among Alaskans and Alaska visitors. One Juneau dealer, the **Nugget Shop** on Front Street, will even sell you plain gold nuggets if you've missed finding any in the streams around the region.

Salmon—smoked, canned, or packaged otherwise—is another popular take-home item, for your own consumption or for friends who had to stay behind. Virtually every community has at least one canning and/or smoking operation that packs and ships local seafood. Throughout the region in food stores and gift shops, you'll likely run into **Silver Lining Seafoods** products, a Ketchikan-based company with a consistently high-quality product in attractive packaging.

Another gourmet delicacy is a product Southeasterners refer to as Petersburg shrimp. Small (they're seldom larger than half your pinky finger), tender, and succulent, they're much treasured by Alaskans and often sent "outside" by them as thank-you gifts. You'll find the little critters fresh in meat departments and canned in gift sections, at food stores throughout the Panhandle. You can buy canned Petersburg shrimp in Petersburg at the Greens and Grains Deli, downtown on First St. or mail order them from Box 5, Petersburg 99833 (tel. 907/772–3392).

A new item in recent years is salmon skin leather—made into wallets, belts, keyholders, purses, and other items. A Juneau firm, **Alas Skins, Inc.** (on S. Franklin St. opposite the cruise ship terminal, tel. 907/780–6900), has pioneered this new industry. See their wares in local shops or visit their showroom.

You can't take it with you because of limited shelf life, but when you're "shopping" the bars and watering holes of Southeast Alaska, ask for Chinook Beer, an amber beer brewed and bottled in Juneau. Alaskans rate Chinook highly—and so did the judges at 1988's national Great American Beer Festival competition in Denver. Against 160 other beers, Chinook brought home a gold medal in the Alt-style category and was elected the people's choice among the 4,500 people attending the festival. Visitors are welcome to visit the mini-brewery's plant and sample the product during the bottling operation on Tuesday and Thursday 11–4. *5429 Shaune Dr., Juneau, tel. 907/780–5866.*

Up the stairs in the restored old Senate Building on S. Franklin Street in Juneau is the **Russian Shop** (tel. 907/586–2778), a depository of icons, samovars, lacquered boxes, nesting dolls, and other items that reflect Alaska's 18th- and 19th-century Russian heritage. One side of the shop is similarly, and surprisingly, devoted to Norwegian wares, including traditional Norwegian wool sweaters.

Participant Sports

Bicycling   In spite of sometimes wet weather, bicycling is very popular in Southeast Alaska communities. There are plenty of flat roads to ride (and some killer hills, too, if you're game) and the cycling can be glorious beside saltwater bays or within great towering forests. Unfortunately, bike rentals in the region seem to cycle in and out of business faster than you can shift derailers. Best bet if you don't bring your own in the back of a car or camper is to call bike shops or the parks and recreation departments in the towns you're visiting. Ask who in town is supplying rentals at the moment. Lodgings at Tenakee and Gustavus have bikes on hand for the use of their guests.

Canoeing/Kayaking   Paddling has been a pleasant way for visitors to see Southeast Alaska since the first Russians arrived on the scene in 1741 and watched the Indians do it. In Ketchikan, contact **Alaska Travel Adventures** (tel. 907/225–2840) for an Indian canoe excursion on Connel Lake north of town; smoked fish and other Indian delights are part of the experience. The **Ketchikan Parks and Recreation Department** (tel. 907/225–3111) rents kayaks. At Sitka, **Baidarka Boats** (tel. 907/747–8996) offers seakayak rentals and custom guided trips. In Juneau, **Alaska Discovery** (tel. 907/586–1811) is the company to see for escorted boat excursions in Glacier Bay National Park and Preserve or Admiralty Island, or for kayaking in the lake in front of Mendenhall Glacier.

Kayak rentals for unescorted Glacier Bay exploring and camping can be arranged through **Glacier Bay Sea Kayaks** (Box 26, Gustavus 99826, tel. 907/697–2257). Twice a day, at 9 AM and 6 PM, their experienced kayakers give orientations on handling the craft plus camping and routing suggestions. The company will also make reservations aboard the regular sightseeing day boat to drop kayakers off and pick them up in the most scenic country.

Fishing   The prospect of bringing a lunker king salmon or a leaping, diving, fighting rainbow trout to net is the reason many visitors choose an Alaska vacation. Local give-away guidebooks and the State of Alaska's *Official Vacation Planner* contain the names of scores of reputable charter boats and boat rental agencies in every community along the Panhandle coast. Your best bet for catching salmon in salt water is from a boat. Similarly, the very finest angling for freshwater species (rainbows, cutthroat, lake trout) is to be found at fly-in lakes and resorts. Still, there's more than adequate fishing right from saltwater shores or in lakes and streams accessible by roads. To learn where the fish are biting at any given time, call the local office of the Alaska Department of Fish and Game in the community you're visiting, or contact the ADFG's main office (Box 3-2000, Juneau 998023, tel. 907/465–4112).

Golf   Juneau's par-three nine-hole **Mendenhall Golf course** (2101 Industrial Blvd., tel. 907/789–7323) is pretty modest. Still, its location on saltwater wetlands beside the waters of Gastineau

Channel makes it one-of-a-kind. You probably won't haul your clubs all the way to Alaska to sample these fairways and roughs, but rentals are available.

Hiking and Backpacking Trekking woods, mountains, and beaches is Southeast Alaska's unofficial regional sport. Toddlers, teens, young adults, and oldsters can be seen along Southeast's trails and paths. Many of the trails are old, abandoned mining roads. Others are natural routes—in some sections, even game trails—meandering over ridges, through forests, and alongside streams and glaciers. A few, like the backpacking Chilkoot Trail out of Skagway, rate five stars for historical significance, scenery, and hiker aids en route. There's not a community in Southeast Alaska that doesn't have easy access to at least some hiking or backpacking. For more information, contact the visitor bureau or parks and recreation department in the community you're visiting. The Alaska Division of Parks Southeast regional office (400 Willoughby Ave., tel. 907/465–4563) will send you a list of state-maintained trails and parks in the Panhandle. Parks and Recreation/Juneau (tel. 907/586–5226) sponsors a group hike each Wednesday morning for locals and visitors.

Motor Scooters and Mopeds Two-wheeled travel has suddenly sprung upon the Ketchikan and Juneau scenes. **Scooter Rentals, Inc.,** of Ketchikan operates from downtown on the wooden cruise-ship dock. If no one is around, call the number on the door, and someone will rush right down to help you. Only available in good weather.

Running and Jogging The national running craze is alive and well along Southeast streets, roads, and trails. Hotel clerks and visitor information offices will be glad to make route suggestions if you need them. If you plan to run, bring along a light sweatsuit and running rain gear as well as shorts and a T-shirt. The weather can be hot and sweaty one day, chilly and wet the next. If you plan to be in Juneau early in July, call the Parks and Recreation Department (tel. 907/586–5226) and check the date of the annual **Governor's Cup Fun Run.** Hundreds of Juneau racers, runners, joggers, race walkers, and mosey-alongers take part in this three-mile event. Other marathons, half marathons, 5Ks, or similar events take place in various communities throughout the summer. The most grueling race in these parts is the annual fall **Klondike Trail of '98 Road Relay** event, spanning 110 miles between Skagway and Whitehorse on the Klondike and Alaska highways. For details: Carol Clark, Tourism Industry Association of the Yukon (102–302 Steele St., Whitehorse, Yukon, Canada Y1A 2C5, tel. 403/668–3331).

Scuba Considering that the visibility is not very good in most Southeast waters, there's a lot of scuba and skin-diving activity throughout the region. Quarter-inch wet suits are a must. So is a buddy; stay close together. Local dive shops can steer you to the best places to dive for abalone, scallops, and crabs, and advise you on the delights and dangers of underwater wrecks. Shops that rent tanks and equipment to qualified divers include **Mac's Dive Shop** (2214 Muir, Juneau, tel. 907/789–5115), **Scuba Crafts, Inc.** (4485 N. Douglas Hwy., Juneau, tel. 907/586–2341), **Alaska Diving Service** (1601 Tongass Ave., Ketchikan, tel. 907/225–4667), and **Southeast Diving & Sports** (203 Lincoln Ave., Sitka, tel. 907/747–8279).

Skiing *Cross-country* Nordic skiing is a favorite winter pastime for outdoor enthusiasts, especially in the northern half of the Panhandle. Although promoted mostly by and for the locals, visitors are always welcome. In Petersburg, the favorite locale for Nordic types is the end of **Three Lakes Loop.** Old logging roads and trails are popular, as well. If you arrive without your boards, call the Chamber of Commerce Visitor Center (tel. 907/772–3646). They'll try to line up some loaners for you.

In Juneau, ski rentals are available along with many suggestions for touring the trails and ridges around town from **Foggy Mountain Shop** (134 S. Franklin St., tel. 907/586–6780).

From Haines, **Alaska Nature Tours** (Box 491, Haines 99827, tel. 907/766–2876) operates a winter Nordic shuttle bus to flattracking in the Chilkat Bald Eagle Preserve and across the Canadian border atop Chilkat Pass in British Columbia.

Downhill   **Eaglecrest** (155 Seward St., Juneau 99801, tel. 907/586–5284) on Douglas Island, just 30 minutes from downtown Juneau, offers late November to mid-April skiing on a well-groomed mountain with two double-chair lifts, a beginner's platter-pull, cross-country trails, ski school (including downhill, Nordic, and telemark), ski rental shop, cafeteria, and trilevel day lodge. Because this is Southeast Alaska, knowledgeable skiers pack rain slickers along with parkas, hats, gloves, and other gear. Weekends and holidays there are bus pickups at hotels and motels.

Tennis   You won't find the likes of Wimbledon in Southeast Alaska, but you will find courts in Ketchikan, Wrangell, Petersburg, Juneau, and Skagway. The **Juneau Racquet Club,** about 10 miles north of downtown, adjacent to Mendenhall Mall, will accommodate out-of-towners at their first-class indoor tennis and racquetball courts. Facilities include sauna, Jacuzzi, exercise equipment, snack bar, massage tables, and sports shop. *Tel. 907/789–2181. 1-day fee for nonmembers: $5 until 4 PM, $8 until 8:30 PM, $5 8:30–10 PM.*

Spectator Sports

With the possible exception of basketball, Southeast Alaska's spectator sports probably don't offer much visitor excitement. High school sports (basketball, wrestling, track, limited football, skiing, and swimming) and Little League baseball in the summertime attract large numbers of locals, but not very many fans from outside the region. There are no semi-pro or professional baseball teams in the Panhandle. The devotion of large numbers of Southeast adults to summer softball, however, borders on outright addiction.

Basketball   Watching two teams of five trying to shoot balls in hoops is Southeast Alaska's major spectator sport. Each January in Juneau, the local Lions Clubs' Golden North tournament attracts teams from all over the Panhandle and even nearby Canada. And the University of Alaska–Southeast Whales and Lady Whales teams likewise are often in town to offer respectable court action. For schedules, contact University of Alaska–Southeast (11120 Glacier Hwy., Juneau 99801, tel. 907/789–4400).

Dining and Lodging

Highly recommended hotels and restaurants are indicated with a star ★ .

Major credit cards are usually accepted, but there are exceptions. It's best to inquire in advance.

Dining Portions are almost universally generous and the variety of offerings ranges from standard American steak and potatoes to Italian, Mexican, Tex-Mex, Chinese, Japanese, and, in recent years, Vietnamese. Seafood, not surprisingly, comprises a large share of most restaurant menus. In summertime the king salmon, halibut, king crab, cod, or prawns are likely to be fresh from the sea. By late fall through to spring, they may have been frozen—and frankly not as tasty—so it pays to ask if its fresh.

Restaurants and cafes in the Panhandle are uniformly informal. Gentlemen in coats and ties and ladies in dresses will always feel comfortable in the nicer places, but so will diners in more casual slacks, sweaters, and sport shirts. Clean jeans and windbreakers are fine in most places. Restaurant hours vary seasonally. It is best to call ahead before you start out.

Restaurants are listed in the following price categories:

Category	Cost*
Expensive	$40–$60
Moderate	$20–$40
Inexpensive	under $20

per person without tax, service, or drinks

Lodging Hotels, motels, lodges, and inns run the gamut in Southeast Alaska from very traditional urban hostelries—the kind you'll find almost anywhere—to charming small-town inns and rustic cabins in the boondocks.

The most rooms, and the most choices, are to be found in Ketchikan and Juneau. Accommodations in any of the Panhandle communities, however, are usually not hard to come by even in the summer, except when festivals, fishing derbies, fairs, and other special events are underway. To be on the safe side and get your first choice, you should make reservations as early as possible. With the exception of bed-and-breakfasts (B&Bs), most hotels accept the major credit cards. Hotels and lodging places are listed under the following categories:

Category	Cost*
Very Expensive	over $120
Expensive	$90–$120
Moderate	$50–$90
Inexpensive	under $50

double room without tax or service

Glacier Bay/
Gustavus
Dining
★

Glacier Bay Country Inn. Another inn where the emphasis is on gourmet dining, with foods fresh from the sea and the inn's own garden. The inn is a large rambling log structure of marvelous cupolas, dormers, gables, and porches. Among guests' favorites: halibut with fresh sorrel sauce, homemade fettuccine, and rhubarb custard pie. Dinner guests not staying at the inn must make reservations in advance. *On the main road halfway between the airport and Bartlett Cove, tel. 907/697–2288. No credit cards, but personal checks accepted. Moderate.*

★ **Gustavus Inn.** The family-style meals at this former homestead are legendary. Hosts David and Jo Ann Lesh—carrying on a tradition established decades ago by David's parents—heap bountiful servings of seafood and fresh vegetable dishes on the plates of overnight guests and walk-ins who reserve in advance. *On the main road, tel. 907/697–2254. MC, V accepted, but cash or personal or traveler's checks preferred. Moderate.*

Glacier Bay Lodge. If it swims or crawls in the sea hereabouts, you'll find it on the menu in the dining room at this, the only lodge actually in Glacier Bay National Park and Preserve. Steaks and other selections are available as well. Located on the main floor of the massive, timbered lodge, the dining room looks out on the chill waters of Bartlett Cove. *Tel. 907/697–2225. AE, MC, V, DC. Inexpensive–Moderate.*

Open Gate Cafe. Nothing fancy here, just good wholesome cooking that the locals seem to like—fresh baked breads, pastries, deli sandwiches. Monday night is pizza night; Saturdays feature prime ribs. *On the dock road, tel. 907/697–2227. No credit cards, but personal checks accepted. Inexpensive.*

Lodging
★

Gustavus Inn. Established in 1965 on a pioneer Gustavus homestead, the Gustavus Inn continues a tradition of gracious Alaska rural living and vacationing. In the original homestead building and in a new structure completed in 1988, there are rooms with full private bath and a few that share facilities. Glacier trips, fishing expeditions, bicycle rides around the community, or berry picking in season are things-to-do options. The option of choice for many guests is simply to do nothing but enjoy the quiet, tranquillity, and notable food the inn has to offer. *On main road (mailing address: Box 60, Gustavus 99826), tel. 907/697–2254. Courtesy-car pickup at the airport. MC, V accepted, but cash or personal or traveler's checks preferred. Very Expensive.*

★ **Glacier Bay Country Inn.** This is the "new kid on the block" among inns in Gustavus. It opened in 1986 with accommodations for 14 guests in a picturesque but fully modern structure built from local hand-logged timbers. Innkeepers Al and Annie Unrein outfitted the inn with cozy comforters, warm flannel sheets, and fluffy towels in each room for a homelike feeling. The Unreins will arrange sightseeing and flightseeing tours. They also operate charter-boat trips into Glacier Bay and nearby waters aboard their elegant *M/V Pacific*, a 42-foot yacht with teak woodwork, two staterooms (sleeping four to six) and two bathrooms. *On main road halfway between the airport and Bartlett Cove (mailing address: Box 5, Gustavus 99826), tel. 907/697–2288; fax 907/697–2289. No credit cards, but personal checks accepted. Expensive.*

Glacier Bay Lodge. The only hotel accommodations actually within Glacier Bay National Park and Preserve. The lodge is constructed of massive timbers, and in spite of its substantial size it blends well into the thick rain forest that surrounds it on three sides. Room accommodations—fully modern—are accessible by boardwalk ramps from the main lodge. From the Bartlett Cove dock out front, visitors venture on day boats or overnight cruises up bay into the glacier country. *Located at Bartlett Cove (mailing address: Box 108, Gustavus 99826 or 523 Pine St., Seattle, WA 98101), tel. 907/697-2225 or 800/622-2042. Facilities: lounge, gift shop, flightseeing reservations desk. AE, MC, V, DC. Expensive.*

The Puffin Bed & Breakfast. These are attractive cabins located in a wooded homestead. Bath and shower are in a separate building. Bikes are available for guests' use. Full breakfast is included. The owners also operate Puffin Travel, for fishing and sightseeing charters, and Puffin Arts and Crafts Shop at the airport. *In central Gustavus (mailing address: Box 3, Gustavus 99826); tel. 907/697-2260 in summer, 907/789-9787 in winter. AE, MC, V. Inexpensive.*

Haines
Dining

The Lighthouse Restaurant. Located at the foot of Main Street next to the boat harbor, the Lighthouse offers a great view of Lynn Canal, boats, and boaters, along with its fine barbecued ribs, steaks, and seafoods. Its Harbor Bar is a popular watering hole for commercial fishermen. It's colorful but can get a little loud as the night wears on. *Front St. on the harbor, tel. 907/766-2442. AE, MC, V. Moderate.*

The Bamboo Room, Popular for sandwiches, burgers, fried chicken, and seafood. *2nd Ave. near Main St., tel. 907/766-9109. Inexpensive.*

The Catalyst. Serves up seafood, fine pastries, and a generous salad bar in a European atmosphere. *Main St. and 3rd Ave., tel. 907/766-2670. Closed Sun. Inexpensive.*

Chilkat Restaurant and Bakery. Offers family-style cooking in a homelike setting. *5th Ave. near Main St., tel. 907/766-2920. Closed Sun. Inexpensive.*

Commander's Room Restaurant and Lounge. Located in the large white rambling home that served as the former commanding officer's quarters at old Fort Seward, this is the dining room for the Halsingland Hotel. It has been satisfying hotel guests and Haines folk for decades. Seafood is the specialty here and halibut is a consistent pleaser. The restaurant has a full salad bar and full "potato bar" of baked potatoes, boiled red potatoes, rice pilaf, and vegetables with varied toppings (cheese, chili, etc.). Nearby, at the Indian Tribal House on the parade grounds, the Halsingland also prepares a nightly salmon bake called the Port Chilkoot Potlatch, priced at $17.50 for all you can eat. *At Ft. Seward, tel. 907/766-2000. AE, DC, MC, V. Inexpensive.*

Lodging
★

Captain's Choice Motel. A conventional motel, located in downtown Haines and featuring amenities such as cable TV, phones, and rooms with bath and toilet facilities. Ask for a room looking out over the waters of Portage Cove. *2nd St. and Dalton St. (mailing address: Box 392, Haines 99827), tel. 800/478-2345 within Alaska or 800/247-7153 outside Alaska. 40 rooms, including 3 deluxe suites: AE, MC, V. Moderate-Expensive.*

Halsingland Hotel. The officers of old Fort Seward once lived in the big, white structures that today comprise the 60-room Halsingland Hotel. Most of the rooms have private baths, a few do not. All are fully carpeted and have wildlife photos on the walls. *On the parade grounds, Ft. Seward (mailing address:*

Box 1589, Haines 99827), tel. 907/766–2000 or 800/542–6363 outside Alaska. AE, MC, V. Inexpensive–Moderate.

There are several B&Bs in Haines, and one youth hostel. For more information call the visitor information center (2nd Ave. near Willard St., tel. 907/766–2202).

Juneau **The Summit.** Unlikely as it may seem, this small, intimate,
Dining candle-lit restaurant in the Inn at the Waterfront is the city's
★ most prestigious dining place. Of 30 entrees on the menu, 20 are seafood—including abalone sautéed in butter and almonds, scallops, prawns, halibut, and a tender salmon offering called Salmon Gastineau. If you like steak, their New York La Bleu features New York strip steak with blue cheese. *455 S. Franklin St., tel. 907/586–2050. Reservations strongly recommended. AE, DC, MC, V. No lunch. Moderate–Expensive.*

Mike's. For decades Mike's, in the former mining community of Douglas across the bridge from Juneau, has been serving up seafood, steaks, and pastas. Their treatment of tiny Petersburg shrimp is particularly noteworthy. Rivaling the food, however, is the view from the picture windows at the rear of the restaurant. Mike's looks over the waters of Gastineau Channel to Juneau and the ruins of the old AJ mine. *1102 2nd St. in Douglas, tel. 907/364–3271. AE, DC, MC, V. No lunch weekends. Moderate.*

★ **The Fiddlehead.** This is probably Juneau's favorite restaurant, a delightful place of light woods, gently patterned wallpaper, stained glass, hanging plants, and historic photos on the wall. The food is healthy, generously served, and, well, *different.* Would you believe, for instance, a light dinner of black beans and rice? Or pasta Greta Garbo, which is locally smoked salmon tossed with fettuccine in cream sauce? Or chicken and eggplant Szechuan, consisting of chicken and eggplant sautéed with bean paste and served over rice? Homemade bread from their bakery is likewise laudable. *429 Willoughby Ave., tel. 907/586–3150. No smoking. Reservations recommended. MC, V. Inexpensive–Moderate.*

The Silverbow Inn. Here's another place so popular with locals that you should reserve ahead for meals during normal dining hours. The decor is "early Juneau," with settings, chairs, and tables (no two are alike) of the kind you might have found in someone's parlor during the city's gold-mining era. The main structure, for years one of the town's major bakeries, was built in 1912. The wine list is limited but selective; dinner entrées change daily and might include halibut with almonds, salmon Florentine, stir-fry prawns, or red snapper. *120 2nd Ave., tel. 907/586–4146. AE, DC, MC, V. Hours vary Oct.–April. Inexpensive–Moderate.*

El Sombrero. It's tiny and a trifle crowded, but the fare in this north-of-the-border Mexican restaurant would make Poncho Villa homesick. If you eat here at noon you get more food for your dollar than if you dine in the evening. A dinner favorite combines a meat or chicken taco, cheese enchilada, plus rice or beans. Order the same meal at noon, and for the same price you get rice *and* beans. *157 S. Franklin, tel. 907/586–6770. AE, DC, MC, V. Closed Sun. Sept.–April. Inexpensive–Moderate.*

★ **Gold Creek Salmon Bake.** The decor here is the Alaska outdoors. You eat under a roofed shelter on comfortable benches and tables, but all around you are trees, mountains, and the rushing water of Gold Creek (where gold was discovered in 1880). The salmon bake itself is thought to be Alaska's oldest such outdoor offering. Fresh caught salmon (supplemented sometimes by halibut as well) is cooked over an alder-smoke fire until it's tender but done. A simple but succulent sauce of brown sugar, margarine, and lemon juice adds the final appetizing touch. Along with the salmon comes hot baked beans, salad, Jello, sourdough or wheat bread, and a can of beer, soft drink, or coffee. (Fixed price, $17.) After dinner you can pan for gold in the stream (pans are available for your use, no charge, keep all the gold you find) or wander up the hill to the remains of AJ gold-mine buildings. *End of Basin Rd., tel. 907/ 586–1424. Free bus ride from in front of the Baranof Hotel in downtown Juneau. No credit cards. Closed mid-Sept.–April. Inexpensive.*

Lodging   **The Baranof Hotel.** For half a century the Baranof has been— for commercial travelers, legislators, lobbyists, and tourists— the city's prestige address. That designation has been challenged in recent years by the Westmark (like the Baranof, a unit of the Westmark chain), but the nine-story hostelry probably remains the hotel of choice for most visitors to the capital city. The lobby and most rooms have been extensively refurbished in recent years in tasteful woods and a lighting style reminiscent of 1939, when the hotel first opened. Facilities include the Capital City Cafe for coffee and light snacks, the Bubble Room lounge and piano bar, and the Gold Room for fine dining. Also on site: a travel agency and Alaska Airlines ticket office. *127 N. Franklin St., tel. 907/586–2660 or 800/344–0970. 200 rooms. AE, MC, V. Very Expensive.*

Westmark Juneau. A high rise (by Juneau standards), the seven-story Westmark is situated across Main Street from Juneau's Centennial Hall convention center and across Egan Drive from the docks. Rooms are basically modern in decor, and the lobby is distinguished by a massive carved eagle figure. Extensive additional wood-mural carvings may be seen on the wall of the Woodcarver Dining Room. *51 W. Egan Dr., tel. 907/ 586–6900 or 800/544–0970. 105 rooms. AE, MC, V. Very Expensive.*

★ **The Prospector.** A short walk west of downtown and right next door to the State Museum, this smaller but fully modern hotel is what many business travelers and a number of legislators like to call home while they're in Juneau. You'll find very large rooms here, and in The Diggings dining room and lounge you can enjoy what some consider to be the finest prime rib in Southeast Alaska. Steaks and seafood are also popular. *375 Whittier Ave., tel. 907/586–3737 or 800/331–2711. 60 rooms. AE, MC, V. Expensive.*

Airport TraveLodge. The rooms and furnishings are pretty standard fare. The structure, matching Fernando's Restaurant inside, is Mexican in design and decor. The motel is one of only two in the community with an indoor swimming pool—a plus if you want to unwind after a day of touring. *9200 Glacier Hwy., tel. 907/789–9700. 86 rooms. AE, MC, V. Moderate.*

Country Lane Inn. Another motel with a pool and a Jacuzzi, the Country Lane Inn is a Best Western. Baskets of multicolored flowers hang along the entrance walk to rooms, a pleasant welcome indeed. The lobby, though quite small, seems like a country home parlor, with comfortable chairs, pillowed couch and library books available. The coffee is on all the time. *9300 Glacier Hwy., tel. 907/789–5005 or 800/334–9401. 50 rooms. AE, MC, V. Moderate.*

★ Travelers who enjoy staying in restored historic hotels have three to choose from in downtown Juneau: the **Silverbow Inn,** in the old bakery building dating from the late 1890s (120 2nd St., tel. 907/586–4146. 6 rooms. Moderate); the **Alaskan Hotel,** a 1913 structure (167 S. Franklin St., tel. 907/586–1000. 40 rooms. Inexpensive/Moderate); and the 1898 **Inn at the Waterfront** (455 S. Franklin St., tel. 907/586–2050. 29 rooms. Inexpensive–Moderate).

Ketchikan **Salmon Falls Resort.** This is Ketchikan's newest (and many say
Dining nicest) eating place. It's a half-hour drive from town, but the
★ seafood and steaks served up in the huge, octagonal restaurant make the drive more than worthwhile. The chef especially recommends seafood caught fresh from adjacent waters. Locals give high marks to the halibut and shellfish stew. The restaurant is built of pine logs, and at the center of the dining room, supporting the roof, rises a 40-foot section of 48-inch pipe manufactured to be part of the Alaska pipeline. The dining area overlooks the waters of Clover Passage, where sunsets can be vivid red and remarkable. *Mile 17, North Tongass Hwy., tel. 907/225–2752 or 800/247–9059. Reservations recommended. AE, DC, MC, V. Moderate.*

Charley's. Located in the Ingersoll Hotel, Charley's is a favorite breakfast/luncheon spot for Ketchikan business types. It's a popular family place, too, offering dinners that don't devastate the pocketbook. Decor is sort of nostalgic, with brass railings, deep-maroon trim on chairs and tables, and an etched-glass window. Seafood is a specialty here—salmon, halibut, or whatever is fresh. For breakfast, try reindeer sausage with your eggs. For dinner, the lobster is first rate, even though it's not from these waters. Bar service available; music in the evenings. *208 Front St., tel. 907/225–5090. AE, DC, MC, V. Inexpensive–Moderate.*

Gilmore Gardens. Eating or sipping a drink here is another stroll down memory lane. Deep burgundy patterns in the carpets, lace place mats under each china table setting, padded old-fashioned chairs, and hanging lights combine to revive the 1930s and '40s. It's also the city's only cappuccino and espresso bar. Among notable international menu items is the prawns amaretto, prepared with amaretto liqueur, a touch of white wine, cream, and just a hint of orange. Prawns, in fact are a specialty, and the menu also includes prawns scampi and sweet-and-sour prawns. For breakfast try their eggs Alaska, which some may confuse with eggs Benedict, except it's prepared with Alaska smoked salmon, not ham. For dessert, locals recommend the peanut butter pie. *326 Front St., tel. 907/225–9423. AE, DC, MC, V. Inexpensive–Moderate.*

Other better-than-adequate eating places in the community include the **Clover Pass Resort** (Mile 15, North Tongass Hwy., tel. 907/247–2234. Inexpensive–Moderate) for excellent seafood and a view of sport fishermen coming, going, and bringing home their catches; **Grandeli's** (in the Plaza Portwest Mall, tel. 907/225–1414. Inexpensive); and **Kay's Kitchen** (2813 Tongass Ave., tel. 907/225–5860. Inexpensive) for homemade soups and generous sandwiches.

Lodging **Royal Executive Suites.** Nothing in the plain, square exterior of this hotel building or in its Spartan lobby reflects the deluxe accommodations waiting within. Some of the 14 units are split level with circular stairways; all are carpeted in steel grays or other light colors with pastel shaded furniture and natural wood trims. Many of the units have full kitchens and Jacuzzis, and all guests have access to an exercise room with treadmill, hot tub, and sauna. Windows are large and look out on the busy water and air traffic in Tongass Narrows. There is no restaurant on site, but meals can be brought to your room. Located between downtown and the ferry terminal. *1471 Tongass Ave. (mailing address: Box 8331, Ketchikan 99901), tel. 907/225–1900. AE, DC, MC, V. Expensive–Very Expensive.*

★ **Ingersoll Hotel.** Old-fashioned patterned wallpaper, wood wainscoting around the walls, and etched-glass windows on the oak registration desk set a 1930s mood for this three-story downtown hotel (actually built in the mid-'20s). Furnishings are standard, with bright Alaskan art on the walls. Some rooms have a view of the cruise dock and the waters of Tongass Narrows. *303 Mission St. (mailing address: Box 6440, Ketchikan 99901), tel. 907/225–2124. 60 rooms. Charley's restaurant on site. AE, DC, MC, V. Moderate.*

The Landing. The sign outside still says "Hilltop Motel," but the new name is "The Landing," in recognition of the ferry landing site in the waters of Tongass Narrows across the street. The hotel is modern, and the 46 rooms are nicely furnished in typical American motel decor. *3434 Tongass Ave., tel. 907/225–5166. Cafe, lounge on site. AE, DC, D, MC, V. Moderate.*

The Gilmore Hotel. Like the Ingersoll down the street, the Gilmore's narrow lobby sets the mood of the place with 1930s-style wine-colored carpeting, hanging lights, and a comfortable little sitting area (on a landing up the stairs) with easy chairs, table, and a stained-glass window. Rooms are plain but clean, with bright bedspreads of floral and leaf patterns. Standard furnishings include a desk, chairs, chest of drawers, and TV. A few of the hotel's 42 rooms share toilet facilities down the hall. *326 Front St., tel. 907/225–9423. No elevator. AE, MC, V. Inexpensive.*

Petersburg
Dining
★

The Beachcomber Inn. Seafood, with a distinctly Norwegian flair, is the specialty in this restored cannery building on the shores of Wrangell Narrows. If you're there on a smorgasbord night you may sample red-snapper fish cakes, salmon loaf, Norwegian (emphatically *not* Swedish) meat balls, creamed potatoes, and sugary desserts such as *sandbakkelse, lefsa,* or *krumkakke* cones. Petersburg's famed beer-batter halibut is also served here, as are salmon steaks and other traditional seafoods. *Mile 4, Mitkof Hwy., tel. 907/772–3888. AE, MC, V. Inexpensive.*

Helse. Natural foods, including enormous vegetable-laden sandwiches, are a specialty here. Also soups, chowders, home-baked breads, and salads. *Sing Lee Alley and Harbor Way, tel. 907/772–3444. No credit cards. Inexpensive.*

The Homestead. Nothing fancy here, just basic American steaks, local prawns and halibut, salad bar, and especially generous breakfasts. A popular place with the locals. *217 Main St., tel. 907/772–3900. DC, MC, V. Inexpensive.*

Pellerito's Pizza. You'll get authentic pizzas with homemade sausages here. Or try the pizza with local shrimp. *Across from the ferry terminal. Tel. 907/772–3727. No credit cards. Inexpensive.*

One of the most hospitable eateries in town is **Greens and Grains** for deli selections to go or sit-down meals at the restaurant. Try the Petersburg shrimp. *Nordic Dr. and Excel St., tel. 907/772–4433. Inexpensive.*

Lodging
★ **Tides Inn.** This is the largest hotel in town, a block uphill from Petersburg's main thoroughfare. It has 46 rooms, all fully modern, with standard furnishings and full baths, showers, and toilet facilities. There's always coffee on in the small, informal lobby, and in the morning you're welcome to complimentary juices, cereals, and pastries. Some units are equipped with kitchens. Ask for a room in the new wing; these units have a view of the boat harbor. *1st and Dolphin Sts. (mailing address: Box 1048, Petersburg 99833), tel. 907/772–4288. AE, DC, MC, V. Moderate.*

Scandia House. Very old country Norwegian, this 24-unit hotel on Petersburg's main street has been a local fixture since 1910. Here, too, the coffee is always on in a small lobby accented by etched-glass windows on the entrance doors and large oil paintings on the wall showing local old-timers in colorful Norwegian garb. "American" units have full toilet facilities; "European" rooms have showers and toilets down the hall. At least one unit has kitchenette facilities, and all rooms are squeaky clean, with standard furnishings including TV. Norwegian rosemaling designs on the exterior make this a frequent camera subject. *110 Nordic Dr. (mailing address: Box 689, Petersburg 99833), tel. 907/772–4281. AE, DC, MC, V. Inexpensive–Moderate.*

Sitka
Dining
★ **Channel Club.** This is Sitka's number one gourmet eating establishment—the winner on five different occasions of the Silver Spoon award from the Gourmet Club of America. It's a toss-up whether to order steak or seafood here, but whatever you choose will be good. Halibut cheeks are a consistent favorite; if you order steak, don't ask the chef for his steak seasoning recipe—it's a secret. Decor is ship-oriented, with glass fishing balls, whale baleen, and Alaska pictures on the wall. *Mile 3.5, Halibut Point Rd., tel. 907/747–9916. AE, DC, MC, V. Moderate–Expensive.*

Raven Room. Located in the Westmark Shee Atika Hotel, the Raven Room offers seafood, pasta, and steaks in a setting rich in Southeastern Alaska native decor. Dancing in the evening in the Kadataan Lounge. *330 Seward St., tel. 907/747–6241. AE, DC, MC, V. Moderate.*

Also recommended: **Marina Restaurant,** for Mexican or Italian fare (205 Harbor Dr., tel. 907/747–8840. Inexpensive); and **Staton's Steak House** for (you guessed it) steak and seafood (Harbor Dr. and Maksutoff St., tel. 907/747–3396. Inexpensive).

Lodging
★ **Westmark Shee Atika.** If you stay here for a night or two, you will surely come away with an increased appreciation for Southeast Alaska Indian art and culture. Displays throughout the hotel—full wall murals in the lobby and additional artwork in the rooms—tell of the history, legends, and exploits of the Tlingit people. Many of the hotel's nearly 100 rooms overlook Crescent Harbor and the islands in the waters beyond; others have mountain and forest views. *330 Seward St. (mailing address: Box 78, Sitka 99835), tel. 907/747–6241 or 800/544–0970. AE, DC, MC, V. Very Expensive.*

A number of B&Bs have sprung up in Sitka in recent years; ask the visitor center for a referral or write to the **Sitka Convention and Visitors Bureau** (Box 1226, Sitka 99835).

Skagway
Dining
Chilkoot Dining Room. If it's not packed with tourists the Chilkoot offers some of Skagway's most gracious dining. Try, therefore, to avoid the 6:30 PM rush hour. Decor here is gold rush, but a lot grander and more plush than anything the stampeders ever experienced. If it's on the menu, try the family-style crab dinner. *3rd Ave., east of Broadway, tel. 907/983–2291. AE, DC, MC, V. Moderate.*

Golden North Restaurant. This is the dining room in the Golden North Hotel, and to eat here is to return to the days of gold rush con man Soapy Smith, heroic Frank Reid, and scores of pioneers, stampeders, and dance hall girls. The decor is *authentically* Days of '98—because the hotel was actually built that year and has been tastefully restored to the era. Popular choices include sourdough pancakes for breakfasts; soups, salad bar selections, and sandwiches for lunch; salmon or other seafood for dinner. If you're not staying at the Golden North, mosey through the lobby after eating. It's almost like a visit to a historical museum. *3rd Ave. and Broadway, tel. 907/983–2294. AE, DC, MC, V. Inexpensive–Moderate.*

Prospector's Sourdough Restaurant. You'll meet as many Skagway folk here as you will visitors, particularly at breakfast time when the sourdough hotcakes or snow-crab omelets are on the griddle. Salmon steak is a popular favorite in the evening. Decor features the colorful works of local artists on the walls. *4th Ave. and Broadway, tel. 907/983–2865. AE, DC, MC, V. Inexpensive.*

Two other worthy cafés in the inexpensive category are the **Kountry Kitchen** at 4th and State and the **Northern Lights Café** at 4th and Broadway.

Lodging
Westmark Inn. Formerly called the Klondike Hotel, this is Skagway's largest inn (210 rooms). In keeping with the locale, the decor is gold-rush elegant, with rich red carpeting, matching wallpapers, and brass trim. You'll find historical pictures throughout. Room furnishings are first class. Ask for a room in the main structure rather than the annex on the south side of Third Street. The rooms are larger and you don't have to leave the building to visit the restaurant or lounge. *3rd St., east of Broadway, tel. 907/983–2291. Reservations necessary. Facilities: dining room, lounge. Open summer only. AE, DC, MC, V. Very Expensive.*

★ **Golden North Hotel.** No question about it, this is Alaska's most historic hotel. It was built in 1898 in the heyday of the gold rush—golden dome and all—and has been tenderly, lovingly restored to reflect that period. Pioneer Skagway families have contributed gold-rush furnishings from their homes to each of the hotel's 32 rooms, and the stories of those families are printed and posted on the walls of each unit. *3rd Ave. and Broadway (mailing address: Box 343, Skagway 99840), tel. 907/983–2451 or 983–2294. Facilities: dining room, lounge. AE, MC, V. Moderate.*

★ **Skagway Inn Bed & Breakfast.** "More like a home than a hotel" is the way the owner advertises this 12-room inn, with each room bearing the name of a gold-rush gal. The building was constructed in 1897 and is thus one of Skagway's oldest. Rooms are private, but baths are shared. Guests are welcome to lounge and socialize in the home-style living room. Tea is served each afternoon in Miss Suzanne's Tea Room, and dinners (by reservation only) are available each evening. *Between*

6th Ave. and 7th Ave. on Broadway (mailing address: Box 13, Skagway 99840), tel. 907/983–2289. AE, MC, V. Moderate.

Wind Valley Lodge. Located a long walk or a short drive from downtown, the Wind Valley Lodge is one of Skagway's newer hotels. All 30 rooms are modern and there is a free shuttle to downtown. *22nd Ave. and State St. (mailing address: Box 354, Skagway 99840), tel. 907/983–2236. MC, V. Moderate.*

Wrangell
Dining

Dock Side Restaurant. This is the coffee shop and dining room for the Stikine Inn, located right on the dock and offering good views of the harbor. Seafood and steaks are staples here. *One block from ferry terminal, tel. 907/874–3388. AE, DC, MC, V. Inexpensive–Moderate.*

Roadhouse Lodge. The walls here carry practically a museum of early Alaskana. The food is wholesome, tasty, and ample. Specialties include local prawns (sautéed, deep-fried, and boiled in the shell) and deep-fried Indian frybread. A courtesy van will pick you up in town. *Mile 4, Zimovia Hwy., tel. 907/874–2335. AE, DC, MC, V. Inexpensive–Moderate.*

Lodging

Stikine Inn. This is Wrangell's largest hotel—34 rooms with tasteful, modern furniture. Located on the dock in the main part of town, the inn offers great views of Wrangell's harbor. The Dock Side Restaurant is on site, as is the Stikine Bar, which can get pretty loud at night. (Unless you're going to be among the late-night party crowd, ask the registration clerk to assign you a room away from the bar.) There's no extra charge for kids under 12. *Box 990, Wrangell 99929, tel. 907/874–3388. AE, DC, MC, V. Facilities: travel agency, beauty salon. Moderate–Expensive.*

Harding's Old Sourdough Lodge. This lodge is located on the docks, in a beautifully converted construction camp. The Harding family welcomes guests in the big open dining/living room with home-baked sourdough breads and local seafood. The 16 guest rooms are paneled—the building's exterior with cedar hand-milled by Lloyd Harding. *Box 1062, Wrangell 99929, tel. 907/874–3613. AE, MC, V. Facilities: conference room, charter boats. Inexpensive–Moderate.*

Roadhouse Lodge. This is not a large facility (10 rooms and 1 suite), but it's fully modern and offers a variety of services including bar, restaurant, car rentals, courtesy car, laundry facilities, and gift shop. The lodge will also arrange fishing and sightseeing charters. *Mile 4, Zimovia Hwy. (mailing address: Box 1199, Wrangell 99929), tel. 907/874–2335. AE, DC, MC, V. Inexpensive–Moderate.*

Clarke Bed & Breakfast. Marlene Clarke offers B&B housing in her comfortable A-frame facing the harbor. Breakfasts include sourdough waffles, freshly ground coffee, and juice. *732 Case Ave. (mailing address: Box 1020, Wrangell 99929), tel. 907/874–2125 or 874–3863. No credit cards. Inexpensive.*

Southeast Region
Lodging

Alaska Bed & Breakfast Association (Box 21890, Juneau 99802, tel. 907/586–2959. Inexpensive–Moderate). Contact this association for B&B accommodations in Juneau, Sitka, Skagway, Petersburg, Haines, Angoon, and Gustavus.

The Arts

Theater   Southeast Alaska's only professional theater company, **Perseverance Theater of Juneau** (914 3rd St., tel. 907/364–2421), covers everything from Broadway plays to Shakespeare to locally written material throughout the fall-winter-spring season.

Haines hosts a statewide drama competition called ACTFEST in April every other year. The festival is held at the Chilkat Center for the Arts at Fort Seward, with entries from community theaters both large and small. For details: City of Haines Tourism Office (Box 576, Haines 99827).

It may be stretching the word "theater" beyond its logical limits, but several communities stage summer musicals or melodramas for the entertainment of visitors. In Haines it's called "The Lust for Dust"; in Juneau, "The Lady Lou Revue"; in Ketchikan, "The Fish Pirate's Daughter"; and in Skagway, the "Days of '98 Show."

More cultural are the Chilkat Indian Dancers, who demonstrate Tlingit dancing twice weekly in Haines, and the New Archangel Dancers of Sitka, who perform authentic Russian Cossack–type dances whenever cruise ships are in port.

Call local information centers for times and dates.

Music Festivals   At least three music festivals are worthy of attention. The annual week-long **Alaska Folk Festival** (Box 21748, Juneau 99802) is staged each April in Juneau, drawing singers, musical storytellers, banjo masters, fiddlers, and even cloggers from all over the state and Yukon Territory.

Early in the summer Juneau is the scene of yet another musical gathering, this one called **Juneau Jazz 'n Classics** (Box 22152, Juneau 99802). As the name implies, it celebrates things musical from Brubeck (the trio having been guests during the 1988 gathering) to Bach.

Southeast Alaska's major classical music festival is the annual **Sitka Summer Music Festival** (Box 3333, Sitka 99835), a three-week June celebration of workshops, recitals, and concerts. Held in the Centennial Building, downtown.

Nightlife

Bars and Nightclubs   Socializing at a bar or "saloon" is an old Alaska custom, and the towns and cities of the Southeast Panhandle offer no exception. Following are some of the favorite gathering places in these parts:

Haines/Fort Seward   **The Harbor Bar** (Front St. at the Harbor, tel. 907/766–2442). Commerical fisherfolk gather here nightly at this old (1907) bar and restaurant. Sometimes live music.

Juneau   **Alaskan Hotel Bar** (167 S. Franklin St., tel. 907/586–1000). Equally popular with locals and distinctly less touristy. If live music isn't playing, an old-fashioned player piano usually is.

Bubble Room (127 N. Franklin St., tel. 907/586–2660). This comfortable lounge off the lobby in the Baranof Hotel is quiet—and the site (so it is said) of more legislative lobbying and decision making than in the nearby state capitol building. The chairs are soft, and so is the music from the piano bar.

The Red Dog Saloon (159 S. Franklin St., tel. 907/463–3777). Unquestionably the state's best-known frontier watering hole, it's in a new location but carries on in a tradition of sawdust on the floor, mounted bear and other game animals on the walls, and lots of historic photos. Live music and lively crowds when the cruise ships are in port.

Ketchikan   **Charley's** (208 Front St., tel. 907/225–5090). Located in the Ingersoll Hotel, and sort of '40s in character, Charley's is popular for sipping as well as for suppering. There's usually live music.

Frontier Saloon (127 Main St., tel. 907/225–9950). Don't expect gold-rush music or even country-western here. It's rock 'n' roll all the way.

Pioneer Bar (122 Front St., tel. 907/225–3210). This is the place for country-western, a popular spot for Ketchikan folk who like to listen well into the wee hours.

Petersburg   **The Harbor Bar** (Nordic Dr. near Dolphin St., tel. 907/775–4526). The name suggests the decor here, a place of ship's wheels, ship pictures, and a mounted 50-pound red snapper.

Kito's Kave (Sing Lee Alley, tel. 907/772–3207). Pretty loud as the night wears on, but most tourists seem to want to at least peek inside. Walls are covered with a variety of items, from Mexican paintings on velvet to stuffed fish and sports pennants. There are also pool tables and dart boards.

Sitka   **Kadataan Lounge** (330 Seward Ave., tel. 907/747–6241). Live soft rock music plays here in the lounge of the Westmark Shee Atika Hotel.

Skagway   **Moe's Frontier Bar** (Broadway between 4th and 5th Sts., tel. 907/983–2238). A long-time fixture on the Skagway scene, Moe's is likewise a bar much frequented by the local folk.

The Red Onion (Broadway at 2nd St., tel. 907/983–2222). You'll meet at least as many Skagway people here as you will visitors. Madame Jan, the proprietress of the establishment, will tell you all about the Red Onion's colorful past. (The upstairs was a gold-rush brothel.)

Wrangell   **The Stikine Bar** (107 Front St., tel. 907/874–3388). This can be a louder-as-the-night-gets-later bar when a rock band is playing, but it's a friendly place to meet the locals.

8 South Central Alaska

By Kent Sturgis

Updated by
Barbara Hodgin

Anchorage may dominate the region in size, recognition, and political clout, but don't let that mislead you into thinking Anchorage is South Central Alaska. Anchorage is an anomaly, a modern urban environment amid historic ports, wilderness outposts, and fishing towns.

South Central starts with the port towns on the Gulf of Alaska—Cordova, Valdez, Whittier, Seward, Seldovia, Kodiak, Homer, Kenai—with their harbors, ferries, glaciers and ocean life. Then come the mountains curled like an arm embracing the region. Talkeetna, at the western limits of South Central, is where mountaineers gather to launch their assaults on towering Mt. McKinley. On the eastern border, the landmark copper mine in McCarthy lies at the foot of the Wrangell Mountains. South Central is also Alaska's farm country. In the Matanuska Valley, under an ever-present summertime sun, 75-pound cabbages are a common occurrence.

Portage Glacier is an accessible ice field near Anchorage. Kenai Fjords National Park and the Kenai National Wildlife Range provide outstanding opportunities for viewing wildlife—from whales, seals, and otters to herds of moose.

Unlike Interior Alaska, where the common theme of gold-rush history links most of the communities, South Central towns and cities have very different personalities. Kodiak, for example, is a busy fishing port, while Homer is a funky fishing and tourist town on beautiful Kachemak Bay.

Essential Information

Getting Around

By Plane Anchorage is the air hub of the South Central region, served by major national and international airlines and well-stocked with smaller carriers and local air-taxi operators (*see* Getting Around in Chapter 6).

Markair (tel. 907/243–1414 or 800/426–6784) flies scheduled service to Kodiak, Katmai, and other destinations. **ERA Aviation** (tel. 907/243–3300) and **Southcentral Air** (tel. 907/561–4193) fly to Homer, Kenai, Valdez, Kodiak, and Denali National Park. **Wilbur's** (tel. 907/243–7878) serves Valdez, Cordova, Aniak, and McGrath.

By Car Driving may be the best way to see Alaska, but keep in mind that all but a few miles of the road system consists of two-lane highways, not all of it paved.

Two highway routes offer a choice for travel by car between Fairbanks and Anchorage. Heading north from Anchorage, the Parks Highway (turn left off Glenn Highway near Palmer) passes through Wasilla and up the Susitna River drainage area and through a low pass in the Alaska Range, then down into the Tanana Valley and Fairbanks. This route passes the entrance to Denali National Park and roughly parallels the Alaska Railroad.

A longer route (436 miles) follows the Glenn Highway to the Richardson Highway, then north to Fairbanks through the Copper River Valley. This route makes possible a side trip to

Valdez, and it offers the most direct connection to the Alaska Highway, joining it at Tok.

Anchorage can be used as a base for side trips over the Seward and Sterling highways to the Kenai Peninsula and its smorgasbord of outdoor recreation. And watch the side roads for short trips to such places as Portage Glacier, off the Seward Highway near Anchorage, and Hope, an isolated community across Cook Inlet.

For hot-line reports on highways during snow season, call the State Department of Transportation in Anchorage (tel. 907/337–9481).

By Train The state-owned **Alaska Railroad** (tel. 907/265–2623 in Alaska, 800/544–0552 outside) is said to be the last railroad in North America that still makes flag stops to accommodate the homesteaders, hikers, fishing parties, and other travelers who get on and off in remote places.

President Warren Harding drove the golden spike at Nenana in 1923 to mark completion of this once-federal railroad from the Gulf of Alaska to the Interior.

The 470-mile main line runs up Alaska's Railbelt between the port town of Seward north to Fairbanks via Anchorage. A spur south of Anchorage connects to Whittier on nearby Prince William Sound.

Following are several options for train travel.

Denali National Park: Between late May and early September, daily passenger service is offered between Anchorage and Fairbanks by way of Wasilla, Talkeetna, Denali National Park, and Nenana. Passengers have a choice of riding in a Vistadome car operated by one of two competing tour companies (with luxury seating and gourmet dining) or in more conventional and considerably less expensive seating in reconditioned coach cars with a snack bar and lounge car nearby. Because of the scenery, there is no such thing as a poor seat on the Alaska Railroad. Beyond your window, a panaroma will unfold: scenes of the sea, alpine meadows and snowcapped peaks, and the muddy rivers and taiga forests of the Interior.

Whittier spur by way of Portage: There's no road through the Chugach Mountains to the Prince William Sound port of Whittier, but you can take your car on the train with you. Whittier has ferry service to other communities on Prince William Sound. Daily service between late May and early September.

Seward: Passenger service offered Friday, Saturday, and Sunday during the summer season into this railroad/port community on the edge of the Kenai Fjords National Park.

Between mid-September and late May, passenger service is spartan and less frequent, consisting of self-propelled rail diesel cars with no meal service (snacks only). Still, a northbound run through the Alaska Range in mid-winter, when the low-lying sun casts a pink glow on snow-covered mountains, is worth a trip.

Each adult passenger on the railroad is allowed three pieces of luggage, to a maximum of 150 pounds. If there is room on the train baggage car, you may be able to check your bicycle and other camping equipment. *Information: Alaska Railroad*

Corp., Box 107500, Anchorage 99510. For information about the luxury-class Vistadome service between Anchorage and Fairbanks, contact the owner companies directly: Midnight Sun Express (tel. 206/728–4202) and Gray Line of Alaska (tel. 800/544–2206).

By Ferry The **Alaska Marine Highway** (tel. 800/642–0066), the state-run ferry operator, offers scheduled service to Valdez, Cordova, Whittier, Seward, Homer, and Seldovia on the mainland and to Kodiak and Port Lions on Kodiak Island. The same agency runs the ferries that operate in southeast Alaska, but the two systems connect only once a year when ferries come up from dry dock to South Central.

The state requires reservations for cabin and vehicle space on all ferries, and passenger reservations are required on some routes. *Information: Alaska Marine Highway, Box R, Juneau 99811, tel. 907/465–3941 or 800/642–0066.*

Ferries are a great way to explore the South Central coast with its glaciers, mountains, fjords, and sea mammals—not to mention some of the best salmon fishing anywhere. The summer ferries between Valdez and Whittier run by way of Columbia Glacier, where it is not unusual for passengers to witness giant fragments of ice "calving" from the face of the glacier into Prince William Sound.

By Bus The most common run is between Fairbanks and Anchorage by way of Denali National Park. However, you also can take side trips by bus or van to Homer and its famous sand spit at the very end of the Kenai Peninsula, south of Anchorage.

For more information about bus service throughout South Central, contact:

Alaska Direct Bus Lines (tel. 907/277–6652 or 800/328–9730). Serves Anchorage and Fairbanks to Whitehorse and Minneapolis. Year-round.

Alaska-Yukon Motorcoaches (tel. 800/637–3334). Serves Anchorage, Fairbanks, Haines, and Valdez. Seasonal.

Denali Overland Transportation (tel. 907/733–2384). Serves Anchorage, Talkeetna, and Denali National Park. Seasonal.

Gray Line of Alaska (tel. 800/544–2206). Serves Anchorage and Fairbanks. Year-round.

Seward Bus Line (tel. 907/337–3425). Serves Anchorage, Moose Pass, and Seward. Year-round.

Valdez Anchorage Bus Line (tel. 907/337–3425). Serves Anchorage and Valdez. Year-round.

Guided Tours

Cooper Landing Unless otherwise indicated, most of the guided tour services listed here operate during the summer only, usually between Memorial Day and Labor Day. As a rule, the nearest visitor center (*see* Important Addresses and Numbers, below) can answer questions year-round about guided tours offered in this area.

Alaska Wildland Adventures (Box 389, Girdwood 99587, tel. 907/783–2928 or 800/334–8730) operates a tidy, pleasant cabin compound on the Kenai River at Milepost 50.1 on the Sterling Highway. Drift boats and raft trips are available.

Cordova **Alaska Sea Coast Charters** (tel. 907/424–7742) will take you bird-watching, fishing, clamming, and beachcombing at Goose Cove Lodge, a major Pacific Coast bird-migration stop.
Cordova Air Service (tel. 907/424–3289) offers aerial tours of Prince William Sound on planes with wheels, skis, or floats.
Cordova Charters (tel. 907/424–3475) offers flexible, hourly tours for fishing, hunting, and sightseeing.

Denali Park **Denali Dog Tours & Wilderness Freighters** (tel. 907/683–2644) can put you into one of 15 cabins throughout Denali National Park, via dogsled or cross-country skis, between November and April.
Denali Raft Adventures (tel. 907/683–2234 summer, 907/337–9604 winter) launches its rafts seven times daily on two- or four-hour scenic and white-water floats on the Nenana River. Courtesy pickup at hotels and train depot.
McKinley Raft Adventures (tel. 907/683–2392) offers several raft trips daily on the Nenana River.

Eagle River Bob Dittrich's **Wilderness Birding Adventures** (Box 10–3747, Anchorage 99510, tel. 907/694–7442) offers guided birding throughout the region.

Homer **Alaska Sunshine Charters** (tel. 907/235–8566) schedules both daytime and overnight charters in search of halibut.
Central Charters Booking Agency (tel. 907/235–7847) can arrange fishing, sailing, a hydrofoil to Seldovia, and ferry trips to Halibut Cove.
Homer Ocean Charters (tel. 907/235–6212) will take you where the halibut are. Call ahead for a reservation.

Kenai/Soldotna Numerous guides offer Kenai River fishing tours, but the best-known is **Harry Gaines** (Box 624, Kenai, 99611, tel. 907/262–5097)

Kodiak **Gray Line of Alaska** (tel. 907/277–5581) offers one- or two-day sightseeing tours of Kodiak, starting in Anchorage.
Kodiak Adventures (tel. 907/373–2285) will take you fishing, hiking, hunting, or on a photography expedition.
Kodiak Island Charters (tel. 907/486–5380) operates boat tours for fishing, hunting, clamming, and sightseeing.

McCarthy McCarthy Bed and Breakfast is the home of **St. Elias Alpine Guides** (Box 11241, Anchorage 99511, tel. 907/277–6867), where owner Bob Jacobs, an experienced mountaineer, offers introductory mountaineering lessons and other less strenuous treks.

Palmer **Alaska Guides and Outfitters** (tel. 907/745–3772) puts together trips for hunting, fishing, photography, and backpacking in the Brooks Range and Talkeetna Mountains, and on the Alaska Peninsula.
The Musk-Ox Farm (tel. 907/272–9225) has 30-minute guided tours on the hour and half-hour during the summer.
Naturalist Hiking (tel. 907/745–5143) offers guided hiking daily or overnight in the Chugach and Talkeetna mountains.
Nova Riverrunners of Alaska (tel. 907/745–5753) are based in nearby Chickaloon for family float trips or white-water runs on the Matanuska River.

Seldovia **Seldovia Fishing Adventures** (tel. 907/234–7417) offers a combination of halibut fishing, bed-and-breakfast, beachcombing, clamming, and hiking in this remote fishing village one hour from Anchorage by air.

Seward **Fish House** (tel. 907/478–8007) is Seward's oldest booking agency for fishing, sailing, and marine sightseeing.
Harbor Air (tel. 907/224–3133) will take you over the Kenai Fjords National Park and Harding Icefield. Commuter service available from Anchorage.
Kenai Fjords Tours (tel. 800/478–8068) has a fleet of five charter boats for sightseeing and fishing.
Mariah Charters (tel. 907/243–1238) has fishing, sightseeing, and drop-off/pickup tours.
Quest Charters (tel. 907/224–3025) has cruises departing daily to explore the Kenai Fjords National Park, featuring humpback whales, sea lions, glaciers, and waterfalls. Bus or rail/cruise package available from Anchorage.
Trails North (tel. 907/224–3587) will arrange local bus tours, kayaking, and an Iditarod sled-dog demonstration.

Sterling **Angler's Lodge & Fish Camp** (tel. 907/262–1747 summer, 907/345–4834 winter) offers guided fishing trips ranging from a half-day Kenai River outing to a seven-day extravaganza that takes in both silver salmon and halibut fishing. Roger Byerly and his crew handle everything from airport pickups to shipping your catch home.

Soldotna **Sports Den** (tel. 907/262–7491) will take you king-salmon fishing and offers customized fly-out fishing, hunting, and sightseeing as well. Boat/trailer and canoe rentals available.

Talkeetna **Alaska-Denali Guiding** (tel. 907/733–2649) puts together hiking and rafting trips into remote wilderness areas, and it offers mountaineering seminars in the Alaska Range. Operates year-round.
Doug Greeting Aviation (tel. 907/733–2366) offers glacier landings and fly-in fishing cabins.
K2 Aviation (tel. 907/733–2291) lands you on a glacier and offers overnight trips to Denali Park. Anchorage departures also available.
Mahay's Riverboat Service (tel. 907/733–2223) offers guided powerboat tours and fishing on the Susitna River.
Talkeetna Air Taxi (tel. 907/733–2218) offers a breathtaking exploration flight close to the massive Mt. McKinley. Flights start in both Talkeetna and Anchorage.
Talkeetna Riverboat Service (tel. 907/733–2281) offers float trips, fishing, and river cabins.

Valdez **Alaska Sightseeing Tours** (tel. 907/276–1305 or 800/637–3334) takes its plush yacht, the *Glacier Seas*, right up to the face of Columbia Glacier. Rates include a two-day package from Anchorage.
Alpine Aviation Adventures (tel. 800/478–4304) has scenic aerial tours to Columbia Glacier and the Wrangell Mountains.
Columbia Glacier Cruises (tel. 907/276–8866) runs the *Glacier Queen II* between Valdez and Whittier by way of Columbia Glacier and the tanker terminus of the trans-Alaska pipeline.
Glacier Charter Services (tel. 907/835–5141 summer, 206/789–2204 off season) specializes in small group tours to Columbia Glacier.

Hook Line and Sinker (tel. 907/835–4410) offers salmon, halibut, and bottom-fish charters.

Keystone Raft & Kayak Adventures (tel. 907/835–2606) provides all gear for guided raft and kayak tours on rivers up to Class V.

Prince William Sound Trophy Charters (tel. 907/835–2282) combines bed-and-breakfast, glacier tours, remote cabins, and customized fishing and hunting trips.

Stan Stephens Charters (tel. 907/835–4731) has various Prince William Sound options: glacier cruises, island cookouts, overnight trips, and wilderness camps.

Wasilla **Northern Wilderness Adventures** (tel. 907/376–0502) wants you to catch salmon, rainbow and lake trout, Arctic char, grayling, Dolly Varden, and pike.

Whittier **Phillips' Cruises & Tours** (tel. 907/276–8023) offers a 100-mile day cruise (lunch included with a full-service saloon) on which you will see 26 glaciers. Transportation from Anchorage to Whittier available.

Prince William Sound Charters (tel. 907/344–3632) will escort you to meet the whales. This service specializes in overnight charters.

Important Addresses and Numbers

Tourist Information Visitor centers and information hot lines are operated by convention and visitor bureaus in the larger communities and by several state and federal agencies concerned with parks and outdoor recreation. They include:

Alaska Lands Public Information Center (in Anchorage, downtown at 605 W. 4th Ave., Anchorage 99501, tel. 907/271–2737).
Cordova (Box 99, Cordova, 99574, tel. 907/424–7443).
Homer (Homer Spit, Homer 99603, tel. 907/235–5300).
Kenai (402 Overland Ave., Kenai 99611, tel. 907/283–7989).
Kodiak Island (100 Marine Way, Kodiak, Kodiak 99615, tel. 907/486–4782).
Palmer (Independence Mine State Historical Park, tel. 907/745–3975; or Palmer Chamber of Commerce, Palmer 99645, tel. 907/745–2880).
Seward (3rd Ave. and Jefferson St., Box 749, Seward 99664, tel. 907/224–3094 summer, 907/224–8051 winter).
U.S. Fish and Wildlife Service (1101 Tudor Rd., Anchorage 99504 tel. 907/276–3487); or Anchorage Public Affairs, tel. 907/786–3487).
U.S. Forest Service (2221 E. Northern Lights Blvd., Suite 238, Anchorage 99508, tel. 907/345–5700), for information about the Chugach National Forest and reservations for U.S. Forest Service cabins.
Valdez (245 N. Harbor Dr., Valdez 99816, tel. 907/835–2330).
Wasilla Chamber of Commerce (East Lake Mall at Big Lake, Wasilla 99687, tel. 907/376–1299).

Emergencies Dial 911 for local **police** or **ambulance** emergency assistance in Anchorage and other larger communities.

The **Alaska State Troopers** also maintain detachments throughout the region. They include *Anchorage* (tel. 907/269–5511), *Cordova* (tel. 907/424–7331), *Glennallen* (tel. 907/822–3263), *Healy* (tel. 907/683–2232), *Homer* (tel. 907/235–8239), *Kodiak* (tel. 907/486–4121), *Palmer* (tel. 907/745–2131), *Seward* (tel.

907/224–3346), *Soldotna* (tel. 907/262–4453), *Valdez* (tel. 907/835–4359), and *Wasilla* (tel. 907/745–2131).

Hospital and Clinic **Anchorage:** Humana Hospital (tel. 907/276–1131); Providence Hospital (tel. 907/562–2211); U.S. Air Force Hospital (tel. 907/552–5555). **Cordova** Hospital (tel. 907/424–8000). **Glennallen** Clinic (tel. 907/822–3203). **Homer:** South Peninsula Hospital (tel. 907/235–8101). **Kodiak:** Kodiak Island Hospital (tel. 907/486–3281). **Palmer** Hospital (tel. 907/745–4813). **Seward** General Hospital (tel. 907/224–5205). **Seldovia** Medical Clinic (tel. 907/234–7825). **Soldotna:** Central Peninsula General Hospital (tel. 907/262–4404). **Valdez:** Community Hospital (tel. 907/835–2249).

Dentist In case of emergency, 24-hour service can be arranged in Anchorage (tel. 907/279–9144).

Exploring South Central Alaska

Numbers in the margin correspond to points of interest on the South Central Alaska map.

Orientation

The Alaska Range to the north mirrors the gentle curve of the Gulf of Alaska in the south, creating natural borders for the South Central region. Anchorage is the central hub. Whittier and Seward are connected to Anchorage by rail; Seward also has a highway connection, Whittier does not. Valdez can be reached by a rather indirect but often interesting road route (the Glenn Hwy./Tok Cutoff to the Richardson Hwy.) out of Anchorage.

The Seward Highway runs to most of the places you would want to see in the Kenai Peninsula, south of Anchorage, including the small towns of Hope, Soldotna, and Homer. South Central's "other" highway, the ferry-driven Marine Highway, connects with Kodiak, Whittier, Seward, Valdez, and Cordova via the Gulf.

Heading north of Anchorage, the Parks Highway is the route of choice, as it skirts Denali National Park and heads on to Fairbanks.

Air taxis are also viable means of transportation around South Central. Compared to the Interior and Fringe regions, South Central is somewhat more compact, and the distances you will have to travel between destinations are less vast.

Denali National Park

If big mountains and big country are on your travel agenda, ❶ **Denali National Park and Preserve** is the place for you. Here you will find *Mt. McKinley*, at 20,320 feet the highest peak in North America, with its unmatched vistas of mountains, glacial rivers, and alpine meadows. You will also find the best wildlife viewing in the state. Nearly every wild creature that walks or flies in South Central Alaska inhabits the park, and many of them are readily visible along the 91-mile road that winds from

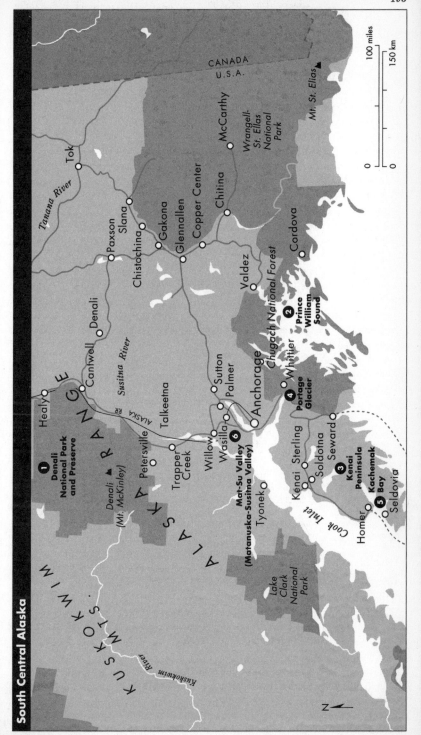

South Central Alaska

CANADA
U.S.A.

Mt. St. Elias

McCarthy

Wrangell-
St. Elias
National
Park

Chitina

Copper Center

Cordova

Gakona

Glennallen

Valdez

Chugach National Forest

Prince
William
Sound **2**

Slana

Chistochina

Paxson

Tok

Tanana River

Denali

Cantwell

Susitna River

Sutton

Palmer

Whittier **4**

Anchorage

Portage
Glacier

Healy

1
Denali
National Park
and Preserve

Denali ▲
(Mt. McKinley)

Petersville

ALASKA RANGE

Talkeetna

ALASKA RR

Trapper
Creek

Willow

Wasilla

6
Mat-Su Valley
(Matanuska-Susitna Valley)

Kenai

Sterling

Soldotna

Seward

Kenai
Peninsula
3

Kachemak
Bay

Homer

5
Seldovia

Cook Inlet

Tyonek

Lake
Clark
National
Park

KUSKOKWIM MTS.

KUSKOKWIM River

N

the park entrance to Wonder Lake in the heart of Denali *(see* Chapter 4).

Denali is readily accessible by highway (Parks Hwy., which connects Anchorage and Fairbanks), the *Alaska Railroad* from Fairbanks or Anchorage, and various air charters from either city. Railroad reservations are recommended *(see* Getting Around, above).

Admission to Denali is $3. Inside and out of the park, accommodations vary from simple public campsites to privately operated hotels. Denali has seven camping areas spotted along the park road. The camping fee is $10 per night except for free camping at the walk-in Morino campsite (no vehicles allowed) just inside the park entrance. Register at the *Riley Creek Information Center.* The park is heavily used, particularly on weekends, and a percentage of sites can be reserved in person in advance. You may reserve campsites and bus passes between 7 and 21 days in advance in Anchorage or Fairbanks at the Public Lands Information centers. You can try your luck on arrival at the park itself, but you may wind up having to stay at one of the private campgrounds outside the park entrance.

To enhance wildlife viewing opportunities, traffic is restricted on the park road past the *Savage River Checkpoint,* about 14 miles inside the park. Private vehicles are not allowed in the park. There is, however, free shuttle bus service along the length of the park road. Making the entire trip to *Wonder Lake* and back will take 10 hours or more, but the shuttle schedule is such that you can get off along the route and catch another bus in either direction about every half hour. Privately operated bus trips also are available for $35, which include a box lunch.

Hikers will find ample opportunities, and overnight packing into the backcountry is possible with a permit from rangers at Riley Creek. This is bear country and the bears are quite wild and fear people. The Park Service provides backpackers with bear-proof food containers. No weapons are permitted in the park.

Denali summer weather can vary from hot and sunny to near-freezing and drizzly, and those changes can occur within a few hours, so you'll want to bring along appropriate clothing: a medium-weight jacket and sturdy walking shoes. Don't forget insect repellent.

The Riley Creek Information Center near the park's entrance can supply all your information needs, including the daily schedule for naturalist presentations and sled-dog demonstrations by the park rangers. Information: Denali National Park and Preserve (Box 9, Denali Park 99755, tel. 907/683–2294) or National Park Service (2525 Gambell St., Room 107, Anchorage 99503, tel. 907/271–2737).

Prince William Sound

❷ Prince William Sound was heavily damaged by the Exxon Valdez oil spill in 1989. However, vast parts of the Sound remain pristine, with abundant wildlife.

A visit to **Columbia Glacier,** which flows from the surrounding Chugach Mountain range, certainly should be on the agenda. Its deep aquamarine face is five miles across, and it calves (gives birth to) new icebergs with resounding cannonades. This glacier is one of the largest and most readily accessible of Alaska's coastal glaciers. The state ferry travels past the face of the glacier and scheduled tours of the glaciers and the rest of the sound are available by boat and aircraft from Valdez *(see* Guided Tours, above).

Of the three major Prince William Sound communities—Valdez, Whittier, and Cordova—only **Valdez** (val-DEEZ) can be reached by road. It lies at the southern end of the Richardson Highway. This community, with its year-round ice-free port, originally was the entry point for people and goods going to the Interior during the gold rush. Today that flow has been reversed, with Valdez harbor being the southern terminus of the trans-Alaska pipeline, which carries crude oil from Prudhoe Bay and surrounding oil fields nearly 800 miles to the north. This region, with its dependence on commercial fishing, is still feeling the aftereffects of a massive oil spill in Prince William Sound in March 1989. *Pipeline Terminus Tour, Gray Line of Alaska. Tours depart from Westmark Valdez Hotel, 100 Fidalgo Dr., tel. 907/835–2357. Cost: $14 adults.*

Much of Valdez looks new because the business area was relocated and rebuilt after being destroyed by the devastating Good Friday Earthquake in 1964. A few of the old buildings were moved to the new town site.

Many Alaskan communities have summertime fishing derbies, but Valdez may hold the record for the number of such contests, stretching from late May into September for halibut and various runs of salmon. The Valdez Silver Salmon Derby is held the entire month of August. Fishing charters abound in this area of Prince William Sound, and for a good reason, too: These fertile waters provide some of the best saltwater sport fishing in all of Alaska.

A pleasant attraction on a rainy day, if you ever tire of gazing at the 5,000-foot mountain peaks surrounding Valdez, is the new **Valdez Heritage Center Museum.** It depicts the lives, livelihoods, and events significant to Valdez and surrounding regions. Exhibits include a 1907 steam fire engine, a 19th-century saloon, and a model of the pipeline terminus. *Corner of Egan St. and Chenega St., tel. 907/835–2764. Admission free. Open early June–early Aug. 9–8, off-season 9–6.*

Access to **Whittier,** a small community on Passage Canal east of Anchorage, is generally by railroad or state ferry; the area is not connected to the state's highway system. Whittier came into being as a major supply port for the U.S. Army during World War II. The railroad was extended to the community from Portage, 50 miles south of Anchorage on the Seward Highway. The army is long since gone, but the rail line and some of the large buildings remain. The Alaska Railroad maintains a schedule to Whittier, carrying freight, passengers, and autos. You will probably find little reason to linger long in Whittier—there are other towns more picturesque and entertaining.

Cordova, located on Orca Inlet in eastern Prince William Sound, began life early this century as the port city for the Copper River & Northwestern Railroad, which was built to serve the Kennecott copper mines 115 miles away in the Wrangell Mountains. With the mines and the railroad shut down since

1938, Cordova's economy now depends heavily on the fishing industry. Attempts to develop a road along the abandoned railroad line, connecting to the state highway system, were dashed by the 1964 earthquake, so Cordova remains isolated. Access to the community is limited to airplane or ferry.

A small town backed by the spectacular backdrop of snowy Mt. Eccles, Cordova is the gateway to the Copper River Delta—one of the great birding areas of the North American continent. Spring migration here provides some of the finest avian spectacles in the world. Cordova is still relatively unvisited; the Reluctant Fisherman Hotel is a good place to stay. You may want to explore nearby iceberg-choked Miles Lake and the Million Dollar Bridge across the Copper River.

The Cordova Community Museum (tel. 907/424–6665) is strong on native artifacts as well as on pioneer history.

These three Prince William Sound communities are linked by regular service on the state ferry system and by major cruiseship lines. Reservations are required on the ferry system—the earlier the better, because some sailings can be sold out months in advance during the summer season (*see* Getting Around, above). The situation has improved in recent years, but it's still difficult to get through on the ferry-system reservations number. *Valdez Visitors Center, 245 N. Harbor Dr., tel. 907/835–2984. Open daily June–Aug.*

Kenai Peninsula

❸ The **Kenai Peninsula,** thrusting into the Gulf of Alaska south of Anchorage, offers excellent salmon fishing along with scenery and wildlife. Commercial fishing is important to the area's economy, and the city of Kenai, on the peninsula's northwest coast, is the base for the Cook Inlet offshore oil fields.

The area is dotted with roadside campgrounds, and you can explore four major federal holdings on the peninsula—the western end of the sprawling **Chugach National Forest, Kenai National Wildlife Refuge, Kenai Fjords National Park,** and the **Alaska Maritime National Wildlife Refuge** (*see* Chapter 4).

❹ **Portage Glacier,** located 50 miles southeast of Anchorage, is one of Alaska's most-visited tourist destinations. A six-mile side road off Seward Highway leads to the Begich-Boggs Visitor Center on the shore of Portage Lake. Boat tours of the face of the glacier aboard the 200-passenger *Ptarmigan* were begun in 1990. They leave from near the visitor center in Portage. Unfortunately the glacier is receding rapidly, so the view across the lake is not as good as it used to be. *Contact Westours Motorcoaches, tel. 907/277–5581. Cost: $19.50 adults, $9.75 children age 12 and under.*

The mountains surrounding Portage Glacier are covered with smaller glaciers. A short hike to Byron Glacier viewpoint is popular in the spring, when avalanches roar down surrounding slopes. Watch for black bears in all the Portage side valleys in the summer.

The little gold mining commmunity of Hope is 90 miles south of Anchorage by road, but just across the Turnagain Arm. Occasional high tides come right up into town, lapping at the old log cabins and weathered frame buildings. The Gull Rock trail is a nice day-hike, and the Resurrection trail system heads south of here 38 miles through the mountains to Cooper Landing.

One of the peninsula's major communities is the city of **Seward** at the head of Resurrection Bay. It lies at the south end of the Seward Highway, which connects Anchorage and also is the southern terminus of the Alaska Railroad. Cruise lines and the state ferry system call here, and there is air service as well.

Seward was founded in 1903 when survey crews arrived at this ice-free port to begin planning for a railroad to the Interior. Since then the town has come to rely heavily on commercial fishing, and its harbor is important for loading coal bound for the Orient.

Seward, like Valdez, was badly damaged by the 1964 earthquake. A slide show, "Seward is Burning," shown daily at 2 PM in the Seward Community Library, illustrates the upheaval caused by the Good Friday tremor. Paintings by prominent Alaskan artists, together with Russian icons, are exhibited at the library. Photographs of the big quake are on display at the State and City Office Building at 5th Avenue and Adams Street. A museum in the building's basement shows artifacts from the early white pioneers as well as handmade Aleut baskets. For more information: Seward Chamber of Commerce (Box 749, Seward 99664, tel. 907/224–8051).

Charter tours of Resurrection Bay are based here. These tours cruise along the fjords that line the western edge of the bay. They explore the bay's bird rookeries and visit one of the world's major sea lion colonies (*see* Guided Tours, above).

North of Seward, the Sterling Highway branches westward, connecting the cities of Sterling, Kenai, Soldotna, and Homer, as well as numerous smaller coastal communities. Look for moose along this road as it passes through the **Kenai National Wildlife Refuge**—and look for big salmon when you reach the coast. Every river is a hot spot for fishing, as successive waves of salmon make their way upstream from the ocean to their spawning grounds. Because of their proximity to Anchorage and their large population, these streams are extremely popular for fishing.

At the south end of the Sterling Highway lies the city of **Homer,** on the head of a sand spit that juts into Kachemak Bay. This community was founded just before the turn of the century as a gold-prospecting camp and later was used as a coal-mining headquarters. Today the town of Homer is Alaska's answer to Carmel, CA, with picturesque buildings, good seafood, and beautiful Kachemak Bay. It's a favorite weekend spot for the Anchorage people who need a change of scene and weather. Halibut fishing is especially good in this area, and numerous charters are available. In addition to highway and air access, Homer also has regular ferry service to Seldovia.

The galleries on and around Pioneer Avenue, including Ptarmigan Arts, a local cooperative, are good places to find works by the town's residents. The Pratt Museum, just off Pioneer Avenue on Bartlett Street, offers pioneer, Russian, and Indian displays, plus a saltwater aquarium.

❺ Kachemak Bay abounds in wildlife. Tour operators take visitors to bird rookeries in the bay or across the bay to gravel beaches for clam digging. Most fishing charters will include an opportunity to view whales, seals, porpoises, and birds close up. A walk along the docks at the end of the day is a pleasant chance to watch commercial fishing boats and charter boats unload their catch. The bay supports a large population of puffins.

Directly across from the end of the Homer Spit, Halibut Cove is a small community of people who make their living on the bay or by selling handicrafts. The Central Charter (tel. 907/235–7847) booking agency runs frequent boats from Homer. Halibut Cove has an art gallery and a sushi restaurant that serves local seafood. The cove itself is lovely, especially during salmon runs, when fish leap and splash in the clear water. There are also several lodges on this side of the bay, away from summer crowds on pristine coves.

Seldovia, isolated across the bay from Homer, retains the charm of an earlier Alaska. The town's Russian bloodline shows through in its onion-domed church and its name, derived from a Russian place-name meaning "herring bay." Local and visiting fishermen use lots of that small fish for bait, catching record-size salmon, halibut, and king or Dungeness crab. You'll find excellent fishing whether you drop your line into the deep waters of Kachemak Bay or cast into the surf for silver salmon on the shore of Outside Beach, near town.

Matanuska-Susitna Valley

Giant homegrown vegetables and the headquarters of the best known sled-dog race in the world are among the most prominent attractions of South Central's **Mat-Su Valley.**

The valley, lying an hour north of Anchorage by road, draws its name from its two largest rivers, the Matanuska and the Susitna. The area is bisected by the Parks and the Glenn highways. Major cities are **Wasilla** on the Parks Highway and **Palmer** on the Glenn Highway. To the east, the Glenn Highway connects to the Richardson Highway by way of several high mountain passes sandwiched between the Chugach Mountain range to the south and the Talkeetnas to the north. At Mile 103, the massive **Matanuska Glacier** comes almost to the highway.

The valley abounds with good fishing, especially for salmon and trout, and numerous charter services are available, both by boat and air, to carry visitors into remote areas. Gold mining was an early mainstay of the valley's economy and visitors today may enjoy touring the dormant **Independence Gold Mine** on the Hatcher Pass Road, a loop that connects to the Richardson Highway just north of Willow and to the Glenn Highway near Palmer. *Independence Mine State Historical Park, 17 mi from the Glenn Hwy. on the Hatcher Pass Rd., tel. 907/745–3975. Admission free. Visitors center open early June–Labor Day, Thurs.–Mon. 11–7; weekends only the rest of the year.*

In the 1940s, as many as 200 workers were employed by the mine. Today it is a 271-acre state park. Only the wooden buildings remain, one of them a red-roof mine manager's building used as a visitors center. Self-guided tours available. Meals and lodging are available nearby at the *Hatcher Pass Lodge* (tel. 907/745–5897).

In 1935 the federal government relocated about 200 farm families from the Depression-ridden Midwest to the Mat-Su Valley.

Some elements of these early farms remain around Palmer, and the valley has developed into the state's major agriculture region. Good growing conditions result in some outsize vegetables such as 100-pound cabbages. You'll find these giants as well as numerous other attractions during the last week of August at the **Alaska State Fair** in Palmer. *Alaska State Fairgrounds, Mile 40.2, Glenn Hwy., tel. 907/745–4827. Admission: $6 adults, $1 children.*

On a sunny day, Palmer looks like a Swiss calendar photo, with its old barns and log houses silhouetted against craggy Pioneer Peak. On the nearby farms (on the Bodenburg loop off the old Palmer Hwy.) you can pick your own raspberries and other fruits and vegetables.

The **Museum of Alaska Transportation and Industry,** on a 4.2-acre site in Palmer, features exhibits of some of the machines that helped develop Alaska, everything from a rare C-123 aircraft to a sheepherder's wagon. The Don Sheldon Building houses aviation artifacts as well as antique autos and photographic displays. Guided tours are available. *Alaska State Fairgrounds, tel. 907/745–7719 or 907/745–4493. Admission: $3 adults, $1.50 children under 12, $7 family rate. Open year-round Tues.–Sat. 8–4.*

Talkeetna lies at the end of a spur road near Mile 99 of the Parks Highway. Modern-day mountaineers congregate here to begin their assaults on Mt. McKinley in Denali National Park. The Denali mountain rangers maintain their climbing headquarters here as do most of the glacier pilots who fly climbing parties to the mountain. The community maintains a museum of the history of Mt. McKinley climbs.

Just south of **Wasilla** is the headquarters and starting point for the **Iditarod Trail Sled-Dog Race,** run each March from here to Nome, more than 1,000 miles to the northwest. The headquarters is open year-round with its displays of dogsleds, musher's clothing, and trail gear as well as video highlights of past races. *Iditarod Trail Headquarters, Mile 2.2, Knik Rd., tel. 907/376–5155. Admission free. Open year-round, weekdays 8–5; in summer, weekends 8–noon.*

What to See and Do with Children

If your children like zoos, touring **Denali National Park** or the **Kenai Wildlife Refuge,** with their abundance of wildlife in their natural habitat—free from limited quarters and cage bars—should delight them.

For the more adventurous, a flightseeing plane over the **Columbia** or **Portage** glaciers should be a thrill not soon forgotten.

Several tour operators offer **family floats** on rubber rafts down a variety of scenic, gentle rivers (*see* Guided Tours, above).

Enter the budding fisherman in one of the many **Valdez** fishing derbies held during the summer.

The **Alaska State Fair,** held each August in Palmer, combines all the best parts of a circus, amusement park, concert, and museum into one big event.

Clam digging at **Clam Gulch** is a favorite with local children who love the really muddy, sloppy digging. Ask locals on the beach how to find the giant razor clams (by their dimples in the sand).

Off the Beaten Track

Kodiak Island, Alaska's largest, is accessible only by air from Anchorage and by the state ferry system from Homer and Seward.

Russian explorers discovered the island in 1763, and Kodiak served as Alaska's first capital until 1804, when the government was moved to Sitka. Situated as it is in the northwestern Gulf of Alaska, Kodiak has been subjected to several natural disasters. In 1912 a volcanic eruption on the nearby Alaska Peninsula covered the town site knee-deep in ash and pumice. A tidal wave resulting from the 1964 earthquake destroyed the island's large fishing fleet and smashed Kodiak's low-lying downtown area.

Today, commercial fishing is king in Kodiak. Despite its small population—about 15,000 people scattered across some 200 islands in the Kodiak group—the city is the second-largest fishing community in the United States.

The harbor is also an important supply point for small communities up and down the Aleutian Islands and the Alaska Peninsula.

Float-plane and boat charters are available from Kodiak to visit numerous remote attractions not served by roads. Chief among these areas is the 1.8-million-acre **Kodiak National Wildlife Refuge,** lying partly on Kodiak Island and partly on Afognak Island to the north.

Seeing the Kodiak grizzlies, cubs of less than a pound at birth but weighing 1,200 pounds when full grown, is worth the trip to this rugged country. The bears are spotted easily in July and August feeding along salmon-spawning streams. Local airlines make charter flightseeing trips to the area, and tales of encounters with these impressive beasts are heard frequently (and often are exaggerated!).

It's also possible to use one of 12 free recreation cabins within the refuge for up to seven days. Contact the **Fish and Wildlife Service** (tel. 907/276–3487) in Anchorage for details. Four cabins also are available in nearby **Shuyak Island State Park** by contacting the state Department of Natural Resources (tel. 907/486–6339) in Kodiak.

Kodiak figured in America's North Pacific defense in World War II and was the site of an important naval station, now occupied by the coast guard fleet that patrols the surrounding fishing grounds. Part of the old military installation has been incorporated into **Abercrombie State Park and Campground,** 3.5 miles north of Kodiak on the Rezano Road.

The **Baranof Museum** in Erskine House portrays the area's Russian origins. Now listed on the National Register of Historic Places, Erskine House was built in 1808 by Alexander Baranov to warehouse precious sea otter pelts. It was sold to the Alaska Commercial Co., probably in 1867, then sold to W.J.

Erskine, who turned the structure into a home in 1911. On display today are Russian samovars, Russian Easter eggs, native baskets, and other relics from the Koniag and Russian eras. *101 Marine Way, tel. 907/486–5920. Admission: $1, children under 12 free. Open weekdays 10–3, weekends noon–4 summer; weekdays 11–3, Sat. noon–3 winter; closed Thurs. and Sun.*

Shopping

Most communities have outposts selling native crafts and jewelry. Look for jade, ivory, and gold pieces, as well as ceramics, beadwork, and leather. A true Alaskan gift, widely available, is the *ulu*, a knife used by Eskimo hunters to skin animals, now used by Alaska cooks for chopping vegetables.

Gakona   **The Little Alaska Cache** sells Athabaskan baskets, moccasins, mittens, jewelry, and beadwork. *North junction of Glenn and Richardson Hwys., open May–Oct.*

Homer   **Alaska Wild Berry Products** (528 Pioneer Ave., tel. 907/235–8858) manufactures jams, jellies, sauces, syrups, and juices made from wild berries hand-picked on the Kenai Peninsula. Yes, they ship. Across the bay at Halibut Cove, **Diana Tillion's Gallery** (tel. 907/296–2207) sells drawings done in octopus ink, which she milks herself from resident octopi. The Tillions have lived on the bay for two generations. Husband Clem operates a water taxi and works as a ships' pilot in the winter. They frequently raise orphan seal pups on their docks.

Soldotna   **Northcountry Fair** (junction of Kenai Spur and Seward Hwy.) sells gifts and locally made bent-willow furniture.

Participant Sports

Boating   Canoe and kayak parties are attracted to the **Tangle Lakes** region of South Central. Access is off the Denali Highway, 20 miles west of Paxson. This mountainous country on the south flank of the Alaska Range forms the headwaters of the north-flowing **Delta River.** Possibilities for paddling here range from a few lazy hours near the road to an extended trip requiring overnight camping and portages. The Bureau of Land Management (tel. 907/267–1246) maintains two campgrounds on the Tangle Lakes.

Visitors with a taste for white-water adventures will find parts of the **Nenana River** near Denali Park to their liking. Several privately owned raft and tour companies operate along the Parks Highway near the entrance to Denali, and they schedule daily rafting, both in the fairly placid areas on the Nenana and through the 10-mile-long Nenana River Canyon, which contains some of the roughest white water in North America. These rafters move thousands of visitors down the Nenana each summer *(see* Guided Tours, above).

Other South Central rivers offer varied rafting opportunities. **Nova Riverrunners** (tel. 907/745–5753) in Chickaloon offers trips on the Chickaloon and Matanuska rivers within an hour's drive of Anchorage, and in other parts of the state.

Several outfitters in Cooper Landing and Soldotna offer fishing or float trips on the Kenai River. The king salmon in this river reach 100 pounds, and drift boats are a popular means of access to the fishing holes. Raft trips are also available if an easy float through spectacular mountain scenery is your goal.

Homer and **Prince William Sound** provide excellent sailing and adventurous kayaking. The Prince William Sound Kayak Center (1106 W. 29th Pl., Anchorage 99503, tel. 907/563–4034) rents kayaks and offers lessons and day trips.

Numerous charter operators offer motorized and sail powered tours of Prince William Sound or Kachemak Bay. Check with the harbormasters in Homer, Valdez, or Whittier for names of charter operators.

Fishing   Boat rentals and guide services are available all along the South Central coastline.

Valdez and the surrounding waters of **Prince William Sound** are prime fishing areas where the salmon congregate before heading up the freshwater streams to spawn.

Another prime fishing ground is found on the west side of the Kenai Peninsula, where the rivers and streams empty into Cook Inlet and along **Kachemak Bay.** Because this area is readily accessible to the large population in and around Anchorage, the hot spots can be lined with people fishing shoulder to shoulder. Campgrounds can be crowded to overflowing at the peak of the salmon runs. Still, at their peaks these salmon runs are so strong that chances are good for a catch.

Soldotna is the headquarters for salmon fishermen on the western Kenai Peninsula. The Kenai River and its tributaries are famous around the world for huge salmon runs. There are salmon of several species in the river throughout the summer. Local guides and charter boat operators can help even novice fishermen find and land a salmon. During king salmon season (June–July), some spots on this river are crowded with fishermen standing shoulder to shoulder on the bank, hoping for a record fish. It is not uncommon for a king salmon to take more than an hour to land.

At the southern tip of the peninsula and the end of the Sterling Highway lies the community of Homer. Salmon are taken in this area, but among Alaskans, Homer is perhaps the best known for landing whopper halibut and for digging razor clams. Halibut of 100 pounds or more are taken here frequently; sometimes a fishing party will land one that weighs well over 400 pounds. Charters are readily available, as is help to clean the delicious fish and air-ship it home.

Clam digging is subject to bag limits and seasons just as other sportfishing is, and it is a skill best learned by observation. There's more to successful clamming than just digging a shovel into the sand. However, Alaskans are known for being friendly —ask a fellow fisherman or clammer about local conditions, and likely you will get an earful of free advice!

Hiking   Trails and footpaths are plentiful to suit every taste, from a leisurely stroll to an extended backpacking trip. Self-guided walking tours are found in the larger communities. Many wilderness trips are accessible from the highway system. Charter flights are available to even more remote regions.

Information on locations and difficulty of trails is available at the Public Lands Information Center at 4th and F Street in Anchorage. Another good resource is *55 Ways to the Wilderness in*

Southcentral Alaska, published by The Mountaineers and available at most local book stores.

Just about all of **Denali National Park** (*see* Exploring South Central Alaska, above) is open to hiking and backpacking, although some areas may be closed from time to time because of bear danger. Check with the park rangers (*see* Chapter 4).

Running The footrace best known among Alaskans is Seward's annual **Mount Marathon** run on the Fourth of July. It doesn't last very long—44 minutes or so—but the route is straight up Mount Marathon (3,022 feet high) and back down to the center of town. They've been running this race in Seward since 1909.

The *Homer News* sponsors an annual Spit Run the first week in July, which goes from downtown Homer to the end of the spit. This 6-mile run is a good one for families.

Skiing Mt. Alyeska Ski Resort, 40 miles southeast of Anchorage on the Seward Highway, is Alaska's largest ski area (*see* Participant Sports in Chapter 6).

Dining and Lodging

Highly recommended establishments are indicated with a star ★.

Dining Seafood is a natural along the coast and it's typically fresh and among the more reasonably priced menu items.

Category	Cost*
Expensive	over $40
Moderate	$20–$40
Inexpensive	under $20

*per person, without tax, service, or wine

Many of the restaurants listed here vary their hours by season. It is a good policy to call ahead to be sure a restaurant is open.

Lodging The range is from rustic and charming to "the only beds in town." You can find unexpected treasures behind a promising-looking facade. Trust your instincts, and the recommendations of locals, if you are traveling independently. Summer rates are quoted; difference in rates between seasons may vary widely in some places.

Category	Cost*
Very Expensive	over $120
Expensive	$90–$120
Moderate	$50–$90
Inexpensive	under $50

*double room without tax or service

Cordova **O.K. Restaurant.** Chinese, Japanese, Korean, and American
Dining dishes are served. *601 6th Ave., tel. 907/424–3433. MC, V. Inexpensive.*

Lodging
★
Reluctant Fisherman Inn. This is probably your best bet in Cordova, with many rooms overlooking the harbor. Don't miss the collection of native art and artifacts. Restaurant and cocktail lounge. *407 Railroad Ave., tel. 907/424–3272. 41 rooms. MC, V. Expensive.*

Prince William Motel. Available here are centrally located motel units, some with kitchens. Restaurant and cocktail lounge. *1st St. and C St., tel. 907/424–3201. 13 rooms. MC, V. Moderate.*

Denali National Park
Dining
Harper Lodge Restaurant. A fine view is offered here, and if a good meal is your top priority, this is the place in the Denali Park area. Picnic lunches are provided. *Just off Parks Hwy. near park entrance, tel. 907/683–2282. MC, V. Moderate.*

McKinley/Denali Salmon Bake. This rustic place, with baked fresh salmon topping the menu, offers shuttle service to all hotels. *Mile 238.5, Parks Hwy., tel. 907/683–2733. DC, MC, V, Inexpensive–Moderate.*

Lodging
Harper Lodge Princess. This is a newer hotel overlooking the Nenana River. There are 1,060 comfortable rooms (two accommodate wheelchairs), outdoor hot tubs, a full-service restaurant, cocktail lounge, gift shop, and tour desk. Complimentary shuttle service to park, airport, and railroad station. *Just off Parks Hwy. near park entrance, tel. 907/683–2282 or 800/426–0442 off-season. Closed mid-Sept.–late May. AE, DC, MC, V. Very Expensive.*

North Face Lodge. There is a country-inn atmosphere at this cozy lodge, located in a remote, quiet haven in the wilderness, in the center of the park. *Tel. 907/683–2290. Closed early Sept.–mid-June. Very Expensive.*

Denali Crow's Nest Log Cabins. Complimentary rides to and from the train station are available to guests at these spartan cantilevered cabins above the highway. *Mile 238.5, Parks Hwy., tel. 907/683–2723. MC, V. Expensive.*

Denali National Park Hotel. This is the "official" hotel, located inside the park entrance and efficiently run by contractors for the National Park Service. *Located next to the train depot in the park, tel. 907/276–7234. 100 rooms. MC, V. Expensive.*

Denali Cabins. Cedar hot tubs and barbecue grills are the attraction here. *Mile 229, Parks Hwy., tel. 907/683–2643. MC, V. Moderate.*

Gakona
Dining
Carriage House Restaurant. American meals and seafood are available at this 60-year-old rustic log dining room overlooking the Gakona River. *In the Gakona Lodge, Mile 2, Tok Cutoff, tel. 907/822–3482. No credit cards. Inexpensive–Moderate.*

Lodging
Chistochina Lodge. This lodge is a busy highway stop and trading post serving mostly tour buses. *Mile 32.8, Tok-Slana Hwy., tel. 907/822–3366. MC, V. Inexpensive–Moderate.*

Glennallen
Dining
Caribou Cafe Family Restaurant. This is a friendly place for lunch or dinner. *Downtown Glennallen, tel. 907/822–3656. No credit cards. Inexpensive–Moderate.*

Homer
Dining
The Fresh Sourdough Express. This bakery offers up incredible baked goods to go, and fine, wholesome local foods in its dining room. Try the halibut omelet for breakfast, or a "stuff" bread pouch filled with reindeer sausage and peppers for lunch. *On Ocean Drive en route to the spit. Open daily 6 a.m.–10 p.m.; tel. 907/235–7571. AE. Moderate.*

The Saltry in Halibut Cove. Fine sushi made from local seafood and a wide selection of imported beers are available here. The deck overlooks the boat dock and the cove. It's a good place to while away the afternoon. *Take the Kachemak Bay Ferry from the Homer harbor; tel. 907/235–7847. AE, V. Reservations required. Moderate.*

Bidarka Inn. The proprietor here specializes in locally caught seafood, including fresh halibut that will melt in your mouth. *575 Sterling Hwy., tel. 907/235–8148. AE, DC, MC, V. Inexpensive–Moderate.*

The Porpoise Room. American meals, seafood, and great views are featured at this restaurant located at the end of the spit. *874 Dock Rd., tel. 907/235–7848. AE, MC, V. Inexpensive–Moderate.*

Lodging **Land's End.** At this hotel, which is past the canneries and campgrounds at the end of the spit, you get great views of the bay. *Box 273, Homer 99603, tel. 907/235–2500. AE, DC, MC, V. Moderate.*

There are a number of secluded bed-and-breakfast homes in Homer. Some are separate cabins with woodstoves. Call **Alaska Private Lodgings** in Anchorage (tel. 907/258–1717) for bookings.

Kenai **Albatross Restaurant and Lounge.** This place is a bit out of town **Dining** but it is popular among the locals for its king-size American meals and seafood. *Mile 13.1 Kalifonsky Beach Rd., tel. 907/283–7052. MC, V. No lunch, closed Sun. Moderate.*

VIP Restaurant and Lounge. American and seafood dishes are offered at this convenient downtown location. *47 Spur View Dr., tel. 907/283–3660. AE, DC, MC, V. Inexpensive–Moderate.*

Italian Garden. Besides traditional Italian dishes, Mexican and American meals are available at this restaurant, which has one of the better salad bars around. *Mile 11 Spur Rd., tel. 907/283–4440. MC, V. Inexpensive.*

Kodiak **Chartroom Restaurant.** American meals and seafood are of-**Dining** fered in a nice setting in the Westmark Hotel overlooking the
★ harbor. *236 S. Benson St., tel. 907/486–5712. AE, MC, V. Inexpensive–Moderate.*

El Chicano Mexican Restaurant. Mexican dishes are offered at this lively restaurant, which is open for lunch and dinner. This place is a favorite among the locals. *104 Center St., tel. 907/486–6116. MC, V. Inexpensive.*

Lodging **Kodiak Buskin River Inn.** There is a restaurant and lounge at this comfortable inn. It is convenient to the airport (airport pickup available) but about three miles from downtown Kodiak. *1395 Airport Way, tel. 907/487–2700. 51 rooms. AE, DC, MC, V. Moderate.*

Westmark Hotel. Several dozen of this hotel's 90 comfortable rooms overlook the harbor. *236 S. Benson St., tel. 907/486–5712, AE, MC, V. Moderate.*

Palmer **Valley Hotel.** This dignified older hotel is on the verge of being **Lodging** historic. Coffee shop and cocktail lounge. *606 South Alaska St., tel. 907/745–3330. AE, DC, MC, V. Inexpensive.*

Seward **Harbor Dinner Club & Lounge.** Local seafood is the best choice **Dining** here; try a halibut burger and fries for lunch. *On 5th Ave., downtown, tel. 907/224–3012. MC, V. Inexpensive–Moderate.*

Lodging **Murphy's Motel.** Small and friendly, this place is where the coffee's always on. *4th St. and D St., downtown, tel. 907/224–8090. AE, DC, MC, V. Moderate.*

Van Gilder Hotel. Considered the best place in town, this aging but dignified hotel with restaurant and lounge is listed on the National Register of Historic Places. *308 Adams St., tel. 907/224–3079. 25 rooms. MC, V. Moderate.*

Breeze Inn. This motel with restaurant and cocktail lounge is in the heart of Seward. Cable TV. *Small Boat Harbor, tel. 907/224–5237. AE, MC, V. Inexpensive–Moderate.*

Soldotna **The Four Seasons Restaurant.** Situated on part of a large tract
Dining that was once a homestead, this restaurant is operated by a local pioneer family. The menu emphasizes locally harvested foods, including salmon, halibut, and wild berries. *On Sterling Hwy. at the Kenai turn-off; tel. 907/262–5006. Open for lunch and dinner daily and Sunday brunch. No credit cards. Moderate.*

International Riverside Inn. Located conveniently on the banks of the Kenai River and close to shopping, this inn serves traditional American meals and seafood. *44611 Sterling Hwy., tel. 907/262–4451. AE, DC, MC, V. Inexpensive–Moderate.*

Sea Wind Restaurant. American meals and seafood are served in this restaurant in the Kenai River Lodge overlooking the river. *44788 Sterling Hwy., tel. 907/262–9300. MC, V. Inexpensive–Moderate.*

Lodging **International Riverside Inn.** This full-service hotel is the town's best. *44611 Sterling Hwy., tel. 907/262–4451. 26 rooms. AE, MC, V. Moderate.*

Bed-and-Breakfast There are a number of B&Bs in Soldotna; contact Alaska Private Lodgings (tel. 907/248–2292) for a booking.

Talkeetna **Talkeetna Roadhouse.** Home-style cooking is available at this
Dining log roadhouse. It's a popular place with locals, who gather when they come in from the woods. *Right on Main St., tel. 907/733–2341. MC, V. Inexpensive–Moderate.*

Lodging **Swiss-Alaska Inn.** They'll recommend fishing and hunting at this comfortable inn with an Alpine flavor. *East Talkeetna by the boat launch, tel. 907/733–2424. 12 rooms. AE, MC, V. Moderate.*

Talkeetna Motel. This all-purpose motel is complete with restaurant, cocktail lounge, and dancing in roadside A-frame splendor. *Downtown Talkeetna, tel. 907/733–2323. 25 rooms. MC, V. Inexpensive–Moderate.*

Valdez **Pizza Palace.** Not much to look at, but this place is popular with
Dining local fishermen and serves some Greek specialties. *On the boat harbor on N. Harbor Dr., tel. 907/835–4686. DC, MC, V.*

Lodging **Westmark Valdez Hotel.** This is another efficient hotel in the Westmark chain, located next to the small-boat harbor, *100 Fidalgo Dr., tel. 907/835–4391. 97 rooms. AE, DC, MC, V. Expensive.*

Wasilla **Mat-Su Resort Restaurant.** American food is the specialty. This
Dining is where Wasilla people take visitors they want to impress. *1850 Bogart Rd., tel. 907/376–3228. AE, MC, V. Moderate.*

Lodging **Lake Lucille Lodge.** Basic Best Western lodging. Try the jumbo Jacuzzi after a hard day of play. *1300 W. Lake Lucille Dr., tel. 907/373–1776. 54 rooms. MC, V. Moderate.*

Mat-Su Resort Motel. There is always something going on at this rambling complex with restaurant, float-plane dock, and boat rentals. *1850 Bogart Rd., tel. 907/376–3228. 36 rooms. AE, MC, V. Moderate.*

Yukon Don's B & B. Visitors to this converted barn have a choice of decor. The log-partitioned rooms are decorated with bearskins and antlers, with stuffed fish and fishnets, or with a dogsled and snowshoes. The recreation room contains a barrel stove and a bar fashioned as a log cabin. Facilities include a sauna and exercise room. Host "Yukon Don" is a dog musher and conducts guided tours. *Box 5086, Wasilla 99687; tel. 907376–7472. 6 rooms. No credit cards accepted. Inexpensive–Moderate.*

Nightlife

Homer
Dance to lively bands at **Alice's** (tel. 907/235–7650) in town and **Land's End** (tel. 907/235–2500) in Homer's Spit. The spit's **Salty Dawg Saloon** (no phone) has an old-fashioned atmosphere and great views of boats and glaciers. Close by is the **Waterfront Bar** (tel. 907/235-9949), a favorite of fishermen.

Kodiak
The B&B Bar (tel. 907/486–3575) at the downtown waterfront is a popular fishermen's hangout. **Solly's Office** (tel. 907/486–3313) and **The Mecca Lounge** (tel. 907/486–3364), downtown on the mall and close to the boat harbor, are among the many bars that serve food and have entertainment that lean toward country-rock music.

9 The Interior

By Kent Sturgis

The image of turn-of-the-century Alaska, with its heady gold rushes set to the jangling accompaniment of honky-tonk saloons, has its roots in the Interior. Gold fever struck in Circle and Eagle in the 1890s, spread into Canada's Yukon Territory in the big Klondike gold rush of 1898, then came back to Alaska when Fairbanks hit paydirt in the 1900s. The broad, swift Yukon River was the rush's main highway. Flowing almost 2,300 miles from Canada to the Bering Sea just below the Arctic Circle, it carried prospectors back and forth across the border in search of instant fortune.

While Fairbanks has grown up into a modern-day small city, many towns and communities in the Interior seem little changed. Soaking in the hot springs of the Chena Hot Springs Resort, it seems you can almost hear the whispers of the gold seekers—exaggerating their finds and claims, ever alert for the newest strike.

Unlike the western United States, where white settlers routed the natives they encountered as their communities spread, Interior Alaska is still flecked with Indian villages. Fort Yukon on the Arctic Circle is the largest Athabaskan village in the state.

Alaska's most recent gold rush—the pipeline carrying black gold from the oil fields in Prudhoe Bay south to the port of Valdez—snakes its way through the heart of the Interior. The pipeline itself is something of an enigma; it's a symbol of commercial interests against the land yet also a monumental construction that hugs the land as a giant necklace. The Richardson Highway, which got its start as a gold stampeders' trail, parallels the trans-Alaska pipeline on its route south of Fairbanks.

Essential Information

Getting Around

By Plane **Alaska Airlines** (tel. 800/426–0333), **United Airlines** (tel. 800/241–6522), **Delta Airlines** (tel. 800/843–9378), and **MarkAir** (tel. 800/426–6784) fly the Anchorage–Fairbanks route. All but MarkAir have connecting routes to the lower 48 states, and MarkAir has an extensive schedule to rural areas.

Air North (tel. 403/668–2228) has the only direct, scheduled air service between Alaska and Canada, flying DC-3s and DC-4s on regular runs from Fairbanks and Juneau to the Yukon Territory towns of Dawson City and Whitehorse.

In much of Bush, federally subsidized mail runs make regular air schedules possible. From Fairbanks, you can easily catch a ride on the mail run to small, predominantly Indian villages along the Yukon River or to Eskimo settlements on the Arctic coast. However, there are no hotels in most villages.

Airlines with Bush service originating from Fairbanks include **Audi Air** (tel. 907/474–0834), **Larry's Flying Service** (tel. 907/474–9169), **Friendship Air** (tel. 907/474–0411), **Tanana Air Service** (tel. 907/474–0301), **Wright Air Service** (tel. 907/474–0502), and **Frontier Flying Service** (tel. 907/474–0014). For commuter flights out of Anchorage, try **Peninsula Airways** (tel. 907/249–2295), **Southcentral Air** (tel. 907/561–4193), **ERA Aviation** (tel.

907/243–3300), **Wilbur's** (tel. 907/243–7878), or **Raven Air** (tel. 907/243–5586).

If you fly from Fairbanks to Anchorage, sit on the right side of the plane for a dazzling view of Mt. McKinley (if the weather cooperates).

By Car In the Interior, your choices of side trips by road from Fairbanks include the Steese Highway to historic Circle City on the Yukon with its legacy of gold mining; the Dalton Highway across the Yukon and along the trans-Alaska pipeline as far as the foothills of the Brooks Range; the Elliott Highway connecting the Alaska Highway near Tok with the historic towns of Eagle on the Alaska side of the border and Dawson City, Y.T., in Canada. These are mainly well maintained gravel roads. However, in summer rain can make them slick and dangerous.

For hot-line reports on highways during the snow season, call the State Department of Transportation in Fairbanks (tel. 907/456–7623). In Canada's Yukon Territory, the government also provides a road report (tel. 403/667–5644).

By Bus The most common run is between Fairbanks and Anchorage by way of Denali National Park. However, you can take side trips by bus or van to such places as Circle Hot Springs, on the Steese Highway north of Fairbanks, and into the Yukon Territory.

For more information about bus service throughout the Interior, contact: **Alaska-Yukon Motorcoaches** (tel. 206/441–8690): seasonal service. **Gray Line of Alaska** (tel. 907/452–2853 or 800/544–2206): year-round. **Royal Highway Tours** (tel. 907/452–8801 or 800/426–0442): seasonal. **Alaska Direct Bus Lines** (tel. 907/277–6652 or 800/328–9730): year-round.

Guided Tours

Dawson City, Y.T. **Cheechako Trail Tours** (tel. 403/993–5460) runs gold-field and city tours.

Delta Junction **Granite Mountain Ranch** (tel. 907/895–4671) will guide you into the wilderness on horseback by the day, week, or month.

Eagle **Eagle Historical Society** (tel. 907/547–2230) offers a two-hour walking tour beginning at 10 AM each day from June 1 to September 1, visiting four museum buildings and telling tales of the famous people who have passed through this historic Yukon River border town.

Fairbanks **Alaska Wilderness Inc.** (tel. 907/455–6060) specializes in university-accredited tours of wilderness areas statewide, dedicated to low-impact camping, outdoor education, and wilderness preservation.
Arctic Grayling Guide Service (tel. 907/452–5201) is a family-run operation offering riverboat fishing and overnight cabins.
Brooks Range Aviation (tel. 907/692–5444) flies rafters and hikers into the Brooks Range from Bettles (regular air service available from Fairbanks). They can provide rental gear.
Family Adventures (tel. 907/455–6502) offers two- to seven-day hiking and rafting trips; also offers to design special trips for tots to teenagers.
General Bull Moose Canoe Tours (tel. 907/479–4061) provides airport transportation, supplies, and all necessary gear for guided one- to four-day canoe trips on Interior rivers.

KAK Tours (tel. 907/488–2649) operates small van service to Arctic Circle Hot Springs and the mining community of Central on the Steese Highway.

Northern Alaska Tour Co. (tel. 907/479–3402) offers a one-day Arctic Circle tour over the Elliott and Dalton highways along the trans-Alaska pipeline to the Yukon River.

Teklanika Tours (tel. 907/457–7194) escorts visitors deep into the wilderness on backpacking and river-float tours ranging from two to 10 days.

Wilderness Birding Adventures (tel. 907/694–7442) offers high-quality guided wilderness raft trips in the Brooks Range and other interior areas.

Wynfromere Trail Rides (tel. 907/457–7902) will show you the pipeline on horseback.

Whitehorse, Y.T. **Atlas Tours** (tel. 403/668–3161) operates two-hour Yukon River cruises, including a run through Miles Canyon aboard the *Schwatka*. Hotel pickups are available.

Important Addresses and Numbers

Tourist Information **Delta Junction** (Milepost 1422, Alaska Hwy., tel. 907/895–5068).
Fairbanks (550 First Ave., tel. 907/456–5774).
Nenana (Second and C Sts., tel. 907/832–5441).
Tok (Milepost 1314, Alaska Hwy., tel. 907/883–5667).
Whitehorse, Y.T. (302 Steele St., tel. 403/667–2915).

Emergencies Dial 911 for local **police** or **emergency** assistance in Fairbanks and other larger communities.

The **Alaska State Troopers** also maintain detachments throughout the region. They include **Delta Junction** (tel. 907/895–4600), **Fairbanks** (tel. 907/452–2114), **Nenana** (tel. 907/832–5554), and **Tok** (tel. 907/883–5111).

The **Royal Canadian Mounted Police** have offices in **Whitehorse** (tel. 403/667–5555) and **Dawson** (tel. 403/993–5444).

Hospital and Clinic **Dawson** (Y.T.): Father Judge Memorial Hospital (tel. 403/993–5333). **Fairbanks:** Fairbanks Memorial Hospital (tel. 907/452–8181); Bassett Army Hospital (tel. 907/353–5281). **Tok:** Public Health Clinic (tel. 907/883–4101). **Whitehorse** (Y.T.): General Hospital (tel. 403/668–9444).

Dentist In case of emergency, 24-hour service can be arranged in Fairbanks (tel. 907/452–8051).

Exploring the Interior

Orientation

Interior Alaska is neatly sandwiched between two monumental mountain ranges—the Brooks Range to the north and the Alaska Range to the south. Important cities and towns are spread along two major transportation routes. The Yukon River flows east–west in the northern half of the region. The Alaska Highway shoots northwest from Dawson Creek in British Columbia to Delta Junction, where it joins up with the Richardson Highway. Hardy motorists driving up from the lower 48 states will enter Alaska at Beaver Creek in the Yukon Territory.

212

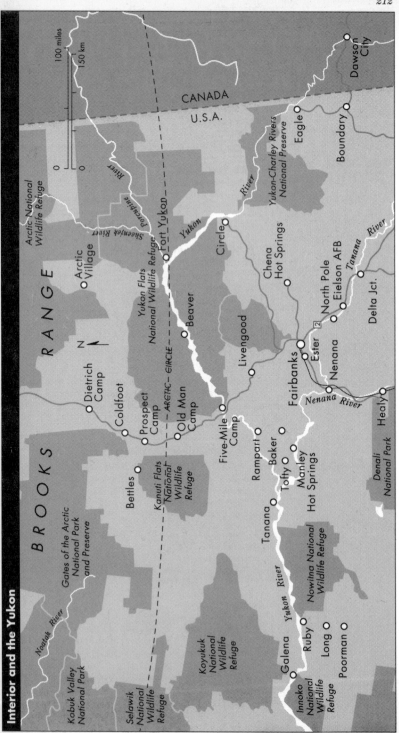

Interior and the Yukon

At Tok comes the first major dilemma for Alaska Highway travelers. Continue northwest into the Interior to Delta Junction and on to Fairbanks, Alaska's second-largest city? Head north and a touch east on the Taylor Highway to Eagle and the Yukon? Or turn southwest onto the Tok Cutoff and make for Valdez or Anchorage?

The Parks Highway south of Fairbanks leads to the northern gates of Denali National Park, a good halfway point for a Fairbanks-to-Anchorage route (*see* Chapters 4 and 8).

Planning a good circle route, whether you are driving, flying, floating, or any combination of the three, will enable you to cover a lot of ground without retracing your steps. For example, from Tok, take the Richardson Highway to Fairbanks; from there you can head south on the Parks Highway to Denali National Park and Anchorage. The Tok Cutoff/Glenn Highway gets you back to Tok from Anchorage.

Fairbanks is a relatively young town, founded in 1901, and the people here are still living amid their own history. This is especially true in the older downtown area, with its narrow, winding streets following the contours of the Chena River. Many of the old homes and commercial buildings trace their history to the early days of the city.

The **Fairbanks Convention and Visitors Bureau,** on the river at the Cushman Street Bridge, offers twice-daily guided historical walking tours at 10 AM and 3 PM through the downtown area. Each lasts about an hour. The bureau also offers maps for a self-guided walking tour and for a similar two-hour, do-it-yourself driving tour.

A few points of interest: **Golden Heart Park,** home of the Unknown First Family statue; the **Clay Street Cemetery** with its marked and unmarked graves of early pioneers; the **Empress Theater** building, first cement structure in interior Alaska; the stately **Falcon Joslin Home,** oldest frame house in Fairbanks still on its original location; **The Line,** home of the red-light district until the mid-1950s; **Oldfellows Hall,** a bathhouse for gold miners until the pipes froze in the winter of 1910–11; and the historic **Immaculate Conception Church,** which was raised off its foundation in 1911 and rolled across the Chena River on logs, pulled by horses. *Fairbanks Walking Tour meets at visitors bureau, 550 First Ave., tel. 907/456–5774. Admission free.*

Fairbanks

Numbers in the margin correspond to points of interest on the Fairbanks map.

Riverboats are to Fairbanks as railroads are to Chicago and airplanes are to Kitty Hawk. This is a river town that was served by proud steamboats in its first two decades. There was no event more exciting than the arrival of the first steamboat with passengers, mail, perishables, even the previous year's Christmas presents from "outside," as many Alaskans refer to the rest of the world.

The excitement and color of the city's riverboat history and the Interior's cultural heritage are relived each summer aboard the popular **Riverboat Discovery cruise,** a four-hour narrated trip by stern-wheeler along the Chena and Tanana rivers to a rustic Indian village setting on the Tanana.

This is no ordinary boat ride. Minutes after departure, passengers experience a sense of the wilderness aboard one of the Binkley family's three stern-wheelers. Sailing twice daily from mid-May through mid-September, the cruises offer a glimpse of the lifestyle of the dog mushers, subsistence fishermen, trappers, traders, and Alaska natives who populate the Yukon River drainage. Captain Jim Binkley, his wife Mary, and their three sons and a daughter have operated the Discovery cruises for 40 years. Their family, with its four generations of river pilots, has run great rivers of the north for 90 years.

Photo opportunities abound: operating fish wheels, a Bush airfield, float planes, a smokehouse and cache, and log cabins. *Alaska Riverways, Dale Road Landing near Fairbanks International Airport, tel. 907/479–6673. Cruises depart at 8:45 AM and 2 PM daily. Fare for adults is $25.*

Time Out **Pump House Restaurant and Bar.** You might wish to get off the
❶ riverboat at this last stop before the end of the cruise. Listed on the National Register of Historic Places, this riverside building once housed a pump that moved water through a pipeline over a nearby ridge into the Ester Valley, scene of extensive gold-mining operations off and on most of this century. There is no better place to be on a hot, sunny day in Fairbanks than the deck overlooking the Chena River. *1.3 Mile Chena Pump Rd., tel. 907/479–8452. No reservations. AE, DC, MC, V.*

A magazine article comparing colleges in the United States
❷ once proclaimed that the **University of Alaska–Fairbanks** offered the best view from any college dorm in the country. On the more serious side, the university has an international reputation for its Arctic research, including study of the aurora borealis, or northern lights.

An eight-foot-nine-inch grizzly bear guards the entrance to the **UA Museum,** a history and natural sciences collection divided into the five regions of Alaska: Southeast, Interior, Aleutians, Southwest, and Arctic.

A featured artifact is the Blue Babe, a mummified steppe bison that lived 38,000 years ago during the Pleistocene epoch. The creature was preserved in permafrost (permanently frozen ground), complete with claw marks indicating attack by a saber-tooth tiger. The bison's remains were found by gold miners a few years ago. *University Museum, West Ridge of UAF campus, tel. 907/474–7505. Admission: $3 adults, $2.50 seniors, military, and students, Fri. (off-season) and under 12 free. Open June–Aug. daily 9–9, off-season 9–5.*

The university offers a host of guided tours June through August, and by arrangement at other times. These include:

A tour of the **Large Animal Research Station,** which houses caribou, musk-oxen, and reindeer, among other animals. It is located on Yankovitch Road, off Ballaine Lake Road behind the university.

The **Geophysical Institute,** the center of atmospheric and earthquake research at the university, located on West Ridge about a mile from the center of the campus.

Fairbanks

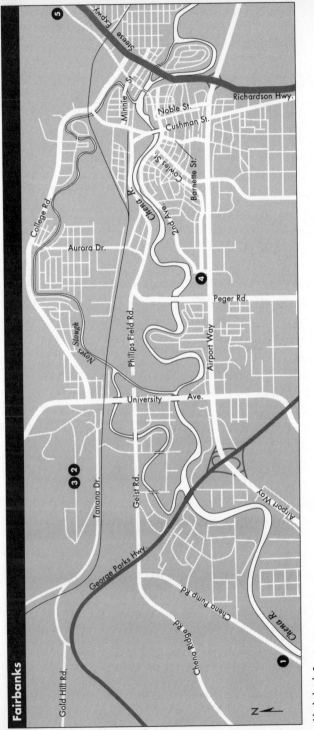

Steese Expwy.

Richardson Hwy.

Noble St.

Cushman St.

Minnie St.

Cowles St.

Barnette St.

2nd Ave.

Chena R.

College Rd.

Aurora Dr.

Noyes Slough

Peger Rd.

Philips Field Rd.

Airport Way

University Ave.

Tanana Dr.

Geist Rd.

George Parks Hwy.

Gold Hill Rd.

Chena Ridge Rd.

Chena Pump Rd.

Airport Way

Chena R.

N

Alaskaland, **4**
Alaska Range
viewpoint, **3**
Gold Dredge No.8, **5**
Pump House
Restaurant and Bar, **1**
University of Alaska-
Fairbanks, **2**

Poker Flat Research Range (sounding rocket range), where the university launches its own rockets studying the aurora borealis, as well as the rockets of other universities and research agencies. It is located 33 miles northeast of Fairbanks on the Steese Highway.

The **Agricultural and Forestry Experiment Station Farm,** where researchers study Interior Alaska's unique, short-but-intense midnight-sun growing season. The farm is located on the far west end of the campus.

A **guided walking tour,** a two-mile, two-hour tour of the university campus. (If you prefer, guide yourself by picking up a campus map at the Office of University Relations.)

University of Alaska, Office of University Relations, 210 Signers Hall, tel. 907/474–7581. Tour schedule varies from year to year; call for details or inquire at Fairbanks Visitors Center.

❸ The Interior offers many vistas of mountains in the **Alaska Range** to the south. The most accessible **viewpoint** in Fairbanks is on the West Ridge of the UA–Fairbanks campus near the museum. Look for the parking area just east of the museum.

The entire north side of the range is visible. Many of the Alaska Range panoramas seen in magazines and travel brochures are photographed from this point. It also is a favorite spot for time-lapse photography of the mid-winter sun just peeking over the southern horizon on a low arc.

Nearly always distinguishable on a clear day are three major peaks, called the "three sisters" because they appear quite similar to one another. They are, from your left, **Mt. Hayes,** 13,832 feet; **Mt. Hess,** 11,940 feet; and **Mt. Deborah,** 12,339 feet.

Much farther to the right, toward the southwest, lies **Mt. McKinley,** the highest peak in North America. On some seemingly clear days it's not visible at all. At times the base is easy to see but the peak is cloud-covered. Often when Mt. McKinley is entirely visible, Mt. Foraker, second-highest peak in the Alaska Range, also can be seen. It appears as a small pyramid just to the right of the base of Mt. McKinley. Its apparent smallness is caused by the fact that it is 75 miles farther away than Mt. McKinley.

❹ The 44-acre **Alaskaland** park, set along the Chena River near downtown Fairbanks, has a museum, theater, art gallery, civic center, native village, and a gold-rush town comprised of historic buildings saved from urban renewal.

Add to that the only preserved stern-wheeler in the state, log-cabin gift shops, and **Mining Valley,** with its outdoor museum of mining artifacts situated around an indoor/outdoor salmon-bake restaurant.

Then there is the newly restored *Denali,* a plush railcar in which President Warren Harding traveled when he came north in 1923 to hammer the golden spike on the Alaska Railroad. Also being restored is the 227-foot stern-wheeler, *Nenana,* built by the railroad in 1933 to serve the rivers of Interior Alaska.

The **Crooked Creek and Whiskey Island Railroad,** a small-gauge train, circles the park. A tram offers free transportation to and from downtown Fairbanks and nearby hotels and motels. No-frills RV camping is available in the west end of the large parking lot on Airport Way. *Alaskaland Park, Airport Way and Peger Rd., tel. 907/452–4529 or 907/452–4244. Admission free. Open late May–early Sept. daily 11–9.*

Time Out   **Alaska Salmon Bake.** This indoor/outdoor restaurant in Alaskaland's Mining Valley features mouth-watering fresh salmon with a special honey sauce cooked over an open fire. *Airport Way and Peger Rd., tel. 907/452–7274. No reservations necessary, but come early to beat the dinner crowd. No credit cards accepted. Closed mid Sept.–mid May.*

Imagine a giant gold dredge literally making its own waterway as it chews through the gold pay dirt, displacing 1,065 tons of rock and gravel as it crawls along at a snail's pace. Built by **⑤** Bethlehem Shipbuilders in 1928, *Gold Dredge No. 8* was operated by the Fairbanks Exploration Co. until her retirement in 1959. The five-deck ship is more than 250 feet long and took millions of dollars worth of gold out of the Goldstream and Engineer creeks north of Fairbanks. She's now listed on the National Register of Historic Places.

The unique mining vessel came to rest at Mile 9, Old Steese Highway, where she was lovingly restored by Big John Reeves, a friendly, colorful ex-miner and poet who also restored a nearby miners' bunkhouse and dining hall into a bar, restaurant, and hotel.

The admission price of a tour on the dredge includes gold panning. Keep what you find. *Gold Dredge No. 8, Mile 9, Old Steese Hwy., tel. 907/457–6058. Admission: $5. Open May–Sept., dredge tours start at 9 AM, bar and restaurant open at 5:30 PM Mon.–Sat.; Sun. brunch served 10 AM–2 PM.*

There are several places where you can pan for gold without fear of jumping a claim. Try **Mining Valley** (Alaskaland, Airport Way and Peger Rd., tel. 907/452–4244), **Alaska Prospectors Supply** (504 College Rd., tel. 907/452–7398), **Little El Dorado Camp** (Mile 10, Old Steese Hwy., tel. 907/456–4598), **Old F.E. Co. Camp** (Mile 27.5, Steese Hwy., tel. 907/389–2414).

Hot Springs Retreats

Forty below zero isn't a temperature that brings thoughts of going for a swim, but that's what visitors have done for many years at one of the three developed hot springs resorts in the Interior.

To early miners, these springs found in the wilderness seemed almost heaven-sent, and small communities sprang up around each one. As mining waned the springs fell into general disuse, but in recent years all three are seeing better days and are open all year, complete with lodging and dining. All three are privately owned and accessible by road and air from Fairbanks.

Nearest to Fairbanks is **Chena Hot Springs Resort** (Drawer 25, 1919 Lathrop St., Fairbanks 99701, tel. 907/452–7867), which lies at the end of the 60-mile-long road bearing the same name. Its proximity to Fairbanks, plus the good Chena River fishing along the way, makes it popular among local residents out for the day. A campground is available on the grounds, and there is good grayling fishing, hiking, and cross-country skiing nearby.

A feature at **Arctic Circle Hot Springs** (Central 99730, tel. 907/520–5113) is the original hotel dating from 1930. It has been restored and offers rooms plus a hostel on the fourth floor. This resort is at the end of an eight-mile spur road that begins at Central on the Steese Highway. There is a small campground along the road about two miles from the resort.

Manley Hot Springs (Manley Hot Springs 99756, tel. 907/672–3611) is in the small community at the end of the Elliott Highway, 160 miles west of Fairbanks. Manley is a colorful, close-knit "end-of-the-road" place. This town originally was a trading center for placer miners who worked the nearby creeks. Residents maintain a small public campground. Northern pike are caught in the nearby slough, and a dirt road leads to the Tanana River with its summer runs of salmon.

Fortymile Country

A trip through the **Fortymile Country** up the Taylor Highway will take you back in time nearly a century—when gold was the lure that drew hardy travelers to Interior Alaska. It's still one of the few places to see active mining without leaving the road system.

The 160-mile Taylor Highway runs north from the Alaska Highway at Tetlin Junction southeast of Tok. It's a narrow, winding, rough gravel road that passes along mountain ridges and through valleys of the Fortymile River. The road passes the tiny community of Chicken (country store, bar, liquor store, cafe, and gas station) and ends in Eagle at the Yukon River. This is one of only three places in Alaska where the river can be reached by road. A cutoff just south of Eagle connects to the Canadian Top of the World Highway leading to Dawson in the Yukon Territory. This is the route many Alaskans take to Dawson. The highway is not plowed in the winter, so it is snowed shut from fall to spring. Watch for road reconstruction.

Chicken was once at the heart of major gold-mining operations, and the remains of many of these works are visible along the highway. Be careful not to trespass on private property. Miners rarely have a sense of humor about trespassing.

Canoeing on the **Fortymile River** is popular among Alaskans, and the Taylor offers several access points. This is one of a number of Alaskan rivers that have been added to the National Wild and Scenic Rivers Program. The Fortymile has some Class 3 and 4 white water. Only experienced canoeists should attempt boating on these rivers, and rapids should be scouted beforehand.

Eagle was once a seat of government and commerce for the Interior. An army post (Fort Egbert) was operated here until 1911, and Territorial Judge James Wickersham had his headquarters in Eagle until Fairbanks began to grow from the gold strike there. The population peaked at 1,700 in 1898. Today it is less than 200.

These days Wickersham's courthouse is part of the walking tour conducted at 10 AM daily between Memorial Day and Labor Day by the **Eagle Historical Society.** There are footpaths and a campground at the old army post.

Eagle is headquarters for the **Yukon-Charley Rivers National Preserve.** This sprawling national preserve straddles the Yukon River downriver from Eagle. Week-long float trips down the river to Circle, 150 miles away, are popular (*see* Chapter 4).

If you can't travel into the Fortymile Country itself, you can catch the flavor of the region at the **Tok Visitors Center** (Milepost 1314, Alaska Hwy., tel. 907/883–5667), which has information on the area.

Dalton Highway

The **Dalton Highway** is a road of "onlys." It's the only road that goes to the Beaufort Sea. It's the only Alaskan road to cross the Arctic Circle, and it has the state's only bridge across the Yukon River.

The 415-mile gravel road runs from the Elliott Highway northwest of Fairbanks to the North Slope oil fields at Prudhoe Bay. It was built in 1974–75 to open a truck route necessary to build the facilities at Prudhoe and the northern half of the trans-Alaska pipeline. For a few months a ferry was used to carry loads across the Yukon River, until the present bridge was completed late in 1975.

Today the road still is used to carry oil-field supplies, but the southern half of the highway is open to visitors as far as **Chandalar,** 320 miles north of Fairbanks. At first the road was called simply the Haul Road. Those wanting a fancier name referred to it as the TAPS road (Trans-Alaska Pipeline System). More recently it was named for James Dalton, a pioneer Alaskan engineer who recognized early the potential of oil on the North Slope.

Overnight lodging, restaurants, fuel, and minor repairs are available at the Yukon River and 120 miles farther north at **Coldfoot.** Travel beyond the Disaster Creek checkpoint on the south flank of the Brooks Range requires a special commercial permit.

The road passes near the **Yukon Flats National Wildlife Refuge** and just east of **Gates of the Arctic National Park and Preserve,** so chances of seeing wildlife are fairly good. This is grizzly bear and caribou habitat. Grayling fishing is good in the creeks along the highway, and there are five camping areas, plus many scenic turnouts along the road.

Tour buses now operate over the Dalton from Fairbanks all the way to Prudhoe Bay, with an overnight at Coldfoot, a tour of the oil field, and air service from Prudhoe back to Fairbanks or Anchorage (*see* Guided Tours, above).

Yukon Territory

Gold! That's what called Canada's **Yukon Territory** to the world's attention with the Klondike gold rush of 1898. And, while Yukon gold mining today is mainly in the hands of a few large companies that go almost unnoticed by the visitor, the territory's golden history is alive and thriving.

Though the international border divides Alaska from Yukon Territory, the Yukon River tends to unify the region. Early prospectors, miners, traders, and camp followers moved readily up and down the river with little regard to national boundaries. An earlier Alaska strike preceded the Klondike find by years, yet Circle was all but abandoned in the stampede to the creeks around Dawson. Later gold strikes in the Alaskan Fortymile Country, Nome, and Fairbanks reversed that flow back across the border into Alaska.

Dawson City

Numbers in the margin correspond to points of interest on the Dawson City map.

Dawson City today forms the heart of the Yukon's gold-rush remembrances. Many of the original buildings are gone, victims of fire, flood, and weathering. But enough of them have been preserved and restored to give more than a glimpse of the city's one-time grandeur. In a period of three years up to the turn of the century, Dawson was transformed into the largest, most refined city north of San Francisco and west of Winnipeg. It had grand new buildings and boasted running water, telephones, and electricity. The city's population, only about 1,500 now, soared to almost 30,000 people in 1899.

Today you may recapture some of that magnificence at the reconstructed **Palace Grand Theatre** (on King St., between 2nd and 3rd aves.) Daily performances of the Gas Light Follies, including authentic cancan dancing, make the theater a popular stop. Another major attraction in Dawson is **Diamond Tooth Gertie's Gambling Hall** (in the Arctic Brotherhood Hall on Queen St.), the only authentic, legal gambling establishment operating in all of the North. Yes, there really was a Diamond Tooth Gertie, Gertie Lovejoy, a prominent dance hall queen who had a diamond between her two front teeth.

The **Dawson City Museum** (in the old Government Administration Building on 5th Ave., tel. 403/993–5291) has gold-rush exhibits, and numerous relics are next door, including trains that operated on the gold creeks.

Scholars still argue the precise details of the tenure of writers Robert Service and Jack London in Dawson, but there's no question that between Service's poems and London's short stories the two did more than anyone else to popularize and romanticize the Yukon. Service's little cabin in town has been restored, and twice daily his poetry is read. London's cabin has been moved into town from Henderson Creek, and performances of his work take place there every day. Both houses are located on 8th Avenue, on the southern side of downtown.

Local tours visit the old "diggings." A highlight is a visit to **Bonanza Creek and Dredge #4**, a wooden-hulled gold dredge.

Regular air service to Dawson is available from Fairbanks. You also may drive the Taylor Highway route, leaving the Alaska Highway at Tetlin Junction and winding through the Fortymile Country past the little communities of Chicken and Jack Wade Camp into Canada. The border is open 8 AM to 8 PM in summer. The Canadian section of the Taylor Highway is called Top of the World Highway. Broad views of range after range of tundra-covered mountains stretch in every direction. Travelers heading

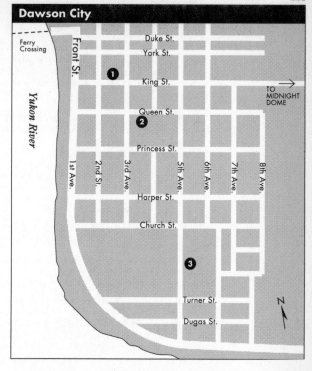

north on the Alaska Highway can turn north at Whitehorse to Dawson City then rejoin the Alaska Highway by taking the Taylor south. This adds about 100 miles to the trip.

Whitehorse is the largest city and governmental center for the Yukon Territory. It is near here that the gold stampeders had to navigate the feared Whitehorse Rapids as they moved down the Yukon River to Dawson. Numerous historical tours and museums are operated in Whitehorse, and there is a large collection of documents comprising the Yukon Archives at the government administration building.

Whitehorse's main attractions include Miles Canyon and the dam-tamed Yukon flowing through it; the McBride Museum, which features the Sam McGee cabin, built in 1899; the Hydro Dam and Fish Ladder; the spirit houses in the Indian cemeteries; the Anglican Old Log Church, built in 1900 and now a church museum; and the stern-wheeler *Klondike*, now a national historic site.

In recent years Whitehorse and Fairbanks have organized the **Yukon Quest International Sled-Dog Race** in March; the race's starting line alternates between the two cities year to year. This is one of the longest and toughest distance races in the North.

The southwestern corner of the Yukon Territory contains **Kluane National Park,** site of Canada's tallest mountain, Mt. Logan, and of numerous spectacular glaciers. Access to the park is along the Alaska Highway in the vicinity of Kluane Lake and Haines Junction. For information contact the Superintendent, Kluane National Park (Box 5495, Haines Junction, Yukon, YOB 1L0, tel. 403/634–2251).

Information: Tourism Yukon, Box 2703, Whitehorse, Y1A 2C6, tel. 403/667–5340; Whitehorse Visitor Information Center, 101–302 Steele St., Y1A 2C5, tel. 403/667–7545; Klondike Visitors Association, Box 389, Dawson City, YOB 1G0, tel. 403/993–5575.

What to See and Do with Children

Alaskaland. The Crooked Creek & Whiskey Island Railroad trip around this 44-acre theme park is popular with kids *(see* Fairbanks in Exploring the Interior).

Creamer's Wildlife Refuge (1300 College Rd., tel. 907/452–1531). A two-mile nature trail walk to see some of the more than 100 species of birds can be a pleasant family outing. Take plenty of mosquito repellent!

Large Animal Research Station at the University of Alaska *(see* Fairbanks in Exploring the Interior).

Wien Memorial Library (Airport Way and Cowles St., tel. 907/452–5177). This library has a well-equipped children's room.

Pleasant Valley Animal Park (Mile 22.5, Chena Hot Springs Rd., tel. 907/488–3967). A variety of Alaskan critters, large and small, reside at this park, an easy drive out of Fairbanks. Horseback riding, buggy rides, and petting zoo available.

Riverboat Discovery. Children of all ages will be thrilled by a stern-wheeler voyage down the Chena and Tanana rivers *(see* Fairbanks in Exploring the Interior).

Santa Claus House (Mile 15, Richardson Hwy., tel. 907/488–2200). It's Christmas 365 days a year at this one-of-a-kind store on Santa Lane, North Pole, southwest of Fairbanks on the Richardson Highway.

Tivi Kennels (Mile 2, Kallenberg Rd., tel. 907/457–2047). Learn about the official state sport from a family of dog mushers. Ride on the "Arfmobile," powered by 12 sled dogs.

Off the Beaten Track

A predominantly Athabaskan Indian village of 444 people, **Tanana** is situated at the confluence of the Tanana and Yukon rivers, 135 miles northwest of Fairbanks. Tanana is a historic trading center and former transfer point for early stern-wheeler traffic headed for Fairbanks. Each June the community has a festival and a potlatch called Nuchalawoya (an Indian word meaning "place where two rivers meet"). Lodging available at Tanana Lodge (inquire at Tanana Store, tel. 907/366–7253). Check with Tanana Air Service (Box 60713, Fairbanks 99706, tel. 907/662–2445) for schedules.

Lying between Tanana and Galena on the Yukon River, **Ruby,** an attractive village of 283, is perched on a hillside overlooking the big river, 220 miles west of Fairbanks. Once a gold-rush town, Ruby is now home to Athabaskan Indians who engage in commercial and subsistence fishing, hunting, and trapping. The Ruby Roadhouse (Box 149, Ruby 99768, tel. 907/468–4400) is listed on the National Register of Historic Places.

About 55 miles northwest of Circle City, **Fort Yukon** lies just above the Arctic Circle, that invisible line that marks the southern end of the earth's frigid zone at latitude 66 degrees 33 minutes north. Several commuter airlines *(see* Getting Around, above) offer one-day trips from Fairbanks in summer, and you'll receive a certificate attesting to your crossing of the invisible line.

A log-cabin Athabaskan Indian village, Fort Yukon is tucked into the northernmost bend in the Yukon River. Summers here are mild, sometimes hot. The mercury has climbed to 100 degrees at Fort Yukon—but winter temperatures have plunged to 78 degrees below as well. The 24-hour summer sunshine results in 10-foot sunflowers and giant strawberries.

Athabaskan women engage in handicrafts, such as elaborate beadwork. A prized example is an intricately beaded white moosehide altar cover, displayed in a log church, one of many historic buildings dating from 19th-century Hudson's Bay trading days when Fort Yukon was the company's westernmost outpost.

Grave markers in the Fort Yukon cemetery date back to 1868, a year after the United States purchased Alaska from Russia. On display in the **Dinjii Zhuu Enjit Museum** are collections relating to life and culture of the people of the Yukon Flats. Fur trapping and fishing, in which fish wheels are used to catch migrating salmon, are main elements of the subsistence lifestyle. Husky dogs, which pull wheel-equipped sleds for summer visitors, are regular sights around town. In winter, both dogs and snow machines pull sleds for pleasure and work.

Shopping

Most communities have outposts selling native crafts and jewelry. Look for jade, ivory, and gold pieces, as well as ceramics, beadwork, and leather. A true Alaskan gift, widely available, is the *ulu*, a unique knife used by Eskimo hunters to skin animals. The stores listed below are just a few of the places you can hunt out special finds.

Fairbanks For branches of fur stores, try the **Fur Factory** (121 Dunkel St., tel. 907/452–6240) or **Gerald Victor Furs** (212 Lacey St., tel. 907/456–6890). **The Arctic Travelers Gift Shop** (201 Cushman St., tel. 907/456–7080) has one of the best selections of Athabaskan beadwork and leather in Fairbanks.

North Pole **The Santa Claus House Gift Shop** (14 mi south of Fairbanks, Mile 1506 on the Alaska Hwy., tel. 907/488–2200) is hard to miss, and you can probably guess what season it celebrates.

Tok **The Burnt Paw** (at the intersection of Alaska Hwys. 1 and 2, tel. 907/883–4121) sells jade and ivory, Alaskan ceramics, crafts, paintings, smoked salmon—even dog-sled puppies.

Participant Sports

Bicycling Bicyclists have their own paved paths from the University of Alaska campus around Farmers Loop to the Steese Highway. Another path follows Geist and Chena Pump roads into downtown Fairbanks. A shorter, less strenuous route is via the bike path between downtown and Alaskaland along the south side of the Chena River. Maps showing all the bike paths are available at the Fairbanks Visitors Information Center (550 1st Ave.).

Boating   In the Fairbanks area, the **Chena River** is popular among boaters and paddlers alike. The stream's proximity to the road system makes trips of various lengths possible. The **Chena River State Recreational Area,** along Chena Hot Springs Road from Mile 26 to Mile 51, contains numerous well-marked river access points. The lower sections of the river area are fairly placid, but the area above the third bridge, at Mile 44.1, can be hazardous for inexperienced boaters.

For much tamer boating in or near Fairbanks, use Chena River access points at Nordale Road east of the city, the Wendell Street Bridge near downtown, and the Alaskaland park above the Peger River Bridge and at the campground just above the University Avenue Bridge. A popular pullout is at the Pump House Restaurant, near where the Chena flows into the Tanana River.

Canoeing on the nearby **Tanana River** is not recommended. The current is swift and tricky, and the water is murky from the load of glacial silt it carries. Sweepers and hidden sandbars can be hazardous. The Tanana is riverboat country. On this river and others in the Yukon River drainage, Alaskans use long, wide, flat-bottom boats powered by one or two large outboard engines. The boats include a lifting apparatus to raise the engine a few inches, allowing passage through the shallows, and some of the engines are equipped with a jet unit instead of a propeller to allow more bottom clearance. Arrangements for riverboat charters can be made in almost any river community.

A waterway with more of a wilderness feel to it, the **Chatanika River** north of Fairbanks is a Mecca for canoeists and kayakers. The most northerly access point is at the BLM campground near Mile 60 of the Steese Highway. Other commonly used access points are at Long Creek (Mile 45, Steese Hwy.), at the state campground where the Chatanika River crosses the Steese Highway at Mile 39, and at the bridge where the river crosses the Elliott Highway at Mile 11. Below this point, the stream flows into the Minto Flats, and access is more difficult.

Water in the Chatanika River may or may not be clear, depending on mining activities along its upper tributaries. In times of very low water, the upper Chatanika River will be shallow and difficult to navigate. Avoid the river in times of extremely high water, especially after heavy rains, because of the danger of sweepers, floating debris, and hidden bars.

Farther north, in the **Steese National Recreation Area,** lies the **Birch Creek Canoe Trail.** Access is at Mile 94 of the Steese Highway. This stream winds its way north through the historic mining country of the Circle District and also may be muddied from active placer mines on the tributaries. The takeout point is at the Steese Highway Bridge 15 miles below Circle City. From there the Birch Creek meanders on to the Yukon River well below the town.

Fishing   Rainbow trout are not native to the Interior, but they have been planted in some lakes. **Birch** and **Quartz lakes,** easily accessible from the Richardson Highway between Fairbanks and Delta Junction, are popular trout-fishing spots.

For lake trout and large grayling in the Interior, try the lakes along the Richardson Highway south of Delta Junction, particularly **Summit Lake,** which is alongside the road.

Popular fishing trips off the Interior highway system include air charters to **Lake Minchumina** (about an hour's flight from Fairbanks), known for good pike fishing and a rare view of the back sides of Mt. McKinley and Mt. Foraker.

Another popular charter trip by riverboat or float plane will take you pike fishing in the **Minto Flats,** below Fairbanks off the Tanana River, where the mouth of the Chatanika River spreads through miles of marsh and sloughs.

Inland migrating salmon can be found in the **Gulkana River** (which is also a terrific trout stream) between Delta Junction and Glennallen, and on the **Salcha River** 40 miles below Fairbanks on the Richardson Highway. Salmon run up the **Tanana River,** too, most of the summer, but they're not usually caught on hook-and-line gear. Residents take them from the Tanana with gill nets and fish wheels under special commercial and subsistence permits.

Golf Golfers have two choices: North America's northernmost course at the **Fairbanks Golf and Country Club** (tel. 907/469–6555), whose nine-hole course straddles Farmers Loop just north of the university; or **Chena Bend** (tel. 907/355–6749), a nine-hole spread on nearby Fort Wainwright. The army course is open to civilians.

Hiking The Bureau of Land Management maintains two trails that are particularly popular for backpacking. One is the 22-mile **White Mountain Trail** from the Elliott Highway, near Wickersham Dome, north into the White Mountains. The other is the **Pinnell Mountain Trail,** connecting Twelve-Mile Summit and Eagle Summit on the Steese Highway. This trail, 27 miles long, passes through alpine meadows and along mountain ridges, all above the tree line. No water is available in the immediate vicinity. Most hikers spend three days making the trip. Cross-country skiers sometimes use the White Mountain Trail, but Pinnell is too high and rugged for winter use. The **Alaska Public Lands Information Center** (250 Cushman, Suite 1A, Fairbanks 99701, tel. 907/451–7352) has information about these trails.

Closer to Fairbanks, the **Chena River State Recreation Area,** which straddles Chena Hot Springs Road from Mile 26 to about Mile 51, is a hiker's and cross-country skier's paradise. A popular day-long trip is the **Granite Tors Trail,** which offers a view of the upper Chena Valley. A popular shorter hike is the **Angel Rocks Trail** near the eastern boundary of the area. This area is maintained by the **Alaska Division of Parks** (tel. 907/451–2695).

The **Chena Lakes Recreation Area,** off the Richardson Highway just south of North Pole, also offers hiking and cross-country skiing. This area was created by the Army Corps of Engineers as part of the Chena River flood-control project and is now operated by local government, the Fairbanks North Star Borough (Parks and Recreation Dept., tel. 907/488–1655).

A relatively new hiking area is the **Circle-Fairbanks Historic Trail,** stretching 58 miles from the vicinity of Cleary Summit to Twelve-Mile Summit. This route follows the old summer trail used by gold miners; in the winter they generally used the ice in the Chatanika River to make this journey. The trail has been roughly marked and cleared, but there are no facilities for hikers. Water is scarce along the trail, so most backpackers carry their own. Much of the trail is on state land, but it does cross valid mining claims, and those must be respected.

This trail is not for a novice. While there are rock cairns and mileposts along it, there is no well-defined tread the whole way, so it's easy to become disoriented. The State Department of Natural Resources strongly recommends that backpackers on this trail equip themselves with the following USGS topographical maps: Livengood (A-1) and Circle (A-6), (A-5), and (B-4). The state Department of Natural Resources (tel. 907/479–2243) has detailed information about the trail.

Running Runners can find plenty of action in Alaska. Many of the cross-country ski trails are used for running in the warmer months. In addition, there are numerous organized running events. Fairbanks has the community-wide **Midnight Sun Run** each June on the weekend nearest the summer solstice and a tough **Equinox Marathon** up and down the large hilly domes northwest of the city in September.

Skiing The Interior has some of the best weather and terrain in the
Cross-country nation for cross-country skiing, especially during the late fall and early spring.

Interior residents enjoy cross-country skiing on the developed trails in the Fairbanks area. The trail at the **Birch Hill Recreation Area** on the city's north side is lighted to extend its use into the winter nights. Cross-country ski racing is a staple at several courses on winter weekends. And the season is a long one, stretching from the first heavy snowfall, generally in October, to trail breakup in late March or early April. Other developed trails can be found at the **University of Alaska Fairbanks** campus, **Chena Hot Springs Resort, White Mountains, Chatanika,** the **Chena Lakes** recreation areas, and the **Two Rivers Recreation Area.**

Downhill The 2,233-foot Cleary Summit has two privately operated downhill ski areas: the **Cleary Summit Ski Area** (tel. 907/456–5520) and **Skiland** (tel. 907/389–3624). Both are located on the Steese Highway about 20 miles from Fairbanks.

Spectator Sports

Baseball Scores of baseball players, including Tom Seaver, have passed through Fairbanks on their way to the major leagues.

The Interior city is home of the Alaska Goldpanners (tel. 907/452–5488), a member of the Alaska League, a string of semi-professional baseball organizations throughout the state.

Players are recruited from among college teams nationwide, and the summer season (late June to early Aug.) generates top-caliber competition. In Fairbanks, home games are played at **Growden Field** along Lower 2nd Avenue at Wilbur Street, not far from Alaskaland.

This baseball park is home of the traditional **Midnight Sun Baseball Game,** in which the Goldpanners play baseball at midnight without benefit of artificial lights. This is thrilling to watch on a clear, sunny evening when the daylight never ends (and possibly chilly—bring a thermos of something hot).

Curling Hundreds of Fairbanksans participate each year in curling, an odd game in which men and women with brooms play a giant version of shuffleboard on ice. This ancient Scottish game was brought to Alaska and the Yukon during the Klondike gold rush. Visitors are welcome at the **Fairbanks Curling Club** (tel. 907/452–3011) at 1962 2nd Avenue. The club hosts an annual international "bonspiel" in March.

Hockey During the winter, the **Gold Kings** professional hockey team (tel. 907/456–7825) holds sway on the sports schedule, hosting teams from other states and from several Canadian provinces. At the nearby University of Alaska Fairbanks, the **Nanooks** (tel. 907/474–6868) play NCAA Division I hockey.

Mushing Dog mushing is the top winter draw. From November to March, there is a constant string of sled-dog races throughout the region, culminating in the **North American Open Sled-Dog Championship,** which attracts international competition to Fairbanks. An increasing number of mushers drive north from New England and the Northern Tier states in their pickups with small dog cubicles in the back, following the racing circuit from one town to another each weekend in the spring.

Throughout Alaska, sprint races, freight hauling, and long-distance endurance runs are held in late February and March, that popular Alaska season when the winter's snow remains but there's more daylight in which to enjoy it. Men and women compete in the same classes in the major races. And for the children, there are various racing classes based on age, starting with the one-dog category for the youngest.

In Fairbanks, many of the sprint races are organized by the Alaska Dog Mushers Association (tel. 907/457–6874), one of the oldest organizations of its kind in the Arctic, at its **Jeff Studdert Sled Dog Race Course** at Mile 4, Farmers Loop.

The **Yukon Quest International** is an endurance race covering more than 1,000 miles between Fairbanks and Whitehorse, Y.T., via Dawson and the Yukon River. It's held in March; you can get more details from the visitors centers in either city.

Riverboat Racing Another summer highlight is riverboat racing sanctioned by the **Fairbanks Outboard Association** (tel. 907/456–5774). These specially built 22-foot racing boats are powered by fairly evenly matched 60-horsepower engines and reach speeds of 70 mph. Weekend races throughout the summer and fall begin and end either at the Pump House Restaurant on Chena Pump Road or at Pike's Landing, just off Airport Way near Fairbanks International Airport.

The season's big event in late June is the **Yukon 800 Marathon,** a two-day, 800-mile race between Fairbanks and Galena by way of the Chena, Tanana, and Yukon rivers. The **Roland Lord Memorial Race** from Fairbanks to Nenana and back is held in early August.

Dining and Lodging

Highly recommended hotels and restaurants are indicated with a star ★.

Dining Why fight it? Salmon and freshwater fish are plentiful and among the better values on most menus; unless you're a confirmed fish hater, try the local specialty. There will, of course, be other dishes available. Ask your waiter to recommend something. He or she will almost always be glad to steer you to the best course.

Category	Cost*
Expensive	over $40
Moderate	$20–$40
Inexpensive	under $20

**per person, without tax, service, or wine*

Opening hours for Fairbanks restaurants are listed in the reviews; restaurants in outlying areas, which are mostly small, family-run establishments, vary their hours with the season. Call ahead to be sure.

Lodging The Interior has a surprising range of lodging, from wilderness lodges to hot springs spas and up-to-date modern lodges.

Category	Cost*
Expensive	over $90
Moderate	$50–$90
Inexpensive	under $50

**for a double room without taxes or service*

Dawson City, Y.T.
Dining
Midnight Sun Cafe. This pleasant restaurant offers a salad bar, Asian specialties, and the usual American road fare. *3rd Ave. and Queen St., tel. 403/993–5495. AE, DC, MC, V. Moderate.*
Jack London Grill. This is a best bet: go for the Canadian/American regional specialties. *2nd Ave. and Queen St. in the Downtown Hotel, tel. 403/993–5346. AE, MC, V. Inexpensive–Moderate.*

Lodging
Westmark Dawson City. This is an upscale, classic accommodation. *5th Ave. and Harper St. tel. 403/993–5542 or 800/544–0970. 132 rooms, including 2 wheelchair-accessible rooms. Closed Sept. 10–May 14. AE, DC, D, MC, V. Expensive.*
Eldorado Hotel. Considered the best in town, this hotel's Sluice Box Lounge is home of the famous Sour Toe Cocktail. *3rd Ave. and Prince St., tel. 403/993–5451. 48 rooms. MC, V. Moderate.*
Triple "J" Hotel. This clean establishment is next to Diamond Tooth Gertie's, home of Canada's only legal casino. Rooms with kitchenettes are available. *5th Ave. and Queen St., tel. 403/993–5551. 47 rooms. MC, V. Inexpensive–Moderate.*

Delta Junction
Dining
Trophy Lodge Restaurant. This is the best nearby place to eat in the area, and the offering is a mixed bag of American, Chinese, and Korean dishes. *Mile 1420.3, Alaska Hwy., tel. 907/895–4685. MC, V. Inexpensive–Moderate.*

Lodging
Black Spruce Lodge. Ten comfortable cabins on nearby Quartz Lake, with a boat provided for each, are available at this comfortable rustic lodge. Bring on the fish! *2740 Old Richardson Hwy., tel. 907/895–4668. Closed Oct.–May. Inexpensive–Moderate.*

Kelly's Motel. Delta residents most often put visitors up here. Modern units newly remodeled; kitchenettes available. *Downtown Delta Junction, tel. 907/895–4667. MC, V. Inexpensive–Moderate.*

Alaska 7 Motel. Cheap and clean accommodations are provided here; some units have kitchenettes. *Mile 270.3, Richardson Hwy., tel. 907/895–4848. MC, V. Inexpensive.*

Fairbanks
Dining
★
A Moveable Feast. Excellent American and French food is offered at this restaurant, which is a great place for a fast breakfast or lunch, and there is outside seating for sunny days. *North Gate Square, 338 Old Steese Hwy., tel. 907/456–4701. Dress: informal. MC, V. Closed Sun. Moderate.*

Clinkerdagger, Bickerstaff & Pett's. American meals and seafood are offered. A good selection of fish is served up in an English antique atmosphere. Lunch and dinner only. *24 College Rd., tel. 907/452–2756. AE, MC, V. Moderate.*

Tiki Cove. Polynesian and Cantonese. Popular among residents, but not widely advertised, this restaurant and cocktail lounge serve up a bird's-eye view of downtown Fairbanks from the top of the 12-story Polaris Hotel. *427 1st Ave., tel. 907/452–1484. No reservations. AE, DC, MC, V. No lunch. Moderate.*

★ **Pump House Restaurant.** American and seafood. There is a lovely atmosphere in this mining pump station-turned-restaurant built alongside the Chena River. You can't go wrong with the daily family special; the gorgeous Sunday buffet is a work of culinary art. *Mile 1.3, Chena Pump Rd., tel. 907/479–8452. Dress: informal. No reservations. AE, DC, MC, V. Moderate.*

Lodging
★
Westmark Fairbanks. This is a full-service hotel with two restaurants, two cocktail lounges; close to downtown Fairbanks. *813 Noble St., tel. 907/456–7722. 240 rooms. AE, DC, MC, V. Expensive.*

Regency Fairbanks Hotel. Comfortable and clean, this is a new hotel and most rooms have a whirlpool bath to ease a traveler's aches after a long day. *95 10th Ave., tel. 907/452–3200. 128 rooms. Moderate–Expensive.*

★ **Sophie Station Hotel.** This spacious, new, and well-appointed hotel near Fairbanks International Airport offers the best accommodations in Fairbanks. Some rooms have kitchens. *1717 University Ave., tel. 907/479–3650. 147 rooms. Moderate–Expensive.*

Bed-and-Breakfast Just-like-home accommodations are offered by **Ah, Rose Marie B&B** (tel. 907/456–2040), **An Old Alaskan Country Inn B&B** (tel. 907/451–8522), **Bev & John's B&B** (tel. 907/456–7351), **Fairbanks Downtown Bed & Breakfast** (tel. 907/452–4967), and **Punton's B&B** (tel. 907/456–4452). *All Inexpensive–Moderate.*

Nenana
Dining
Tamarack Inn. American. Best bet on the Parks Highway. Dine by the light of a fireplace at this inn, which provides one of the best-known restaurants on the road from Anchorage to Fairbanks. *Mile 298, Parks Hwy., 6 mi. south of Nenana, tel. 907/832–5455. No credit cards. Inexpensive–Moderate.*

Tok
Dining
Fast Eddie's Restaurant. Living up to its name, this restaurant takes pride in its fast service. Summer hours 6 AM–midnight. *Mile 1313.3, Alaska Hwy., tel. 907/883–4411. No credit cards. Inexpensive–Moderate.*

Lodging
Westmark Tok. Reliable, comfortable, and well appointed, the hotel offers a dining room, lounge, and gift shop. *Junction of Alaska and Glenn Hwys., tel. 907/883–5174. Expensive.*

Golden Bear Motel. This motel is located in a nice, quiet spot. You can pan for gold nearby. *1/4 Mile Glenn Hwy., tel. 907/883–2561. AE, MC, V. Inexpensive–Moderate.*

Whitehorse, Y.T.
Dining
★

Westmark Hotel dining room. Canadian/American. Nightly entertainment is offered here with dinner. *2nd Ave. and Wood St., tel. 403/668–4700. AE, MC, V. Moderate–Expensive.*

Lodging

Westmark Hotel. Centrally located, this full-service hotel has a restaurant, beauty salon, and free parking. *2nd Ave. and Wood St., tel. 403/668–4700 or 800/544–0970. AE, MC, V. Expensive.*

★ **Regina Hotel.** Available here are spartan but comfortable rooms, dining room, cocktail lounge, and heated underground parking. *102 Wood St., tel. 403/667–7801. AE, MC, V. Moderate.*

The Arts

Fairbanks supports a year-round arts program that would be the envy of many larger communities. Museums, art galleries, musical groups, theater companies, and various other performing arts are active here. The community also is host to a major annual summer arts festival, and name entertainers and artists come and go year-round.

The **Fairbanks Summer Arts Festival,** which in 1990 celebrates its tenth anniversary, has grown from a small arts camp for young people to a major annual event attracting staff and students nationwide. The festival is spread over two weeks in late July and early August, featuring music, dance, theater, musical theater, and visual arts instruction. The program is run in conjunction with the University of Alaska–Fairbanks.

Dozens of noted guest artists attend to perform and to present workshops. Entertainer Cab Calloway has been a headliner; so has his daughter, singer Chris Calloway. Members of the Boston Pops Jazz Ensemble are regular visitors. For more information about the festival, contact its founder and organizer, Jo Scott (Box 80845, Fairbanks 99708, tel. 907/479–6778).

In addition, various performances are offered during the fall, winter, and spring by the **Fairbanks Concert Association** (tel. 907/452–8880), the **Fairbanks Symphony Orchestra** (tel. 907/479–3407), the **UA Fairbanks Music Department** (tel. 907/474–7555), and by three theater groups: the **Fairbanks Drama Association** (tel. 907/456–7529), the **Fairbanks Light Opera Theater** (tel. 907/456–5631), and the **UA Fairbanks Drama Workshop** (tel. 907/474–7751).

Fairbanks has two public art galleries: **The Bear Gallery,** in the civic center at Alaskaland; and the **Fine Arts Complex Gallery** on the UA Fairbanks campus. The community also supports numerous private art galleries.

Nightlife

Summer visitors to Fairbanks will find that the lack of a true "night"—thanks to the midnight sun—doesn't seem to hinder nightlife at all.

The **Palace Theatre & Saloon** at Alaskaland (tel. 907/456–5960) is one of the livelier summer spots. The Palace's "Good as Gold" show, a musical comedy revue about life in Fairbanks, runs at 7:30 and 9 every night from the end of May to mid-September. Reservations are advised.

Those who want a bit of the gold-rush poetry with their evening entertainment will find it in the **Malemute Saloon** (tel. 907/479–2500), part of the Cripple Creek Resort. The saloon is in Ester, a former gold-mining town six miles south of Fairbanks and just off the Parks Highway. The resort includes a dining room and hotel restored from the mining era and an unusual "photo-symphony" that combines photography and music to describe the northern lights and the seasonal changes of Alaska.

The resort's major attraction is the nightly show at the Malemute Saloon—a gold-rush theme with melodramatic readings from the poetry of Robert Service, Bard of the Yukon. It's rustic. The management invites visitors to throw their peanut shells on the sawdust-covered floor and to "look over the historical artifacts (and junk!) that dangle from the walls and ceiling."

A favorite watering hole among miners, truckers, university students, homesteaders, ex-hippies, and the younger set is the **Howling Dog Saloon** (tel. 907/457–8780) in Fox, 11 miles north of Fairbanks on the Steese Highway. This get-down bar has been written up in the *New York Times*. Be ready for a big crowd and loud, authentic rock 'n' roll. All-night volleyball games out back are part of the ambience of the "Dog."

Country music and dancing with an occasional dash of rock is on the evening menu at the **Sunset Inn** (tel. 907/456–4754), near the Richardson Highway on the south side of Fairbanks.

Folk music with some pop is the featured entertainment in the lounge at **Clinkerdagger, Bickerstaff & Pett's** (tel. 907/452–2756), a restaurant and lounge next to the Bentley Mall on the north side of the city. Dinner reservations advised.

The **Senator's Lounge** at the Pump House Restaurant (tel. 907/479–8452) is the place for easy-listening music alongside the Chena River on a warm summer evening.

More upscale, the **Kobuk Room** (tel. 907/456–7722) in the Westmark Hotel complex (formerly the Travelers Inn) offers a variety of evening entertainment—piano, pops, and soft rock—in a comfortable lounge.

The Center (tel. 907/479–3800), an entertainment complex on Airport Way about halfway between downtown Fairbanks and the city's major airport, combines a variety of entertainment and recreation. Dancing, rock 'n' roll, and stand-up comedy are scheduled throughout the week.

Speaking of dancing, there are square-dancing clubs in Fairbanks, North Pole, Delta Junction, and Tok. The groups are part of the **Northern Lights Council of Dancers** (tel. 907/452–5699), and they welcome visitors. Call for current dance schedules.

First-run movies are available at the theater complex in **The Center** and at **Goldstream Cinemas** (tel. 907/456–5113), both on Airport Way near downtown Fairbanks and Alaskaland park.

10 The Fringe Areas of Alaska

*By Stanton H.
Patty*

Alaskans call it the "Bush"—those wild and lonely bands of territory beyond cities and towns, stretching from the Aleutian Islands in the south through the Yukon and Kuskokwim rivers and into the northern High Arctic.

It is a land where caribou roam and the sun really does shine at midnight.

It is a land that knows the soft footsteps of the Eskimos and the Aleuts, the scratchings of those who still search for oil and gold, and the ghosts of almost-forgotten battlefields of World War II.

It is a vast, misunderstood wonderland—bleak yet beautiful, harsh yet bountiful. A look across the Arctic tundra in summer yields the miracle of bright wildflowers growing from a sponge of permafrost ice water. In the long, dark Arctic winter, a painter's-blue kind of twilight rises from the ice and snowscapes at midday.

The brown bears of Katmai (KAT-my) on the Alaska Peninsula rule a vast national park, sharing salmon and trout streams with wary sport fishermen and always receiving the right-of-way. The polar bears of the Beaufort Sea (of the Arctic Ocean), stained a light gold from the oil of seals they have killed, pose like monarchs on ice floes, swinging their heads with the fluid motion of athletes, warning humans to stay their distance. Great herds of caribou, hundreds of thousands of animals, move in slow waves across the tundra, feeding, fattening for the next winter. Close to the Aleut (ALLEY-oot) village of St. Paul in the Pribilof Islands, far out in the Bering Sea, between Alaska and Siberia, the world's largest herds of northern fur seals haul out on wave-lashed breeding rookeries—while far above, on sheer cliffs, puffins, cormorants, and other seabirds put on a show that delights birders equipped with binoculars and zoom lenses.

The chain of islands called the Aleutians were the stepping stones of history that beckoned Russian explorers to Alaska in the 18th century. Along the islands, weathered, onion-domed Russian Orthodox churches in Aleut villages brace against the fierce Pacific winds. The debris of war, rusted Quonset huts, weed-covered bunkers, and shell casings still litter the foggy Aleutians, where American and Japanese forces fought bitter campaigns during World War II. And yet in the treeless, windswept Aleutians, there are occasional summer sightings of wild orchids.

Dutch Harbor, in the Aleutians, a former U.S. Navy base pounded by Japanese bombs in 1942, is one of America's busiest commercial-fishing ports. Deep-sea trawlers and factory ships venture from Dutch Harbor into the stormy North Pacific Ocean and the Bering Sea for harvests of bottom fish, crab, and other catches. One of the most profitable and abundant species these days is Alaska pollack, which is turned into a paste called *surimi*, reformed, flavored, and sold as the imitation crab we buy for seafood salads and casseroles. Unalaska, an ancient Aleut village, is Dutch Harbor's across-the-bay neighbor and is home to the Holy Ascension Cathedral, one of the oldest Russian Orthodox churches in Alaska.

Nome is one old gold-rush town where you can still pan for gold. In the spring, the going gets wild when Nome hosts a zany golf tournament with "greens" painted on the ice of the Bering Sea coast. Eskimo ceremonial dances are demonstrated at the Living Museum of the Arctic in Kotzebue, as is the Eskimo blanket toss, a sport dating to ancient times, when Eskimo hunters were bounced high in the air to see across ice ridges in search of seals and other wildlife.

Roads in the Bush are few, and only one (the Dalton Highway, between Prudhoe Bay in the Arctic and the Fairbanks area in the Interior) leads toward a few of Alaska's major communities. But the Bush also is where America's largest oil field, Prudhoe Bay, was discovered in 1968. Now more than a million barrels a day of North Slope crude from Prudhoe and lesser basins nearby flow southward by an 800-mile pipeline to the port of Valdez, on Prince William Sound, in South Central Alaska, to help fuel the lower 48 states. The sound was the site of the huge oil spill in March 1989, when the *Exxon Valdez* hit a reef and dumped 10 million gallons of crude oil into it. The oil still coats many beaches, but most are not accessible to tourists.

Airplanes, from jetliners to small bush planes, are the lifelines of Bush Alaska. This is where the legendary Bush pilots of the Far North that visitors hear about all through Alaska—Noel and Sig Wien, Bob Reeve, Ben Eielson, Harold Gillam, Joe Crosson, Jack Jefford, and the others—won their wings in the early years. They are Alaska's counterparts of the cowboy heroes of the Wild West. And the Bush is where America's favorite humorist, Will Rogers, died in a crash with Wiley Post, the famed aviator, in 1935. It happened just a few miles from Barrow, America's northernmost community. Today's pilots in Alaska, with instrument ratings and dependable aircraft, make Bush flying seem almost routine. Regional Bush centers such as Nome, Kotzebue (KOTS-eh-bew), Barrow, and Bethel, though with smaller populations than most Lower Fortyeight small towns, can count on daily jet service. The jets carry more than passengers; they also bring the freight—from fresh vegetables to disposable diapers—that makes life livable in rural Alaska.

The Bush Alaskans have a deep affection for their often-raw land that is difficult to explain to strangers. They talk of living "close to nature," a cliché, perhaps, until one realizes that these Alaskans reside in the Bush all year long, adapting to brutal winter weather and isolation. They talk of a love for free-wheeling frontier life, yet there is hardly a Bush family that hasn't been touched by tragedy, from drownings to airplane crashes. They have accepted the Bush for what it is, dramatic and unforgiving. They have swapped big-city cultural amenities and supermarkets for wide-open spaces and distance from bureaucracy. They couldn't recite the poet's lines about the "spell of the Yukon," but they'll tell you there really is such a feeling. It has to do with mystery, excitement, natural beauty, and peace.

Fortunately for travelers, airlines and rural air-taxi services have made the Fringe areas of Alaska as accessible in recent years as, say, a flight between New York and Chicago.

Visitors, still in city clothes, hop aboard jets in Anchorage and Fairbanks and head into the Bush like pampered explorers. Tour companies are waiting at the end of the line in the Arctic and near-Arctic with warm parkas (jackets with fur-trimmed hoods) that travelers can borrow for their stays. For, even in summer, the weather can be chilly in the Arctic.

Elsewhere in the Bush, away from usual tour patterns, you are more or less on your own. Hopefully, your travel agent has advised you to pack some warm clothing, rain gear, sturdy walking shoes, and plenty of mosquito repellent.

Those tales you've heard about Alaska's mosquitoes are true. One Alaskan writer files his folder on mosquitoes under the heading of "Wildlife" and swears he is not stretching the truth.

Expect hotel and restaurant prices in the Bush to be higher than in your hometown. The Bush communities depend on costly air freight and/or infrequent, long-distance tug-and-barge supply runs for food, building materials, and other necessities.

Visitors should be aware that many of the Bush communities, including Barrow, Kotzebue, and Bethel, have voted themselves "dry" recently to fight alcohol-abuse problems affecting populations of Alaskan natives. Enforcement is strict. The 1988 session of the Alaska Legislature passed a bill making bootlegging a felony. Nome, of course, remains "wet" with its several lively saloons.

Essential Information

Getting Around

By Plane **Alaska Airlines** (tel. 206/433–3100 or 800/426–0333) is among the major carriers serving Alaska from Seattle, and it flies within Alaska to most major communities. Alaska Airlines has tours to Nome and Kotzebue. **MarkAir** (tel. 907/243–1414 or 800/426–6784) serves Barrow, Prudhoe Bay, Dutch Harbor, King Salmon, Dillingham (hubs in the Bristol Bay–Alaska Peninsula areas), and such Bush villages as McGrath, Galena, Unalakleet, Aniak, and Iliamna. MarkAir offers package tours to Barrow, Prudhoe Bay, Katmai National Park and Preserve, and Dutch Harbor/Unalaska. **Reeve Aleutian Airways** (tel. 907/243–4700 or 800/544–2248) has scheduled service to points on the Alaska Peninsula, the Aleutian Islands, and the Pribilof Islands.

Many Anchorage and Fairbanks air taxis serve the Bush in addition to Bush-based carriers such as **Bering Air Inc.** (Box 929, Nome 99762, tel. 907/443–5464), which, weather and politics permitting, offers flights to Providenya, on the Siberian coast across the Bering Straits of Alaska; **Cape Smythe Air Service** (Box 549, Barrow 99723, tel. 907/852–8333); **Hermens/MarkAir Express** (Box 7010, Bethel 99559, tel. 907/543–4220); **Frontier Flying Service** (3820 University Ave., Fairbanks 99701, tel. 907/474–0014); **Wright Air Service** (Box 60141, Fairbanks 99706, tel. 907/474–0502); **Friendship Air Alaska** (Box 1168, Bethel 99559, tel. 907/543–4280); **Peninsula Airways** (Box 36, King Salmon 99613, tel. 907/246–3372). If time permits, arrangements often can be made to ride along on mail flights that serve the native villages.

By Car The **James W. Dalton Highway**—formerly the construction road for the trans-Alaska pipeline—is Alaska's only highway to the High Arctic. The 414-mile, all-gravel road begins about 73 miles north of Fairbanks, connecting with the Steese and Elliott highways to points south. Only the first 320 miles of the Dalton Highway, to a checkpoint at Chandalar, are open to the public. Commercial vehicles only are now allowed to travel farther north, because the highway is still a busy route for trucks hauling freight to the Arctic oil fields.

Vehicle services are limited along the highway, with fuel and repairs available at only two places: the Yukon River crossing (Mile 56) and Coldfoot (Mile 175). Motorists are cautioned not to expect assistance from truckers shuttling between Prudhoe Bay and Fairbanks.

Despite the difficulties of traversing this route, the rewards are high. Open to the public less than 10 years, the Dalton presents a rare opportunity to see unspoiled northern Alaska.

The **Steese Highway** connects Fairbanks with Circle, a small settlement on the Yukon River, 162 miles north of Fairbanks, 50 miles south of the Arctic Circle. The drive is scenic, with traces of old gold-mining operations and plenty of wilderness, but only the first 44 miles of the Steese Highway out of Fairbanks are paved. The Arctic and near-Arctic communities of Nome, Kotzebue, and Barrow do not have highway connections to the rest of Alaska.

By Bus   In the summer tourist season, two companies—**Princess Tours** (2815 2nd Ave., Suite 400, Seattle, WA 98121, tel. 206/441–8428 or 800/647–7750) and **Gray Line of Alaska** (300 Elliott Ave. W., Seattle, WA 98119, tel. 206/281–3535 or 800/544–2206)—operate package tours by motor coach the full length of the Dalton Highway, between Fairbanks and Deadhorse, the support community for Prudhoe Bay. Travelers go one way by air, the other by motor coach. The route crosses the rugged Brooks Range, (which divides the High Arctic from the Interior), the Arctic Circle, and the Yukon River. It also brushes by the edges of the Gates of the Arctic National Park and the Arctic National Wildlife Refuge, the latter currently the scene of a major battle between the oil industry and environmentalists.

By Boat   The Alaska state ferry *Tustumena* (Alaska Marine Highway System, Box R, Juneau 99811, tel. 907/465–3941 or 800/642–0066) makes monthly trips to Dutch Harbor/Unalaska and several other Bush communities in southwestern Alaska.

Guided Tours

The most popular Bush package tours are those from Anchorage to Nome, the colorful old gold-rush town just south of the Arctic Circle, and to Kotzebue, a major Eskimo community in the Arctic. Other Arctic tours visit Barrow, the Eskimo town near the top of the world, and the Prudhoe Bay oil field.

Air tours and sportfishing packages are available to Katmai National Park and Preserve (on the Alaska Peninsula, west and south of Anchorage), and there are nature tours to the Pribilof Islands in the Bering Sea. Most of the rest of the Bush holds adventures mostly for a bold breed of independent traveler.

The package tour operators listed below rely primarily on air travel to get to and between various points of interest along Alaska's Fringes (*see* Tour Groups in Chapter 1).

Exploration Holidays & Cruises (tel. 206/625–9600 or 800/426–0600) offers package tours to the Arctic and the Pribilof Islands.

Holland America Line Westours (tel. 206/281–3535 or 800/426–0327) and **Alaska Sightseeing Tours** (tel. 206/441–8687 or 800/621–5557) cover the Arctic and Katmai National Park and Preserve. **Katmailand** (tel. 907/243–5448 or 800/544–0551) is a local operator with tours of Katmai National Park.

MarkAir (tel. 907/243–1414 or 800/426–6784) has packages to the Aleutian Islands.

Some of the Fringe area tours offered by these operators can be combined with the comprehensive cruise tours of Alaska covering the famed Inside Passage and/or the glacier-studded Prince William Sound in South Central Alaska (*see* Cruise Tours in Chapter 3).

Important Addresses and Numbers

Tourist Information
Alaska State Division of Tourism, (Box E, Juneau 99811, tel. 907/465–2010), **Alaska Visitors Association** (Box 10-2220 Anchorage 99510, tel. 907/276–6663), **Nome Convention & Visitors Bureau** (Box 251, Nome 99762, tel. 907/443–5535), **Arctic Circle Chamber of Commerce** (Box 284, Kotzebue 99752, tel. 907/442–3401), **Barrow Convention & Visitors Bureau** (Box 1060, Barrow 99723, tel. 907/852–5211), and **Kodiak Island Convention & Visitors Bureau** (100 Marine Way, Kodiak 99615, tel. 907/486–4782).

For information about camping, hiking, fishing, etc.: **National Park Service** (Alaska Regional Office, 2525 Gambell St., Anchorage 99503, tel. 907/271–4243), **U.S. Bureau of Land Management** (Alaska State Office, 701 C St., Anchorage 99513), and **Alaska Department of Fish and Game** (Box 3-2000, Juneau 99802, tel. 907/465–4112).

Dalton Highway information: **Alaska State Department of Transportation and Public Facilities** (2301 Peger Road, Fairbanks 99709, tel. 907/451–2209).

For ferry travel to Kodiak and the Aleutian Islands: **Alaska Marine Highway System** (Box R, Juneau 99811, tel. 907/465–3941 or 800/642–0066).

Emergencies
Hospital
A statewide air ambulance service operates through **Humana Hospital** in Anchorage (tel. 907/258–3822). **The Norton Sound Regional Hospital** (tel. 907/443–3311) is the major hospital in the Nome area. The U.S. Government Public Health Service operates a **PHS Hospital** in Barrow (tel. 907/852–4611) and in Kotzebue (tel. 907/442–3321).

Police
Nome (tel. 907/443–5262), Barrow (tel. 907/852–6111), and Kotzebue (tel. 907/442–3351).

State Troopers
Nome (tel. 907/443–2835), Barrow (tel. 907/852–3783), and Kotzebue (tel. 907/486–4121).

Exploring the Fringe Areas

Orientation

Alaska's Fringe is roughly defined by a long arc covering the state's western and northern edges. The Alaska Peninsula is its southernmost point, jutting out between the Pacific Ocean and the Bering Sea. The **Aleutian Islands** start where the peninsula ends and sweep off towards Japan.

The **Pribilof Islands** lie north of the Aleutians, 200 miles off Alaska's coast. Head farther north and you encounter the undeveloped wilderness of **Nunivak Island.** Due east, back on the mainland, is the town of **Bethel,** an important Fringe outpost.

Continuing in a clockwise direction, the next major stop is **Nome,** a predominantly white community with a gold-rush heritage just below the Arctic Circle. **Kotzebue,** just above the circle, is an Eskimo town surrounded by tundra.

Barrow sits at the very top of the state, the northernmost point in the United States. Follow the Arctic coastline to the southeast and you reach **Deadhorse,** on Prudhoe Bay, the custodian to the region's important oil and gas reserves.

Package tours are the most common way of traveling the Fringe, where making your flight connections and having a room to sleep in at the end of the line are no small feats. Independent travel, particularly for campers and hikers, can be highly rewarding, but it takes careful planning. During peak season—late May through Labor Day—planes, state ferries, hotels, and sportfishing lodges are likely to be crowded with travelers on organized tours. Booking well ahead is recommended; many Alaska travelers make their reservations a year in advance.

The Katmai and the Valley of Ten Thousand Smokes

The **Katmai National Park and Preserve** is a wild, remote landscape on the Alaska Peninsula, bordering Shelikof Strait across from Kodiak Island.

Moose and almost 30 other species of animals, including fox, lynx, and wolves, share the scene with bears fishing for salmon from stream banks or in the water. Ducks are common; so are whistling swans, loons, grebes, gulls, and shorebirds. Bald eagles can be seen perched on rocky pinnacles by the sea. More than 40 species of songbirds alone can be seen during the short spring and summer season. Marine life abounds in the coastal area, with the Steller's sea lion and hair seal often observed on rock outcroppings.

Compared with roads and facilities at Denali National Park, Katmai is quite primitive, but therein lies its charm.

The first visitors to the Katmai area arrived over 4,000 years ago. There is some evidence, in fact, that native Alaskan people inhabited Katmai's eastern edge for at least 6,000 years. The attraction was plentiful fish and game, and a peaceful, green valley.

The Fringe Areas (Alaska's Western Coast)

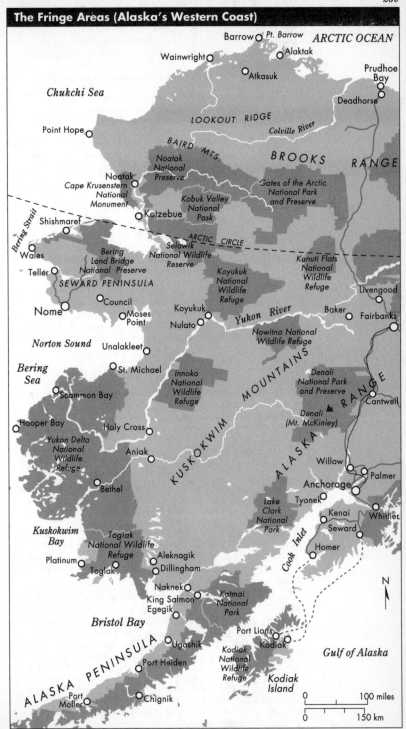

ARCTIC OCEAN

Barrow
Pt. Barrow
Alaktak
Wainwright
Atkasuk
Prudhoe Bay
Deadhorse

Chukchi Sea

LOOKOUT RIDGE
Colville River

Point Hope

BAIRD MTS.
BROOKS RANGE

Noatak National Preserve

Noatak
Cape Krusenstern National Monument
Kobuk Valley National Park
Gates of the Arctic National Park and Preserve

Kotzebue

ARCTIC CIRCLE

Shishmaref

Bering Strait

Wales
Selawik National Wildlife Reserve

Teller
Bering Land Bridge National Preserve

SEWARD PENINSULA

Koyukuk National Wildlife Refuge

Kanuti Flats National Wildlife Refuge

Livengood

Council

Nome
Moses Point

Koyukuk
Yukon River
Baker
Fairbanks

Nulato

Norton Sound

Unalakleet

Nowitna National Wildlife Refuge

Bering Sea

St. Michael

Scammon Bay

Innoko National Wildlife Refuge

KUSKOKWIM MOUNTAINS

Denali National Park and Preserve

Cantwell

Hooper Bay

Holy Cross

Denali (Mt. McKinley)

RANGE

ALASKA

Yukon Delta National Wildlife Refuge

Aniak

Willow
Palmer

Bethel

Anchorage
Tyonek
Whittier

Lake Clark National Park

Kenai

Kuskokwim Bay

Togiak National Wildlife Refuge

Seward

Platinum

Aleknagik

Homer

Cook Inlet

Toglak
Dillingham

Naknek

N

King Salmon
Egegik

Katmai National Park

Bristol Bay

Ugashik

Port Lions
Kodiak

Gulf of Alaska

Port Heiden

Kodiak National Wildlife Refuge

Kodiak Island

ALASKA PENINSULA

Port Moller
Chignik

0   100 miles

0   150 km

On the morning of June 1, 1912, a 2,700-foot mountain called Novarupta decided to disturb Katmai's peace. The earth quaked and erupted into violent tremors for five straight days. When the quakes subsided, rivers of white-hot ash poured over the valley. A foot of ash fell on Kodiak, 100 miles away. Winds carried the ash to eastern Canada and as far as Texas.

While Novarupta was belching pumice and scorching ash, another explosion occurred six miles east. The mountaintop peak of Mt. Katmai collapsed, creating a chasm almost three miles long and two miles wide. The molten andesite that held up Mt. Katmai had rushed through newly created fissures to Novarupta and been spewn out. Sixty hours after the first thunderous blast, more than seven cubic miles of volcanic material had been ejected, and the green valley lay under 700 feet of ash. Though no one was killed, the natives fled from Katmai and other villages.

By 1916, things had cooled off. A National Geographic expedition, led by Dr. Robert F. Griggs, reached the valley and found it full of steaming fumaroles. The report on what Griggs dubbed the Valley of Ten Thousand Smokes inspired Congress to set it and the surrounding wilderness aside as a national monument in 1918.

The natives never did come back, but they have since been replaced by sightseers, fishermen, hikers, and outdoor enthusiasts who migrate here in summer. Fish and wildlife are still plentiful, and a few "smokes" still drift through the volcano-sculpted valley.

No roads lead to the national park, at the base of the Alaska Peninsula, 290 miles southwest of Anchorage. Getting there is an all-Alaskan fly-in experience. Planes wing from Anchorage along Cook Inlet, rimmed by the lofty, snowy peaks of the Alaska Range. They land at **King Salmon,** near fish-famous Bristol Bay, where passengers transfer to smaller planes that are at home on land and water. After a 20-minute hop, the amphibian plane splashes down in Naknek Lake, in front of the Park Ranger Station, next to **Brooks Lodge.** Most visitors stay at the lodge or at the adjacent park service campground. Campers can pay to eat and shower at the lodge. Each campsite comes equipped with a cache to protect food from the ever-present brown bears that live around Brooks Lake.

From Brooks Lodge, a daily tour bus with a naturalist aboard makes the 23-mile trip through the park to the Valley Overlook. Hikers can walk the 1½-mile trail for a closer look at the pumice-covered valley floor. (Some consider the return climb strenuous.)

A flightseeing tour—with an operator such as **Katmai Air Services** (tel. 907/246–3079)—will allow you to view from the air early trade and hunting routes, perhaps a deserted native village or roaming brown bear and moose in season. Jade-green water now fills Katmai Crater, and the sulfur smell of some smokes, still sending up signals in the valley, wafts into the plane.

Brooks River and **Naknek Lake** are hot spots for fly-fishing. In fact, the trophy rainbow trout fishing is so good that only fly-fishing is permitted. A short walk upriver to **Brooks Falls,** salmon are easily seen and photographed from a viewing platform (on a trail separated from the river to avoid confrontations with bears) as they leap an eight-foot barrier.

This "angler's paradise" has other fly-in camps and lodges. From **Grosvenor Lake** and **Kulik Lodge** on Novianuk Lake, avid fishermen can fly off with a pilot/guide to fish for Arctic char and grayling, northern pike, and rainbow trout that reach trophy size. Nonfishers can take boat trips, hike, rock hound, and observe and photograph birds and wildlife.

Lodge accommodations are mostly shared cabins, with hot and cold water, private bathroom with shower, heat, and lights. Additional information, including other camps and lodges, is available from park headquarters (Katmai National Park and Preserve, Box 7, King Salmon 99613, tel. 907/246–3305).

Bethel

Huddled on a sweeping curve of the Kuskokwim River is one of the lesser known Bush destinations. Bethel is a rough-hewn frontier town of 4,500 or so residents and is one of rural Alaska's most important trading centers, a hub for more than 50 native villages in a region roughly the size of the state of Oregon. Hit-and-run journalists unfairly describe Bethel as "one of Alaska's ugliest ducklings." While Bethel might not win a beauty contest, those writers must have failed to see the surrounding tundra woven with pastel hues in summer and the handsome faces of the native Eskimo people, or experience how good the fishing for salmon, Arctic grayling, and Dolly Varden trout is just a few miles outside town.

Bethel is one of several of Alaska's Bush communities that has voted itself "damp" to combat alcoholism problems; liquor may be imported for personal consumption. Check with your air carrier before departure for current laws governing alcohol importation.

Though visitor accommodations are limited, Bethel boasts a library, museum, radio and television stations, theater, hotel, bank, newspaper, child-care center, regional office of the Alaska State Troopers, and the largest Alaska Native Service field hospital in the state.

The **Yugtarvik Regional Museum** holds Eskimo artifacts and is the marketplace for contemporary crafts of western Alaska and the Yukon-Kuskokwim Delta Area. *Tel. 907/543–2098. Admission free. Open Tues.–Sat. 10–6.*

The **Kuskokwim Delta Area,** about 80 miles west of Bethel at the mouth of the river, abounds with moose, wolf, beaver, and muskrat. To the northwest, the **Yukon Delta Wildlife Refuge** encompasses one of the largest waterfowl breeding grounds in the world. Despite modern encroachment, Yupik Eskimos in the delta continue their centuries-old subsistence lifestyle. For information, contact Alaska Public Lands Information Center (605 W. 4th Ave., Anchorage 99501, tel. 907/271–2737).

Nome

It has been almost 90 years since a great stampede for gold put a wilderness speck called Nome on the map of Alaska. But for visitors to this frontier community on the icy Bering Sea, it is almost as if the stampede never ended. Gold mining and noisy saloons are still mainstays in Nome.

No roads or rails lead to Nome, 539 air miles northwest of Anchorage—and only 165 miles from the coast of Siberia. To get there, one must fly or mush a team of sled dogs. And mush some do: Front Street in Nome is the finish line of the famed, 1,049-mile Iditarod Trail Sled Dog Race between Anchorage and Nome.

Nome, mainly a collection of ramshackle homes and low-slung commercial buildings, still looks like a vintage gold camp or a neglected Western-movie set—rawboned, rugged, and somewhat shabby. Visitors are charmed not by the architecture but by Nome's cheerful hospitality and colorful history.

"Well," you might hear a tour guide say as he greets a busload of tourists, "it looks like the churches here are finally outnumbering the drinking holes. We have 15 churches and nine saloons now. Ask me for a tally again next year; those numbers have been seesawing up and down ever since Nome began."

Nome's golden years began in 1898, when three prospectors—known as the "Lucky Swedes"—struck rich deposits on Anvil Creek, about four miles from what became Nome. The news spread quickly. When the Bering Sea ice parted the next spring, ships from Puget Sound, down by Seattle, arrived in Nome with eager stampeders. The rush was on. But that was only the first wave. Historians estimate that 15,000 people landed in Nome between June and October of 1900.

It was a brawling time, with a cast of memorable characters. Among the gold-rush luminaries were Wyatt Earp, the old gunfighter from the O.K. Corral, who mined the gold of Nome by opening a posh saloon; Tex Rickard, the boxing promoter, who operated another Nome saloon; and Rex Beach, the novelist.

Nome is also proud to be the home town of General James H. Doolittle, the Tokyo raider of World War II. When Doolittle's bombers hit Japan in a daring raid in 1942, the headline in the *Nome Nugget* proudly announced: "NOME TOWN BOY MAKES GOOD!"

The gold-dust tales and historic trails merge with the present, as visitors tour Nome on buses, pan for gold, watch sled-dog demonstrations, buy walrus ivory carvings, and dine on reindeer stew.

And there is still gold in the hills around Nome. Several years ago, a local miner (reportedly answering a call of nature at the time) scooped up a whopper nugget weighing nine pounds.

The folks here enjoy teasing visitors with tall stories. But that one's true.

Nome has no highway link to the rest of Alaska, but there is a network of 250 miles or so of gravel roads around Nome that lead to creeks and rivers for gold panning or fishing for trout, salmon, and Arctic grayling. There are also opportunities to view reindeer, bear, fox, and moose in the wild while venturing on the back roads that used to connect early day mining camps and hamlets.

Independent travelers with hardy vehicles (you can rent a Jeep, pickup truck, or van in Nome for $65 to $80 a day) should go exploring. Because the sun stays up late in the summer months, drive to the top of Anvil Mountain, near Nome, for a panoramic view of the old gold town and the Bering Sea. Be sure to carry mosquito repellent.

The Carrie McClain Museum, on Front Street, remodeled with new exhibits, is well worth a visit. Friendly volunteers will even give you a personal guided tour upon request. On display are exhibits depicting Eskimo art and culture and the gold-rush history of Nome, as well as historic photo collections. Ask the Visitors Bureau (Box 251, Nome 99762, tel. 907/443–5535) for hours.

Kotzebue

It happens all the time. An Alaska Airlines jetliner bound for Kotzebue nears the Arctic Circle.

"Please fasten your seat belts," the pilot cautions. "We usually get a bump when we cross the circle." Moments later, the plane takes a roller-coaster dip that has passengers shrieking and laughing.

"Big fun," a flight attendant says of the traditional welcome to the Arctic for air travelers.

Kotzebue, Alaska's second-largest Eskimo community (Barrow is the largest), lies 26 miles above the Arctic Circle, on Alaska's northwestern coast. Population: about 3,000 and growing.

"We have four seasons—June, July, August, and winter," a tour guide jests.

But don't worry about the sometimes-chilly weather. The local sightseeing company has snug, bright-colored loaner parkas for visitors on package tours.

Strung out in clusters of weather-bleached, little homes and a few public buildings on the gravelly shore of Kotzebue Sound, Kotzebue provides visitors with a glimpse of the way Alaska's Eskimos live today.

For this part of the world, Kotzebue is something between a village and a town. It was an ancient Eskimo trading center; now it is an example of the new spirit that is nudging Alaska's natives into the mainstream of Alaska without wrecking cultural traditions.

There is great dignity in the simple surroundings. Walking along the unpaved main street, a visitor sees racks draped with air-drying seal meat and salmon. Eskimo fishermen mend nets and pack their skiffs. Roofs of homes are storage places for caribou antlers and between-seasons snowmobiles.

The NANA (Northwest Alaska Native Association) Regional Corp., one of the 13 Native corporations formed when Congress settled the Alaskan natives' aboriginal land claims in 1971, has its headquarters in Kotzebue. It was NANA that built the $1-million Living Museum of the Arctic in 1977 and turned it into one of Alaska's top-rated museums.

Eskimo skin drums throb as the lights go down at the museum. Then traditional Eskimo dances are presented, including one in which visitors are invited to join.

Soon everyone goes outdoors to witness an Eskimo blanket toss.

It may look like a game, but it was serious business in the early days, when Eskimo hunters were launched high in the air from blankets of walrus or seal hide to scan the seas for game. You even may be urged to take a turn on the bouncing blanket.

In late July, Kotzebue holds the Northwest Native Trade Fair with Eskimo games, dances, and other activities. Write the trade fair (Box 49, Kotzebue 99752) for information.

Ootukahkuktuvik (Place Having Old Things) is the name of Kotzebue's other very worthwhile museum. It contains masks, whaling guns, and many more of the fascinating antique items relating to Kotzebue's early trading history, including Russian trading beads made of blue glass. *2nd Ave., tel. 907/442–3401. Donations only. Open summer weekdays 8–4:30; by appointment rest of the year.*

Time Out   The Eskimo-owned and -operated **Nullagvik Hotel** features two local specialties on its menu: reindeer stew and Arctic sheefish.

Visitors hiking the wildflower-carpeted tundra around Kotzebue enter a living museum dedicated to permafrost, the permanently frozen ground that lies just a few inches below the spongy tundra. Even Kotzebue's 6,000-foot airport runway is built on permafrost—with a six-inch insulating layer between the frozen ground and the airfield surface to assure landings are smooth, not slippery.

Not to be missed, for travelers with a sense of humor, is **Kotzebue National Forest.** Consisting of a single spruce tree on the otherwise treeless tundra, enclosed by a white picket fence, the "forest" was planted and nurtured by the men of the local air force Distant Early Warning Line radar station.

Don't let that little bit of irony keep you from considering an outing to any of the three exceptional national wilderness areas for which Kotzebue serves as a gateway. **Noatak National Preserve** is ideal for river trips and for running rapids on the Noatak River, which empties into Kotzebue Sound. **Kobuk Valley National Park,** accessible by air taxi and boat from Kotzebue, includes two desert areas and more runnable rivers. **Cape Krusenstern National Monument** is rich in cultural and archaeological treasures; it lies only 10 miles northwest of Kotzebue (*see* Interior and Arctic Alaska in Chapter 4).

Barrow

The northernmost community in the United States, Barrow sits just 1,300 miles from the North Pole. It is the best place in Alaska to catch the legendary midnight sun. For 82 days, from May to August, the sun stays above the horizon in logic-defying fashion.

Photographers with tripods can record multiple exposures as the sun arcs from east to west, making it appear to be a bouncing ball on the horizon over the Arctic Ocean. Try to set an interesting foreground for your photos, such as an *umiak* (Eskimo skin boat) or fish-drying rack. Drifting Arctic pack ice, often close to shore, can add to the scene.

Prudhoe Bay

Most towns offer museums that chronicle local history and achievements. **Deadhorse,** the town anchoring life along Prudhoe Bay, could well be preserved as a huge museum complex itself, dedicated to man's hunt for energy and his ability to adapt to harsh conditions.

The costly, much-publicized Arctic oil and gas project is complex and varied. One-day tours explore the tundra terrain from oil pipes to sandpipers. Along with spotting caribou, wildflowers, and an unusual stand of willow trees at the edge of the Arctic Ocean, the field tour surveys oil wells, stations, and oil-company residential complexes—small cities themselves. Your guide will discuss the multimillion-dollar research programs aimed at preserving the region's ecology and point out special tundra vehicles known as Rolligons. The great weight of these vehicles is carefully distributed so that it scarcely makes a dent as it passes over delicate terrain.

Most visitors arrive in the summer, but you can sample the Arctic in winter for dog-sledding, snowmobiling, and ice-fishing. In May and June, you may encounter the "breakup," when the shore ice splits and winter gives way to a fleeting spring season.

Off the Beaten Track

The Aleutian Islands Beyond the Katmai and the Alaska Peninsula lie the farthest reaches of Alaska. Separating the North Pacific Ocean from the Bering Sea, the Aleutian Islands, termed "The Chain," stretch from the Alaska Peninsula in a southwesterly arc toward Japan. The distance from the point nearest the Alaska mainland, Unimak Island, to the most distant island, Attu, is more than one thousand miles. This semivolcanic, treeless archipelago consists of about 20 large islands and several hundred smaller ones.

Before the Russians came, the islands were dotted with Aleut villages. Today's communities include: **Nikolski,** on Umnak Island; **Unalaska,** on Unalaska Island; **Atka,** on Atka Island; **Pilot Point,** on the Alaska Peninsula, and **Cold Bay** at its tip. The hardy Aleuts work at commercial fishing or in canneries and as expert guides for hunters and fishermen. With the exception of U.S. military bases, the settlements are quite small, and accommodations scarce. Visitors are not allowed to visit Adak or Shemya without special permission. By air, the chain is served by Reeve Aleutian Airways (*see* Getting Around, above).

The Pribilof Islands In the Bering Sea some 200 miles northwest of Cold Bay are the Pribilof Islands, misty, fog-bound breeding grounds of fur seals. Five islets make up the Pribilof group—a tiny, green, treeless oasis, with rippling belts of lush grass contrasting with red volcanic soil. In May, the mating seals come home from far Pacific waters, and the islands are overwhelmed with scenes of frenzied activity. When a thousand bulls scold at the top of their lungs or roar jealously, the sounds roll out several miles to sea.

Tours fly primarily to **St. Paul** and sometimes to **St. George,** the two largest Pribilof Islands. For the most part, these outposts are visited (by air and sometimes by sea) by those who have business there or by persistent, independent travelers addicted to way-out destinations. On most flights, space is blocked off for freight, and there are usually 30 or so seats left over for passengers. Typical passengers include native Aleuts and government workers, many in wildlife jobs, along with travelers heading out for a wildlife tour.

The islands are a 2,000-mile round-trip from Anchorage, over the massive snowy peaks of the Alaska Peninsula, tapering down to the rocky sea-level islands of the Aleutian Islands. This was the supply route for U.S. forces during World War II, when Japan invaded Attu and Kiska islands toward the tip of the Aleutian chain. The flight passes over old lava flows, some still-smoking volcanic peaks, rustic debris, and Quonset huts left at Cold Bay and other American bases after the war. During the Bering Sea leg, there may be a playful pod of whales below.

At St. Paul Airport, tours are met by the resident guide. Nature lovers are given the chance to watch members of the largest northern fur seal herd in the world and more than 180 varieties of birds. In town, you can visit with local residents; about 500 descendents of Aleut-Russians live here now, in the shadow of the Old Russian Orthodox Church and the vestiges of Aleut culture.

Nunivak Island Farther north, just past Kuskokwim Bay and due west of Bethel, is another important wildlife refuge. Nunivak Island, home of the **Nunivak National Wildlife Refuge,** is noted regionally for its large herd of reindeer, a transplanted herd of musk-oxen, and the Eskimo settlement of Mekoryuk. This is one of the least-touristed parts of Alaska. Visitors, lured by fine ivory carvings, masks, and items knit from qiviut (musk-oxen) wool, should check with airlines flying to the island about accommodations, which are limited and far from deluxe.

Shopping

Alaska's Arctic is known for Eskimo arts, ranging from wildlife figures carved from creamy walrus ivory to bracelets and other jewelry fashioned from ivory, gold, Alaska jade, and other local materials. Nome, Kotzebue, and Barrow all have reputable gift shops. Prices range from about $10 for tiny earrings to several hundred dollars for ceremonial masks and other major pieces.

Barrow Stuaqpak ("The Big Store"; no phone) is the largest store in town for both groceries and Eskimo products, including furs, parkas, mukluks, and ceremonial masks. However, make sure to visit the lobby of the **North Slope Borough Building** (tel. 907/852–2611), which has a fine display case of Eskimo arts and crafts for sale from all the villages along the North Slope. This is a nonprofit operation, so the money goes directly to the artisans. For sale are such items as baleen baskets and artwork, seal-skin bags, and ivory carvings.

Bethel The **Yugtarvik Regional Museum** (tel. 907/543–2098) is also a nonprofit marketplace for all the villages of the Kuskokwim area. Items for sale here include water grass baskets, wooden spirit masks, ivory-handled knives, grass and reindeer beard dancebands, yo-yos, dolls, and seal-gut parkas. The **Moravian Bookstore,** located next door, stocks much of the same material along with books about Eskimo culture.

Kotzebue The **Nul-luk-vik Hotel Gift Shop** and **Hansons** on Front Street, **Alaska Commercial Co.** (4th Ave. and Bison St.) and **Val-U-House** (2nd St. and Tundra Way) stock native crafts such as masks and other items of skin, ivory, jade and fur.

Nome Nome is considered one of the best places to buy ivory, because many of the Eskimo carvers from outlying villages come to Nome first to offer their wares to dealers. **The Arctic Trading Post** (Bering St. and Front St.) has an extensive stock of authentic Eskimo ivory carvings and other Alaskan artwork and books. Also try **Jim West's Ivory Shop, Maruskyika's,** and the other shops on Front Street in downtown Nome.

Participant Sports

Cross-country Skiing The many national parks, wilderness areas, and wildlife refuges of the Fringe offer spectacular trails for cross-country skiing. Local visitors bureaus and park offices can direct you to resources for equipment rentals (*see* Important Addresses and Numbers, above).

Fishing/Hunting Outfitters scattered throughout the Fringe will arrange lodge accommodations and supply you with equipment and guides. Hunting is arranged with guns, bow and arrow, or camera. Two are **Brooks Range Arctic Hunts** (Mile 329-AT, Rte. 1 Parks Hwy., Nenana 99760, tel. 907/479–6128) and **Alatna Guide Service** (Box 80424-AT, Fairbanks 99708, tel. 907/479–6354). Alatna is open only March to late Sept.

River Rafting From family float trips to wild rapid running, there are numerous rivers to choose from. Contact **Sourdough Outfitters** (Box 90-AT, Bettles 99726, tel. 907/692–5252) or **Wilderness Alaska** (6710-AT Potter Heights, Ketchikan 99516, tel. 907/225–6664). In South Central, try **Nova Riverrunners** (Box 1129, Chickaloon, 99674, tel. 907/745–5753) or Bob Dittrich's **Wilderness Birding Adventures** (Box 10-3747, Anchorage 99510, tel. 907/694–7442).

Sled-Dog Mushing Several outfitters offer winter dog-sled rides; some offer lessons and overnight sled-dog trips. In Nome, try **Flat Dog Kennels** (Box 1103-AT, Nome 99762, tel. 907/443–2958). In Anchorage, try **Chugach Express Dog Sled Tours** (Box 261, Girdwood 99587, tel. 907/783–2266).

Spectator Sports

Sled-Dog Mushing The famed 1,049-mile Iditarod Trail Sled Dog Race—the Olympics of sled-dog racing—reaches its climax in Nome in mid-March. Racers start in Anchorage, with the trip taking an average of two weeks. The 1991 race was won for the fifth time by Rick Swenson of Manley Hot Springs. He beat four-time winner Susan Butcher. The arrival of the mushers heralds a winter carnival. For information, contact the Iditarod Trail Committee (Box 870800, Wasilla 99687, tel. 907/376– 5155).

Dining and Lodging

In the Fringes, accommodations and dining opportunities are few, and prices may seem relatively high. Keep in mind that these towns are small outposts of civilization. Restaurant food supplies are barged or flown in and limited lodging space is often reserved by tour groups. Add to that a short visitor season, lasting only about 110 days, from mid-May through mid-September.

Accommodations in outlying areas are plain but comfortable; meals are hearty, often with too much deep-fat cooking for cholesterol- and calorie-conscious travelers. Water supplies are often limited in the Artic. Your shower water may be draining into your toilet tank to conserve water. Independent travelers are advised to make reservations early, because most of the major hotels and motels are occupied by tour groups in the summer season. Ask about bed-and-breakfasts; their numbers are slowly growing. It's also sometimes possible to arrange to stay with a local family through the Bush airlines serving outlying villages.

Addresses are listed whenever possible. In some towns, residents literally do not refer to their main street as anything other than "in town." Don't worry. These are places small and friendly enough to make getting lost impossible.

Highly recommmended restaurants and hotels are indicated with a star ★.

Dining Restaurants in Alaska's Fringes are categorized as follows:

Category	Cost*
Expensive	$16–$20
Moderate	$10–$15
Inexpensive	under $10

based on a complete meal, with tax and tip

Virtually all restaurants in the Fringes of Alaska are small, family-run establishments whose hours vary widely from one season to the next. We have not listed opening hours because of this unpredictability. Your best bet is to call ahead.

Lodging Hotel and motel rates are as follows:

Category	Cost*
Expensive	over $80
Moderate	$60–$80
Inexpensive	under $60

double occupancy without taxes or service

Aleutian Islands: Dutch Harbor/ Unalaska
Dining
★

The Unisea Inn. Excellent fresh seafood and pizza are served here. The decor is standard rural Alaska—utilitarian. The attached bar has live, loud music most nights. Look for locally caught salmon and halibut on the summer menu. *Dutch Harbor, tel. 907/581–1325. MC, V. Expensive.*

Linn's. This restaurant serves surprisingly good Asian—Vietnamese and Chinese—food in a non-Asian cafe atmosphere. *Near the Walafhek shipyards in downtown Dutch Harbor, tel. 907/581–1625. No credit cards. Moderate.*

Stormy's Restaurant. Mexican, Italian, and American foods are served, but featured dishes include Greek chicken as well as Acapulco shrimp, caught locally and prepared Mexicanstyle with rice, beans, and red peppers. The decor is kitsch Italian: there are red checked tablecloths and prints of Italy on the walls. *In the center of Unalaska village, across the bridge from Dutch Harbor, tel. 907/581–1565. MC, V. Moderate.*

Lodging **The Unisea Inn.** This downtown hotel features a lounge with live country music six nights a week, a restaurant, gift shop, beauty parlor, and liquor store. Each room comes equipped with cable TV and telephone. *Pouch 503, Dutch Harbor 99692, tel. 907/581–1325. 47 rooms. MC, V. Expensive.*

Barrow **Pepe's North of the Border.** Its 18 Mexican dishes are ranked
Dining highly in the Bush area. An amazing decor features walls painted with bullfighting and Mexican village scenes. *Adjoins Top of the World Hotel, tel. 907/852–8200. MC, V. Expensive.*

Sam & Lee's Chinese Restaurant. Fine food available at the only place in town open until 2 AM. Ask to sit in the back room—it's more pleasant than you might think from the restaurant's dingy exterior. *1052 Kiogak St., tel. 907/852–5555. MC, V. Expensive.*

U.I.C.-NARL. This former Naval Arctic Research Lab was leased to the village and converted into a hotel with a cafeteria-style restaurant. It features great food and selection; all-you-can-eat for about $20, half price for children. *Tel. 907/852–7800. MC, V. Moderate–Expensive.*

Ken's Restaurant. Basic burgers and bakery goods are available at this restaurant, with good daily specials at the best prices in town. *Located above the airport terminal building, tel. 907/852–8888. No credit cards. Moderate.*

Señor Sam's. Although there's no place to sit, and the menu is limited to burgers, steak, and chicken, their steak sandwich is reportedly the best in all of Alaska. The downtown restaurant is not well marked, so it's wise to ask for directions. *1059 Kiogak St., tel. 907/852–2244. No credit cards. Inexpensive–Moderate.*

Lodging **Barrow Airport Inn.** Rated the city's best, this inn is located
★ one block from the airport; limousine service is available on request. It features an in-house travel agency and cable TV and telephones in all 16 rooms. *Box 933, Barrow 99723, tel. 907/852–2525. AE, MC, V. Rates include Continental breakfast served in the lobby. Expensive.*

Top of the World Hotel. This far-north hotel is located on the shore of the Arctic Ocean in Barrow's business district. All 40 rooms have been or are being remodeled and have full baths, cable TV, and telephones. Two stuffed polar bears welcome guests in the lobby. Facilities include a gift shop and adjoining restaurant. *Box 189, Barrow 99723, tel. 907/852–3900. AE, DC, MC, V. Expensive.*

Bethel **Kuskokwim Inn.** Located downtown, not far from the river of
Dining the same name, the Kuskokwim Inn is Bethel's only full-service restaurant, and it serves passable American and Chinese food. Halibut is usually available, and it is fresh in summer. *Box 888, Bethel 99559, tel. 907/543–2207. No credit cards. Moderate–Expensive.*

Standard Alaskan greasy-spoon menus can be found at **Isan's Pizza** (tel. 907/543–4335), **Riverfront** (tel. 907/543–3408), **Corina's** (tel. 907/543–4430), and **Dimitri's** (tel. 907/543–3434). *All Inexpensive–Moderate.*

Lodging **The Kuskokwim Inn.** This hotel serves mostly Alaskans in the winter and a few tourists in the summer. Rooms are basic, with inexpensive wood paneling, showers and tubs. The place is likely to be noisy. *Box 888, Bethel 99559, tel. 907/543–2207. AE, MC, V. Expensive–Moderate.*

The Bethel Inn. Proprietor Janie promises the friendliest service in Alaska and a home-cooked meal, even if you wake her up for one at 3 AM. Each room has a TV. *454 Ptarmigan St., Bethel 99559, tel. 907/543–3204. No credit cards. Inexpensive.*

Katmai **Katmailand Inc.** offers Brooks Lodge, Grosvenor Camp, and
Wilderness Lodges Kulik Lodge, accessible by air, available summers only. Fish for rainbow, Arctic char, grayling, lake trout, and salmon. *4700 Aircraft Dr., Anchorage 99501, tel. 907/243–5448 or 800/544–0551.*

Kotzebue **Arctic Dragon.** Serves above-average Chinese food. *301 Front*
Dining *St., downtown, tel. 907/442–3770. MC, V. Moderate–Expensive.*

Nullagvik Hotel Restaurant. This hotel coffee shop-style restaurant offers standard American fare in addition to a few local specialties, such as reindeer stew and Arctic sheefish. Reindeer is a mild, lean meat reminiscent of veal. The reindeer are herded locally by the Eskimo-owned NANA Regional Corporation. *Downtown, tel. 907/442–3331. AE, DC, MC, V. Moderate–Expensive.*

Kotzebue Pizza House. Despite the name, native Alaskans passing through tout its burgers as among the best. *Downtown at 2nd Ave. and Bison St., tel. 907/442–3432. No credit cards. Moderate.*

Lodging **Nullagvik Hotel.** Located downtown, it overlooks Kotzebue Sound. Facilities include a gift shop, beauty parlor, and restaurant. The hotel is built on pilings driven into the ground because the heat of the building would melt the underlying permafrost and the hotel would sink slowly into the ground. There's no elevator. *336, Kotzebue 99572, tel. 907/442–3331. AE, MC, V. Expensive.*

Nome **Fort Davis Roadhouse.** The roadhouse is the place locals go for a
Dining night out. It specializes in steaks and seafood, including local reindeer steaks. Some visitors fall for the proffered "Bering Ball," a potent cocktail which locals avoid. *3 mi east of town on the Nome-Council Rd., tel. 907/443–2660. Taxis serve the area. No credit cards. Dinner only; closed Sun. and Mon. Expensive.*

★ **Fat Freddie's Beef, Reef and Roost.** Located behind a bar overlooking the Bering Sea, this utilitarian restaurant serves an ample, inexpensive buffet lunch. *Downtown, adjacent to the Nugget Inn Hotel on Front St., tel. 907/443–5899. MC, V. Inexpensive.*

Nacho's Mexican Restaurant. Authentic Mexican food, along with good breakfasts, are served at this restaurant, popular with the locals. The place holds only 25 people, so you may have a short wait. *Front St., downtown, tel. 907/443–5503. MC, V. Inexpensive.*

Polar Club. Bakery goods are the specialty here. Locals like to linger over coffee, making it a good place to eavesdrop on area issues. *Downtown, next to the seawall by the Bering Sea, tel. 907/443-5191. MC, V. Inexpensive.*

Lodging **Nugget Inn.** Situated on Front Street downtown, this inn offers
★ 47 rooms with private baths and has attractive gold-rush decor in its lobby and lounge. This is where the Arctic tour groups stay. *Box 430, Nome 99762, tel. 907/443-2323. 47 rooms. AE, DC, MC, V. Expensive.*

Polar Arms. Fully furnished apartments with kitchens, TV, and telephones are available here. On Front Street, with some rooms overlooking the Bering Sea. *Box 880, Nome 99762, tel. 907/443-5191. DC, MC, V. Expensive.*

Nome Outfitters. If you want a house to yourself, this house-keeping outfit may fill your needs. Up to four people in one party only can be accommodated here. Facilities include a bedroom, kitchen, utility room, bath, and TV. Cooking facilities and basic foodstuffs are also provided. *Box 1045, Nome 99762, tel. 907/443-2880. MC, V. Moderate–Expensive.*

Aurora House Bed & Breakfast. Located in a quiet residential area of Nome, this place is five blocks from downtown. No smoking or drinking allowed in guest rooms. Full breakfasts include reindeer sausage. *Box 1318-B, Nome 99762, tel. 907/443-2700. 2 rooms. DC, MC, V. Moderate.*

Oceanview Manor. This bed-and-breakfast, on Front Street, four blocks from downtown, overlooks the Bering Sea. Rooms are individually decorated, some quite ruffled and feminine. Ask for a room facing the ocean. Baths are shared. *Box 65, Nome 99762, tel. 907/443-2133. DC, MC, V. Moderate.*

St. George Hotel. On nearby St. George Island, this place offers spartan accommodations with shared bath and kitchen. *4000 Old Seward Hwy., Anchorage 99503, tel. 907/562-3100 for reservations. V. Moderate.*

Wilderness Lodges **Camp Bendeleben** is open year-round, by reservation. It's located at Council, an early-1900s gold-mining camp, about 75 miles northeast of Nome. Expert hunter/fisherman John Elmore guides small-game hunting and ice-fishing trips in winter. The rest of the time he leads the way to the best Arctic char, grayling, pike, and salmon fishing, combined with sightseeing and photography expeditions. *Box 1045-S, Nome 99762, tel. 907/443-2880. MC, V. Expensive.*

White Mountain Lodge, Accessible by plane from Nome. Some of the best fishing in Alaska for pike, grayling, trout, or salmon. *Box 81, White Mountain 99784, tel. 907/638-3431. AE. Moderate.*

Pribilof Islands: It is unusual, but not unheard of, for tourists to travel to the
St. Paul Pribilofs independently. Check with tour operators before you go, since a package price may be cheaper than what you can arrange on your own. One tour operator offering special packages is **Reeve Aleutian Airways** (4700 W. International Airport Rd., Anchorage 99502, tel. 800/544-2248).

Dining **King Eider Restaurant.** The one restaurant in St. Paul serves basic American food. *Village Center, tel. 907/546-2312. Moderate–Expensive.*

Lodging **King Eider Hotel.** Filled in summer, mainly with tour groups who travel by air to this remote island to view fur-seal rookeries and cliffs crowded with seabirds. In summer, the hotel may be completely booked by bird-watching groups. *Tel. 907/546–2312. No single rooms and no private baths. Expensive.*

Prudhoe Bay   It's almost unheard of for individual travelers to turn up in Prudhoe Bay. Virtually everyone who visits works here or comes on a tour with **Alaska Airlines** (tel. 907/243–3300 or 800/426–0333) or **MarkAir** (tel. 907/243–6275 or 800/478–0800).

Lodging   **NANA Hotel.** This 175-room hotel, the oldest continuous operating one in the area, is owned by native Alaskans. All rooms have twin beds, and bathrooms are shared. There is a buffet-style restaurant, exercise room with sauna, TV lounge, and recreation room. *Box 340112, Prudhoe Bay, 99730. Tel. 907/659–2840. MC, V. Expensive.*

Index

Personal Itinerary

Departure *Date*

Time

Transportation

Arrival *Date* *Time*

Departure *Date* *Time*

Transportation

Accommodations

Arrival *Date* *Time*

Departure *Date* *Time*

Transportation

Accommodations

Arrival *Date* *Time*

Departure *Date* *Time*

Transportation

Accommodations

Personal Itinerary

Arrival *Date*   *Time*

Departure *Date*   *Time*

Transportation

Accommodations

Arrival *Date*   *Time*

Departure *Date*   *Time*

Transportation

Accommodations

Arrival *Date*   *Time*

Departure *Date*   *Time*

Transportation

Accommodations

Arrival *Date*   *Time*

Departure *Date*   *Time*

Transportation

Accommodations

Personal Itinerary

Arrival *Date*   *Time*

Departure *Date*   *Time*

Transportation

Accommodations

Arrival *Date*   *Time*

Departure *Date*   *Time*

Transportation

Accommodations

Arrival *Date*   *Time*

Departure *Date*   *Time*

Transportation

Accommodations

Arrival *Date*   *Time*

Departure *Date*   *Time*

Transportation

Accommodations

Personal Itinerary

Arrival *Date*   *Time*

Departure *Date*   *Time*

Transportation

Accommodations

Arrival *Date*   *Time*

Departure *Date*   *Time*

Transportation

Accommodations

Arrival *Date*   *Time*

Departure *Date*   *Time*

Transportation

Accommodations

Arrival *Date*   *Time*

Departure *Date*   *Time*

Transportation

Accommodations

Personal Itinerary

Arrival *Date* *Time*

Departure *Date* *Time*

Transportation

Accommodations

Arrival *Date* *Time*

Departure *Date* *Time*

Transportation

Accommodations

Arrival *Date* *Time*

Departure *Date* *Time*

Transportation

Accommodations

Arrival *Date* *Time*

Departure *Date* *Time*

Transportation

Accommodations

Addresses

Name	*Name*
Address	*Address*
Telephone	*Telephone*
Name	*Name*
Address	*Address*
Telephone	*Telephone*
Name	*Name*
Address	*Address*
Telephone	*Telephone*
Name	*Name*
Address	*Address*
Telephone	*Telephone*
Name	*Name*
Address	*Address*
Telephone	*Telephone*
Name	*Name*
Address	*Address*
Telephone	*Telephone*
Name	*Name*
Address	*Address*
Telephone	*Telephone*
Name	*Name*
Address	*Address*
Telephone	*Telephone*

Name | *Name*

Address | *Address*

Telephone | *Telephone*

Name | *Name*

Address | *Address*

Telephone | *Telephone*

Name | *Name*

Address | *Address*

Telephone | *Telephone*

Name | *Name*

Address | *Address*

Telephone | *Telephone*

Name | *Name*

Address | *Address*

Telephone | *Telephone*

Name | *Name*

Address | *Address*

Telephone | *Telephone*

Name | *Name*

Address | *Address*

Telephone | *Telephone*

Name | *Name*

Address | *Address*

Telephone | *Telephone*

Fodor's Travel Guides

U.S. Guides

Alaska
Arizona
Boston
California
Cape Cod, Martha's Vineyard, Nantucket
The Carolinas & the Georgia Coast
The Chesapeake Region
Chicago
Colorado
Disney World & the Orlando Area
Florida
Hawaii
Las Vegas, Reno, Tahoe
Los Angeles
Maine, Vermont, New Hampshire
Maui
Miami & the Keys
National Parks of the West
New England
New Mexico
New Orleans
New York City
New York City (Pocket Guide)
Pacific North Coast
Philadelphia & the Pennsylvania Dutch Country
Puerto Rico (Pocket Guide)
The Rockies
San Diego
San Francisco
San Francisco (Pocket Guide)
The South
Santa Fe, Taos, Albuquerque
Seattle & Vancouver
Texas
USA
The U. S. & British Virgin Islands
The Upper Great Lakes Region
Vacations in New York State
Vacations on the Jersey Shore
Virginia & Maryland
Waikiki
Washington, D.C.
Washington, D.C. (Pocket Guide)

Foreign Guides

Acapulco
Amsterdam
Australia
Austria
The Bahamas
The Bahamas (Pocket Guide)
Baja & Mexico's Pacific Coast Resorts
Barbados
Barcelona, Madrid, Seville
Belgium & Luxembourg
Berlin
Bermuda
Brazil
Budapest
Budget Europe
Canada
Canada's Atlantic Provinces
Cancun, Cozumel, Yucatan Peninsula
Caribbean
Central America
China
Czechoslovakia
Eastern Europe
Egypt
Europe
Europe's Great Cities
France
Germany
Great Britain
Greece
The Himalayan Countries
Holland
Hong Kong
India
Ireland
Israel
Italy
Italy's Great Cities
Jamaica
Japan
Kenya, Tanzania, Seychelles
Korea
London
London (Pocket Guide)
London Companion
Mexico
Mexico City
Montreal & Quebec City
Morocco
New Zealand
Norway
Nova Scotia, New Brunswick, Prince Edward Island
Paris
Paris (Pocket Guide)
Portugal
Rome
Scandinavia
Scandinavian Cities
Scotland
Singapore
South America
South Pacific
Southeast Asia
Soviet Union
Spain
Sweden
Switzerland
Sydney
Thailand
Tokyo
Toronto
Turkey
Vienna & the Danube Valley
Yugoslavia

Wall Street Journal Guides to Business Travel

Europe
International Cities
Pacific Rim
USA & Canada

Special-Interest Guides

Bed & Breakfast and Country Inn Guides:
Mid-Atlantic Region
New England
The South
The West
Cruises and Ports of Call
Healthy Escapes
Fodor's Flashmaps New York
Fodor's Flashmaps Washington, D.C.
Shopping in Europe
Skiing in the USA & Canada
Smart Shopper's Guide to London
Sunday in New York
Touring Europe
Touring USA